Retaking the Universe

DISCARD

Retaking the Universe

William S. Burroughs
in the Age of Globalization

Edited by
Davis Schneiderman and Philip Walsh

Pluto Press

LONDON • STERLING, VIRGINIA

First published 2004 by Pluto Press
345 Archway Road, London N6 5AA
22883 Quicksilver Drive, Sterling, VA 20166–2012, USA

www.plutobooks.com

British Library Cataloguing in Publication Data
A catalogue record for this book is available from the British Library

ISBN 0 7453 2082 1 hardback
ISBN 0 7453 2081 3 paperback

Library of Congress Cataloging-in-Publication Data
Retaking the Universe: William S. Burroughs in the Age of Globalization/
edited by Davis Schneiderman and Philip Walsh.
    p. cm.
Includes bibliographical references.
ISBN 0-7453-2082-1 (hbk.)—ISBN 0-7453-2081-3 (pbk.)
1. Burroughs, William S., 1914—Criticism and interpretation
2. Homosexuality and literature—United States—History—20th century.
3. Sexual orientation in literature. 4. Beat generation in literature.
5. Narcotic habit in literature. I. Schneiderman, Davis. II. Walsh,
Philip, 1965–

PS3552.U75Z835 2004
813'.54—dc22

                                                    2003025963

10 9 8 7 6 5 4 3 2 1

Designed and produced for Pluto Press by
Chase Publishing Services, Fortescue, Sidmouth, EX10 9QG, England
Typeset from disk by Newgen Imaging Systems (P) Ltd, India
Printed and bound in the European Union by
Antony Rowe Ltd, Chippenham and Eastbourne, England

Contents

List of Abbreviations

The many editions and printings of Burroughs's large body of work present multiple challenges to any type of standardized reference system. Stories, essays, and entire novels appear in multiple publications, and in forms often distinct from their previous incarnations. This list of abbreviations should help the reader to not only identify but also locate the texts to which the contributors refer. To this end, we have listed, whenever possible, widely available editions of Burroughs's work.

Major and single-volume text-based works written by or produced in concert with Burroughs are cited throughout this collection according to this list. Sound works attributed in whole or in part to Burroughs, when cited in the essays, are also noted by abbreviations. Essays and stories that appear outside of the works listed below, unpublished letters, collections of interviews, and critical works about Burroughs referenced by the contributors, as well as other Burroughs's written/sound/film work mentioned (but not specifically cited) in this collection are listed in the References section of the individual essays when appropriate.

A note on the text: Throughout the references in this collection, the year that appears in the first parenthesis of a citation signals the year of initial publication, and the second date indicates the year of the edition, printing, or publication cited in the collection.

For more specific information and overviews of these issues in relation to Burroughs's work, see Joe Maynard and Barry Miles's *William S. Burroughs: A Bibliography, 1953–73*, and Barry Miles's *William Burroughs: El Hombre Invisible*.

AM	(1985) *The Adding Machine: Selected Essays* (New York: Arcade, 1993).
APH	(1979) *Ah Pook is Here and Other Texts* (London: John Calder).
Best	(1998) *The Best of William Burroughs from Giorno Poetry Systems*, Disc 4 (Mouth Almighty Records, 314 536 704-2).
BF	(1984) *The Burroughs File* (San Francisco: City Lights).
BR	(1979) *Blade Runner, a Movie* (Berkeley: Blue Wind, 1990).

BTGR	(1986) *Break Through in Grey Room* [Sub Rosa, CD006-8]. Compilation of recordings from the 1960s and 1970s.
CI	(1986) *The Cat Inside* (USA: Penguin, 1992).
CMB	(1965) *Call Me Burroughs* [Rhino Records, reissue 1995 R2 71848].
CRN	(1981) *Cities of the Red Night* (New York: Picador, 2001).
E!	(1973) *Exterminator!* (New York: Penguin, 1979).
Elvis	Burroughs, W. S. and Van Sant, G. (1985) *The Elvis of Letters* [TK Records, 91CD001].
ER	(1970) *Electronic Revolution* (Bonn, Germany: Expanded Media Editions, 1976).
GC	(1991) *Ghost of Chance* (New York: Serpent's Tail, 1995).
J	(1953) *Junky*, unexpurgated edition (London: Penguin, 1977). Originally published as *Junkie* by 'William Lee'.
Job	[with Odier, D.] (1969) *The Job: Interviews with William S. Burroughs*, rev. edition, Grove, 1974 (New York: Penguin, 1989).
LTG	(1982) *Letters To Allen Ginsberg 1953–1957* (New York: Full Court).
LW	(2000) *Last Words: The Final Journals of William S. Burroughs*, Grauerholz, J. ed. (New York: Grove).
LWB	(1993) *The Letters of William S. Burroughs 1945–1959*, Harris, O. ed. (New York: Viking).
MTG	[with Gysin, B., Beiles, S., and Corso, G.] (1960) *Minutes to Go* (Paris: Two Cities).
NE	(1964) *Nova Express* (New York: Grove, 1992).
NL	(1959) *Naked Lunch* (New York: Grove, 1992).[1]
PDR	(1983) *The Place of Dead Roads* (New York: Picador, 2001).
PG	(1992) *Painting and Guns* (New York: Hanuman).
POS	(1973) *Port of Saints*, rev. edition (Berkeley, CA: Blue Wind, 1980).
Q	(1985) *Queer* (New York: Viking Penguin, 1987).
SAA	(1993) *Spare Ass Annie and Other Tales* [Island Records 162-535 003-2].
SM(2)	(1966) *The Soft Machine*, 2nd edition (New York: Grove, 1992).[2]
TE(2)	(1967) *The Ticket that Exploded*, 2nd edition (New York: Grove, 1992).[3]
3M	[with Gysin, B.] (1964–65, unpublished version) *The Third Mind* (New York: Seaver Books/Viking, 1978).

WB   (1971) *The Wild Boys: A Book of the Dead* (New York: Grove, 1992).

WL   (1987) *The Western Lands* (New York: Viking Penguin).

WS   (1973) *White Subway* (London: Aloes seolA).

WV   (1998) *Word Virus: The William S Burroughs Reader*, Grauerholz, J. and Silverberg, I. eds (New York: Grove Press).

YL   [with Allen Ginsberg] (1963) *The Yage Letters* (San Francisco: City Lights, 1990)

1. Several editions of *Naked Lunch* from the early 1990s use the same ISBN but have different pagination. The edition cited here contains a Foreword by Terry Southern and an introductory piece called '*Naked Lunch* on Trial'.

2. Burroughs produced three distinct versions of *The Soft Machine*, including the second edition listed above, which is the most widely available. Oliver Harris's essay, 'Cutting Up Politics', specifically references the second and third editions. The other two editions: (1961) *The Soft Machine*, 1st edition (Paris: Olympia) and SM3 (1968) *The Soft Machine*, 3rd edition (London: John Calder).

3. Burroughs produced two distinct versions of *The Ticket that Exploded*, including the 2nd edition, listed above, which includes an appendix essay, 'The Invisible Generation' (1966). The first editing: (1962) *The Ticket that Exploded*, 1st edition (Olympia: Paris).

Acknowledgments

We owe lavish thanks to the many people and institutions that have helped this book find its way to publication. First, without a chance meeting at Tompkins Cortland Community College in 2000, and a chance discovery of a mutual interest in Burroughs, we would never have formed the friendship and intellectual partnership that has produced this text.

Sincere thanks must be offered to the three Lake Forest College students who dedicated the summer after their freshman years (as participants in the Richter Scholar Program) to shepherd various stages of this project toward completion. First, both Michael Haining and Logan Dick provided valuable support in the proposal stage of the project, and their attention and interest carried from the summer of 2002 through their careful editing during the following year and a half. Second, Michael Wakcher dove fiercely into editorial work in the summer of 2003, distinguishing himself with a fine attention to detail and a desire to meet the highest standards of accuracy and scholarship.

Also, the generous support of Lake Forest College in the form of summer research grants, departmental encouragement, and collegiality, helped to make this a project whose long work was punctuated by the best sort of academic camaraderie.

Many others, of course, have contributed in all sorts of tangible and intangible ways. In no particular order, and with great fear of omission, we wish to thank: Lisa Schneiderman, Ruth Schneiderman, Philip Schneiderman, Lennard J. Davis, John Vernon, William Haver, Joseph Bisz, Carlos Hernandez, J. Elizabeth Clark, Matt Laferty and, of course, Nicola East and Kelly Haramis.

Finally, we also wish to thank Pluto Press for their support, and Kieran Macdonald for his excellent copy-editing.

Foreword

Jennie Skerl

In our survey of the critical response to Burroughs from 1959 to 1989, Robin Lydenberg and I observed that, decade by decade, Burroughs's work has been seen as emblematic of his times. As J. G. Ballard remarked upon Burroughs's death, 'his weird genius was the perfect mirror of his times' (cited by Caveney 1998:217). The 1950s saw Burroughs as a spiritual hero of an underground movement that sought to create not only a new bohemia, but also a new consciousness. The legend of William S. Burroughs as a controlling and uncontrollable construct began before he published his first novel, *Junkie* (1953), through the shaping of his persona by other writers in his circle (Jack Kerouac, Allen Ginsberg, John Clellon Holmes, Alan Ansen) and the gossip of the bohemian subculture coming into being.

The publication of *Naked Lunch* and the Nova trilogy in the early 1960s led to intense critical debate on the morality or lack thereof in Burroughs's work, beginning with the attempts at censorship that were made before the 1962 publication of *Naked Lunch* in the US. Critical reactions were extravagant and irreconcilable: from '[g]lug, glug, it tastes disgusting' (*TLS* reviewer) to 'possessed by genius' (Norman Mailer, *Naked Lunch* dust jacket). But both detractors and defenders saw Burroughs as representative of the era—either an example of a sick society or its most incisive critic. The montage structure of *Naked Lunch* was itself seen as a moral issue: lack of coherence was equated with lack of a moral point of view or praised as the source of the novel's visionary power. Burroughs's cut-up experiments of the 1960s and the trilogy of novels that resulted (*The Soft Machine, The Ticket that Exploded, Nova Express*) were dismissed at the time as producing incomprehensible and boring texts. Everyone—friends, editors, reviewers—thought that cut-ups were a dead end. Censorship, legend, expatriation, association with the much-ridiculed Beat movement, montage and collage prose techniques, taboo subject matter, fragmented audiences not in communication with each other—all contributed to the conflicted arena of Burroughs criticism in the 1960s and into the 1970s as well.

However, the 1970s also saw the beginning of serious academic criticism and the appropriation of Burroughs by the rock scene and associated youth cultures—both of which trends grew stronger in the 1980s and 1990s. Although Burroughs continued to be discussed as a social critic, there was greater acceptance of cut-ups and the beginning of an analysis of Burroughs's radical challenge to identity, language, and psychosexual systems of control. Critics such as Tony Tanner (1971), Cary Nelson (1973), John Tytell (1976), and Eric Mottram (1971, 1977) turned from a focus on Burroughs's shocking imagery and questions about moral purpose to an assessment of his theoretical constructs and stylistic effects. Burroughs in the 1970s continued to move on in his fiction toward a more sparing use of cut-ups and the introduction of more narrative in works such as *The Wild Boys*.

The publication of a second trilogy in the 1980s (*Cities of the Red Night, The Place of Dead Roads, The Western Lands*) renewed critical interest in Burroughs's writing and led to reassessments of his career and literary significance. The latter was marked by Burroughs's 1983 induction into the American Academy and Institute of Arts and Letters, a full-length biography by Ted Morgan (1988), a film biography by Howard Brookner (1983), and three critical books devoted to Burroughs by Michael B. Goodman (1981), Robin Lydenberg (1987), and myself (1985). In the 1980s, Burroughs was seen as emblematic again—as an exemplar of postmodernism. From this decade on, Burroughs criticism has reflected the development of postmodern theory and poststructuralist thought in general, with many pointing out that Burroughs's linguistic and social analysis parallels that of several prominent French theorists taken up by American literary critics. Burroughs himself began to be taken more seriously as a theoretician/artist. In this context, ambivalence toward the morality of his work was transformed into contradictory interpretations of his politics. Increased use of narrative in the later trilogy also resulted in more positive reviews in the mass media, in contrast to the almost universally negative reviews of the 1970s.

In the last decade, books by Timothy S. Murphy (1997) and Jamie Russell (2001) attempted comprehensive overviews that situated Burroughs historically and within current ideological debates. In addition, throughout the 1990s, Burroughs's image as a transgressive artist became gradually consolidated as a popular icon. His name, his image, and the titles of his works have become the index of 'hip' or 'cool' and are recognized by many who have never read his works. David Cronenberg's film entitled *Naked Lunch* (1991) honored the legend, rather than the novel, and contributed to a normalized (even heterosexualized) portrait of the artist. Most recently, Oliver Harris has taken up the problematics of this image in *William Burroughs and the Secret of Fascination* (2003).

The present volume continues to see Burroughs as emblematic of our times and illustrative of current theoretical preoccupations, attesting to his continuing power as a writer. These twenty-first-century essays confirm Graham Caveney's assertion that, 'Burroughs's project has never seemed so urgent [...] Far from being the end of an era, Burroughs has been instrumental in creating the one in which we now live. The man may be dead, his legacy has never been more alive' (1998:217). The essays in this volume read Burroughs within the context of theories about globalization and resistance. This perspective emphasizes Burroughs's analysis of control systems, especially his theories of word and image control (language as a virus), of the constructed nature of reality (the reality film), the social and cognitive effects of the electronic media (the Soft Machine), and the anarchist power of his utopias and dystopias (cities and zones). Several essays also continue to affirm Burroughs's status as an influential avant-garde experimentalist with discussions of the grotesque, humor, cut-ups, and cinematic prose techniques in his work. What is striking to this reader is the general agreement among the authors in this collection that Burroughs's moral and political position is clear: he opposes the sociopolitical control systems of late capitalism in the era of globalization, and his writing is a form of resistance. The icon of transgressive artist and the experimental artwork merge into one project: the creation of alternative subjectivities and resistance by 'turning the machine against itself'. Burroughs's avant-garde goal of deconstructing the art versus reality binary is seen as the political act of modeling resistance and of demonstrating practices for transforming everyday life.

Practically every critic writing during Burroughs's lifetime felt constrained to take a defensive position at some point—to defend the work against censorship, scandal, legend, moral and political condemnation, or critical incomprehension. It is refreshing to read a volume of new essays that see Burroughs unambiguously as an established authority—or is it anti-authority? The question confirms that Burroughs the icon and Burroughs the oeuvre continue to resist easy closure.

REFERENCES

Brookner, H. dir. (1983) *Burroughs*, Giorno Video, 1985 [video:VHS].

Burroughs, W. S. and Balch, A. (1990) *Towers Open Fire and Other Short Films*, Mystic Fire Video [video:VHS].

Caveney, G. (1998) *Gentleman Junkie: The Life and Legacy of William S. Burroughs* (Boston: Little, Brown).

Cronenberg, D. dir. (1991) *Naked Lunch*, Twentieth Century Fox.

Goodman, M. B. (1981) *Contemporary Literary Censorship: The Case History of Burroughs' 'Naked Lunch'* (Metuchen, NJ: Scarecrow).

Harris, O. (2003) *William Burroughs and the Secret of Fascination* (Carbondale: Southern Illinois University Press).

Lydenberg, R. (1987) *Word Cultures: Radical Theory and Practice in William S. Burroughs' Fiction* (Urbana: University of Illinois Press).

Morgan, T. (1988) *Literary Outlaw: The Life and Times of William S. Burroughs* (New York: Henry Holt).

Mottram, E. (1971) *William Burroughs: The Algebra of Need*, rev. edition (London: Marion Boyars, 1977).

Murphy, T. S. (1997) *Wising Up the Marks: The Amodern William Burroughs* (Berkeley: University of California Press).

Nelson, C. (1973) *The Incarnate Word: Literature and Verbal Space* (Urbana: University of Illinois Press).

Russell, J. (2001) *Queer Burroughs* (New York: Palgrave).

Skerl, J. (1985) *William S. Burroughs* (Boston: Twayne).

Skerl, J. and Lydenberg, R. (1991) *William S. Burroughs at the Front: Critical Reception 1959–1989* (Carbondale: Southern Illinois University Press).

Tanner, T. (1971) *City of Words: American Fiction, 1950–1970* (New York: Harper).

TLS reviewer/Willett, J. (1963) 'Ugh…', unsigned review, *Times Literary Supplement*, 14 November 1963, p. 919.

Tytell, J. (1976) *Naked Angels: The Lives and Literature of the Beat Generation* (New York: McGraw-Hill).

Introduction: Millions of People Reading the Same Words

Davis Schneiderman and Philip Walsh

Whether as novelist, essayist, painter, filmmaker, recording artist, mystic, countercultural icon, queer hero, science fiction guru, junkie, or media theorist, William S. Burroughs (1914–97) casts a larger-than-life shadow over the second half of the twentieth century. His alternately arcane and exoteric perspectives on the control systems of modern life first became familiar to segments of the postwar generation through the cosmic opera *Naked Lunch* (1959), the notoriety of his revolutionary cut-up method and, later, his iconic persona as a counterculture anti-hero. Burroughs wrote dozens of significant prose works, from his first novel *Junky* (1953) through the posthumous release of *Last Words: The Final Journals of William S. Burroughs* (2000). *Naked Lunch* was adapted into a film by David Cronenberg (1991), and Burroughs appeared in Gus Van Sant's *Drugstore Cowboy* (1989) as well as the video for U2's 'The Last Night on Earth' (1997); he collaborated on numerous recordings with musicians as diverse as Kurt Cobain, Tom Waits, Laurie Anderson and Bill Laswell, and engaged in various radical image experiments ranging from cut-up films in underground London to 'shotgun' paintings and text/image collaborations with artists such as Keith Haring, Robert Rauschenberg and Philip Taaffe. In short, William S. Burroughs has become not only a literary innovator, but also a major force within popular media and aesthetic culture.

Yet, for all his dynamic prescience, academic and popular criticism has managed only to scratch the surface of Burroughs's significance. With the exception of such notable recent texts as Timothy S. Murphy's *Wising Up the Marks: The Amodern William S. Burroughs* (1997), Jamie Russell's *Queer Burroughs* (2001) and Oliver Harris's *William S. Burroughs and the Secret of Fascination* (2003)—a corpus which signals a critical renaissance for Burroughs—the increasingly important social and political elements of his work have been only sporadically treated in the past four decades.

1

This collection functions as a partial corrective to this state of affairs by connecting Burroughs's work to the theme of 'globalization' and its emerging dominance as a key theoretical transdisciplinary paradigm. This connection involves what Jennie Skerl, in the Foreword to this collection, identifies as a key challenge: to move beyond the 'easy closure' of seeing Burroughs as an icon or prophet, and to situate his work within the *critical* discourse engendered by the prevailing reality of globalization.

We have selected a group of contributors that includes not only scholars at the forefront of Burroughs studies but also critics, novelists and theorists from a range of disciplines and backgrounds. These authors attack their material with enough energy to infuse the cogent issue—literary explication that moves beyond its own rarefied limits—with vital connections that present Burroughs's work as a 'blueprint' for identifying and resisting the immanent control mechanisms of global capital. Additionally, the editors come to this collection as children of Bretton Woods, of IMF and World Bank 'structural adjustment' policies, of ballooning world debt, of a globalizing 'junk culture', of a rapidly unfolding new imperialism, and of a symbolic culture dominated by the logic of the commercial logo. These forces demand an engagement that goes beyond the traditional literary or sociological work of the past decades. Schooled in the 1990s viability of cultural studies, Davis Schneiderman has found his work evolving from literary analysis into investigations of literature as a global commodity, analogous in many important ways to the world trade in coffee beans, microcomputers, and information. Philip Walsh comes to this project with a special interest in the critical theory of the Frankfurt School and in the sociology of globalization. Together, we wish to produce both a 'sociological literature' and a 'literary sociology'—a hybrid discipline that acknowledges the fact that the world does not break apart into separate domains, each accessible only to discrete specialized disciplines.

The 16 essays have been commissioned specifically for this collection (with the exception of John Vernon's study, which because of its special relevance, we have reprinted from an earlier era of Burroughs criticism). Their aim, en masse, will not be to cover the targets already pierced by earlier arrows, but to claim new areas for debate and discovery in the work of a writer who defiantly cast off the linear conventions of the world—and with whose work the world has perhaps only now begun fully to catch up.

THE GLOBALIZATION PARADIGM

A key debate within globalization theory concerns the connection between globalization and '(post)modernity'. This debate is nested within a larger question that concerns the precedents for globalization: Does globalization describe an explosive set of social changes suddenly erupting in the wake of a structural transformation? Or is it simply an end-stage to what has been called 'modernization'? The first position focuses on the new possibilities of human society set forth by the current processes; the second maintains the tendency of human institutions to replicate themselves and reintroduce the old order within the new. There is also dispute about the salient features of globalization. Although global connections have been developing for centuries, the term may be understood in its current context, broadly speaking, to refer to the flow of capital, goods, technologies, ideas, forms of culture and people across previously minimally related spaces, to create an intensified form of interconnectedness. In response, a network of specialized theory-types have come to form a 'globalization theory' paradigm, but a paradigm, which, somewhat like the processes it purports to describe, simultaneously splits and hollows out at the same time as it unifies and consolidates.

A first axis of globalization—and for some, the only axis—is that of economics. Economic globalization theorists emphasize the power and penetrative power of markets. Neo-liberalism, represented in the writings of Milton Friedman and Francis Fukuyama, emphasizes the unfettered expansion of market relations, the lowering of trade barriers (mainly to the advantage of the fully industrialized countries of the Northern hemisphere), and the construction of regulatory organizations such as the WTO. Such hulking neo-liberalism is based on an implicit and unnerving compound of determinism and millennialism. Indeed, for Fukuyama (1992), globalization is marked not only by the unprecedented expansion of capitalist social relations, but also by its unprecedented legitimation.

Opposed to such reductionism, but with a similar emphasis on economics, contemporary Marxist theorists such as Immanuel Wallerstein (1998) agree that capitalist social relations tend toward universality and totality, but see this process as marked by increasing social conflict and the polarization of economic resources, with political and military conflict as 'lag effects' of this general process.

For Fredric Jameson (1991), globalization is 'capitalism', but, inasmuch as it is 'late' capitalism, it implies an emergent 'cultural logic' that breaks with the logic of global commodity production, emphasizing instead the production of a global culture of consumer capitalism. For Joseph E. Stiglitz (2002:206–13), former World Bank chief economist and senior vice-president, globalization has come to mean unfettered global capitalism: supranational regulatory organizations such as the IMF, originally charged with ensuring global financial stability and providing funds for countries faced with recession conditions, have moved away from this goal and now operate under a mandate of promoting the financial interest of parties that put the organization in direct conflict with its original charge. Such pronouncements in Stiglitz's *Globalization and its Discontents*, along with similar re-estimations by ex-insiders such as Harvard economist and former IMF advisor Jeffrey Sachs, suggest that Jameson's 'logic of late capitalism' is becoming inescapably self-propelling.

A second perspective privileges the emergence of global communication networks, and emphasizes changes brought about by both the increasing scale and speed of the global flow of information. According to such thinkers as Manuel Castells (1996), Marshall McLuhan (1989) and Paul Virilio (2002), globalization consists of the eclipse of the localized experience of time and place brought about by the properties of high information flow, what Virilio refers to as 'an audiovisual derealization as a result of which the worldly public [...] would end up believing what it would not touch and could not have "seen" ' (37–8). This derealization radically changes the framework of human experience and destabilizes the intersubjective bases of enframing institutions, such as the nation state and the news media. Jean Baudrillard (1983) extrapolates from these tendencies to argue for the emergence of the 'hyperreal' as a distinct domain of experience, specific to a global system based on the smoke and mirrors of replicated simulacra.

A third perspective, which may be said to combine elements of the previous two, emphasizes the changes in the industrial order brought about by new technologies. For such thinkers as Daniel Bell (1999) and Anthony Giddens (1990), we are living in a post-industrial society in which changes in culture and politics are *secondary* phenomena, subordinate to alterations in the technological order. Benjamin Barber (1995) plays upon the same theme in his analysis of the effects of the 'McWorld' virus—the products, imagery and culture deriving from new symbol-based technology—which flows, significantly, from West to East and North to South, absorbing and replacing local sources of identity. The case of Bhutan, which in 1999 became the last country in the world to introduce television, an innovation rapidly followed by the collapse of the local economy, obliteration of its traditional Buddhist culture and rapid descent into a miasma of crime and corruption, serves as merely the most extreme example of the corrosive power of symbolic technologies.

We may identify a fourth perspective that analyzes globalization through the prism of power. Michael Hardt and Antonio Negri, drawing on the work of Gilles Deleuze and Félix Guattari, present globalization as a contradictory, 'Empire'-driven impulse of rapidly spreading global markets and processes of production, new media and technology, together with changes in modes of governance, class relations and questions of sovereignty.

RESISTANCES

While these vectors of 'structural' globalization—economics, technology, culture and power—are intrinsic to world development in the last several decades, for many of Burroughs's primarily 'literary' readers, the application of such sociopolitical concepts to his work may appear as no more 'real' than the threat of Venusian invaders in *The Place of Dead Roads* (1983) or the 'Alien Mind-Screens' that threaten Agent K-9 on the first track of the *Break Through in Grey Room* recording (circa 1965).

Nevertheless, we must insist on reading the products of Burroughs's fantastic imagination as *more* than tropes that simply teach the reader 'facts of general validity' (*J* xvi). His repeated entreaty to 'take a broad general view of things' can be read as part of the systemic logic of globalization that executes its agenda by separating the 'subject' from the point of production. Just as the workers in a Haitian Export Processing Zone are shocked to discover the price that Disney charges for the clothing produced in their factory (see the National Labor Committee [NLC] film *Mickey Mouse goes to Haiti*), so do Burroughs's subjects find themselves shocked and invaded by the insidious tentacles of their 'alien' controllers. In the famous 'Biologic Court' section of *Nova Express*, Life Form A requires 'oxygen' not present on the planet they have crashed on to, and so inhabits Life Form B (without Life Form B's knowledge), directing all activity to the *telos* of 'oxygen' production for Life Form A.

Aside from the instrumentality of producers working for unseen consumers, the trick is to maintain separation: 'Life Form A remains invisible to Life Form B by a simple operation scanning out areas of perception where another life form can be seen' (*NE* 134). Significantly, Burroughs's work consistently implies that both the sweatshop and the film medium (the latter used, à la the NLC, to expose the operations of the former) offer the same obfuscations due to the ubiquitous *mediation* of 'reality'. As Theodor Adorno and Max Horkheimer point out in their famous analysis of the 'culture industry', the cinema show is often little more than the extension of the workplace; Burroughs extrapolates this point to the plane of the 'reality film' or 'reality studio', reminding us that even when multinational power makes shift to 'clean up' its act, it responds with the typical misdirection to which it has become accustomed.

This raises a further issue associated with the globalization para-digm: namely, the sites and sources of protest against the 'agents' of global capital. Transnational 'opposition' movements are perhaps misnamed, in that the groups that mobilize against the perceived abuses of globalization 'agents' (ranging from Médecins Sans Frontières to the United for Peace and Justice website that helped mobilize 400,000 protestors opposed to the Iraq war in New York City on 15 February 2003) are as diverse as those agents themselves, and by no means universally opposed to leveraging global eco-nomic, communicative and technological developments for a counter-offensive. In this sense, the worldwide press coverage of the dismantling of a semi-constructed McDonald's restaurant in Millau, France, on 12 August 1999 (led by farmer-activist José Bové) and the early 2001 text-message-inspired protest of 100,000 Filipinos that helped oust former President Joseph Estrada both represent globally mediated forms of resistance that would have been impossible only decades ago.

Remarking upon the now (in)famous 'Battle of Seattle' that disrupted a meeting of the World Trade Organization in late 1999, Gilles Luneau writes that the 'new idea' offered by the loose but determined confederation of protestors was that, 'as capitalism at its most rampant and ruthless was sweeping the world, a global stance in favor of democracy was now required' (2001:xii). Burroughs anticipated the need for just such a mass movement that would continue the gains of the 1960s, while also maintaining a healthy skepticism necessary to deal with the contradictions of concerted action. This is evident in the ambivalence of his novels, which often conflate a reactionary aggression with ideals of autonomy and self-possession (see Russell 2001:131). Burroughs's distrust of all narrative-based critiques qualifies his support (to use Luneau's phrase) for a 'global stance'. While texts such as *The Job* and *The Wild Boys*, which follow the events of the 1968 Democratic Convention week in Chicago, offer some of Burroughs's most 'clearly' enunciated political statements, the totality of his work remains distanced from explicitly organized political aims.

This is no less the case with respect to the problem of Burroughs's medium: 'The Word'. Lennard J. Davis writes: 'Look any day and in any place and you will see its victims [...] Solitary people [...] sitting passive, silent, hunched almost fetally over a small pack of papers. Most often their lips are still, their faces expressionless, their eyes fixed on some invisible moving point. In order to remain in this state, they must block outside stimuli, become virtually autistic' (Davis 1987:2). While this excerpt from Davis's opening to *Resisting Novels* may be facetious, Burroughs's series of reflexive language games highlights a parasitism of language that limits the efficacy of 'the Word'. His junkies, hooked on everything from heroin to 'heavy metal' (*TE* 52), search eternally and empty-eyed for the immaculate fix of *silence*—because the talking cure *is* the parasitic condition, and 'the Word' functions as the ultimate narcotic. Burroughs's junk is omnidirectional; it effects a cold blue absence *and* presence all at once; it sparkles dully inside us like the aurora borealis set across the length of the intestines; it is J. G. Ballard's 'lost symmetry of the blastophere' (1990:14), the medium of our understanding, the pusher, the product, and—in an age of accelerated 'Word' technology—the very definition of the 'global' itself.

Three central concerns for this collection thus emerge from Burroughs's creative and critical production as relevant to questions surrounding the emergent global order: The essays in Part I, 'Theoretical Depositions', link Burroughs's articulation of the global control systems that emerged in the post-World War II era with the dominant strands of twentieth-century theory. These essays establish the importance of reading Burroughs through the lens of a sophisticated oppositional politics beyond the tradition of the merely literary. The essays in Part II, 'Writing, Sign, Instrument: Language and Technology', investigate the application of Burroughs's theory to his diverse methods of production—typewriter and cut-up, recording, painting, film—as well as the extrapolation of his work to the worldwide web. Part III, 'Alternatives: Realities and Resistances', investigates the possibilities that arise from such combinations of production and theory—through magic, violence, laughter and excess. Together, these essays argue for the significance of Burroughs's own version of a 'global stance'—a position keenly aware of its own failures and missed chances. The Burroughsian engagement with the 'global' will never be completely that of Hakim Bey's 'Temporary Autonomous Zones' (1991)—carnivals that emerge fully born outside World Economic Forum meetings. For Burroughs, such temporary victories are simply that, and we must be wary of false stances that celebrate too soon and that reject the necessity of understanding that resistance must always encounter its real limits in the process of creation.

Anything less establishes Burroughs as a false hero, a messianic media icon whose image becomes part of the mass consolidation *of the image*. Instead, these essays locate Burroughs's work within a space beyond the familiar safe channels of literary analysis. As he writes in *Cities of the Red Night*, articulating the limits of 'the Word':

> Faced by the actual practice of freedom, the French and American revolutions would be forced to stand by their words. The disastrous results of uncontrolled industrialization would also be curtailed [...] Any man would have the right to settle in any area of his own choosing [...] The escalation of mass production and concentration of population would be halted. The land would belong to those who used it. (*CRN* xiv)

This collection situates Burroughs's work within the tenuous forces of the global field, and in doing so, stakes a bold new claim.

REFERENCES

Ballard, J. G. (1990) *The Atrocity Exhibition*, rev., expanded, annotated, illustrated edition (San Francisco: Re/Search).
Barber, B. (1995) *Jihad vs. McWorld* (New York: Times).
Baudrillard, J. (1983) *Simulations* (New York: Semiotext[e]).
Bell, D. (1999) *The Coming of Post-Industrial Society*, Anniversary Edition (New York: Basic Books).
Bey, H. (1991) *T.A.Z.: The Temporary Autonomous Zone, Ontological Anarchy, Poetic Terrorism* (New York: Autonomedia).
Castells, M. (1996) *The Network Society* (Oxford: Blackwell).
Davis, L. J. (1987) *Resisting Novels: Ideology and Fiction* (New York: Methuen).
Fukuyama, F. (1992) *The End of History and the Last Man* (New York: Farrar, Strauss and Giroux).

Giddens, A. (1990) *The Consequences of Modernity*. (Stanford, CA: Stanford University Press).

Jameson, Fredric (1991) *Postmodernism, or, the Cultural Logic of Late Capitalism* (London: Verso).

Luneau, G. (2001) 'Preface', IN Bové, J. and Dufour, F., *The World is Not for Sale: Farmers Against Junk Food*, de Casparis, A. trans. (New York: Verso), pp. ix–xii.

McLuhan, M. and Powers, B. R. (1989) *The Global Village: Transformations in World Life and Media in the 21st Century* (New York: Oxford University Press).

National Labor Committee (1996) *Mickey Mouse goes to Haiti*, National Labor Committee [video:VHS].

Russell, J. (2001) *Queer Burroughs* (New York: Palgrave).

Stiglitz, J. (2002) *Globalization and its Discontents* (New York: Norton, 2003).

Virilio, P. (2002) *Ground Zero* (New York: Verso).

Wallerstein, I. (1998) *The End of the World as We Know It* (Minneapolis: University of Minnesota Press, 1999).

Part I
Theoretical Depositions

1
Shift Coordinate Points: William S. Burroughs and Contemporary Theory

Allen Hibbard

William S. Burroughs was way ahead of the theory game. As early as the 1950s, in works such as *Queer* and *Naked Lunch,* and continuing into the 1960s with the Nova trilogy (*The Soft Machine, The Ticket that Exploded* and *Nova Express*), Burroughs grappled head-on with issues that later became central concerns of deconstruction, cultural studies and queer theory. Subsequent works, up through the Red Night trilogy (*Cities of the Red Night, The Place of Dead Roads, The Western Lands*), written in the 1980s, also are susceptible to a variety of theoretical occupations. We are now in a position to look back at Burroughs's production through the lens of theory and appreciate how prescient he was. An artist with his antennae up, Burroughs responded to the same cultural landscape that spurred and shaped so much of contemporary theory: the manipulation of images by mass media, space travel, Cold War politics, genetic engineering, sophisticated surveillance systems, chemical/biological warfare, nuclear arms proliferation, genocide, environmental disaster, global inequalities in the aftermath of colonialism, a surge of religious fundamentalism, electronic communications, more open expressions of various forms of sexual desire, and so on. Indeed, as many have suggested, in the midst of these phenomena, Burroughs helped forge what became known as a distinctly new and innovative postmodern literary style. With so many and varied ports of entry, it is not surprising that Burroughs's work has become a host for so many strains of theory (which themselves act like viruses, taking hold, multiplying and spreading). My purpose here is to examine how various theoretical tools have been employed to help us understand and develop greater appreciation for Burroughs's project.

Foremost among the preoccupations Burroughs shares with literary theorists is an abiding, intense interest in the operation of language. Throughout the last century, a host of theorists including Ferdinand de Saussure, Ludwig Wittgenstein, Hilary Putnam, Noam Chomsky, J. L. Austin, John Searle and Jacques Derrida have toyed with the riddles associated with meaning formation in and through language. Ferdinand de Saussure's seminal thinking, found in his 'Course in General Linguistics' (1916), remains an important touchstone for subsequent theorists, and provides concepts that help us understand Burroughs's project. Crucial to Saussure's theory of language is his now classic distinction between thing or idea and word, and between signified and signifier. There was, he proposed, a certain arbitrariness associated with the sign, and meanings could change from community to community, from time to time. Saussure's groundbreaking work opened fresh space to discuss how language functioned, how meanings were formed, and how particular meanings can be controlled and used for political purposes.

Frequently, in interviews, Burroughs referred to the theories of Alfred Korzybski, whose notions about the relationship between signifier and signified resemble those of Saussure. Burroughs saw Korzybski as a natural philosophical ally, and heralded the linguist's challenge to strict dichotomies of 'either/or': a thing must be this or that. Relying on Korzybski, Burroughs submits, in a 1987 interview with Larry McCaffery and Jim McMenamin, that '[e]very act is not either instinctive or intellectual; it's instinctive *and* intellectual, involving the organism's entire body' (1990:190). The copula was the culprit. The word 'is', Burroughs noted (again relying on Korzybski), and carries 'the implication that there is some sort of eternal status being conveyed' (1990:184). Once identifications are established through language, they are extremely difficult to pry apart.

Burroughs, in much the same way as Martin Heidegger in his essay 'Language' (1950) (published when Burroughs was off in Mexico), saw man and language as integrally intertwined. Man lives in language and is shaped by language. Man speaks, to be sure, yet it is also language that speaks man, Heidegger asserts. Language makes itself at home in us—inhabits us—just as we inhabit language. While Heidegger seems relatively untroubled by this condition, Burroughs acutely felt the political implications of such a situation. Certain dominant ideologies are constructed and maintained *through* language. We are apt to be trapped by the language we hear and inherit. Thus, it would behoove us to think more about how meanings are created and controlled, and then explore ways of breaking the hold of conventional language on our thought and behavior. This project clearly has much in common with deconstruction and poststructuralist textualism, both of which insist upon a certain free play or arbitrariness of the sign. Burroughs, whose dictum was 'rub out the word forever', was guided by similar presuppositions. It was necessary, he posited, to disrupt established patterns of language in order to destabilize and transform dogmatic, rigid social, moral and political structures. Therein lies the revolutionary potential of his thinking.

One of Burroughs's famous formulations is that language (the 'Word') works like a virus. This metaphor enables us to think afresh about the operation of language, how things take hold and spread: over the airwaves, through the television, from mass-produced newspapers and books and the Internet, words travel, finding— wherever they can—the susceptible eye, ear or mind. They take hold, reproduce themselves and are passed on in similar fashion. The writer, aware of this process, acts as a secret agent, surreptitiously huggermugger, putting words together in new combinations and disseminating them as a sort of inoculation or counter-virus, attempting to curb or eliminate the harmful effects of the dominant, most prevalent and pernicious forms of virulent word.

Robin Lydenberg, one of the first Burroughs critics to use theory to elucidate his work, dwells on the issue of language in her book *Word Cultures*. Lydenberg comes to Burroughs with an arsenal of analytic explosives supplied by theorists such as Roland Barthes, Julia Kristeva and Jacques Derrida. She notes in the Preface that 'the ideas we now recognize as characteristic of poststructuralism and deconstruction were being developed independently by Burroughs almost thirty years ago' (1987:xi). Clearly, her intent in bringing contemporary theory to bear on Burroughs is to advance a more serious discussion of his work, which had so often been dismissed (or celebrated!) as incomprehensible rubbish, the effluvia of a debased drug addict and pervert. With her close readings of *Naked Lunch* and the cut-up novels of the Nova trilogy, infused with theoretical insights, Lydenberg does indeed help elevate Burroughs's status, and with it, the sophistication of critical discussion.

Burroughs subverts established ideologies through the nature of the stories he tells and the means by which he tells them, as well as through his radical deployment of language. The writer serves as a guardian of knowledge. What is more, he can be a force for the creation of new values. If there is any chance of opposing dominant meanings, possibility comes from the creative writer's ability to conjure counter-narratives. Thus, the writer in *The Place of Dead Roads*, William Seward Hall (one of Burroughs's fictional alter egos), takes to both concealing and revealing knowledge 'in fictional form' so that 'only those for whom the knowledge is intended will find it' (*PDR* 115). Burroughs effects a radical rupture from established circuits of energy and rut-worn storylines by continually disturbing or breaking the narrative thread. His narratives do not move the way conventional narratives move, with a logically developed plot and chronologically unfolding story. His fictive worlds are fluid, moving nomadically from one time to another, from one place to another, purposefully derailing strict linearity. Aspects of Mexico and Latin America blur with those of North Africa, London, Paris, Cairo and the Midwest of the United States. Burroughs creates a visionary space (much in the way utopian fiction does) where rules, practices and structures of our ordinary life are suspended or displaced by new ones born from the creative act.

Burroughs thereby participates (no doubt unwittingly) in a project that Jean-François Lyotard identifies in his highly influential *The Postmodern Condition: A Report on Knowledge* as 'the crisis of narratives'. Noting the firm grasp scientific discourse and knowledge have maintained on modern culture, Lyotard posits strategies to dislodge pervasive 'master narratives' associated with the Enlightenment ideal of progress—psychoanalysis, dogmatic Marxism, or absolutist religious paradigms. 'Postmodern knowledge is not simply a tool of the authorities', Lyotard writes in the Introduction. 'It refines our sensitivity to differences and reinforces our ability to tolerate the incommensurable. Its principle is not the expert's homology, but the inventor's paralogy' (1979:xxv). Like Lyotard, Burroughs acknowledges the powerful influence of science and technology on our lives, granting both their potential to constrain individual choice as well as to create new spaces for free thought and action (for example, through space travel).

In a manner consistent with Lyotard and with other poststructuralist thinkers, Burroughs champions the heterogeneous over the homogeneous, a scattered diversity over a coherent unity. Similarly, he challenges the very notion of an autonomous self, particularly a singular, discrete author. In 'The Death of the Author', Roland Barthes directs our attention to the text itself, noting that 'it is language which speaks, not the author' (1968:1467). The author's 'only power is to mix writings, to counter the ones with the others, in such a way as never to rest on any one of them' (1968:1468), and 'the book itself is only a tissue of signs, an imitation that is lost, infinitely deferred' (1968:1469). It is, then, in the act of reading that the text and its meaning are created, Barthes proclaims. In a similar vein, responding to Barthes, Michel Foucault examines the question, 'What Is An Author?'. Cultures have not universally acknowledged the singular author or granted him privileged status, he notes. What we have is an 'author-function' that 'is not formed spontaneously through the simple attribution of a discourse to an individual' but rather 'results from a complex operation whose purpose is to construct the rational entity we call an author' (1969:1629).

To be sure, we associate the name William S. Burroughs with a set of texts, just as we associate Barthes and Foucault with the works they wrote. (Their names are on the covers, and the associations are repeated, over and over, by convention.) Nonetheless, Burroughs employed various methods to undermine his own singular authority as author. One was by composing, much like a *bricoleur*, moving blocks of language from some previous linguistic construction (for example, the works of Kafka or his own previously published works) to use them in the construction of a 'new' text. Like many other postmodern artists (Kathy Acker comes to mind at once), Burroughs quoted, borrowed or plagiarized as a means of challenging the notion of literary ownership.

Collaboration was another means by which Burroughs called into question the notion of autonomous author. His collaborative projects with his St Louis friend Kells Elvins, Allen Ginsberg, Jack Kerouac, Brion Gysin, James Grauerholz and a host of musicians and visual artists are well known. When one creative talent joins another to produce something that exceeds their individual aesthetic, they form a 'third mind'. (We might think of those photos of Burroughs and Gysin in *Ports of Entry* [Sobieszek 1996], as well as the many pieces the two produced jointly.) Finally, in his fiction, Burroughs challenges the conventional notion of the autonomous character, creating multiple selves in response: one character may split off from another, assume a disguise, submit to cloning, find his organs transplanted into another body, or unite with another species to form some novel hybrid. The author himself is described as composed of many selves: 'William Seward Hall, the man of many faces and many pen names, of many times and places ... pilgrim of adversity and danger, shame and sorrow. The Traveler, the Scribe, most hunted and fugitive of men, since the knowledge unfolding in his being spells ruin to our enemies' (*PDR* 115). The principle of diversity is biologically driven; the chances of survival are greater when there are differences even within a species.

It is perhaps Giles Deleuze and Félix Guattari who provide the most fitting theoretical tools for elucidating Burroughs's life and work. Timothy S. Murphy, in his study *Wising Up the Marks: The Amodern William Burroughs*, examines the connections between Burroughs and Deleuze and Guattari. Murphy identifies a strain of literature, subsequent to modernism, which at once liberates itself from the totalizing claims of modernism and resists the groundlessness of so much of postmodernism. As he puts it, '[t]he amodernist alternative to (post)modernism, briefly, shares the modernist and postmodernist suspicion of representational art and politics, but rejects both the constitutive asymmetries of modernist myth-mongering and the postmodern abandonment of critique in the face of the procession of simulacra' (1997:29). Burroughs's amodernism— like Ralph Ellison's in *Invisible Man*—carves out a space/place in which constructive, positive resistance is possible. Rather than simply launching attacks on the existing structures, it allows alternative forms of organization based on libertarian principles to emerge.

The analytical tools and vocabulary of Deleuze and Guattari, Murphy suggests, like Burroughs's literary project, provide routes toward new ways of thinking. In *A Thousand Plateaus*, for instance, Deleuze and Guattari (who, they note at the outset, are fused and transformed through their collaboration) distinguish between what they call 'rhizomatic' and 'root' thinking. The image of root thinking is the tree; thought moves and multiplies along the lines of a strict binary logic. The image of rhizomatic thinking is the bulb or tuber; the rhizome follows principles of 'connection and heterogeneity', 'multiplicity' and 'asignifying rupture' (1980:7–9). The very nature of a book, Deleuze and Guattari submit, has traditionally been bound by root thinking. *A Thousand Plateaus* is conceived and composed rhizomatically. That is, theoretically, the book does not *depend* upon linear reading. The reader can dip in and out of the book, constructing his or her own logic, skipping around, moving backwards or forwards, setting the book aside to read another book by another author, coming back, jumping in at another point, depending upon the reader's own will or whim. Burroughs's own books certainly have this rhizomatic quality. They are arranged rather than plotted. They do not operate according to the logic of conventional narratives (though, as many critics have noted, the later works have more of a narrative thread). There is always an element of spontaneity and surprise, with radical shifts from one point to another, from one character to another, without warning, thus challenging the notion of one singular 'logic'. What we have, then, is simply juxtaposition: one element placed beside another, if not randomly, at least not wholly and inviolably dependent on that which came before: thus the potential for radical change.

Certainly, Burroughs's thinking is rhizomatic, as it celebrates hetereogenity and intentionally creates points of rupture, ways of breaking loose from old, calcified patterns. Not surprisingly, Deleuze and Guattari were drawn to Burroughs's work. Indeed, Robin Lydenberg has even suggested that Burroughs influenced the composition of *A Thousand Plateaus*. They recognized Burroughs's cut-up method as a way of 'making series proliferate or a multiplicity grow', and challenging singular, unitary, wholly linear notions of knowledge, though they wonder whether an implied 'supplementary dimension' might point toward a unity that 'continues its spiritual labor' (1980:6). And, in *Naked Lunch*, they found a superb example of their notion of the Body without Organs (BwO), which they define in *Anti-Oedipus* as 'the unproductive, the sterile, the unengendered, the unconsumable', the 'imageless, organless body' that can resist being integrated into the established machines producing desires and products, ready-made for consumption (1972:8).[1] As an example of the 'drugged body' (one of the forms of a body inclined to BwO, along with the hypochondriac body, the paranoid body, the schizo body and the masochist body), they cite this passage from *Naked Lunch*: 'The human body is scandalously inefficient. Instead of a mouth and an anus to get out of order why not have one all-purpose hole to eat *and* eliminate? We could seal up nose and mouth, fill in the stomach, make an air hole direct into the lungs where it should have been in the first place' (*NL* 119; cited by Deleuze and Guattari 1980:150).

A key (perhaps *the* key) feature of Deleuze and Guattari's thought is to make available routes of resistance to fascism, in both its internal and external manifestations. This battle is played out over and over again in Burroughs's work, as individuals and groups of individuals fight for free expression against those aligned with dominant power structures—politicians, captains of industry, military leaders, police, bigots, and so on. In *Nova Express*, a battle wages between the Nova Police and the Nova Mob. In various places, Burroughs distinguishes between the 'shits' (those who are always determined to *impose* their views and ways) and the 'Johnsons' (those who mind their own business and leave you alone).² *The Place of Dead Roads* features Kim Carsons, assassin and sharpshooter, whose targets include bigots and intolerant Christian fundamentalists. (He only responds with violence when provoked.) And, of course, the figure of the legendary Hassan i Sabbah, the Isma'ili renegade who perfected the use of assassination for strategic political purposes (to counter the growing power of dogmatic forms of Islam in the twelfth century), is a recurring and vastly important leitmotif throughout Burroughs's oeuvre. Such binary oppositions seem to serve much the same purpose as they do for William Blake. They are posited as a necessary means by which change can be effected.

Insofar as Burroughs sought to reveal the workings of corporate and governmental control mechanisms, it would seem that he would be sympathetic to the Marxist theory that serves as the basis for so much work in cultural studies. As Murphy writes, 'Burroughs's work [...] constitutes an exacting critique both of the social organization of late capital and of the logic of representation or textuality that abets it' (1997:74). Indeed, few, if any, contemporary American writers have so assiduously unmasked the fundamental architecture and internal operations of late capitalism. Murphy usefully points out ties between Burroughs and various important Marxist theorists of the past century: Adorno and Horkheimer (notably their critique of the culture industry), Fredric Jameson (in his attempts in *Postmodernism, or, The Cultural Logic of Late Capitalism* [1991] to resuscitate a Marxist-historical mode of analysis in a resolutely anti-historical context), and Louis Althusser (in his identification of Ideological State Apparatuses such as schools, courts, unions, political parties, media, and families that reproduce themselves, thus maintaining underlying capitalistic structures).

Despite these affinities between Burroughs's project and those of various Marxist critics, Murphy is quick to point out that Burroughs is no strict Marxist thinker. Indeed, Burroughs would likely assert that a dogged, inflexible adherence to any ideology would be anathema to the artist. Ann Douglas, in her introduction to *Word Virus*, seeks to clarify Burroughs's relationship to Marxism:

> Burroughs had no sympathy for the regimented, Marxist-based Communist regimes of Eastern Europe. He saw the Cold War

administrations of the U.S. and the U.S.S.R. not as enemies but as peers and rivals vying to see who could reach the goal of total control first. Yet both Burroughs and Karl Marx had an acute understanding of just how revolutionary the impact of plain common sense could be in a world contorted by crime and self-justification, and in a number of areas their interests ran along parallel lines [...] Like Marx, he was certain that 'laissez-faire capitalism' could not be reformed from within: 'A problem cannot be solved in terms of itself.' He, too, saw the colonizing impulse that rewrote the world map between the sixteenth and nineteenth centuries as a tactic to 'keep the underdog under,' an indispensable part of capitalism's quest for new markets and fresh supplies of labor. (1998:xxi–xxii)

Burroughs's work can also be fruitfully situated within the context of gender and queer theory. Burroughs lived and wrote through a period marked by a gradual reduction of the stigma associated with marginalized sexualities and a burgeoning of critical activity in all literary periods related to the formation of sexual subjectivity. Foucault's *History of Sexuality* (1976) and Eve Sedgwick's *The Epistemology of the Closet* (1990), among many other studies, advanced critical discussions on the relationship between discourse and sexuality. Desires and means of sexual expression were created, monitored and controlled by a variety of social mechanisms. The notion of a norm—say, the norm of 'compulsory heterosexuality'—has been challenged by feminist critics such as Adrienne Rich and Bonnie Zimmerman.[3]

Burroughs's fiction has always been marked by strong, often graphic depictions of homosexual acts, and even in the relatively conservative 1950s, Burroughs did little to conceal or mask his homosexuality, which, for him, became but one more method (along with drug use and writing) of acting subversively, asserting a self outside the boundaries of law and social norms. The radical force of Burroughs's work was quickly acknowledged. Leslie Fiedler was one of those who recognized early on the power of Burroughs's vision. In the mid-1960s, Fiedler linked Burroughs to the Dionysian, hippie uprisings, and the feminization of man in popular culture. He saw Burroughs as 'the chief prophet of the post-male post-heroic world'; in *Naked Lunch* were 'clues to the new attitudes toward sex that will continue to inform our improbable novels of passion and our even more improbable love songs' (1965:517–18).

Given that Burroughs has often been perceived as a misogynist (women: a biological mistake) and that his work promotes an all-male utopian vision, it is not surprising that he has not been roundly applauded by feminist critics and theorists. Despite the validity of various charges (not a debate I wish to enter into here), it should be pointed out that the kind of critique Burroughs develops (particularly his interest in how various means of sexual expression are socially shaped and controlled) is analogous to and consistent with the feminist project. Two early pioneers in Burroughs criticism, Jennie Skerl and Robin Lydenberg, have felt and acknowledged this link. Lydenberg describes how Burroughs's project can be aligned with feminist concerns: 'Burroughs adopts an anti-patriarchal perspective from which he isolates sexual dualism as the basic problem in Western civilization and thought. There are some surprising affinities between this position and radical feminist theory' (1987:171).

One would think that given the fairly graphic (sometimes surreal) depiction of sex between men in his work, Burroughs might have become a poster boy for the gay liberation movement and that his work would have been brought into the canon of gay literature. Burroughs and the 'gay community' (posed here as a useful fiction, but also understood as the guardians of the canon of gay literature) have never wholeheartedly embraced one another, however. Burroughs has never strictly been categorized as a 'gay' writer. He likely would have been uncomfortable with such restrictive, impre-cise, reductive labeling (he could just as well be thought of as a science fiction writer, or a satirist along the lines of Vonnegut, for instance). His writings and comments frequently register disdain for the 'fag', or feminized man. And while he spoke openly about his sexuality in places such as the *Gay Sunshine* interviews in the 1970s, his second novel, *Queer*, written in the early 1950s, was not published until 1985, in large part, it seems, because of concerns about the book's subject matter.

Only recently has Burroughs criticism squarely focused on sexual issues in his life and work. No doubt this move comes in response to the growing interest in queer theory. Richard Dellamora has con-sidered Burroughs in light of Cronenberg's film version of *Naked Lunch*, asserting that Cronenberg drains the work of its homosexual content. Dellamora also suggests that Burroughs himself 'lacks a concept of minority sexual identity. And he lacks an erotics, which might provide a locus at which ethical and social relations could be developed. In short, he has no readily available way in which to validate desire for sexual and emotional ties with other men'

(1994:114). Despite these criticisms, Dellamora does admit that 'the intersection of perverse sexual behavior with bohemian existence in the 1940s and 1950s contributed to the development of gay male politics', and that 'reading Burroughs provides an opportunity to begin to rewrite the relations of desire in "hip" culture' (1994:117).

Jamie Russell's recent book *Queer Burroughs* pulls Burroughs criticism out of the closet. Russell begins his study with the observation that 'silence over Burroughs' literary output as *queer* has been a consistent feature of his reception' (2001:2) and then embarks on a sustained, penetrating analysis that seeks to account for that silence and situate Burroughs within discussions of queer theory and the history of gay literature. He argues that 'Burroughs' texts do offer a complete (as opposed to *discontinuous*) pronouncement of a radical gay subjectivity that is in stark opposition to the heterosexual dominant's stereotypes of gay identity' (2001:6). Russell's critique calls attention to the ways in which Burroughs, while challenging dominant moral values, is yet still bound by those values. 'What is so interesting about the search for sexual freedom', he writes, 'is the extent to which Burroughs remains unable to divorce himself from the restrictive nature of American social morality' (2001:15). In particular, he clung to a culturally constructed idea of 'the masculine' even as he moved away from compulsory heterosexuality. His was a search for 'a narcissistic relationship in which each of the participants reflects the masculine status of the other' (2001:19–20).

Burroughs's vision, including the way he conceived of and depicted sexuality, evolved alongside the gay liberation movement. 'The post-Stonewall novels', Russell notes, 'center on a vision of a new, queer social order based on all-male (and all-gay) communes in which women and effeminate gay men have no place' (2001:57). Here, of course, he is referring to works such as *The Wild Boys* (1971), *Port of Saints* (1973, rev. 1980) and, perhaps, the Red Night trilogy of the 1980s. In these works, the gay characters 'are always prepared to defend their sexuality and prove their status as men through violence' (2001:91). In these later novels, Russell sees a 'political failure of the texts' (2001:138). Burroughs's primary deficiency, it seems, lies in his inability to wriggle loose from essentialist notions of 'male' and 'female' that have been challenged by recent theorists, notably Judith Butler, who sees gender as being primarily performative and thus highly fluid. Burroughs's views on gender, Russell suggests, are out of line with recent work in gender and queer theory.

The global dimension of Burroughs's writing anticipates concerns of those in postcolonial studies or even recent interest in considering American studies within a global context.[4] In his recent book, *Colonial Affairs: Burroughs, Bowles, and Chester Write Tangier*, Greg Mullins draws upon both queer theory and postcolonial theory as he seeks to understand the importance of Tangier for these three American writers. Burroughs belongs to a long and distinguished tradition of American expatriate writers who have gone abroad for various reasons. Mullins emphasizes the importance of Burroughs's expatriation, noting that roughly half of his works were written abroad. Quite likely, Burroughs would never have become a writer had he not left the US and lived elsewhere, relatively free from obligation and constraint. In Mexico he wrote his first two books, *Junky* and *Queer*; in Tangier, in the late 1950s, he composed *Naked Lunch* (whose working title was *Interzone*), creating a truly radical style that later would be identified as postmodern. Just as it had done for Paul Bowles earlier and Alfred Chester later, Tangier provided Burroughs with unique conditions conducive to imaginative breakthroughs. The place had a reputation for being a haven for travelers seeking various drugs or sex with boys.[5] As Mullins writes, Tangier was 'a space where national, religious, and cultural interests could be blurred and where unrestrained and proliferating desire could supplant bounded identities and ideologies' (2002:69). It was precisely that 'interzone' condition that allowed these writers to 'construct and call into question narratives of national, racial, and sexual identity' (2002:3).

As early as the 1940s, Allen Ginsberg recalled Burroughs talking to him and Jack Kerouac about the 'end of empire'. His journeys in search of *yagé* in Peru and his time in Tangier afforded him a better sense of both the reach and effect of American imperialism, in both cultural and political terms. Out of his experiences he formed a distinct distaste for the nation-state system and forged a vision, revealed in various places in his fiction, of a kind of utopian space where men of all races, colors and kinds could live together harmoniously, without social, economic or political distinctions based on those markers. *Cities of the Red Night*, for instance, is a kind of historical science fiction, re-imagining the history of the eighteenth century in a way that tilts the power to marginal groups of pirates and independent social projects that forbid slavery and colonization. Among the Articles proposed by Captain Mission: '[A]ll decisions with regard to the colony to be submitted to vote by the colonists; the abolition of slavery for any reason including debt; the abolition of the death penalty; and freedom to follow any religious beliefs or practices without sanction or molestation' (*CRN* xii). In these communities there would be '[n]o white-man boss, no Pukka Sahib, no Patrons, no colonists' (*CRN* xiv). Their character would be mixed and diverse: 'Negro, Chinese, Portuguese, Irish, Malay, Japanese, Nordic boys with kinky red and blond and auburn hair and jet-black eyes, Chinese with bright red hair and green eyes, mixtures of Chinese and Indian of a delicate pink color, Indians of a deep copper red with one blue eye and one brown eye, purple-black skin and red pubic hairs' (*CRN* 221).

Despite this fictive utopian vision, in his own life and travels, Burroughs was bound by the colonial legacy as he sought smooth places on the fringes of the Empire beyond the reach of law and rigid moral structures. It was not always clear whether his own struggle for liberation extended to embrace the collective (or even personal) struggles of those who were still living in oppressive conditions. As Greg Mullins notes, 'he accepted rather than critiqued his desires and accepted the neocolonial political relationships through which those desires became acts' (2002:81). 'Both his erotic practice and his politics', Mullins writes, 'depend upon sustaining his distance from and ignorance of his "third world" sex partners' (2002:85). (Significantly, Burroughs's partners—Angelo in Mexico City and Kiki in Tangier—are known to us merely by their first names.)

Burroughs was caught in an age-old critical bind: How can we overcome the blindnesses of our particular historical, subjective positions? At the outset of *Prisms*, Theodor Adorno clearly characterizes the ambivalent position of the cultural critic, as he stands within the very system he critiques: 'The cultural critic is not happy with civilization, to which alone he owes his discontent. He speaks as if he represented either unadulterated nature or a higher historical stage. Yet he is necessarily of the same essence of that to which he fancies himself superior' (1955:10). Burroughs—white, male, Harvard-educated, privileged, and American—bore the marks of the insider, yet always felt outside of those structures, realizing that to pledge allegiance to them would be to align himself with the machinery of oppression.

This bind or tension takes on a distinct character and is felt most acutely within the colonial or postcolonial scene. How can one, as a product and representative of an empire, speak purely and unequivocally against the very forces that have composed and nourished him? Burroughs's position was rather like that Ali Behdad describes in *Belated Travelers: Orientalism in the Age of Colonial Dissolution*. The writers in his study (Nerval, Flaubert, Kipling, Lady Anne Blunt, and Isabel Eberhardt) are caught between their alliances to home/empire and their sympathies for the countries through which they travel, a situation that produces 'elliptical discourses, uncertain about their representations and melancholic about their inability to produce an alternative mode of writing about the desired Other' (Behdad 1994:15). These travelers (like Burroughs), 'arriving too late to the Orient, at a time when tourism and European colonialism had already turned the exotic into the familiar [...] encountered the difficulty, if not the impossibility, of finding an elsewhere, of finding alternative horizons to explore, discover, and conquer' (1994:92). Burroughs's travels to Mexico and Morocco certainly heightened his consciousness of difference. And even if he may not have completely resolved these questions, his work at least brings to the surface many of these vexed issues related to global economic inequalities and political domination.

As is the case in so much contemporary theory, Burroughs's project is propelled by an unswerving, fervent desire to protect and exercise individual liberty. In his life and fiction, he sought to find or create spaces beyond legalistic, nationalistic forms of domination that dictated the contours and limits of thought and morality. He lamented the shrinking of freedoms he saw occurring in his own times. In the 'Fore!' of *Cities of the Red Night*, he concludes:

> There is simply no room left for 'freedom from the tyranny of government' since city dwellers depend on it for food, power, water, transportation, protection, and welfare. Your right to live where you want, with companions of your choosing, under laws to which you agree, died in the eighteenth century with Captain Mission. Only a miracle or a disaster could restore it. (*CRN* xv)

The prognosis seems now to be even more dire, as the pernicious machinery created to maintain Empire—a vast, intricate network involving check points, identity cards, increased police powers, electronic surveillance, a curbing of civil liberties—is being calibrated and lubricated to control actions and spaces that had previously lain beyond its reach and jurisdiction. In order for humans to resist, to seek out or reclaim space for free thought and action, Burroughs would say, we will need to evolve, to develop biological capacity for travel into space. Just as we evolved from aquatic forms, giving up gills for lungs, we must now—in order to survive, in order to find free and open spaces—transform ourselves from land creatures to space creatures.

Meanwhile, one of the last really free spaces seems to be the space of the imagination, the space of creative activity, the space of writing. Burroughs put his imagination to work, letting it loose to conceive of provocative, perverse and subversive fictions that challenged dominant political paradigms and regimes. There is no doubt in my mind that in the years to come, Burroughs will increasingly be recognized as one of the most innovative, prophetic American voices of the last half of the twentieth century. One vivid indication of his staying power has been the extent to which his work has served as such a ready, viable host to so many strains of the theory virus. We should expect that Burroughs will continue to be a prime target of whatever new forms of the virus lie waiting to be born.

NOTES

1. In *A Thousand Plateaus*, Deleuze and Guattari say that the Body without Organs 'is not at all a notion or a concept but a practice, a set of practices. You never reach the Body without Organs, you can't reach it, you are forever attaining it, it is a limit. People ask, So what is this BwO?—But you're already on it; scurrying like a vermin, groping like a blind person, or running like a lunatic: desert traveler and nomad of the steppes. On it we sleep, live our waking lives, fight—fight and are fought—seek our place, experience untold happiness and fabulous defeats; on it we penetrate and are penetrated; on it we love' (1980:150).
2. See, for instance, 'My Own Business' (in *AM* 15–18).
3. See Adrienne Rich, 'Compulsory Heterosexuality and Lesbian Existence', IN Leitch, V. B. 2001, pp. 1762–80 (first published in *Signs: Journal of Women in Culture and Society* [1980]; an abridged version published in *Adrienne Rich's Poetry and Prose*, edited by Barbara Charlesworth Gelpi and Albert Gelpi [1993]); and Bonnie Zimmerman, 'What Has Never Been: An Overview of Lesbian Feminist Literary Criticism', IN Leitch, V. B. 2001, pp. 2340–59 (first published in 1981 in *Feminist Studies*).
4. The January 2003 issue of *PMLA*, for instance, features a handful of articles devoted to 'America: The Idea, the Literature', many of which specifically address global contexts. Djalal Kadir's introduction, 'America and Its Studies', is particularly significant.
5. See Joseph Boone, 'Vacation Cruises; or, The Homoerotics of Orientalism', *PMLA* 110 (January 1995), pp. 89–107.

28   Theoretical Depositions

REFERENCES

Adorno, T. (1955) *Prisms*, Weber, S., and Weber, S. trans. (Cambridge, MA: MIT Press, 1981).
Barthes, R. (1968) 'The Death of the Author', IN Leitch, V. B. 2001, pp. 1466–70.
Behdad, A. (1994) *Belated Travelers: Orientalism in the Age of Colonial Dissolution* (Durham, NC: Duke University Press).
Deleuze, G., and Guattari, F. (1972) *Anti-Oedipus*, vol. 1 of *Capitalism and Schizophrenia*, Hurley, R., Seem, M., and Lane, H. R. trans. (New York: Viking, 1977).
—— (1980) *A Thousand Plateaus*, vol. 2 of *Capitalism and Schizophrenia*, Massumi, B. trans (Minneapolis: University of Minnesota Press, 1987).
Dellamora, R. (1994) *Apocalyptic Overtures: Sexual Politics and the Sense of an Ending* (New Brunswick, NJ: Rutgers University Press).
Douglas, A. (1998) ' "Punching a Hole in the Big Lie": The Achievement of William S. Burroughs', IN *WV* pp. xv–xxix.
Fiedler, L. (1965) 'The New Mutants', *Partisan Review*, 32(4) (Fall 1965) pp. 505–25.
Foucault, M. (1969) 'What is an Author?', IN Leitch, V. B. 2001, pp. 1622–36.
—— (1977–84) *The History of Sexuality*, vols 1–3, Hurley, R. trans. (New York: Pantheon, 1978–86).
Heidegger, M. (1950) 'Language', IN Leitch, V. B. 2001, pp. 1121–34.
Jameson, Fredric (1991) *Postmodernism, or, the Cultural Logic of Late Capitalism* (London: Verso).
Leitch, V. B. general ed. (2001) *The Norton Anthology of Theory and Criticism* (New York: W. W. Norton).
Lydenberg, R. (1987) *Word Cultures: Radical Theory and Practice in William S. Burroughs' Fiction* (Urbana: University of Illinois Press).
Lyotard, J. F. (1979) *The Postmodern Condition: A Report on Knowledge*, Bennington, G., and Massumi, B. trans. (Minneapolis: University of Minnesota Press, 1984).
McCaffery, L., and McMenamin, J. (1990) 'An Interview with William S. Burroughs', IN Hibbard, A. ed., *Conversations with William S. Burroughs* (Jackson: University Press of Mississippi, 1999), pp. 171–95.
Mullins, G. A. (2002) *Colonial Affairs: Bowles, Burroughs, and Chester Write Tangier* (Madison: University of Wisconsin Press).
Murphy, T. S. (1997) *Wising Up the Marks: The Amodern William Burroughs* (Berkeley: University of California Press).
Russell, J. (2001) *Queer Burroughs* (New York: Palgrave).
Saussure, F. de (1916) 'Course in General Linguistics', Bally, C., and Sechehaye, A. eds, IN Leitch, V. B. 2001, pp. 960–76.
Sedgwick, Eve (1990) *Epistemology of the Closet* (Berkeley: University of California Press).
Sobieszek, R. A. (1996) *Ports of Entry: William S. Burroughs and the Arts* (Los Angeles: Los Angeles County Museum of Art/Thames and Hudson).

2
Exposing the Reality Film: William S. Burroughs Among the Situationists

Timothy S. Murphy

> What you want is always smthng
> within a complex situation in (of)
> present time.
> We will provide the situation
> without which what you desire
> will remain a phantom...
> > the situation
> > the complex of
> > contents
> > or
> > conditns
> > —Alexander Trocchi, 'Advt.' (1972:81)

The opening thesis of Guy Debord's 1967 *Society of the Spectacle*, the most sophisticated and influential document produced by the Situationist International (SI) in the course of its stormy 15-year existence, proposes that '[t]he whole life of those societies in which modern conditions of production prevail presents itself as an immense accumulation of *spectacles*. All that once was directly lived has become mere representation' (1967:12). Three years earlier, in his cut-up novel *Nova Express*, William S. Burroughs wrote that ' "Reality" is simply a more or less constant scanning pattern—The scanning pattern we accept as "reality" has been imposed by the controlling power on this planet, a power primarily oriented toward total control' (*NE* 53). The following year, in conversation with Conrad Knickerbocker of *The Paris Review*, Burroughs clarified that '[i]mplicit in *Nova Express* is a theory that what we call reality is actually a movie. It's a film, what I call a biologic film' (Knickerbocker 1965:70).

What is the relationship between these two surprisingly similar claims, made by two of the most enigmatic figures to emerge from the global cultural ferment of the 1950s and 1960s? They never met or corresponded, as far as I have been able to determine, and they hardly make any direct reference to each other, yet they arrived at critical models of contemporary society that are remarkably congruent not only at the highest level of theoretical generality, but also at the more focused level of practical tactics for resistance. The key to this convergence, I would claim, lies not only in Burroughs's and Debord's parallel sensitivities to the postwar economy of the image, but also in the heretofore under-appreciated and unexamined role played by their common friend and ally Alexander Trocchi in translating between Debord's primarily political analysis and Burroughs's primarily aesthetic one and (perhaps) vice versa. Today, more than 30 years later, these critical models are still relevant to the extent that they retain their ability to dissect and displace the increasingly integrated economy of the image, whose global reach has only widened in the intervening decades. Despite the setbacks and even defeats they experienced, Burroughs and the Situationists continue to provide us with suggestive means to comprehend, and in so doing to resist, the spectacle of the present.

I: A LOOSE CULTURAL VENTURE

Let us begin by examining Trocchi's unacknowledged role as a conduit and translator between Burroughs and Debord. Glasgow-born Trocchi met Debord in Paris in 1955, while dividing his time between editing the avant-garde literary review *Merlin* and writing pseudonymous pornographic fiction for the Olympia Press (which would later publish Burroughs's *Naked Lunch*). For the next eight years, even after his relocation to the US in 1956, Trocchi would move relatively freely between the discrete bohemian worlds of the Lettrist International (and after 1957 its successor, the Situationist International) on the one hand and the expatriate Anglophone literary community on the other (Marcus 1989:385–7). In his 1960 novel, *Cain's Book*, which would soon bring him into contact and later friendship with Burroughs, Trocchi obliquely acknowledged his continuing involvement with Debord and company: late in the book, his junkie narrator writes: '*Il vous faut construire les situations*' (Trocchi 1960:236). When Trocchi was arrested in the US that year on drug charges, his fellow Situationists published a resolution appointing Debord and others to 'take immediate action on behalf of Alexander Trocchi' and to 'demand [his] setting free' (*IS* 1997:160). Unsurprisingly, the years immediately following the publication of *Cain's Book* would see Trocchi's most ambitious attempt to participate in the articulation of the Situationist project—that is, to 'construct situations'—an attempt that also involved Burroughs, whom he had gotten to know well during their scandalous joint attendance at the 1962 Edinburgh Festival (Morgan 1988:332–41). This would be, in essence, an attempt to construct a practical conduit between his two bohemian worlds, to establish an alliance between two distinct but overlapping modes of cultural resistance.

The opening move of Trocchi's effort was the composition of 'Invisible Insurrection of a Million Minds', a manifesto for what can only be called a revolution in consciousness and at the same time a proposal for the foundation of a 'limited liability company', initially called 'International Cultural Enterprises Ltd', which would manage the economic exploitation of the work of countercultural artists working toward such a revolution (1963a:190). This company would be a first step toward the establishment of a 'spontaneous university' similar to Black Mountain College that would in turn act as the 'detonator of the invisible insurrection' of the title (Trocchi 1963a:186–8, 191). I will examine these linked notions further in Section III, below. 'Invisible Insurrection' was first published in French in *Internationale Situationniste* 8 (January 1963) under the title 'Technique du coup du monde', which may be translated as 'Technique for World Takeover'—'*coup du monde*' in contrast to the 'coup d'état of Trotsky and Lenin' (*IS* 1997:346; see also Trocchi 1963a:177). Trocchi was also listed as a member of the journal's editorial committee for that issue. Later that year, the essay appeared in English under its original title, and in the following year it was incorporated into Trocchi's open-ended *Sigma Portfolio*, along with a further elaboration of the notion of a countercultural company and university entitled 'Sigma: A Tactical Blueprint' (1964a; see also Trocchi 1964b, #2 and 3).

A few months before the initial distribution of the *Portfolio*, Trocchi wrote Burroughs to invite him to join the board of directors of Sigma (as the countercultural company had been re-christened), which was apparently incorporated in London in the summer of 1963. 'The bricks and mortar of our enormous factory', he wrote, 'are contingent upon the eventual assent of our nuclear cosmonauts to operate it' (Trocchi 1963b:208). Trocchi hoped to raise capital for the

Sigma 'factory' by signing up high-profile writers and artists, the 'nuclear cosmonauts' he mentions, as directors and clients of Sigma's artist management service; in addition to Burroughs, Robert Creeley was invited to become a director, and Anthony Burgess, Lawrence Ferlinghetti, Allen Ginsberg, R. D. Laing, Timothy Leary and Michael McClure were named as 'people interested' in Sigma (Trocchi 1964b, #17). Along with the letter, Trocchi 'enclose[d] a copy of the ["Sigma: A Tactical Blueprint"] essay to acquaint [Burroughs] with the methods we have already evolved' (Trocchi 1963b:207); thus it seems fair to assume that Burroughs was at least superficially acquainted with Trocchi's revolutionary ambitions and his Situationist perspectives by this time. There is no evidence that Burroughs was ever formally 'registered as a director in the company' as Trocchi wanted (Trocchi 1963b:208), but he did contribute a piece entitled 'Martin's Folly' to the project, which was incorporated into a poster that became the first item in the *Portfolio* as it was originally distributed (Trocchi 1964b, #1). If we assume further that Burroughs later received a copy of the entire *Portfolio*, he would also have been able to read Trocchi's translation/adaptation of the 1960 'Manifesto Situationniste' that was included as well (for the original, see *IS* 1997:144–6; for Trocchi's translation, see Trocchi 1964b, #18). Thus the conduit that Trocchi was trying to build between the Anglophone counterculture and the Situationist International began to take shape, although it would have little opportunity to function.

All this work of independent but parallel practical organization did not go unnoticed by the leading members of the SI, who no doubt received copies of the *Portfolio*. In *Internationale Situationniste* 10 (March 1966), the editorial committee (headed by Debord and including the influential Situationists Michèle Bernstein, Mustapha Khayati and Raoul Vaneigem) published the following note of clarification regarding the group's relationship with Trocchi:

> Upon the appearance in London in autumn 1964 of the first publica-
> tions of the 'Project Sigma' initiated by Alexander Trocchi, it was mutu-
> ally agreed that the SI could not involve itself in such a loose cultural
> venture, in spite of the interest we have in dialogue with the most exi-
> gent individuals who may be contacted through it, notably in the
> United States and England. It is therefore no longer as a member of the
> SI that our friend Alexander Trocchi has since developed an activity of
> which we fully approve of several aspects. (*IS* 1997:495; trans. Knabb
> 1989:373)

Thus, despite the SI's 'interest in dialogue' with his 'exigent' friends like Burroughs (whose *Naked Lunch* had appeared in French translation in the spring of 1964), Trocchi was effectively expelled from the group just as he was beginning to contribute to it, though in a kinder and gentler fashion than most of the others who were excluded earlier and later. Indeed, in Christopher Gray's tabular summary of the SI's membership, Trocchi is listed as one of 19 'mutually agreed' 'resignations' (*démissions*) from the SI, rather than one of the 45 involuntary and rhetorically harsh 'exclusions' (Gray 1974:132–3). Debord's recently published letters to Trocchi confirm this (Debord 2001:299–300, 309–10). In any case, cut off from one of his bohemian worlds, Trocchi was left without a strong political basis for his fundamentally artistic Project Sigma, which seems to have dissolved thereafter, along with his plans for another novel, into junkie recidivism. He spent the bulk of his remaining years dealing in used books, and died of pneumonia in 1984.

II: RETAKE THE UNIVERSE

If we accept the thesis that Trocchi did act as a conduit and translator between the SI's milieu and Burroughs's, then the first questions that follow from this are, what exactly did he translate or conduct, and in which direction? Pending a comprehensive investigation of still-unpublished archives (including Trocchi's and Burroughs's personal correspondence of the period, much of which is still in private hands), the evidence suggests that the direction of influence, if it indeed took place, was most often from the Situationists to Burroughs rather than the reverse. Most of the key statements of Situationist theory and method to which I will refer hereafter predate, sometimes by many years, the parallel texts by Burroughs that bear the closest similarities to those statements. However, the claim of direct or indirect influence must remain speculative until all the evidence becomes available, no matter how suggestive the similarities may be between Burroughs's ideas and Debord's. Nevertheless, a passage in one unpublished letter from Burroughs to his French translator Mary Beach does confirm some degree of recognition of their shared interests, strategies and tactics:

> Do you know of a French group called Situationist International—correspondence: B.P. 307-03 Paris? Seemingly a sophisticated anarchist group. I think they would be an excellent outlet for the short

pieces I am writing now. Just read a very intelligent analysis of the Watt [sic] race riots by this group. (Burroughs 1967)

This letter was written long after Burroughs's brief involvement with Trocchi's Project Sigma, during which time he presumably first learned about the SI, so his description of it as 'a sophisticated anarchist group' may be forgetful or ironic. His interest in the SI's analysis of the Watts riots, however, is quite direct, and it will serve as our password into the extended comparison that follows.

The convergence between Burroughs's notion of the reality film and the Situationist theory of the spectacle manifests itself in a number of ways, some of which only become apparent when viewed through the lens of Trocchi's Project Sigma. First of all, despite their common language of visuality, neither model is simply a critique of some perceived misuse of film, television or the mass media generally. As I noted above, for Burroughs, the very reality that the media claim to depict is 'a more or less constant scanning pattern' that 'has been imposed by the controlling power on this planet, a power primarily oriented toward total control' (*NE* 53). Similarly, for Debord, '[t]he spectacle is not a collection of images; rather, it is a social relationship between people that is mediated by images' (1967:12). It is a control system of which the media are only a subordinate part, for it is 'the self-portrait of power in the age of power's totalitarian rule over the conditions of existence' (Debord 1967:19). As Burroughs argues, to understand the present it is necessary to '[p]ostulate a biologic film running from the beginning to the end, from zero to zero as all biologic film run in any time universe—Call this film X1 and postulate further that there can be only one film with the quality X1 in any given time universe' (*NE* 8 [note]). The issue of the film's singularity connects it to Burroughs's earlier and better-known theory of language as a totalitarian virus that people unwittingly internalize, expressed in *Naked Lunch* as follows: 'The Word is divided into units which be all in one piece and should be so taken, but the pieces can be had in any order being tied up back and forth, in and out fore and aft like an innaresting sex arrangement' (*NL* 207). Although '[t]he word cannot be expressed direct' (*NL* 105) in its totality, it is nevertheless the immediate condition of human reality. The reality film, like the Word or the spectacle, is a totality that is not so much a set of words that we speak or images that we watch as it is a general condition in which we are immersed, even and especially when we are apparently not focused on words or images. It is the material horizon of our existence in that '[t]he spectacle is *capital* accumulated to the point where it becomes image' (Debord 1967:24). Despite the fact that we are allowed to make certain limited choices that are provided by that segment of the spectacle or film known as the market, we are not free because we are deprived of genuine activity. The spectacle imposes isolation and passivity as conditions of its control.

This material reality of the spectacle thus constitutes a form of economic domination, but unlike earlier forms of domination, it is not organized so as to combat a fundamental scarcity of resources and a concomitant limit to production. Instead, the spectacular reality film produces and distributes scarcity as a subordinate component of a general economy of material abundance, which is the most significant consequence of the global mechanization of commodity production. Trocchi takes this shift for granted when he writes, in 'Invisible Insurrection', that '[c]learly, there is in principle no problem of production in the modern world. The urgent problem of the future is that of distribution which is presently (dis)ordered in terms of the economic system prevailing in this or that area' (1963a:179). That is, the massive growth of production under global capitalism (understood in Debord's terms as referring both to the Western capitalist nations of the 'diffuse spectacle' and to the Eastern-bloc socialist nations of the 'bureaucratic' or 'concentrated spectacle' [1967:41–3], an identification with which Burroughs agrees: '[T]he same old formulas' define both sides [*Job* 72]) has resulted in a general situation of abundance that could in principle provide every living person with an acceptable standard of living— if a radical redistribution of consumption were carried out.

Of course, it hasn't been carried out, and instead scarcity and its correlates, poverty and passivity, are represented and reproduced through the spectacle itself. Even the struggle against poverty is determined by the logic of the spectacle, in that 'reform' (within the sphere of the diffuse spectacle) and 'revolution' (within the sphere of the concentrated spectacle) are equally denied the possibility of addressing the basic axioms of the system. Thus a new form of resistance is called for.

Freedom now is the password of all the revolutions of history, but now for the first time it is not poverty but material abundance which must be dominated according to new laws. Dominating abundance is not just changing the way it is shared out, but *redefining its every orientation,* superficial and profound alike. This is the first step of an immense struggle, infinite in its implications. (*IS* editorial committee 1965:156)

For Trocchi as for Debord, the new focus of resistance is not the sphere of production but rather its dialectical mirror image: '[O]ur anonymous million [minds] can focus their attention on the problem of "leisure" ' (Trocchi 1963a:180). Like the Frankfurt School Marxists, the Situationists recognized that leisure was not relief from work but its continuation in another form—'[t]he forms that dominate [the worker's] life are carried over into leisure which becomes more and more mechanized; thus he is equipped with machines to contend with leisure which machines have accorded him' (Trocchi 1963a:180). And thus the spectacle spreads its unfreedom into all the corners of everyday life, colonizing leisure time as it previously colonized non-capitalist spaces.

At the limit, then, our unfreedom is defined by the fact that we are not allowed to turn the spectacle of the reality film off or to step outside it, to take back the material reality of abundance and action from the controlling image of poverty and passivity. To do so would not only trigger a defensive reaction from the administrators of image-capital, it would also threaten the very structure of the spectator's subjectivity. One of the most disturbing consequences of the domination of the spectacle is the isolation it imposes on the people subjected to it. The spectacle inserts itself into all relationships and alienates them by proposing itself as a necessary point of exchange and communication. As Debord notes, '[s]pectators are linked only by a one-way relationship to the very center that maintains their isolation from one another' (1967:22). The result is, in fact, the very opposite of communication considered as an inter-subjective or dialogical process of exchange, for in the spectacle ' "communication" is essentially *one-way*; the concentration of the media thus amounts to the monopolization by the administrators of the existing system of the means to pursue their particular form of administration' (Debord 1967:19–20). Burroughs had already recognized this in *Naked Lunch* when he satirized the fascistic 'Senders' who seek to establish control by means of 'one-way telepathic broadcasts instructing the workers what to feel and when' (*NL* 148). Thus even the emotional and psychological behavior of the individual is pre-programmed by the ubiquitous image: 'The spectacle's externality with respect to the acting subject is demonstrated by the fact that the individual's own gestures are no longer his own, but rather those of someone else who represents them to him' (Debord 1967:23).

This insidious invasion of the subject's consciousness (and unconscious) by the spectacle is thorough, but it is not complete. It can be successfully resisted, and has been for brief moments like the Watts riots of 1965 (to which the Situationist essay that Burroughs found so intelligent, 'The Decline and Fall of the Spectacle-Commodity Economy' [*IS* editorial committee 1965], responds). What both civil rights leaders and institutional leftist organizations fail to realize about the Watts rioters is that,

> [b]y wanting to participate really and immediately in affluence, which is the official value of every American, they demand the egalitarian *realization* of the American spectacle of everyday life: they demand that the half-heavenly, half-terrestrial values of this spectacle be put to the test. (*IS* editorial committee 1965:157)

It's not a question of living up to the abstract political ideals of the US Constitution, as the civil rights leaders would have it, nor of controlling the means of production as the institutional left insists, but rather of attacking the arbitrary limits imposed on consumption and activity, and hence on life itself, by the hierarchical power of the spectacle. It is a matter of replacing the spectacular logic of mere survival with an affirmation of abundance and the active life that should correspond to it. As Burroughs said with regard to Black Power a few years later, '[f]ind out what they want and give it to them [...] [W]ho has a better right to it?' (*E!* 99).

Chief among the tactics by means of which such resistance expresses itself is what the Situationists called '*détournement*', which is quite similar to the practice of cut-ups that Burroughs carried on throughout the 1960s. *Détournement*, 'the signature of the situationist movement, the sign of its presence and contestation in contemporary cultural reality' (*IS* editorial committee 1959:55–6), is the tactic of using the throwaway images of the spectacle against it by removing images or signs from their original or authorized spectacular contexts and placing them in completely different subversive contexts.

> Any elements, no matter where they are taken from, can serve in making new combinations. The discoveries of modern poetry regarding the analogical structure of images demonstrate that when two objects

are brought together, no matter how far apart their original contexts may be, a relationship is always formed [...] The mutual interference of two worlds of feeling, or the bringing together of two independent expressions, supercedes the original elements and produces a synthetic organization of greater efficacy. (Debord and Wolman 1956:9)

Drawing on Dadaist and Surrealist precedents, Situationist propaganda made extensive use of *détournement* in comic strips (the dialogue of which was replaced with dialectical aphorisms), advertising images (which were given ironic new juxtapositions and captions), and most importantly, films.

'It is obviously in the realm of the cinema that *détournement* can attain its greatest efficacy, and undoubtedly, for those concerned with this aspect, its greatest beauty' (Debord and Wolman 1956:12). Cinematic *détournement* can operate effectively through the accumulation of small detourned elements, as in Debord's famous film version of *Society of the Spectacle* (Debord 1973), which detourns a huge mass of pornographic photos, ads, journalistic images, scenes from Nicholas Ray's *Johnny Guitar*, Sergei Eisenstein's *Battleship Potemkin* and *October*, Josef von Sternberg's *Shanghai Gesture* and Orson Welles's *Mr Arkadin*, among other things. However, it can also function integrally in the *détournement* of entire existing works, like D. W. Griffith's *Birth of a Nation*, which could in principle be detourned 'as a whole, without necessarily even altering the montage, by adding a soundtrack that made a powerful denunciation of the horrors of imperialist war and of the activities of the Ku Klux Klan' (Debord and Wolman 1956:12). Onetime Situationist René Vienet's film *Can Dialectics Break Bricks?* applies the process of integral *détournement* to an absolutely generic Chinese martial arts film, which by the total substitution of soundtracks becomes an amusing dramatization of worker revolt against the bureaucratic administration of the spectacle (Vienet 1973).

Burroughs's work with cut-ups, the method to which he was introduced in 1959 by his painter friend Brion Gysin, parallels virtually all of these points. As he wrote in 'The Cut-Up Method of Brion Gysin' (1961), '[t]he cut-up method brings to writers the collage, which has been used by painters for fifty years. And used by the moving and still camera' (*3M* 29). He found precedents in the work of the Dadaist Tristan Tzara and the American modernists T. S. Eliot and John Dos Passos (Knickerbocker 1965:66). At first, Burroughs treated cut-ups as simply another poetic technique, but soon he realized that their implications went beyond mere aesthetics. By physically cutting printed texts, written by himself and by others, into pieces of various sizes and then reassembling them in random order, he had found a way to evade conscious and unconscious patterns of thought, association and choice that had been dictated by the binary structure of the Word and the reality film itself (see Murphy 1997:103–7). Cut-ups were a form of practical demystification and subversion that could uncover the ideology at work in the political lines of the media—for example, revealing the structural collusion between the police and the drug market in the US and UK (see *NE* 52–3). Ideology is a constantly repeated pre-recording, and as Burroughs writes in his unpunctuated essay 'the invisible generation' (1966), the 'only way to break the inexorable down spiral of ugly uglier ugliest recording and playback is with counterrecording and playback' (now in *TE* 217). Through this insight, Burroughs realized that '[c]ut-ups are for everyone. Anybody can make cut-ups. It is experimental in the sense of being *something to do*. Right here right now. Not something to talk and argue about' (*3M* 31). Cut-ups, like *détournement*, are directly subversive methods that can be practiced and engaged by everyone because they use the omnipresent material of the reality film against itself.

Like the Situationists, Burroughs also applied his subversive methods to film. He too realized that cut-up recontextualization can function both on a local level, as in *Nova Express* (which cut together Shakespeare, Joyce, Rimbaud, Genet, Kafka, Conrad, pulp science fiction and other texts [Knickerbocker 1965:68–9]) and his films *Towers Open Fire* and *The Cut-Ups* (in Burroughs and Balch 1990), and also on an integral level, as he argued in 'the invisible generation':

> what we see is determined to a large extent by what we hear you can verify this proposition by a simple experiment turn off the sound track on your television set and substitute an arbitrary sound track prerecorded on your tape recorder street sounds music conversation recordings of other television programs you will find that the arbitrary sound track seems to be appropriate and is in fact determining your interpretation of the film track [...] (now in *TE* 205)

The closest Burroughs came to realizing this integral form of the cut-up was in his short film collaboration with Antony Balch, *Bill and Tony*, in which the talking heads of Burroughs and Balch swap names and voices halfway through the film and in the process become one another (in Burroughs and Balch 1990; see also Murphy 1997:206–16). Though less immediately seductive than Vienet's detourned martial arts film, *Bill and Tony* is nevertheless an accessible and indeed pedagogical example of the potentials of the cut-ups.

For both Burroughs and the Situationists, the final goal of this systematic deployment of guerilla citation is the total transformation of everyday life. The Situationists called the 'tendencies for *détournement* to operate in everyday social life' ultra-*détournement*, and insisted that 'when we have got to the stage of constructing situations, the ultimate goal of all our activity, it will be open to everyone to detourn entire situations by deliberately changing this or that determinant condition of them' (Debord and Wolman 1956:13–14). In the wake of a successful revolution, therefore, *détournement* would change its modality from being purely critical of the organization of the spectacle to being creative of new conditions of living. The result would then be the simultaneous realization and suppression of art: that is, the elimination of art as a particular sector in the social division of labor, access to which is limited to specialized producers (artists) and consumers (collectors and critics), at the same time that creative activity becomes the general condition of human life in all its aspects. As Trocchi put it, '[a]rt can have no existential significance for a civilization which draws a line between life and art and collects artifacts like ancestral bones for reverence'; in contrast, 'we envisage a situation in which life is continually renewed by art, a situation imaginatively and passionately constructed to inspire each individual to respond creatively, to bring to whatever act a creative comportment' (1963a:181). Such would be the revolution of everyday life made possible by the new economy of abundance.

Burroughs too offers a model for this final goal of revolutionary theory, again as a consequence of his conception of the cut-ups. The cut-ups render visible or 'make explicit a psycho-sensory process that is going on all the time anyway' in every mind: '[A] juxtaposition of what's happening outside and what you're thinking of' (Knickerbocker 1965:67–8). Burroughs encourages his readers to experiment not only with the cutting-up of printed texts but also with the experiential cutting-up of everyday life, as in 'The Literary Techniques of Lady Sutton-Smith':

> Sit down in a café somewhere drink a coffee read the papers and *listen* don't *talk* to yourself [...] Note what you see and hear as you read

what words and look at what picture. These are *intersection points*. Note these intersection points in the margin of your paper. Listen to what is being said around you and look at what is going on around you. (Burroughs 1966:28)

The reality film operates to integrate all these elements as coherently as possible into a seamless whole and thus prevent the reader from imagining that there is something outside of it, some other principle of juxtaposition; this is its ideological function. But multimedia cut-ups can challenge this integration. In his own practice, Burroughs compiled elaborate collage scrapbooks of found juxtapositions between places visited, words read, sounds overheard, and images and objects seen, many of which served as source material for his novels (see the reproductions in *BF* 156–83 and Sobieszek 1996:38–53). These mixed-media collages, which 'spill off the page in all directions, kaleidoscope of vistas, medley of tunes and street noises, farts and riot yipes and the slamming steel shutters of commerce' (*NL* 207), do not simply resemble Debord and Asger Jorn's collages in *Mémoires* (see the reproductions in Sussman 1989:128–9); rather, like Debord and Jorn's assemblages, they point toward and demand a practice of everyday life that would realize art on a mass scale and suppress it as a specialized market niche.

The key to the large-scale success of ultra-*détournement* and multimedia cut-ups is the reconceptualization and reconstruction of the human environment, especially the urban environment. The SI called this reconceptualization 'unitary urbanism', by which they meant 'the theory of the combined use of arts and techniques for the integral construction of a milieu in dynamic relation with experiments in behavior' (*IS* editorial committee 1958:45). To counter modern urban planning, the spectacular integration of the human environment around the production and distribution of economic scarcity, the SI proposed the total reorganization of lived space around patterns of human affect and association. This would be the ultimate realization and suppression of art and the triumph of life over mere economic survival. Although Burroughs never conceived such a comprehensive project of urban reorganization, he was consistently interested in the unevenness and alienating effects of modern urban space. As I have argued elsewhere (Murphy 1997:47–50), Burroughs's first novel, *Junky* (1953), examines the heroin addict's navigation of the economic organization of urban space, and demonstrates that his reliance on the underdetermination of that space converts what was intended as a productive spatial order into an intermittently anti-productive one. That is, the junkie gravitates toward those parts of the urban landscape that undergo only inconstant and predictable surveillance by the authorities, and there he carries on his economy of theft and fencing as a parodic mirror image of capitalist production and exchange. While this economy of anti-production is not strictly analogous to the Situationist concept of non-economic unitary urbanism, it does identify and criticize the link between capitalist control and the experiential organization of urban space.

Given their small numbers and bohemian attitude toward the accumulation of capital, it's not surprising that the members of the SI never managed to put their grandiose dreams of unitary urbanism into construction. They got only as far as the mapping of urban space according to contours of affect and association, a mapping that parallels Burroughs's focus on derelict spaces of anti-production. Indeed, in his later works, Burroughs favored Trocchi's description of them both as 'cosmonauts of inner space' and considered his job to be that of 'a mapmaker [...] an explorer of psychic areas. ... And I see no point in exploring areas that have already been thoroughly surveyed' (cited by Morgan 1988:338). Similarly, the Situationists called their program 'psychogeography', 'the study of the specific effects of the geographical environment, consciously organized or not, on the emotions and behavior of individuals' (IS editorial committee 1958:45). Since most cities are organized into well-defined sectors, neighborhoods and quarters according to the demands of economic production, psychogeographical mapping sometimes involved 'detourning' or 'cutting up' city maps in order to defamiliarize the given economic landscape (for example, Debord's psychogeographical map of Paris entitled Naked City [1957], reproduced in Sussman 1989:135 and on the cover of Knabb 1989).

The theory of psychogeographical mapping was materialized by the Situationist practice of the dérive or 'drift' through a city. The dérive is 'a mode of experimental behavior linked to the conditions of urban society: a technique of transient passage through varied ambiances' (IS editorial committee 1958:45). Instead of following the planned lines of circulation through a metropolis, lines that are almost exclusively designed to smooth the turbulent flow of capital, commodities and their producers, the drifter would follow contours of personal affect, aesthetic juxtaposition, unplanned encounter and/or psychic association, and in the process discover an alternative city (or cities) within the spatial confines of the economically rationalized urban environment. Drifters would 'let themselves be drawn by the attractions of the terrain and the encounters they find there. The element of chance is less determinant than one might think: from the *dérive* point of view cities have a psychogeographical relief, with constant currents, fixed points and vortexes which strongly discourage entry into or exit from certain zones' (Debord 1956:50). Clearly this notion of the *dérive* bears a striking resemblance to Burroughs's advice to his readers for creating a multimedia experiential cut-up, including the clarification about the comparatively minor role that is played by chance.

The *dérive* is also the nodal point of Trocchi's understanding of the fundamental category of 'situation' as a kind of artistic 'happening'. In his adaptation, the 'Manifesto Situationiste' (sic) included in the *Sigma Portfolio*, he insists that: 'Within an experimentally constructed context, due attention paid to what we call "psychogeographic" factors, the situation is the gradual and spontaneous realization (articulation: happening) of a superior game in which each participating individual is vitally involved' (Trocchi 1964b, #18/3).

The other Situationists were, perhaps predictably, less inclined to see any genuine similarity between their covert, unspectacular *dérives* and the garish public spectacles of the professional (and thus integrative) artistic 'happenings' that proliferated throughout the 1960s:

> Our project has taken shape at the *same time* as the modern tendencies toward integration. There is thus not only a direct opposition but also an air of resemblance since the two sides are really contemporaneous. We have not paid enough attention to this aspect of things, even recently. Thus, it is not impossible to interpret Alexander Trocchi's proposals in issue #8 of this journal as having some affinity—despite their obviously completely contrary spirit—with those poor attempts at a 'psychodramatic' salvaging of decomposed art [...] (*IS* editorial committee 1964:136)

In fact, the further development of this aspect of Trocchi's interpretation of the Situationist project may have been the spur that led the other Situationists to expel him, rather gently, later that same year.

Thus the SI's concept of revolution as life taking control over the real production of abundance and eliminating the spectacular distribution of scarcity dovetails nicely with Trocchi's demand for an 'invisible insurrection' of those trapped by their own commodified and spectacular leisure time and Burroughs's appeal to the 'invisible generation' for a cut-up, detourned rebellion of 'counterrecording and playback' against the reality film's insidious control:

> there was a grey veil between you and what you saw or more often did not see that grey veil was the prerecorded words of a control machine once that veil is removed you will see clearer and sharper than those who are behind the veil whatever you do you will do it better than those behind the veil this is the invisible generation it is the efficient generation (now in *TE* 209)

Appropriately enough, and in confirmation of his intuition that the Situationist milieu would offer 'an excellent outlet for the short pieces I am writing now' (Burroughs 1967), Burroughs's essay 'Electronic Revolution' (1971), the sequel to 'The Invisible Generation', was published in French in 1974 by Editions Champ Libre, the publishing house run by Debord's close friend Gérard Lebovici that kept all the major Situationist texts in print through the 1970s and 1980s (now in *Job*). Burroughs's rallying cries of 'Total Exposure', 'Wise up all the marks everywhere', 'Show them the rigged wheel of Life-Time-Fortune', 'Storm the Reality Studio', and 'retake the universe' (*NE* 59) resonate with the Situationist-inspired slogan directing the reader to '[t]ake your desires for reality' and thereby abolish the society of the spectacle (*IS* editorial committee 1969: 244). Only if we do so will we ever see 'The Reality Film giving and buckling like a bulkhead under pressure' (*NE* 59).

III: SPONTANEOUS UNIVERSITY

As noted above, the Watts riots offered the Situationists an example of the revolutionary interruption or realization of the spectacle that they sought, and so did the radical students' takeover of the university quarter of Paris in May 1968. The Situationists had been attentive to the specific constraints faced by students for some time; indeed, they first attracted the attention of the mainstream mass media as a result of their collaboration with the militant students of the University of Strasbourg on a withering exposé of the 'poverty of student life, considered in its economic, political, psychological, sexual and especially intellectual aspects' (*IS* et al. 1966:319). In that pamphlet they argued that the spectacle 'allots everyone a specific role within a general passivity. The student is no exception to this rule. His is a provisional role, a rehearsal for his ultimate role as a conservative element in the functioning of the commodity system' (*IS* et al. 1966:320). Consequently, 'the student cannot revolt against anything without revolting against his *studies*' first of all (*IS* et al. 1966:325) because 'the suppression of alienation necessarily follows the same path as alienation' (*IS* et al. 1966:319). Or, as Burroughs later put it, '[t]he way out is the way through' (*WB* 82). The early, abortive efforts of the international student radical movements, according to the SI, constituted a confused but nonetheless real

> *revolt against the whole social system based on hierarchy and the dictatorship of the economy and the state.* By refusing to accept the business and institutional roles for which their specialized studies have been designed to prepare them, they are profoundly calling into question a system of production that alienates all activity and its products from their producers. (*IS* et al. 1966:328)

Trocchi had anticipated the SI's contemptuous analysis of student discontent two years earlier, when he insisted that '[w]e can write off existing universities', which are 'hopelessly geared and sprocketed to the cultural-economic axles of the status quo', as 'factories for the production of degreed technicians' (1964a:197).

But Trocchi was also more optimistic, indeed utopian, about the politics of education and university reorganization than his fellow Situationists, who lampooned the fictitious spectacular 'politicization' of students (*IS* et al. 1966: 324–5), and Burroughs came to share that utopian optimism, though somewhat belatedly. Trocchi recognized that his 'invisible insurrection of a million minds' would need a 'detonator', and in that role he cast the spontaneous university, which he conceived as 'a vital laboratory for the creation (and evaluation) of conscious *situations*; it goes without saying that it is not only the environment which is in question, plastic, subject to change, but men also' (1963a:186). Unlike the existing university, the spontaneous university would not reflect the alienating divisions of labor from consumption, of art from life, of living space from affect that characterize modern survival; rather, it would attack those divisions through Situationist methods of *détournement* and unitary urban reconstruction in order to bring creativity to everyday life. There would be no fixed departments, exams or career paths, but rather constant experimentation. 'What is essential is a new conscious sense of community-as-art-of-living; the experimental situation (laboratory) with its "personnel" is itself to be regarded as an artefact, a continuous making, a creative process, a community enacting itself in its individual members' (Trocchi 1964a:200). Instead of reflecting and reinforcing the hierarchical totality of the spectacle, '[t]he community which is the university must become a living model for society at large' (1964a:201).

Events would prove Trocchi right, to a certain extent. When the series of occupations and strikes that now go by the name of 'May 1968' broke out in Paris, the Situationists were quick to leap into the fray despite their distrust of the students' inadequate politicization. These events were very complex and are too well known to be summarized here, but the Situationist interpretation of them is quite relevant to our inquiry (see also Vienet 1968). The '*May movement was not a student movement*', according to the SI, but rather 'a revolutionary proletarian movement' that 'was able to concretely express itself and take shape only on the very unfavorable *terrain* of a student revolt' (*IS* editorial committee 1969:229). What this means is that while the student movement did not ultimately dominate or determine the significance of the events that occured, the student uprising did act as precisely the 'detonator' of insurrection that Trocchi had been looking for. The student occupation of the Sorbonne and the Latin Quarter triggered the very first 'wildcat general strike' of industrial workers in history, and effectively though belatedly brought down the De Gaulle government (*IS* editorial committee 1969:225, 252).

For the Situationists, this was 'the complete verification of the revolutionary theory of our time and even here and there the beginning of its partial realization' (*IS* editorial committee 1969:225), and by 'the revolutionary theory of our time' they of course meant their own conception of the spectacle and of the necessary means for its overcoming. 'Situationist theory had a significant role in the origins of the generalized critique that produced the first incidents of the May crisis and that developed along with that crisis' (*IS* editorial committee 1969:241). The strikes and university occupations constituted, they insisted, a 'critique in acts of the spectacle of nonlife' that corresponded to and dialectically realized Situationist theory (*IS* editorial committee 1969:226). Despite the high-profile presence of several Situationists at the Sorbonne during its occupation, they did not claim to have led any part of the revolt—neither the student struggles that detonated it, nor the workers' strikes that gave it material force. All they claimed was the accuracy of their theory, which had been adopted in whole or part by a crucial subset of the rebels. 'If many people *did* what we *wrote*, it was because we essentially wrote the negative that had been lived by us and by so many others before us' (*IS* editorial committee 1969:227).

Indeed, the Situationist interpretation of May 1968 downplayed its members' activities during the occupation, and claimed that their only crucial contribution to its progress lay in their insistence upon mechanisms of direct democracy, in the form of students' and workers' councils, for all decision-making during the revolt. The refusal of delegation or political representation had always been a key element in Situationist models of radical organization, and in May they got a chance to practice it. Their dedication to radically democratic organization made them unreservedly hostile to all attempts to appropriate or reform existing non-democratic institutions, however. For example, although other factions of the student movement saw the Sorbonne occupation as an opportunity to create an autonomous popular university to replace the integrated spectacular university, the Situationists did not: '[I]n our eyes the Sorbonne was of interest only as a *building seized by the revolutionary movement*' and not 'as a *university*– albeit "autonomous and popular"– something we despise in any case' (*IS* editorial committee 1969:250–1). For them, the university was an essential functional component of the spectacle and therefore not something that could be detached from the spectacle for relocation to a different position— that is, not an institution that could be detourned as a whole.

Like the Situationists, Burroughs reacted affirmatively to the events of May 1968, and to the broader international cycle of struggles of which they were a part, but like Trocchi's, his attitude toward the students was more generous. In an interview with French writer Daniel Odier just a few months after the riots and occupations of May, he called for 'more riots and more violence', which were justified because '[y]oung people in the West have been lied to, sold out and betrayed [...] The student rebellion is now a worldwide movement. Never before in recorded history has established authority been so basically challenged on a worldwide scale' (*Job* 81). Though he was more supportive of the students' specific claims and objectives than the Situationists were, he did implicitly agree with the SI in seeing the student uprising as a symptom of a deeper conflict and as the detonator of a more far-reaching revolutionary offensive against the basic structure of the reality film. He noted that 'the incidents that trigger student uprisings are often insignificant [...] [for example,] a refusal to change the examination system' (*Job* 81), but much more significant intersection points can be found in the universities. Perhaps the most

> crucial reason for all young people to rebel is the issue of top secret research carried on in universities or anywhere else. *All knowledge all discoveries belong to everybody* [...] *A worldwide monopoly of knowledge and discoveries for counterrevolutionary purposes is the basic issue* [...] *All knowledge all discoveries belong to you by right. It is time to demand what belongs to you.* (*Job* 81–2)

At that point, in the middle of the Cold War, universities constituted key links in the military-industrial complex just as today they act as research partners for private enterprise; in both cases, institutions supposedly dedicated to the non-partisan search for and humanitarian dissemination of knowledge restrict access to that knowledge according to the demands of the global image economy (as universities always have, of course, from their origins in the Middle Ages to the present). Contrary to this, Burroughs tried to convince the students to ask for the free and equal distribution of all knowledge, which is another way of formulating the Situationist demand for the freedom to live in place of the coercion of mere survival: 'If you want the world you could have in terms of discoveries and resources now in existence be prepared to fight for that world. To fight for that world in the streets' (*Job* 224).

The street fighting soon stopped, at least in the US and France, but in the months following May 1968, Burroughs often revisited the issue of education and its role in stabilizing (or destabilizing) the order imposed by the reality film. He realized that training in conformity, the prefabrication of expectations and opinions, was essential to the continued functioning of the film, and so he began to theorize alternative educational institutions to counteract the conformist socialization inculcated by the existing universities instead of simply denouncing the latter as the Situationists did. He called these alternative institutions 'academies', and defined 'academy training' as 'precisely *decontrol* of opinion [...] The program proposed is essentially a disintoxication from inner fear and inner control, a liberation of thought and energy to prepare a new generation' (*Job* 138). This program, which is essentially congruent with

Trocchi's model of the spontaneous university, would promote a new way of thinking that would correspond to a different, more critical apprehension of reality:

> Like a moving film the flow of thought seems to be continuous while actually the thoughts flow stop change and flow again. At the point where one flow stops there is a split-second hiatus. The new way of thinking grows in this hiatus between thoughts [...] The new way of thinking is the thinking you would do if you didn't have to think about any of the things you ordinarily think about if you had no work to do nothing to be afraid of no plans to make. (*Job* 91)

One of the academies' key elements is the negation of the division of labor that is embodied in the departmental structure of the traditional university. Students would be offered instruction in a variety of disciplines, '[a]ny one of [which] could become a way of life but [...] [the] point is to apply what we have learned from one discipline to another and not get stuck in one way of doing things' (*Job* 95). The ultimate goal of the new way of thinking and the academics that foster it would be the extinction of work along with fear and control, an extinction that the Situationists intended to implement through the simultaneous revolutionary realization and suppression of the spectacle. Thus the students would indeed be an 'invisible generation', with a different kind of consciousness and subjectivity than the spectator–participants of the reality film.

Burroughs's most important literary expression of his conception of radical education is to be found in *The Wild Boys* and *Port of Saints*. As I have argued elsewhere, Burroughs's wild boys must be understood in part as a hyperbolic intensification of countercultural revolt (Murphy 1997:145–7). They represent a break with the reality film so profound that it requires a new calendar: 'The wild boys have no sense of time and date the beginning from 1969 when the first wild boy groups were formed' (*POS* 73). In this, they constitute a step beyond the radicals of 1968. They are the graduates of the academies that Burroughs theorized in his essays and interviews of the period in that they conform to no division of labor, no dominant model of public opinion, and no onerous work discipline. They copulate and consume at will, unfettered by the reality film's iron logic of scarcity and passivity, work and leisure, and in the end they are the only ones who can carry out the electronic revolution.

On the penultimate page of *The Wild Boys*, the narrator blows up
the time barrier separating present time from the wild boys' future,
and in so doing ruptures the reality film. 'The screen is exploding in
moon craters and boiling silver spots' (*WB* 184), and then the film
is done and everyone is invisible, unspeakable, free ...

IV: SWIRLS AND EDDIES AND TORNADOES OF IMAGE

But the invisible insurrection, the electronic revolution, the revolution of everyday life, did not take place—at least not according to
the expectations of Trocchi, Burroughs and the Situationists. What
did happen is well known, if still poorly understood. In the wake of
the worldwide radical movements, the spectacle briefly lost its lus-
ter; the reality film momentarily slipped its sprockets; then the
process of image circulation and accumulation incorporated the
bulk of the movements and picked up where it had left off.
Détournement and the cut-ups were taken up by advertising, to no
one's surprise, not even their authors'. Even in their first articulation of the method, the Situationists recognized that 'it is in the
advertising industry, more than in a decaying aesthetic production,
that one can find the best examples' of *détournement* (Debord and
Wolman 1956:10). By the mid-1960s, Burroughs too admitted that:
'I've recently thought a great deal about advertising. After all,
they're doing the same sort of thing [I am]. They are concerned
with the precise manipulation of word and image' (Knickerbocker
1965:76). Ultra-*détournement* and the *dérive*, the experiential cut-ups
that Burroughs advocated, had to wait a little longer to be recuper-
ated in the form of multimedia, computer games and virtual reality.
No longer content to be even apparently external to its subjects, the
spectacle drew them into its own representational substance—with
their enthusiastic approval.

The new media that form the cornerstone of the contemporary
version of the spectacular reality film often lay claim to the educational imperatives of Trocchi's and Burroughs's utopian project as
well as Burroughs's cut-up methods and the psychogeography of the
SI. In a recent report on the use of three-dimensional animation in
advertising, video consultant Jeff Sauer profiles a media company
that specializes in 3D: Reality Check Studios. One of their most
impressive projects, from the spectacular point of view, is a multimedia CD-ROM designed for the telecommunications giant SBC

(Southwestern Bell Communications). Sauer's description is worth quoting in full:

> The CD-ROM starts with an amazing four-minute, high-speed fly-through of a fictitious future city. But the journey isn't just for fun; SBC wanted to educate, too. So the fly-through stops at the metropolis' movie theater to show the entertainment possibilities of broadband service. From there, viewers fly to a concert venue to learn about the music available on the Internet and to an animated shopping mall to learn about commerce on the Web. They can learn about home security and wired smart homes and, of course, how to sign up for DSL. (Sauer 2002)

This fictitious city seems an unlikely example of unitary urbanism, though no doubt that concept too is subject to recuperation within the spectacle. And 'education' here is conceived exclusively as the most seductive method for informing the consumer of the choices the market has made (available) for her. Advertising is our academy and commodities our education, the only education we'll ever need for life in the reality film.

In the same piece, Sauer also discusses the perfect dialectical counterpart to this fictitious city: a 'real' cityscape that becomes just as fictitious, just as mediated, just as spectacular. It's Times Square, of course, in which 'any new construction' must 'have electronically lit signage with a size compensatory to the size of the building', according to a recent New York City ordinance (Sauer 2002). While most buildings have simply been equipped with external billboards and giant pre-programmable TV monitors, the Lehman Brothers Corporation, an investment banking firm, went much further with its office tower, perhaps in an effort to literalize its motto, 'Where vision gets built'. As Sauer notes, not content with simply displaying electronic signs, 'the Lehman Brothers building is itself an electronic sign' (Sauer 2002). And what a sign:

> The sign is a huge system of LEDs, 5340 by 736, that stretches vertically from the third floor to the fifth floor of the building. Horizontally, the sign wraps around the building from halfway down the 49th Street side across the entire length of the building facing Times Square, then halfway down the 50th Street side. (Sauer 2002)

The images projected on this immense three-dimensional screen are not merely prefabricated ads, but real-time mixes of pre-constructed content with live images from the building's environs.

The Lehman Brothers sign content will be controlled by a database that runs on a schedule, but the sign also has the ability to be affected by external input. For example, if the weather in Times Square turns gray and rainy, the sign's mode, color tone, or message may change to match or contrast with the dreariness. Similarly, if the financial markets are up or down on a given afternoon, that input could trigger the sign to change mood. (Sauer 2002)

This is integrative unitary urbanism with a vengeance, and a tidy allegory for the recent mutations of the global economy of the image: a spectacular sign equipped with the resources to steal affect ('mood') from its environment and re-project it as its own. As such screens and images proliferate throughout the world, the functional control of the spectacle increases.

Burroughs anticipated something like this in *Nova Express*, although he expected it to function as a critical cut-up rather than an integrative element of the reality film. In the novel's concluding chapter, 'Pay Color', the Subliminal Kid (in collaboration with the ubiquitous Muslim heretic and revolutionary Hassan i Sabbah) deploys independent media technology against the controllers of the reality film in an effort to force them to 'pay back' the 'stolen colors' of human life (*NE* 149–50). In particular, he

set up screens on the walls of his bars opposite mirrors and took and projected at arbitrary intervals shifted from one bar to the other mixing Western Gangster films of all times and places with word and image of the people in his cafés and on the streets his agents with movie camera and telescope lens poured images of the city back into his projector and camera array and nobody knew whether he was in a Western movie in Hong Kong or The Aztec Empire in Ancient Rome or Suburban America whether he was a bandit a commuter or a chariot driver whether he was firing a 'real' gun or watching a gangster movie and the city moved in swirls and eddies and tornadoes of image [...] (*NE* 148)

The final clause suggests that the key to this sabotage of the reality film lies in its disordering of the carefully integrated images that give the film its consistency and predictability. However, the reality film of the twenty-first century can incorporate the turbulence of these 'tornadoes of image' into its own structure without thereby loosening its hold on the human landscape. After all, chaos theory has taught us that most disorder is only a differential of a higher integration of order. Indeed, to the extent that it more effectively seduces the eye and the other senses, the chaotic image in fact tightens its hold on the mind and body.

Not only does the spectacle continue to seduce us into looking at it, thinking with it and living in it, but now it also looks back at us from a thousand different angles at once. The one-way communication that both Burroughs and the Situationists attacked as the reality film's unilateral chain of command has given way to multi-directional surveillance that masquerades as democratic dialogue and informational collaboration. In a late essay, Gilles Deleuze argues that this shift demonstrates that '[c]ontrol societies are taking over from disciplinary societies [in Michel Foucault's sense]. "Control" is the name proposed by Burroughs to characterize the new monster' of technological monitoring (Deleuze 1990:178), and thus the society of control is a further development of, if not the direct successor to, the reality film or the society of the spectacle. Unlike modern discipline, which was long-term and discontinuous (as Burroughs showed with regard to urban space in Junky), '[c]ontrol is short-term and rapidly shifting, but at the same time continuous and unbounded' (Deleuze 1990:181). We have the security of holographic IDs, the convenience of credit cards, the amusement or edification of web surfing, and the spontaneity of e-mail and instant messaging, but all these forms of instantaneous information transfer leave a residue that is tirelessly collected by credit agencies, merchants, employers, police and the State in order to map our movements, plans, desires and affects. In the US, recent proposals to fully integrate all these presently separate collections of personal data in order to 'mine' it for purposes of national security (such as the joint Pentagon–FBI Total Information Awareness project) have provoked a backlash from civil libertarians, although no doubt such integration is already under way in less monumental and hence less visible enterprises, as the rising tide of personalized junk mail and telemarketing shows.

Following Deleuze's lead, Michael Hardt and Antonio Negri also note that in the contemporary global economy of the image, 'the freedom of self-fashioning is often indistinguishable from the powers of an all-encompassing control' of the sort that Burroughs anatomized (Hardt and Negri 2000:216, 448, n14). They insist as well that like Burroughs's theory, 'Debord's analysis of the society of the spectacle, more than thirty years after its composition, seems ever more apt and urgent' right now (2000:188). In particular, the concept of the spectacle, like Burroughs's notion of control, helps to explain the dematerialization of politics in the contemporary world.

> [The] spectacle is a virtual place, or more accurately, a *non-place* of politics. The spectacle is at once unified and diffuse in such a way that it is impossible to distinguish any inside from outside—the natural from the social, the private from the public. The liberal notion of the public, the place outside where we act in the presence of others, has been universalized (because we are always now under the gaze of others, monitored by safety cameras) and sublimated or de-actualized in the virtual spaces of the spectacle. The end of the outside is the end of liberal politics. (Hardt and Negri 2000:188–9)

Liberal politics, the politics of delegation and representation, have been completely subsumed by the spectacle and in the process have lost their grounding in the populace. They have consequently been replaced by imperial politics, the spectacular politics of Empire.

'Empire' is Hardt and Negri's term for the present global situation of decentralized, transnational capitalism, and should not be mistaken for a reference to classical nationalist imperialism of the British, Spanish or French sort. Empire, the society of control, began to manifest itself in 1968, the 'beginning of an era' as the Situationists put it (and Burroughs's wild boys would agree). Empire is the rule of the spectacle, in that its 'control operates through three global and absolute means: the bomb, money, and ether' (Hardt and Negri 2000:345). All three of these means are directly spectacular—they define and orient the reality film. Thermonuclear weapons, which Burroughs called 'Soul Killer[s]' (*WL* 7), function as a standing threat of total annihilation whose deployment is both unthinkable and constantly expected. Imperial control uses their actual possession (for example, in American hands) as a nightmarish goad that overdetermines and subordinates all other conflicts, and their virtual possession (for example, in Iraqi hands) as a pretext for the direct and violent subordination of recalcitrant groups. Thermonuclear weapons are very real 'tornadoes of image' that destroy even when they aren't actually used.

The other two means are more like swirls and eddies of image, though that doesn't mean they are insignificant. Money and its transnational flows have always been central means of control for the spectacle; after all, Debord did write that '[t]he spectacle is *capital* accumulated to the point where it becomes image' (1967: 24). Burroughs too argued that human reality is being consumed and replaced by money as image: 'the money machine [...] eats youth, spontaneity, life, beauty and above all it eats creativity. It eats quality and shits out quantity [...] People want money to buy what the machine eats to shit money out. The more the machine eats the less remains' (*Job* 73–4). Lastly, by 'ether', Hardt and Negri mean 'the management of communication, the structuring of the education system, and the regulation of culture'; that is, the mass media and educational/creative institutions such as universities, which 'cannot help submitting to the circulating society of the spectacle [...] Communication is the form of capitalist production in which capital has succeeded in submitting society entirely and globally to its regime, suppressing all alternative paths' (2000:346–7). Of the three, in fact, '[c]ommunication has become the central element that establishes the relations of production' (2000:347–8), as Burroughs and the Situationists already knew, and it is communication that is most likely to provide opportunities of resistance, as, for example, the media-savvy Zapatistas showed in 1994 (Hardt and Negri 2000:54).

Despite its acknowledged inability to provide tactics that could replace the now-recuperated techniques of *détournement*, cut-ups, unitary urbanism and the *dérive*, Hardt and Negri's theory of Empire has been taken up by a wide range of groups currently engaged in contesting the globalization of capitalism—including the Tute Bianche and Ya Basta, who protested at Genoa, and many of the organizers of the Porto Alegre World Social Forum, to name just two key sites of struggle (*On Fire* 2001:101–3)—and through it the Situationist critique of the spectacle and Burroughs's subversion of the reality film's control continue to provide critical leverage for the resistance to the present. As Burroughs wrote late in his career, '[m]aybe we lost. And this is what happens when you lose [...] [Yet] there were moments of catastrophic defeat, and moments of triumph' (*WL* 252–3). The Situationists too acknowledged that in the past century, 'revolution has so far not been victorious anywhere, but the practical process through which its project manifests itself has already created at least ten revolutionary moments of an extreme historical importance that can appropriately be termed revolutions' (*IS* editorial committee 1969:236). Those moments have continued to erupt, from Watts 1965 and Paris 1968 to Seattle 1999 and Genoa 2001, and there is no reason to expect them to cease so

56   Theoretical Depositions

long as the spectacle retains control and the reality film remains unexposed. Once again it will be necessary, no doubt, to 'Storm The Reality Studio', and 'retake the universe' (*NE* 59).

The author would like to thank Dan Cottom and Oliver Harris for their advice and assistance in the composition of this essay.

REFERENCES

Burroughs, W. S. (1964) *Le festin nu* Kahane, E. trans. (Paris: Gallimard).
—— (1966) 'The Literary Techniques of Lady Sutton-Smith', IN Berner, J. ed., *Astronauts of Inner-Space* (San Francisco: Stolen Paper Review), pp. 28–9.
—— (1967) Letter to Mary Beach, 28 July 1967. Department of Special Collections, Kenneth Spencer Research Library, University of Kansas [MS 63 B:b:24].
—— (1974) *Révolution electronique*, Chopin, J. trans. (Paris: Editions Champ Libre).
Burroughs, W. S., and Balch, A. (1990) *Towers Open Fire and Other Short Films*, Mystic Fire Video [video: VHS].
Debord, G. (1956) 'Theory of the *Dérive*', IN Knabb, K. 1989, pp. 50–4.
—— (1967) *The Society of the Spectacle*, Nicholson-Smith, D. trans. (New York: Zone, 1994).
—— (1973) *La société du spectacle* (Paris: Simar Films).
—— (2001) *Correspondance* vol. 2: *septembre 1960–décembre 1964* (Paris: Librairie Arthème Fayard).
Debord, G., and Wolman, G. J. (1956) 'Methods of Detournement', IN Knabb, K. 1989, pp. 8–14.
Deleuze, G. (1990) 'Postscript on Control Societies', IN Joughin, M. trans. *Negotiations 1972–1990* (New York: Columbia University Press, 1995), pp. 177–82.
Gray, C. ed. (1974) *Leaving the 20th Century: The Incomplete Work of the Situationist International* (London: Rebel Press, 1998).
Hardt, M., and Negri, A. (2000) *Empire* (Cambridge, MA: Harvard University Press).
[IS] Internationale Situationniste, édition augmentée (1997) (Paris: Librairie Arthème Fayard). Complete re-issue of the journal, 1958–69.
IS editorial committee (including G. Debord) (1958) 'Definitions', IN Knabb, K. 1989, pp. 45–6.
—— (1959) 'Detournement as Negation and Prelude', IN Knabb, K. 1989, pp. 55–6.
—— (1964) 'Now, the S.I.', IN Knabb, K. 1989, pp. 135–8.
—— (1965) 'The Decline and Fall of the Spectacle-Commodity Economy', IN Knabb, K. 1989, pp. 153–60.
—— (1969) 'The Beginning of an Era', IN Knabb, K. 1989, pp. 225–56.
IS et al. (1966) 'On the Poverty of Student Life', IN Knabb, K. 1989, pp. 319–37.

Knabb, K. ed. and trans. (1989) *Situationist International Anthology* (San Francisco: Bureau of Public Secrets).

Knickerbocker, C. (1965) 'White Junk', IN Lotringer, S. ed., *Burroughs Live: The Collected Interviews of William S. Burroughs 1960–1997* (USA: Semiotext[e], 2001), pp. 60–81.

Marcus, G. (1989) *Lipstick Traces: A Secret History of the Twentieth Century* (Cambridge, MA: Harvard University Press).

Morgan, T. (1988) *Literary Outlaw: The Life and Times of William S. Burroughs* (New York: Henry Holt).

Murphy, T. S. (1997) *Wising Up the Marks: The Amodern William Burroughs* (Berkeley: University of California Press).

On Fire: The Battle of Genoa and the Anti-Capitalist Movement (One-Off Press, 2001).

Sauer, J. (2002) 'New Dimensions', IN *Video Systems*, 1 February 2002, <videosystems.com/ar/video_new_dimensions/index.htm>, 18 January 2003.

Sobieszek, R. A. (1996) *Ports of Entry: William S. Burroughs and the Arts* (Los Angeles: LA County Museum of Art/Thames and Hudson).

Sussman, E. ed. (1989) *On the Passage of a Few People Through a Rather Brief Moment in Time: The Situationist International 1957–1972* (Cambridge, MA: MIT Press).

Trocchi, A. (1960) *Cain's Book* (New York: Grove).

—— (1963a) 'Invisible Insurrection of a Million Minds', IN Trocchi, A. 1991, pp. 177–91.

—— (1963b) 'Letter to William S. Burroughs', IN Trocchi, A. 1991, pp. 207–9.

—— (1964a) 'Sigma: A Tactical Blueprint', IN Trocchi, A. 1991, pp. 192–203.

—— (1964b) *Sigma Portfolio* items #1–25 (London: privately duplicated). Cited copy is in the collection of the Lilly Library, Indiana University.

—— (1972) *Man at Leisure* (London: Calder and Boyars). Introduction by William S. Burroughs.

—— (1991) *Invisible Insurrection of a Million Minds: A Trocchi Reader*, Murray Scott, A. ed. (Edinburgh: Polygon).

Vienet, R. (1968) *Enragés and Situationists in the Occupation Movement, France, May '68* (Brooklyn, NY: Autonomedia, 1992).

—— (1973) *La dialectique peut-il casser des bricques?* (Paris: L'Oiseau de Minerve).

3
Reactivating the Dialectic of Enlightenment: Burroughs as Critical Theorist

Philip Walsh

The group of philosophers and sociologists that came to be known as the Frankfurt School and the writer William S. Burroughs are both strongly associated with the themes that engaged the New Left in the 1960s, although their respective backgrounds and primary interests are, of course, very different. Recent commentators on Burroughs's work, including Timothy S. Murphy in his book *Wising Up the Marks*, have made explicit reference to the parallel structure of their concerns (1997:77–96), but details of the relationship between these two bodies of work remain under-explored. In fact, their respective influences may also be detected within the theoretical voices that succeeded the New Left; poststructuralism, cultural studies and, more recently, critics of the accelerating logic of global capital, all draw on themes, angles and theoretical grids that owe much to the influence of both the Frankfurt School and Burroughs. This chapter examines the convergent aspects of Burroughs's and the Frankfurt School's perspectives on social control, subjectivity and representation, and how these are to be understood within the context of globalization.[1]

POINTS OF INTERSECTION

The key members of the first generation of the Frankfurt School (Theodor Adorno, Max Horkheimer and Herbert Marcuse) and Burroughs are all radical critics of certain trends of contemporary *mass* civilization: the growth of instrumental rationality to the detriment of critical rationality; the subjugation of the individual and of nature to the dictates of global capital; the invasion of personal life by dehumanized structures of control; and the proliferation of large-scale socially induced psychological pathology in the form of authoritarianism, police power and other variants on fascism. They are also concerned with the cultural effects of these tendencies, in the spheres of the power/knowledge nexus, culture industries and language. Finally, they contextualize their approaches within a global anthropological perspective on human consciousness: in the case of the Frankfurt School, this perspective is explicit in their Hegelian-Marxist background, while with Burroughs, it emerged more gradually through his later works.

The contemporary relevance of these concerns must be treated through the prism of globalization, since globalization may be said to consist partly in the global projection of these tendencies. The homogenizing, dehumanizing power of globalization is emphasized, for example, by William Greider (1997). George Ritzer (2000) discusses tendencies that the Frankfurt School theorized under the rubric of instrumental reason, and which Burroughs located in the dehumanizing scientism of Western culture. Benjamin Barber's 'McWorld' (1995) looks like the logical outcome of Adorno and Horkheimer's 'culture industry' and an extension of the 'Trak' agency that Burroughs describes in *The Soft Machine*. Barber's 'Jihad' presents an unexpected but nevertheless distinguishable face of fascism in the twenty-first century, while Noam Chomsky (2003) and others have identified the global super-authoritarian ambitions of 'neo-conservativism'. The increased consciousness of the interconnected biological, ecological and economic history of the planet's inhabitants—at least among those who have benefited from the effects of economic globalization—reasserts the importance of a critical anthropological perspective, and this is reflected in the recent mainstream popularity of universal histories.[2] In short, these tendencies, identified by both Burroughs and the Frankfurt School in the freeze of the Cold War and the delirium of the counterculture, have now become global in their scale and reach.

CONTROL AND MASS SOCIETY

Adorno and Horkheimer's *Dialectic of Enlightenment* (1944) is primarily concerned with the baleful influence of 'instrumental rationality' (*Zweckrationalität*), a term derived from Max Weber's economic sociology, and which Weber contrasted with 'substantive rationality' (Runciman 1978:352–4). Substantive rationality involves critical questioning of thought and action in accordance with a concern with the ends or goals of life and human welfare. Instrumental reason concerns itself exclusively with the most efficient and practical means of achieving a given end—an end that is not itself put into question. According to Weber, the modern world is characterized by the dominance of the latter mode of thinking and the progressive weakening of the former; hence his metaphor of modern life as increasingly resembling a 'steel-hard cage'[3] of rationality. The ascendancy of the steel-hard cage is most clearly manifested in such developments as the mathematization of knowledge and experience, the development of a strictly means-oriented ethics and, most importantly, the increasing and unstoppable power of bureaucracies. Bureaucracies allow both an unprecedented concentration of power among a technical elite and the emergence of the phenomenon of the masses (see Runciman 1978:351). Bureaucratic power, for Weber, is inherently 'self-multiplying', and he therefore sees no alternative to the civilizational trend toward the mounting power of bureaucracy, and with it, the reign of instrumental reason.

Adorno and Horkheimer, as well as Marcuse, developed the elements of Weber's theory of rationalization, tracing the origins of instrumental reason to the desire to dominate nature, and tracing its function to the formation and maintenance of Western social hierarchies based on capitalist social relations. They therefore combined Weber's insights with Marxism, pointing to the way bureaucracies become the fulcrum on which social power turns in advanced capitalist societies. They pointed out that bureaucracies achieve exceptional power in economies in which the division of labor is most highly developed, the alienation of labor from its object is most acute, and the everyday decision-making processes have a democratic character. Bureaucracies thereby allow exceptional integration of economic functions, but act to atomize social units—including, but not exclusively, individual human beings (see Marcuse 1941:154). Bureaucracy grows out of tendencies that homogenize and disempower the individual worker while simultaneously democratizing elements of the labor process. The need for bureaucratic control is exacerbated by the tendency of modern capitalist societies to continually colonize new areas of social, political and individual life, including the sphere of leisure, which then assumes the form of an alternate realm of production. The process is accompanied by the application of scientific thinking—precision, quantification, prediction and repetition—to the techniques of modern industry and modern play. The Frankfurt School 'critical theory' of contemporary society, therefore, identifies the triangulation of science, bureaucracy and industrialism—all originally emancipatory forces—as the key elements of instrumental rationality. Horkheimer formulates the critical perspective on this convergence when he notes:

> The basic form of the historically given commodity economy on which modern history rests contains in itself the internal and external tensions of the modern era; it generates these tensions over and over again in increasingly heightened form; and after a period of progress, development of human powers, and emancipation for the individual, after an enormous extension of human control over nature, it finally hinders further development and drives humanity into a new barbarism. (1937:227)

Burroughs's identification of the link between bureaucracy and democracy—'Democracy is cancerous, and bureaus are its cancer' (*NL* 121)—is part of a broader conception, similar to that of the Frankfurt School, of the effects of linking modern science with technologies of mass social control. The combination allows unprecedented increases in the means of domination to subsist with the maximization of *social distance*.[4] Important technologies of mass control such as bureaucracies, media outlets, long-range weaponry, biological/chemical warfare agents and—in the future, Burroughs predicts—other technologies such as electromagnetism or sound, which are capable of effecting direct changes in consciousness, intensify social interaction through interconnectedness while at the same time producing social distance and social atomization. This is complemented, in the case of the mass media and bureaucracies, by a tendency to operate through a process of circulation within social systems, thus, like language, imitating the action of a virus or the metastasis of a cancer. Burroughs's fascination with the phenomenon of control-at-a-distance runs as a thread throughout his work, and also motivates his interest in phenomena such as telepathy, spells and possession, which may be understood as magical correlates or forerunners of modern technologies of social control.

In contrast, Burroughs clearly identifies certain technologies as emancipatory. These are either scaled to the individual or function as defense against social distortion. For example, in *The Western Lands*, the character of Joe the Dead is equipped with an artificial eye. This apparatus presents him with pictures of reality that are exempt from the scanning patterns attaching to ordinary vision—patterns that are acquired through socially conditioned habituation:

> [H]e came to realize to what extent that which we see is conditioned by what we expect to see [...] He found that he could read motives and expressions with great precision by comparing the data of the good eye, which was picking up what someone wants to project, and the data of the synthetic eye. Sometimes the difference in expression was so grotesque that he was surprised it was not immediately apparent to anyone. (WL 34–5)

Guns, typewriters, tape recorders, cameras and—one may speculate—personal computers are all potentially emancipatory by virtue of their scale and purpose as tools for individual action. Modern 'many-to-one' communications technologies (radio, television, the Internet) are organs of circulation and methods of producing social distance, effective for propaganda and control by virtue of the passive state they impose on actors, and their compatibility with bureaucratic organization. Burroughs died in 1997, when the Internet was still in its take-off phase. However, his attitude toward the marrying of the personal computer with the Internet, together with other supposedly individualized communication devices such as the mobile telephone, would likely be negative, since the individualized scale of these devices is deceptive; they are actually the outlying component parts of a larger machine (see Ed Desautels's essay in this collection).

GLOBALISM, UTOPIA AND OGU/MU

Burroughs's perspective on the effects of mass technologies, by which social and economic connections based on locale are swept up and subjected to forces of circulation and the creation of social distance, anticipates contemporary critical analyses of the global effects of such processes. However, as Anthony Giddens has pointed out, the 'push and pull' of global processes often have contradictory effects (1990:139). Both circulation and the production of social distance, by 'disembedding' locale, do not simply negate self-to-self relations, but reintegrate them into abstract systems which can be 'steered' in accordance with norms—which may themselves act against forces of global control and create new localized spaces (see Giddens 1990:151–4). Similarly, the anti-globalization movements have often made effective use of the very tools developed by agents of global control themselves. As Naomi Klein has pointed out, 'Nike, Shell, Wal-Mart, Microsoft and McDonald's have become metaphors for a global economic system gone awry, largely because [...] the methods and objectives of these companies are plain to see: [...] They have become the planet's best and biggest popular education tools' (2000:441). By destroying the privilege of locale, globalization makes possible the radical abstraction of time from place, thus rendering the idea of a localized history obsolete and threatening such oppressive parochial ideas as national mythology and the idea of 'race', which has generally been rationalized in cultural–geographical terms (see Gilroy 2001).

The Burroughsian utopia presented in *Cities of the Red Night*, and in the late novella *Ghost of Chance*, presents a mix of these global and local elements. The denizens of the communities in these novels are acutely aware of their geographical location, the balance of power between the European imperialists (against whom they conduct a defensive guerilla war), and, in the case of Captain Mission's commune in Madagascar, the disastrous ecological effects of transcontinental economic exploitation. The constitutions of the communes, based on the 'Articles' inherited from the French and American revolutions, are universalist, anti-imperialist and anti-statist, and thus truly 'transnationalist'. Social and economic life in the communes is regulated by the Articles, which limit the population to 300 people, and which promote unalienated and unregulated labor, orgiastic (homo)sexual rites and sustainable resource management. This does not constitute reversion to the structure of the village or the autarky of the commune (although Burroughs uses this latter term); rather, it suggests a tribal mentality, nomadic by instinct and origin but, as Burroughs insists, 'on a world-wide scale' (*CRN* xiv), and therefore intrinsically modern and global in outlook. The combination of elements is premised on Burroughs's sensitivity to historical possibilities and on an implicit philosophy of history.

The Frankfurt School affirmed the need for a philosophy of history, but qualified this claim by rejecting any fixed meaning to human history. Closed systems of *interpreting* the past, such as those represented by Hegelian Grand Narrative and Dialectical Materialism,[5] in common with the traditional monotheistic religions, are premised on the need to *control* the past in order to manipulate the future. In contrast, in *Dialectic of Enlightenment*, Adorno and Horkheimer develop a radical historicism that highlights particular transition points in history, where bridges to alternative futures became available. The character of Odysseus (discussed later) stands on the cusp of the transition from a mythological to a scientific world-view, representing both the break and the continuity between reason and myth that is at the heart of the dialectic of enlightenment. Adorno and Horkheimer show that the domination of enlightenment over myth—of the rule of law and reason over the rule of authority and instinct—does not presage emancipation, but the perpetuation of domination within new forms and techniques of deception, and thus of unreason. However, the basic theme of *Dialectic of Enlightenment* is not the exhaustion, but rather the ambivalence of enlightenment. The work has often been misunderstood in this respect, being taken as a purely 'negative' critique of modern technical rationality. Significantly, its critical force cannot be the outright rejection of the process of enlightenment as such, since the critical tools used within the work are explicitly derived from the rationalist philosophical tradition (see Rose 1978, Jarvis 1998). Rather, enlightenment 'reverts to myth' (Adorno and Horkheimer 1944:11–12) when it brings about an unreflective equation of such non-equivalents as truth with freedom, work with labor, and play with consumption.

In the Red Night trilogy, Burroughs makes use of a similar, though loosely cast and equivocal, opposition between the Magical Universe (MU) and the One-God Universe (OGU). At one level, Burroughs is registering a basic metaphysical tension:

> The OGU is a pre-recorded universe of which He is the recorder [...] it has no friction by definition. So He invents friction and conflict, pain, fear, sickness, famine, war, old age and Death.
> [...]
>   The Magical Universe, MU, is a universe of many gods, often in conflict. So the paradox of an all-powerful, all-knowing God who permits suffering, evil and death, does not arise. (*WL* 113)

However, the OGU principle is also used more broadly to denote closed systems of control in general, particularly those that involve the manipulation of meaning. Judaism, Islam and Christianity represent somewhat one-dimensional methods of control, based on the democratization of the fear of death and its correlate, the desire for immortality: they promise 'immortality to everyone simply for obeying a few simple rules. Just pray, and you can't go astray. Pray and believe—believe an obvious lie, and pray to a shameless swindler' (*WL* 70). Modern pseudo-democratic and totalitarian secular states follow a more complex model. They eschew the God-concept for other mythical forms such as National Destiny, Communism, Progress, Science, Civilization, and so forth. These systems also promise a form of immortality, though it is abstract and projected into the collective, according to the principle that ultimately 'immortality is purpose and function' (*WL* 70), not physical individual life.

A different model of control operates in ancient polytheistic or animistic societies, where control is exercised directly by the rulers over the subjects' minds, and in which the need for a 'bribe', the promise of immortality, is not necessary. Ancient Mayan society, as presented in *The Soft Machine*, offers one archetype here. The priests exercise direct control over the consciousness of the populace, by possessing 'codices which contain symbols representing all states of thought and feeling possible to human animals living under such limited circumstances' (*SM* 91). The Mayan control system is therefore direct and total, but by the same token, highly vulnerable. Modern control systems, premised simultaneously on the fully developed individual and her enrollment in her own subordination, are less stable ('riddled with contradictions', according to Burroughs [*AM* 120]), but at the same time less static, and so ultimately less fragile.

The setting for *The Western Lands* is the breakdown of the ancient Near Eastern civilizations, represented by Egypt, allowing Burroughs to mix reflections on various ancient *and* modern forms of organization and control. His focus on this period at least partly derives from a confluence of his interest in the political origins of the West and the implications and origins of the unconscious. The two interests come together in his encounter with Julian Jaynes's *Origins of Consciousness in the Breakdown of the Bicameral Mind* (1977), which Burroughs discusses in two essays, 'On Freud and the Unconscious' and 'On Coincidence' (see *AM*).[6] It is worth recounting Jaynes's theory in some detail, since it bears a striking resemblance to many of the themes present in Adorno and Horkheimer's *Dialectic of Enlightenment* and elsewhere, and was a major influence on Burroughs's thinking during the period of the composition of the Red Night trilogy.

HISTORICITY AND CONSCIOUSNESS

The Origins of Consciousness in the Breakdown of the Bicameral Mind, although nominally a work of psychology, presents an explanation of consciousness similar to Adorno and Horkheimer's account of the emergence of individual consciousness, with its emphasis on the primarily subjective character of time and space, and therefore of all conscious experience, the original dualism of human nature and the social basis of the individual consciousness. Jaynes sketches the origins of this dualism in the physical structure of the brain and proposes an anthropology of the 'bicameral mind', his term for the human mental structure that predominated in the earliest large-scale agrarian civilizations of the Near East—Mesopotamia, Egypt, Minoa and Mycenaea. According to Jaynes, the chaos surrounding the collapse of Mycenaean civilization between 1200 and 800 BCE allowed the emergence of new elements in the human mental structure. These included the capacities of 'spatialization', in which objects could be cast into the representational form of 'mind-space', and 'narratization', in which the world is viewed from the standpoint of a self located imaginatively within time. These characteristics of the self, necessary to what Freud called the ego,[7] did not exist within the ancient bicameral mind. Rather, the bicameral mind was 'split in two, an executive part called a god, and a follower part called a man. Neither part was conscious' (Jaynes 1977:84). This structure was compatible with the development of language, mathematics, construction, coinage and other technologies widespread in the ancient world, but not with individual volition or with any critical questioning faculty.[8] Burroughs interprets Jaynes in overtly Freudian terms as purporting to show that 'the ego [...] is a comparatively recent development that occurred in the period from about 1000 to 800 B.C. Before that, man obeyed the Voice of God, which emanated from the non-dominant brain hemisphere, without question. There was no questioning entity. They literally had no ego but were governed by what Freud calls the Superego and their instinctual drives, the Id' (*AM* 92).

Jaynes's theory entails the historical contingency of the individual ego and traces its origins to a specific time, place and set of environmental factors. Many of Burroughs's key obsessions—his cut-up methodology, his pronouncements on the need for humanity to move from time into space, and his own experiments with time-displacement (for example, 'mirror gazing' [see Morgan 1988:306–7]) are premised on the idea that the conditions of subjective experience, including the basic categories of time and space, are rooted in material and social conditions, and not fixed to an objective 'way the world actually is'. Given Burroughs's lifelong interest in anthropology, it is not surprising that he was drawn to the explanatory power of Jaynes's thesis.

The same theme of the historicity of human experience, and the concomitant denial of the subject–object dualism of contemporary scientific ontology, is also pursued by Horkheimer and Adorno. As Horkheimer expresses it, 'the facts which our senses present to us are socially preformed in two ways: through the historical character of the object perceived and the historical character of the perceiving organ. Both are not simply natural; they are shaped by human activity' (1937:200). In the essay on Homer's *Odyssey* in *Dialectic of Enlightenment*, Adorno and Horkheimer present an account of the emergence of the modern individual in the character of Odysseus, whose abilities—particularly that of reflective cunning—that allow him to survive are linked with the capacity to situate himself in space and time. Odysseus represents the emergence of the ego as a source of power over the mythic forces of nature and of gods, and therefore as the embryonic form of enlightenment.[9] His character exhibits, in an underdeveloped form, the properties of spontaneity, will, self-individuation and apperception capacities of an ego that conceives of space and time as abstract and rationalized forms, and therefore as separated from *place*. Within this mode of consciousness (which corresponds to Jaynes's understanding of the earliest form of the post-bicameral mind),

> the inner organization of individuality in the form of time is still so weak that the external unity and sequence of adventures remains a spatial change of scenery [...] Whenever in later history the self has experienced such debilitation, or the particular representation presupposes such debility in the reader, the narrative account of life has slipped into a [mere] sequence of adventures. (Adorno and Horkheimer 1944:48)

In other words, a self whose self-narrative can only be presented through sequential spatial arrangements is organizationally impoverished; it is not, however, 'primordial', since Horkheimer and Adorno suggest that such a structure of consciousness is compatible with other more recent historical conditions. In other works, Horkheimer and Adorno both explored the changing nature of the individual consciousness in detail, emphasizing the extent to which the supposed invariant properties of reflexive self-awareness, individual initiative and auto-direction of the will—the defining qualities of the Western notion of self—are socially produced and historically variable.

A second line of continuity extends from Jaynes's anthropological account of schizophrenia. Burroughs was particularly interested in schizophrenia, and especially in modern attempts to induce it artificially as a means of social control. According to Burroughs's reading of Jaynes, '[b]icameral man didn't need much consciousness. His environment was vastly more uniform and predictable and he was [...] getting his orders straight from the voice of God in the non-dominant brain hemisphere [...] Introspection was simply impossible' (AM 93). Burroughs's accounts of the Ancient Mayans in *The Soft Machine* and of aspects of ancient Egyptian society in *The Western Lands* suggest a bicameral social structure—obedience among individuals in bicameral societies was not something that was experienced as 'external', and thus did not need continual reinforcement through institutions of social control. Rather, obedience and volition were essentially identical, and commands from the priest/king/god were introduced as direct causal agents into the mental structure of the recipient in the form of auditory hallucinations. Jaynes identifies ego-loss and automatic obedience with schizophrenia, and suggests that '[modern] schizophrenia, at least in part, is a vestige of bicamerality' (405).

Horkheimer's essay, 'The Rise and Decline of the Individual' (1947), argues that the conformist qualities of primitive humanity are once again becoming socially useful: 'In our era of large economic combines and mass culture, the principle of conformity emancipates itself from its individualistic veil, is openly proclaimed, and raised to the rank of an ideal per se' (139). Burroughs pursues the same theme in his explorations of artificially induced schizophrenia, in which the theme of control-at-a-distance recurs. In *Naked Lunch*, Dr Benway experiments with various drugs ('Mescaline, harmaline, LSD6, bufotenine, muscarine' [NL 25]) that induce schizophrenic automatic obedience, and in the essay 'Freud and the Unconscious', Burroughs follows a discussion of a modern schizophrenic patient with the reflection that '[f]ifteen years ago experiments in Norway indicated that voices can be produced directly in the brain by an electromagnetic field. Progress along these lines is probably classified material' (AM 94).

A third point of convergence involves the interest of Jaynes, Burroughs, and Horkheimer and Adorno in the phenomenon of *deception* as a defining quality of the Western psyche, and with the relationship between representation and deception. Curiously, Jaynes also frames his analysis with respect to the Homeric narratives. Jaynes traces the transition from the bicameral to the post-bicameral mind through a genealogical analysis of the language and events recounted in the *Iliad* and *Odyssey*, respectively. Through these texts, which are of course multi-authored and multi-generational re-distillations of past events, Jaynes identifies a radical break in the development of the Western mind within the structure of the *Odyssey*. The defining human quality of the character of Odysseus is his *deviousness*, and '[t]he Odyssey is a journey [...] of guile, its invention and celebration. It sings of indirections and disguises and subterfuges, transformations and recognitions, drugs and forgetfulness, of people in other people's places, of stories within stories, and men within men' (1977:273).

In Adorno and Horkheimer's reading of the *Odyssey*, deception, domination and the emergence of the individual are seen as similarly entwined. In one striking aside, they claim that 'the history of civilization is the history of the introversion of sacrifice' and that deception is therefore an operative principle of culture, since 'all human sacrifices, when systematically executed, deceive the god to whom they are made: they subject him to the primacy of human ends, and dissolve his power' (1944:50). In its origins, however, deception is a phenomenon deriving from the use of language as description, or the triumph of identification over mimesis:

> [t]he mythic destiny, *fatum*, was one with the spoken word. The sphere of ideas to which the decrees of fate irrevocably executed by the figures of myth belong, is still innocent of the distinction between word and object. The word must have direct power over fact; expression and intention penetrate one another. Cunning consists in exploiting the distinction [...] The word is emphasized, in order to change the actuality. (1944:60)

In other words, as Adorno was later to emphasize in his philosophical explorations of the phenomenon of identity-thinking, the advent of language as descriptive instrument inevitably tends toward idealism because it forces the object to conform to subjectively derived categories, 'leaving no remainder' (1966:5).

The same theme emerges from Burroughs's claim that modern language is inherently deceptive—that, like a virus, it invades and occupies not only consciousness, but also the world that issues from the 'scanning pattern' of that consciousness. Burroughs's insights on this issue grew out of his reflections on Alfred Korzybski's theory of general semantics:

> As Korzybski points out [...] there are falsifications built into Western languages that impose aberrative thinking. One of these is the *is* of identity [...] The *is* of identity which equates the word with the object or process to which the word refers is a source of confusion ranging from muddled thinking and purely verbal arguments to outright insanity. (AM/PA 1970:158–9)

Burroughs's calibrated exercises in disengaging language and world may be understood as a literary version of Adorno's notion of metacritique. While epistemological critique attempts to answer the question of what logical categories make experience possible, metacritique alters the equation and asks what social categories and modes of human organization must be present for forms of logic—which are always, for Adorno, misrepresented forms—to arrive at particular answers. Therefore, according to Adorno, the confusion of word with thing that Burroughs, via Korzybski, associates as a problem of (Western) language, and which Adorno dubs as 'identity thinking', has to be understood as a broader problematic, expressing a basic *social* condition. In fact, according to Adorno, identity thinking is an expression of the fetishism of commodities that predominates in Western societies, and which, through the abstract mechanisms of the market—and in particular through the commodification of labor—identifies what is not merely quantitatively unequal but qualitatively incommensurable.

In this respect, the convergence between Burroughs and Adorno can be understood as variations on an appeal to materialism: the conditions under which modern society operates together involve an implicit belief in the original inherent identity of thought and world. The version of secularized Western (post)modernity currently being exported worldwide, which prides itself on its inexorable materialism and devotes such strenuous efforts to the overcoming of outmoded idealistic and anthropomorphic tendencies, in fact ends up as a species of equally misguided solipsism. The fact that solipsism, which involves the total internalization, or *immaterialization*, of the world, may indeed have 'material' consequences for the world is attested to by Burroughs's oft-quoted remark that 'Western man is *externalizing himself* in the form of gadgets' (*NL* 23, emphasis added).

CONCLUSION

The convergence between Burroughs and the Frankfurt School does not extend, perhaps, far beyond their respective diagnoses of the ills of (post)modernity. Adorno, Horkheimer and Marcuse were committed to concrete political action in one form or another, even though they qualified this commitment in important ways.[10] Burroughs did not so much reject politics as remain skeptical about the extent to which the existing system of social relations could be displaced by any existing critical resources, and redefined his own strategies as a writer and agent accordingly. What remains central to their shared concerns, however, is an ambivalence toward certain core elements of Western culture—truth, rationality and individuality; while both the Frankfurt School and Burroughs insisted on both the historical contingency of these elements and their entwinement with domination, in neither case did this translate into a complete rejection or dismissal of other possibilities embedded within them.

NOTES

1. The commentary here is restricted to the principal members of the first generation of the Frankfurt School. I also pass over important differences between Marcuse, Adorno and Horkheimer, which, for the purposes of this essay, are redundant.
2. See, for example, Jared Diamond's technological reductionist but nevertheless ingenious *Guns, Germs and Steel* (1998).
3. The concept is usually rendered as 'iron cage', which is a misleading translation of *stahlhartes Gehäuse*. See Kalberg's (2002) translation, 245–6 n129.
4. Zygmunt Bauman has convincingly argued that the social production of distance has been an ineliminable element of the 'civilizing process', and partly attributes to it the negation of the 'moral urge' that made the Holocaust possible (see Bauman 1989:192–8).
5. Adorno and Horkheimer chiefly criticize the dogmatic interpreters of these thinkers as at fault. Hegel and Marx themselves were both concerned to avoid being misinterpreted in such ways, as a close dialectical reading of their work—as undertaken with respect to Hegel in Adorno's *Negative Dialectics*, for example—would make clear.
6. Jaynes also crops up in several interviews and letters from Burroughs in the early 1980s (see Lotringer 2001:449–50, 454).
7. Jaynes does not use Freudian language, although his argument is very obviously influenced by Freud's basic theoretical paradigm.
8. Jaynes's theory of the emergence of subjectivity is more complex than stated here. In addition to spatialization and narratization, he argues that consciousness consists in excerption, in which detail is picked out from surroundings; the ability to generate the analog of 'I' and the metaphor

'me', linguistically based constructions that allow the abstraction of self from immediate experience and are therefore prerequisites of imagination; and conciliation, the process of assembling experience together in a coherent way. These operations are premised on the existence of language, since they involve an 'analogical' maneuver of mind, but language is only a necessary and not a sufficient condition for consciousness.

9. It should be emphasized that the intent of Adorno and Horkheimer's analysis of the Homeric myths in *Dialectic of Enlightenment* is not intended to be anthropological, but philosophical. Therefore, in drawing attention, for example, to the 'origins' of sacrifice in the character of Odysseus, they are not making a claim to historical causation but asking—as Simon Jarvis has expressed—'what must have happened for our thinking to have become what it is' (1998:21).

10. Adorno and Horkheimer returned to West Germany in the 1950s and were prominent critics of the postwar consolidation of liberalism there. Marcuse's influence on the 1960s student movement is well known.

REFERENCES

Adorno, T. (1966) *Negative Dialectics*, Ashton, E. B. trans. (London: Routledge, 1973).

Adorno, T., and Horkheimer, M. (1944) *Dialectic of Enlightenment*, Cumming, J. trans. (London: Verso, 1979).

AM/PA (1970) 'WSB, Alias Inspector J. Lee of the Nova Police', IN Lotringer, S. ed., *Burroughs Live: The Collected Interviews of William S. Burroughs 1960–1997* (USA: Semiotext[e], 2001), pp. 158–62.

Arato, A., and Gebhardt, E. (1978) *The Essential Frankfurt School Reader* (New York: Urizen).

Barber, B. (1995) *Jihad vs. McWorld* (New York: Times).

Bauman, Z. (1989) *Modernity and the Holocaust* (Oxford: Polity).

Chomsky, Noam (2003) *Rogue States: The Rule of Force in World Affairs* (Cambridge, MA: South End).

Diamond, J. (1998) *Guns, Germs and Steel* (New York: W. W. Norton).

Giddens, A. (1990) *The Consequences of Modernity* (Stanford, CA: Stanford University Press).

Gilroy, P. (2001) *Against Race* (Cambridge, MA: Harvard University Press).

Greider, W. (1997) *One World Ready or Not: The Manic Logic of Global Capitalism* (New York: Simon & Schuster).

Horkheimer, M. (1937) *Traditional and Critical Theory*, O'Connell, M. J. trans., IN Horkheimer 1972.

—— (1947) *Eclipse of Reason* (Oxford: Oxford University Press).

—— (1972) *Critical Theory: Selected Essays*, O'Connell, M. J. et al. trans. (New York: Seabury Press).

Jarvis, S. (1998) *Adorno: A Critical Introduction* (London: Routledge).

Jaynes, J. (1977) *Origins of Consciousness in the Breakdown of the Bicameral Mind* (Boston: Houghton Mifflin).

Klein, N. (2000) *No Logo* (London: Flamingo).

Marcuse, H. (1941) 'Some Social Implications of Modern Technology', IN Arato and Gebhardt 1978.

Morgan, T. (1988) *Literary Outlaw: The Life and Times of William S. Burroughs* (New York: Henry Holt).
Murphy, T. S. (1998) *Wising Up the Marks: The Amodern William Burroughs* (Cambridge, MA: Harvard University Press).
Ritzer, G. (2000) *The McDonaldization of Society* (Thousand Oaks, CA: Pine Forge).
Rose, G. (1978) *The Melancholy Science* (London: MacMillan).
Runciman, W. G. (1978) *Weber: Selections in Translation* (Cambridge: Cambridge University Press).
Weber, M. (1904–05) *The Protestant Ethic and the Spirit of Capitalism*, Kalburg, S. trans. (Los Angeles: Roxbury, 2002).

4
Speculating Freedom: Addiction, Control and Rescriptive Subjectivity in the Work of William S. Burroughs

Jason Morelyle

I am not *an* addict. I am *the* addict. The addict I invented to keep this show on the junk road. I *am* all the addicts and all the junk in the world. I *am* junk and I am hooked forever. Now I am using junk as a basic illustration. Extend it. I am reality and I am hooked, on, reality.

—William S. Burroughs,
'The Beginning is Also the End' (*BF* 62)

Maybe the target is not to discover who we are but to refuse who we are.

—Michel Foucault, 'The Subject and Power'

Addiction and control: in the work of William S. Burroughs, the two issues are inextricably and irrevocably bound together. The concepts of 'power', 'control', 'control machine', and 'control society' are crucial aspects of Burroughs's trajectory; as elements in the equation of his 'lifelong preoccupation' (*Q* xxiii), manifestations of control are treated with varying degrees of intensity throughout his work, and its drives and stratagems within such discursive formations as the mass media, organized religion, the government, the State, the nuclear family, science, institutionalized medicine, Western capitalist technocracies, instrumental reason, and, importantly, language (the Word) are represented in multifarious variations. Moreover, addiction, 'the algebra of need', functions as a kind of counterpoint, a sinister collaborator invested in the machinations of control: addiction to capital, addiction to materialism, addiction to the media, even addiction to the ego, subjectivity and notions of 'self'.

As Timothy S. Murphy proposes in his superb work, *Wising Up the Marks: The Amodern William Burroughs* (1997), subjectivity in Burroughs's work 'itself is a form of addiction to language, to the "I" of self-consciousness and identity as an instrument of control, both of the phenomenal world by the "I" and of the "I" itself by the ideological structure of its socius' (58).

When subjectivity is seen as a form of addiction in Burroughs's work we can begin to chart how he uses addiction as a *trope* for subjectivity, attempting, in effect, to re-inscribe or rescript how subjectivity is formed in a society of control. In other words, Burroughs's work contains resources not simply for theorizing, but also for resisting control, especially in his representations of the so-called drug addict, a figure that is often understood as a subject formed at the limits of 'straight' society. There are many examples throughout Burroughs's work that suggest how the drama of resistance might unfold, and perhaps one of the more compelling means through which he approaches this problem is through the rescripting or rewriting of subjectivity to determine methods of thinking about and moving toward 'freedom' under a regime of control. As Michel Foucault noted some months before his death, it is imperative that we promote 'new forms of subjectivity' through the refusal of certain kinds of individualities and subjectivities that have been imposed on us (Foucault 1983:216). As a figure of subjectivity, Burroughs's rendering of addiction provides a means of grasping how subjectivity is formed by power through the subjectivation (*assujetissement*) of a control society, where this term designates both the 'becoming' of the subject and the processes of subjection itself (Butler 1997:83). In order to understand the implications of what a society of control might be, we must come to terms with new forms of subjectivity that emerge from the new relations or 'diagram' of power that comprises such a society. Burroughs's work not only offers us a way of beginning to grasp what form this new subjectivity might assume, but it also provides blueprints for how we can begin conceptualizing the possibility of a *resistant* subject. In other words, Burroughs's rendering of 'addiction' can be read as a trope of subjectivity, but a subjectivity that is formulated specifically as strategically resistant to a control society: under the regime of control and junk, the addicted subject is a resistant, modulatory subject who realizes, like Mr Martin, 'The Man of a Thousand Lies' quoted in the epigraph, that there are 'realities' alternative to those imposed by control that can be generated by alternative subjectivities.

Although in many respects the emergence of the concept of addiction and the taxonomy of the addict as we have come to know it today are largely symptoms and side-effects of the growing dominance of nineteenth-century Western politico-medical discourse, many commentators have persuasively argued that the concept of 'drug' (the 'supplement') and the 'logic' of addiction are deeply embedded in the historicity of Western culture as a whole, a 'structure that is philosophically and metaphysically at the basis of our culture' (Ronell 1992:13). The meaning of the term 'addiction' can be traced to the Latin verb *addicere*, which in Roman law referred to a formal 'giving over' or delivery by sentence of court and implied a surrender, or dedication, of the sentence to a master. To be both literally and figuratively 'sentenced'—simultaneously condemned and bound by language—suggests, according to David Lenson, that the user has lost control of language and of consciousness itself, and that the user is, in a way, 'spoken' for by another: 'Instead of saying, one is said' (1995:35). It is telling that 'addiction' implies that one is acted upon or spoken for by an external-made-internal entity. One facet of Burroughs's approach to addiction falls very much along these lines, signaling an internalized possession, a kind of subjectivation of a user by some externalized force or entity usually figured as the 'controllers', the Nova Mob, and so on. Yet it is also interesting that the 'addict'—as emerging from the disciplinary enclosure of institutionalized medicine and psychiatry—is traditionally viewed by these disciplines as being 'possessed', because it is just this definition that Burroughs tries to disassemble. In Burroughs, the subject-as-addict, the modulatory subject, attempts to release himself from the nightmare of possession, from the trap of being spoken for by an-other; the definition of addiction in the traditional sense is implicitly a definition of the control society itself, something that Burroughs spent his entire life describing and attempting to eradicate.

POWER, DISCIPLINE, CONTROL

Power, for Foucault, is a 'multiplicity of force relations', the name one attributes to a 'complex strategical situation' in society (Foucault 1976:92–3), and a heterogeneous network that circulates through the sociopolitical whole in a 'capillary' fashion. Because power cannot be 'sought in the primary existence of a central point', power should not be thought of as a 'privilege' that is possessed, or as an 'institution' or 'structure' that assumes the 'sovereignty of the state [and] the form of law' (Foucault 1975:26); power is not a strength one is endowed with (Foucault 1976:93), a material 'thing' that can be consciously transferred, exchanged, and directed at a given class or individual, and is not 'a general system of domination exerted by one group over another' (92). Power, then, is not hierarchical, flowing from the top down, but 'comes from below'—that is, it is a mobile and localized field of relations, 'self-producing', 'everywhere', and 'exercised from innumerable points' not because it can consolidate 'everything under its invincible unity, but because it is produced from one moment to the next [...] in every relation from one point to another' (93–4). Power is decentralized and *relational*, a strategy performed through a variety of social and political practices in society. As such, power is not 'external' to or 'outside' of social relations, but constitutive of and coextensive with them.

Importantly, Foucault conceives of power as positive and productive, and insists that it should not be thought of in negative terms, as dominating, repressive, or exclusionary: 'We must cease once and for all to describe the effects of power in negative terms: it "excludes", it "represses", it "censors", it abstracts, it "masks", it "conceals". Power produces. It produces reality, produces knowledge, and produces domains of objects and rituals of truth' (Foucault 1975:194). This, then, is where the analyst or, to use Foucault's term, *genealogist* of power must focus her attention, on the interrelation between knowledge and power, because just as it is 'not possible for power to be exercised without knowledge' it is 'impossible for knowledge not to engender power' (Foucault 1977:52). For Foucault, discourses are self-referential 'coherent' bodies of statements that produce versions of reality by generating 'knowledge' about concepts or objects; hence, discourses 'write the rules' about what can be known and said about—for example, medical discourses, legal discourses, discourses about science, politics, and the insane. 'Knowledge is that of which one can speak in a discursive practice, and which is specified by that fact: the domain constituted by the different objects that will or will not acquire a scientific status' (Foucault 1969:201). The analysis of discourse must take place at the level of determining how and where subjects or objects of knowledge emerge, what new relations of power they might effect, and how regimes of 'truth' are produced. 'Truth is linked in a circular relation with systems of power which produce and sustain it, and to effects of power which it induces and which extend it into a "regime" of truth' (Foucault 1980b:133). Foucault uses an analytics of power and discourse in an attempt to 'create a history of the different modes [...] [so that] human beings are made into subjects' (Foucault 1983:208). Crucially, the subject is not only constituted *in* power, but constituted *by* it: power does not operate upon or outside relationships, but across and *through* them. Power produces, forms, and initiates the subject through the 'primary submission' of subjection, where 'power is not simply what we oppose but also, in a strong sense, what we depend on for our very existence [...] [what] initiates and sustains our agency' (Butler 1997:2). In this way, we see how the focus is not so much on power per se, but on the subject and the formation of the subject through subjectivation.

In the seventeenth and eighteenth centuries, Foucault contends, disciplinary power began to emerge in response to monarchical-based juridical forms of power that understood power as repressive and negative; disciplinary power, on the other hand, is necessarily positive, a kind of 'nonsovereign' power (Foucault 2002:36) that produces docile bodies with maximum efficiency, a 'unitary technique by which the body is reduced as a "political" force at the least cost and maximized as a useful force' (Foucault 1975:221). Disciplinary power and its technologies, understood as one of 'bourgeois society's great inventions', was instrumental in the formation of industrial capitalism and its corresponding culture (Foucault 2002:36; 1975:221) and materialized in a variety of forms: military barracks, schools, factories, hospitals, and prisons. The point was that such technologies extracted time, labor, and usefulness from consenting, docile bodies, rather than the commodities and wealth that the sovereign model demanded. Hence, since the emergence of disciplinary power, what we have in modern society is the shift from an administration of force (sovereign) to an administration by compliance (discipline).

Taking Michel Foucault's meditations on power and government as an implicit starting point, Gilles Deleuze captures the sense of what a control society may be when he contends that over the course of the twentieth century, our society has been confronted with a general crisis in relation to all 'environments of enclosure' and has registered a new formulation or 'diagram' of power; we have, he claims, been undergoing a transformation from a disciplinary society to a society of control or 'modulation' (Deleuze 1990:3). Although the society of control is defined very differently from the sovereign regimes of the sixteenth and seventeenth centuries and the 'modern' disciplinary regimes of the nineteenth and twentieth centuries, this does not necessarily mean that these two regimes have completely disappeared. As Foucault contends, we must see such transitions not in terms of a 'replacement of a society of sovereignty by a disciplinary society' or the replacement of a 'disciplinary society by a society of government'; rather, we should see it 'as a triangle, sovereignty–discipline–government' (Foucault 1978:102). Just as some features of a sovereign regime remain in a disciplinary society, so do features of disciplinary society remain in a society of control. As Michael Hardt points out, power never leaves a vacuum. Instead, what we are seeing in a society of control is not so much a complete disintegration of environments of enclosure such as the prison, the family, or the factory, but rather the 'generalization of the logics' of disciplinary institutions 'across the entire society, spreading like a virus' (1998:30–1). Control societies will employ many strategies of disciplinary regimes, in that the authority of disciplinary regimes is no longer contained in particular institutions and environments of enclosure, but is spread out in a 'continuous network' (Deleuze 1990:5) in which the *socius* is not 'emptied of the disciplinary institutions but completely filled with the modulations of control' (Hardt 1998:31).

In a society of control, all disciplinary institutions—education, policing, psychiatry, production—subsume every aspect of experience so that the object of these institutions is life itself. Just as discipline entails a discontinuous molding of the individual who is 'always starting again' and who 'never ceases passing from one closed environment to the next' (Deleuze 1990:4, 2), in a society of control 'one is never finished with anything' (4). The distinction between the two can be seen in the difference between a limited, segregated incarceration and the limitless postponements of continuous variation. Where disciplinary practice molded behavior and fashioned subjects, practices of control continuously modulate and integrate. As such, the connection between society and State is no longer seen in the 'mediation and organization' of disciplinary institutions, but rather in how the State is set 'in motion directly through the perpetual circuitry of social production' (Hardt 1998:31). Like a sovereign regime or a disciplinary society, however, the modus operandi of control society is power, and the ways in which power is integrated into social life; the difference is that this integration takes place in an increasingly synthesized, complete and total fashion. Thus, a society of control, like a society of sovereignty or disciplinarity, is still rooted in the 'diagram' (Deleuze 1986:70–93) of power. Although its strategies and relational formulae are modified, the power/knowledge equation still remains the concomitant force. Power may never leave a vacuum, but its strategies and relations *do* shift, especially when it comes to resistance to power itself. A society of control will not set out to contain or limit resistance as in a regime of sovereignty or discipline, but will instead seek to diffuse it.

Burroughs's understanding of control directly addresses this issue because he recognizes that the subject—the 'agent' Inspector Lee, for instance—resists control on a continuous basis while also being thoroughly *dependent* on it. Perhaps one of the more important ways that a society of control is formulated in Burroughs's work is in the figure of junk, where the 'theory' of junk and junk addiction *itself* is troped into a 'general' theory of power, a 'mold of monopoly and possession' (*NL* xxxvi). Throughout Burroughs's corpus of work, not only are subjectivity and language shaped, affected and *infected* by the overriding theme of control/junk, these mechanisms are manifestations of control/junk. However, Burroughs's taxonomy of addiction can be profitably understood as other than being simply 'addiction' in the normative sense; junk and junk addiction can be seen, he writes, as a 'cellular equation that teaches the user facts of general validity' (*J* xvi). Burroughs is implicitly stating that the subject, formed within a control society, is dependent on the relations of power that comprise that society for its sense of self. 'Facts' of general validity here are read as structures of knowledge, regimes of truth, and systems of 'word and image'—the very 'facts' that work in and through subjectivation. The challenge for both Burroughs and Foucault, however, lies in the fact that power does not simply suppress the subject; it *produces* the subject as well. The subject needs power like it needs junk because it is only through such a dependency that it can be recognized within the category of 'subject' itself. Subjectivity—what Burroughs sometimes refers to as the 'human form' (*BF* 64)—is thoroughly dependent on 'word and image' (see 64–5), and as such is both limited and created by the discursive mechanisms of word and image (see 45–6). '[I]mage *is* junk' (*NE* 52) and 'junk *is* image' (9 [note]), Burroughs maintains, and addiction to junk constitutes normative subjectivity itself—that which must be subverted. This, of course, is one of the central problems facing Burroughs, because if subjectivity—addiction—is the system that we must all struggle against, then the only tool we have in this struggle is subjectivity itself. Coming to terms with this problem is a matter of formulating the ways in which power is organized, be it through the stratagems of disciplinarity or the maneuverings of a society of control. In this sense, the troping of junk and junk addiction into a 'general' theory of power is reminiscent of Foucault's notion of power; junk, like power, is everywhere and nowhere, a modulated space without a circumference or a middle, and as such, one 'becomes addicted' to power-as-addiction, dependent on it not only for one's understanding of the world, but for one's sense of self as well:

> There is no true or real 'reality'—'Reality' is simply a more or less constant scanning pattern—The scanning pattern we accept as 'reality' has been imposed by the controlling power on this planet, a power primarily oriented towards total control. (NF 53)

The 'imposition' of 'reality' by the 'controlling power' resonates with the 'pyramid of junk' outlined in the deposition-Introduction to *Naked Lunch*, where 'one level [eats] the level below [...] right up to the top or tops since there are many junk pyramids feeding on peoples of the world and all built on principles of monopoly' (*NL* xxxvi). Given the attributes of 'monopoly', 'imposition', and 'controlling', it would seem that Burroughs is portraying a hierarchical or transcendental model of power: sovereign, top-down, and utilitarian. However, those at the 'top' of the pyramid are just as implicated in the system as those at the 'bottom' because junk, the 'evil virus', like power, is a heterogeneous network and does not recognize or 'need' hierarchical systems to function: '[the] junk merchant does not sell his product to the consumer, he sells the consumer to his product' (*NL* xxxvii).

The 'product'—in this case, in the form of junk and power that 'constitutes' reality—is not an 'object' to be passed around or imposed on another, but is in effect that which is doing the passing. Junk, like power, is not hierarchical, flowing from the top down, but 'comes from below', in a mobile field of relations that is everywhere, and 'exercised from innumerable points'. Burroughs's rendering of the control/power/junk formula as constituent of 'reality' allows for a highly innovative and radicalized understanding of the world and oneself because, as a figuration of power, addiction provides a means of understanding those *relations* of power that make 'possible' the range of ethics, knowledges, actions, and experiences that mold the field of relationships that circumscribes the process of subject formation, a procedure that points to the potential development of new forms of subjectivity. This figuring of junk advances an understanding of control and power alternative to that of a 'top down' structure. Burroughs is adamant that locating power in a sovereign entity such as the State, and resisting it based on that assumption, only results in replicating that oppressive system: 'Doktor Kurt Unruh von Steinplatz writes: "He who opposes force alone forms that which he opposes and is formed by it" ' (BF 106).

RESISTANCE, RESCRIPTION, AND
MODULATORY SUBJECTIVITY

A society of control permeates the entirety of social life, submitting subjects to specific ways of acting, thinking, and existing beyond the confines of disciplinary enclosures where subjectivation takes place on a continuous and contiguous basis. In a control society, discourses are no longer limited to specific domains, but have spilled over and saturated the total field of relations. Recalling that truth is linked in a circular relation with systems of power that produce and sustain it, in a society of control this circular relation is compressed, and truth and power become even more inextricably connected than they were in previous disciplinary regimes. When truth and power are coexistent, there is no need for disciplines, no need for institutions of policing, education, or medicine, because these institutions are everywhere. As Burroughs points out, in a society of complete control, '[n]o police force is necessary' (AM 117). This is why, according to Burroughs, we must avoid reproducing certain forms of control when resisting a society of control; hence, we must move towards initiating new ways of thinking. Towards the end of his life, Foucault became more and more concerned with the notion of detaching power from truth towards the possibility of 'constituting a new politics of truth' (Foucault 1980b:133) and initiating new forms of subjectivity. In a society of control, this mode of thinking becomes more and more difficult: '"New concepts can only arise when one achieves a measure of disengagement from enemy conditions. On the other hand disengagement is difficult in a concentration camp is it not?" ' (BF 106).

The 'altered self' or a 'new form' of subjectivity is represented in the addict-as-subject and emerges as a modulatory subject directly engaged in the strategic games of power and control; such a modulatory subjectivity constantly moves towards, but never transcends, the limits not only of what constitutes a society of control itself, but of what, in effect, constitutes subjectivity. In other words, resistance in a control society emerges at the site of the subject. The addict is a modulatory or 'undulatory' subjectivity that reshapes and reforms itself in a continuously shifting movement that can be seen in Burroughs's shape shifters, in the oscillating perspectives and floating 'authorial I', in the decentralized network of control and junk itself. In *Nova Express*, for example, Inspector Lee, in detailing how arrests are made, explains that Nova criminals are not 'three-dimensional organisms [...] but they need three-dimensional human agents to operate' (*NE* 56). The point at which Nova criminals 'intersect' with human agents are known as 'coordinate points', sites that the criminals—the controllers—can occupy in a limitless series. Yet, the 'one thing that carries over from one human host to another and establishes identity of the controller [...] is *habit*' (*NE* 56). The transitory, modulatory subjectivity of the controllers is still limited in some ways by its addiction to identity. This is also underscored in the narrative point of view of *Nova Express*, especially at those points where the narrative suddenly breaks away from Inspector Lee's 'I' and shifts into the removed third-person narrative of the 'nameless' narrator referred to as 'Bill', 'I&I' and 'Bill&Iam'. These are instances of breaking away, or at least attempting to break away, from the normative confines of junk-identity. As such, Burroughs points to the modulatory-addict as existing at the extremes of control society, constantly testing and interrogating the limits of what constitutes subjectivity. Where or how might resistance to power, 'freedom' in the form of subjectivity, emerge in a society of control? Is there a way to resist strategies of power? This problem relates back to Foucault's proposition that power is productive. When Burroughs writes that the 'illusion of a separate inviolable identity limits your perceptions and confines you in time' (*AM* 133), he is not advocating a destruction of the 'self', a thought that he admitted was 'terrifying' (133); rather, he is proposing a configuration that prompts the shift, alteration, or production of one's notion of self. When power is conceived as functioning not 'on' or 'outside' its subjects, and does not act on them 'from above' but through, within, and 'from below', this indicates that power is not 'despotic' or limiting, but quite the opposite—that it is productive. Seen in this way, the *antithesis* of power is limitation and totalization. This is why Deleuze implies that power, in the guise of politics, is a potentially *creative*, even *experimental* force (Deleuze and Parnet 1977:137).

Power, then, is productive, and must encompass resistance: 'in relations of power, there is necessarily the possibility of resistance, for if there were no possibility of resistance [...] there would be no relations of power' (Foucault 1984:12). And just as power creates its own resistance, a society of control will create its own perforations and undermine its own aspirations to totality. In his essay 'The Limits of Control', Burroughs distinguishes between control and use, and points to the stagnancy of total control as the 'basic impasse' of all 'control machines':

> [C]ontrol also needs opposition or acquiescence; otherwise it ceases to be control [...] I *control* a slave, a dog, a worker; but if I establish *complete* control somehow, as by implanting electrodes in the brain, then my subject is little more than a tape recorder, a camera, a robot. You don't *control* a tape recorder—you *use* it [...] All control systems try to make control as tight as possible, but at the same time, if they succeeded completely, there would be nothing left to control. (*AM* 117)

Similarly, in the essay 'Mind War', Burroughs surmises that a society of 'world control' would look like an 'elitist World State very much along the lines laid down by the Nazis', controlled by a 'theocracy trained in psychic control techniques implemented by computerized electronic devices that would render opposition psychologically impossible' (*AM* 151). If there were no 'points of insubordination' (Foucault 1983:225) or possibilities of dissent within relations of power, there would be, simply, '*complete* control' (*AM* 117) in the form of enslavement, submission, and pure use. Just as a 'society without power relations' is only an 'abstraction' (Foucault 1983:222), the 'relationship between power and freedom's refusal to submit' cannot be separated (221).

Foucault maintained that it is a mode of action that defines a relationship of power, a mode of action that does not act on others, but on their actions—'a set of actions upon other actions' (Foucault 1983:220). Burroughs echoes this sentiment in writing that this 'is a game planet' and that although there cannot be a final victory because that would 'mean the end of the war game', all the players must 'believe in final victory' in order for the game to function (*AM* 155). Yet when we see the relationship of power, the 'game', as a series—or as an array—of actions upon the actions of others, one must include a crucial element: freedom (Foucault 1983:221). It is the alteration of the self that 'produces a modification of one's activity in relation to others, and hence a modification in power relations, even if only at the micro-level to begin with' (O'Farrell 1989:129). Hence, freedom, for Foucault as well as for Burroughs, constitutes the delimitation of domination in order to make space for the freedom of human relations, which is the space of possibility for the creation of new forms of subjectivity. Burroughs's modulatory subject is a subject that experiences itself not only formed within relations of power, but also as having power, capable of relaying and redeploying the strategies of power themselves.

Burroughs's fascination with control and his rendering of the subject-as-addict—the modulatory subject—shores up not so much a 'transcendence' of the limits of cultural norms or a 'moving outside' the limits of the self, but more an exploration of discursive limits. Transgression, as Foucault insists, is not related to limits in the same way that the prohibited is related to the lawful, or the outside to the inside, but it 'takes the form of a spiral which no simple infraction can exhaust' (Foucault 1963:35). It is crucial to understand that Burroughs's work in no way represents a literal moving 'beyond' or standing 'beside' oneself, but an interrogation of the *limits of the self* that points to the possibility of sociopolitical transformation within a society of control. What we tend to see in Burroughs is a 'creation of the self', the representation of the *experience* of self-formation in the face of the social and political forces that are incessantly affecting us on a daily basis. Through the lens of Burroughs's radicalized perspective, the formulation of a modular subjectivity is a generative force, and signals the possibility of promoting new forms of subjectivity, of bringing one to experience oneself as an agent *with* and constituted *by* power; he underscores the necessity of distinguishing alternative modes of liberation and resistance to dominant, normalizing systems of thought exercised in a society of control. Burroughs's representations of control and his re-signification of the subject as a modulatory subject is a gesture toward empowerment, a shift towards perceiving how we can interrupt the flow between power and truth. This, he warns, is perhaps one of the only ways that we can create power relationships that can be viably developed and employed within a society of control.

REFERENCES

Butler, J. (1997) *The Psychic Life of Power: Theories in Subjection* (Stanford: Stanford University Press).
Deleuze, G. (1986) *Foucault*, Hand, S. trans. (Minneapolis: University of Minnesota Press, 1988).
—— (1990) 'Postscript on the Societies of Control', *October*, 1992 No. 59, Winter, pp. 3–7.
Deleuze, G., and Parnet, C. (1977) *Dialogues*, 2nd edition, Tomlison, H., and Habberjam, B. trans. (New York: Columbia University Press, 2002).
Dreyfus, H., and Rabinow, P. (1983) *Michel Foucault: Beyond Structuralism and Hermeneutics* (Chicago: University of Chicago Press).
Foucault, M. (1963) 'Preface to Transgression', IN *Language, Counter-Memory, Practice* (Ithaca: Cornell University Press, 1977).
—— (1969) *The Archaeology of Knowledge*, Smith, S. A. M. trans. [1972] (New York: Routledge, 2002).
—— (1975) *Discipline and Punish: The Birth of the Prison*, Sheridan, A. trans. (New York: Vintage, 1979).
—— (1976) *The History of Sexuality Volume I*, Hurley, R. trans. (New York: Vintage Books, 1980).
—— (1977) 'Prison Talk', Gordon, C. trans., IN Foucault, M. 1980a, pp. 37–54.
—— (1978) 'Governmentality', IN *Power: The Essential Works of Foucault, 1954–1984*, Saubion, J. B. ed., Hurley, R. et al. trans. (New York: New Press, 2000), p. 219.
—— (1980a) *Power/Knowledge: Selected Interviews and Other Writings, 1972–77*, Gordon, C. et al. trans. (New York: Pantheon).
—— (1980b) 'Truth and Power', Marshall, L., Mepham, J., and Soper, K. trans., IN Foucault 1980a, pp. 109–33.
—— (1983) 'The Subject and Power' (Afterword), IN Dreyfus and Rabinow 1983, pp. 208–28.
—— (1984) 'The Ethic of Care for the Self as a Practice of Freedom: An interview with Michel Foucault, January 20, 1984', conducted by Raul Fornet-Betancourt, Helmut Becker, and Alfredo Gomez-Müller. Gautier, J. D., and s. j. trans., IN Bernauer, J., and Rasmussen, D. (1987) *The Final Foucault* (Cambridge: MIT Press, 1988), pp. 1–20.
—— (2002) *Society Must Be Defended: Lectures at the Collège de France 1975–1976*, Macey, D. trans. (New York: Picador). First publication of collected lectures.
Hardt, M. (1998) 'The Withering of Civil Society', IN Kaufman, E., and Heller, K. J. (1998) *Deleuze and Guattari: New Mappings in Politics, Philosophy, and Culture* (Minneapolis: University of Minnesota Press), pp. 23–9.
Lenson, D. (1995) *On Drugs* (Minneapolis: University of Minnesota Press).
Murphy, T. S. (1997) *Wising Up the Marks: The Amodern William Burroughs* (Berkeley: University of California Press).
O'Farrell, C. (1989) *Foucault: Historian or Philosopher?* (New York: St Martin's Press).
Ronell, A. (1992) *Crack Wars: Literature, Addiction, Mania* (Lincoln: University of Nebraska Press).

5

Excursus: Burroughs, Dada and Surrealism

Jon Longhi

William S. Burroughs's experiments with novel literary and media forms have a self-conscious relationship to Dada and Surrealism. Few artists or writers active after the Surrealists' heyday of the 1940s did so much to champion their cause and to reaffirm the fertility of the Dadaists' explorations into the nature of the work of art and its producer. Many of Burroughs's innovative working techniques originated in Dada parlor games; his cut-ups and dream journals employ devices first pioneered by the Surrealists decades earlier; and his interest in the unconscious and the irrational basis of human nature closely parallels the outlook of key Surrealist figures. This excursus examines some of the intellectual and aesthetic similarities between Burroughs's work and that of his Dadaist and Surrealist predecessors, with particular reference to the roles of automatism and dreaming in artistic technique.

The common conceptual origin of both Burroughs's 'routines' of the 1940s and 1950s—the spontaneous comedy monologues delivered as impromptu performances that gave rise to the revelatory and hallucinatory prose of *Naked Lunch*—and the free-form immediacy that characterized Dada is that of 'automatic writing'. Automatic writing, a technique in which text is produced 'spontaneously', was introduced into public consciousness at the beginning of the twentieth century by, among others, W. B. Yeats and the psychic Helen Smith (Jochum 1993). The Dadaists' adaptation of the method involved three elements: 'the psychological concept of the liberation of psychic inhibitions, the mathematical one of the coincidences of chance verbal encounters, and the hermetic one of the oracular function of the medium-poet' (Balakian 1971:61). All three of these themes are echoed in Burroughs's reflections that '[t]he writer is simply someone who tunes in to certain cosmic currents. He's sort of a transcriber, an explorer, a map maker' (Ziegesar 1986:162), and in his 1957 letter to Allen Ginsberg, in which he remarks that '[t]he only way I can write narrative is to get right outside my body and experience it. This can be exhausting and at times dangerous. One cannot be sure of redemption' (*LWB* 375).

The technique of automatic writing was pioneered by the Dadaists in the 'Cabaret Voltaire' performances in the refugee-flooded no-man's land of 1916 Zurich. These performances involved spontaneous poems that, like Burroughs's routines, invoked the elements of unconscious creation. Tristan Tzara's *Zurich Chronicle*—itself a stream-of-consciousness diary of the first days of the Dada movement—describes the free-form spontaneous poems improvised nightly by the Cabaret (Huelsenbeck 1920). Such poems, read 'in various languages, rhythms, intonations, by several people at once' (1920:112), evolved into more elaborate innovations: 'Innovations came pouring in: Tzara invented the static poem, a kind of optical poem that one looks at as at a forest; for my part, I initiated the dynamic poem, recited with primitive movements, as never seen before' (1920:112). Tzara always remained committed to the element of mathematical chance, however: 'choice played no part: the refusal of the conscious self was the essential thing' (Brandon 1999:100). Even four years after the invention of the cut-ups, during the 1919 Dada Parisian debut—a poetry reading organized by Andre Breton's magazine, *Litterature*—Tzara's method of writing was still the same: 'Tzara appeared, blinking in the lights. He proceeded to cut up an article by Leon Dauder, dropped the pieces into a hat, and read out the resulting "poem". In the wings on either side Breton and Aragon rang bells as he spoke, drowning out the words' (Brandon 1999:138-9).

Quite early on, however, two opposite dynamics developed in response to Tzara's technique. Hans Arp interrupted the element of mathematical chance by discarding the poems he didn't deem 'successful'; from here it was a short step to Breton's impatience and rejection of this core element of Dadaism. As Phillipe Soupault later commented, it was always in Breton's nature to 'draw conclusions' (Brandon 1999:148). Two other key figures, Kurt Schwitters and Hugo Ball, however, went in a different direction, going beyond creating clusters of random words to reducing the poems to collections of sound-concoctions of rhythmic grunts, squeals and cries. Ball's 'intention was to free vowels from syntax and meaning, creating nuances and triggering memories' (Huelsenbeck 1920:61), while Schwitters adopted Raoul Hausmann's 'optophonetics', a technique for denoting atomized individual phonemes (which culminated in the 1932 composition 'Die Sonata in Urlauten', a 40-minute sound poem set in traditional sonata form [Nice 1988]).

While Burroughs often attributes the invention of the cut-up technique to Brion Gysin in September of 1959 at the Beat Hotel in Paris (see, for example, Miles 2000:194), there is no doubt that he was aware of Tzara's techniques earlier than this (see, for example, *BF* 63). It is also possible that he was aware of Schwitters's later experiments with collage and montage (a technique Schwitters dubbed *Merz*); certainly Burroughs's visual works in *Ports of Entry* bear many similarities to Schwitters's collages and canvases.

As the connection between Burroughs's techniques and those of Dada may be understood in terms of automatic writing, his adaptation of Surrealist principles can be traced to a shared interest in the nature of the 'unconscious'. The literary paths that Breton chose to travel following his disillusionment with Dada were strongly directed by his immersion in Sigmund Freud's researches. Breton described Surrealism as 'a systematic exploration of the unconscious', and as existing 'firmly in the realm of the non-rational, to be achieved by any number of routes—physical fatigue, drugs, extreme hunger, dreams, mental illness—all inducing similar hallucinatory phenomena' (cited by Brandon 1999:215). Burroughs's literary experiments were also closely linked to a view of human nature that, like psychoanalytic theory, emphasized instinct and the biological, non-rational basis of culture and consciousness. Burroughs experimented intensely with the manipulation and alteration of consciousness through the use of drugs, but he also viewed travel, sex, art, and machines of various types as portals to the unconscious.

The convergence between Burroughs, the Surrealists and psychoanalysis is nowhere more striking, however, than in their shared attitudes towards dreams. Both Burroughs and the Surrealists give the sleeping life an almost equal relevance to the waking world. As Burroughs wrote to Allen Ginsberg in 1958:

> Of course life is literally a dream, or rather the projection of a dream. That is why political action fails, just as attempts to coerce neurosis with so-called will-power always fail. But the whole existing system can be *dreamed away* if we get enough people dreaming on the Gysin level. There is nothing can stop the power of a real dream. (*LWB* 398)

Burroughs also used his dreams 'professionally': 'I get perhaps half my sets and characters from dreams. Occasionally I find a book or paper in a dream and read a whole chapter or short story ... Wake up, make a few notes, sit down at the typewriter the next day, and copy from a dream book' (*AM* 97). Burroughs was a restless sleeper and often woke many times a night, at which instances he recorded his dreams in a notebook kept next to the bed. A selection of these writings was published as *My Education: A Book Of Dreams* (1995).

Surrealist painters such as Salvador Dali and Max Ernst considered their paintings to be essentially recorded dreams. Major Dali works such as *The Great Masturbator* (1929) and The *Lugubrious Game* (1929) owe the majority of their images to Dali's sleeping world (Descharnes and Neret 2001:139). In 1922, immediately following his break with Tzara, Breton initiated the 'séance project' (see Nadeau 1944:80–2). Breton was the lead 'scientist' and Robert Desnos his favorite patient. Desnos had narcoleptic tendencies and was capable of frequent catnaps in public. During these 'sleep fits', as the Surrealists called them, Desnos would scrawl down sponta-neous poems. Breton was entranced by the results of these experi-ments and for months the Surrealists embarked on a series of séances, where groups of Surrealists would study sleeping subjects and prod them to write down or speak messages as a means of accessing their unconscious. The experiments produced only words at first, but the Surrealists rapidly began to externalize images as well. These experiments in the visualization of dreams reached their highest point in Dali and Luis Bunuel's cinematic masterpiece *Un Chien Andalou* (1928). According to Bunuel:

> One morning we told each other our dreams and I decided that they might be the basis for the film we wanted to make. [...] Dali said, 'Last night I dreamed that my hands were swarming with ants.' I said, 'And I dreamed that I cut someone's eye in half.' [...] We wrote the screenplay in six days. Our minds worked so identically that there was no argument at all. The way we wrote was to take the first thoughts that came into our heads, rejecting all those that seemed tainted by culture or upbring-ing. They had to be images that surprised us, and that both of us accepted without question. That's all. (cited by Brandon 1999:317–18)

To cut through the 'taint of culture and upbringing' was a shared ambition of Burroughs and the Surrealists. Indeed, Dali argued that 'I categorically refused to consider the Surrealists as just another literary and artistic group. I believed they were capable of liberating man from the tyranny of the "practical, rational world" ' (1955:22).

The 'logic of disintegration' that may be said to inhabit both Dada and Surrealism as well as Burroughs's work is not, of course, to be understood simply in terms of production, but also as *reflection*: their experiments in fragmentation anticipate—and helped to create the appetite for—the jumbled and confused circus of the nightly media, a spectacle that would not look out of place in the Cabaret Voltaire itself. However, while the Dadaists and Surrealists were marking the decline of Old World hierarchies, giving much of their work a playful and even celebratory dimension, Burroughs was in a position to observe the consequences of the appropriation of their techniques by the rapidly emerging hegemony of the culture industry. Burroughs's vision, while it retains the humor and antinomianism of Dadaism and, to a lesser extent, Surrealism, has the nightmare quality of derangement, a reflection of an incoherent media landscape of constantly changing images, desires, and needs that the Surrealists and Dadaists could have only dreamed of.

REFERENCES

Balakian, A. (1971) *Andre Breton, Magus of Surrealism* (New York: Oxford University Press).

Brandon, R. (1999) *Surreal Lives* (New York: Grove).

Dali, S. (1955) *Diary of a Genius*, Howard, R. trans. (London: Creation, 1994).

Descharnes, R., and Neret, G. (2001) *Dali: The Paintings* (Hamburgh: Benedik Taschen Verlag).

Huelsenbeck, R. (1920) *Dada Almanac*, Green, M. trans. (London: Atlas Press, 1993).

Jochum, K. P. S. (1993) 'Yeats's Vision Papers and the Problem of Automatic Writing: A Review Essay', *English Literature in Transition (1880–1920)* (36)3, pp. 323–36.

Miles, B. (2000) *The Beat Hotel: Ginsberg, Burroughs, and Corso in Paris, 1968–1963* (New York: Grove Press).

Nadeau, M. (1944) *The History of Surrealism*, Howard, R. trans. (New York: MacMillan, 1965).

Nice, J. ed. (1988) *Futurism And Dada Reviewed* [Brussels, Belgium: Sub Rosa Records].

Ziegesar, P. Von (1986) 'Mapping the Cosmic Currents: An Interview with William Burroughs', IN Hibbard, A. ed., *Conversations with William S. Burroughs* (Jackson: University Press of Mississippi, 1999), pp. 160–70.

Part II

Writing, Sign, Instrument: Language and Technology

6
Burroughs's Writing Machines
Anthony Enns

In January 1953, William S. Burroughs traveled to South America in search of *yagé*, a drug he hoped would allow him to establish a telepathic link with the native tribes. He documented this trip in a series of letters to Allen Ginsberg which he wrote on typewriters rented by the hour in Bogotà and Lima and which he eventually published as a book ten years later. Critics have interpreted this period as a seminal point in Burroughs's career, largely due to the fact that the transcriptions of his drug experiences became the starting point for *Naked Lunch*. However, this experience also seems significant because it reveals Burroughs's desire to achieve a primitive, pre-literate state—a goal which remained central to his work, but which later manifested in his manipulations of media technologies. Burroughs's work thus offers a perfect illustration of Marshall McLuhan's claim that the electric age would effect a return to tribal ways of thinking: '[S]ince the telegraph and the radio, the globe has contracted, spatially, into a single large village. Tribalism is our only resource since the electro-magnetic discovery' (1962:219). And Burroughs's rented typewriters seem to stand somewhere between these two worlds, as he used them to translate his primitive/mythic experiences into a printed book, a commodity more appropriate to Western culture and the civilized world of 'typographic man'.

In this chapter, I argue that the representations of writing machines in Burroughs's work, as well as his manipulations of writing machines in his working methods, demonstrate the effects of the electric media environment on subjectivity, as well as its broader impact on the national and global level. I further argue that McLuhan's theories provide an ideal context for understanding the relationship between media, subjectivity, and globalization in Burroughs's work, because they explain how the impact of the electric media environment on human consciousness is inherently linked to a wider array of social processes whose effects can be witnessed on both mental and geopolitical states. McLuhan and

Burroughs were also contemporaries, and there is ample evidence that they drew ideas from one another's work. McLuhan, for example, was the first critic to note that Burroughs's novels effectively replicate the experience of the electric media environment (1964a:517), and he explicitly borrowed the term 'mosaic' from *Naked Lunch* to describe the format of television programming (1964b:204). In the original, unpublished version of *The Third Mind*, which Burroughs and Brion Gysin assembled from 1964 to 1965, Burroughs also included a paragraph from McLuhan's *The Gutenberg Galaxy*, which claimed that electric media technologies were producing new mental states by releasing the civilized world from the visual emphasis of print (McLuhan 1962:183). However, despite the fact that Burroughs was clearly influenced by McLuhan, he also distanced himself from the overt optimism of McLuhan's 'global village', thus avoiding the problem of technological determinism. In other words, rather than claiming that the electric media environment would automatically improve the human condition by enabling a greater degree of involvement and democracy, Burroughs repeatedly emphasized that this possibility was dependent on our ability to take control of the media. Burroughs's representations and manipulations of writing machines thus prefigure much of the contemporary work concerning the potential uses of the Internet and the worldwide web as either corporate environments or new tools of democracy.

WRITING MACHINES AND THE ELECTRIC MEDIA ENVIRONMENT

Although several critics have already discussed Burroughs's work in terms of the impact of media on subjectivity, these discussions generally focus on electric media technologies such as sound and film recording, and they often overlook mechanical machines like the typewriter. In her book *How We Became Posthuman*, for example, N. Katherine Hayles examines the impact of media on subjectivity in *The Ticket that Exploded* through Burroughs's use of sound recording technology. She argues that Burroughs's novel represents the tape recorder as a metaphor for the human body, which has been programmed with linguistic 'pre-recordings' that 'function as parasites ready to take over the organism' (1999:211). She also points out that the tape recorder subverts the disciplinary control of language by externalizing the mind's interior monologue, 'recording it on tape and subjecting the recording to various manipulations', or by producing new words 'made by the machine itself' (1999:211). These manipulations reveal the ways in which electric media are capable of generating texts without the mediation of consciousness, thus enabling 'new kinds of subjectivities' (1999:217). Hayles therefore suggests that information technologies, for Burroughs, represent the threat of language to control and mechanize the body; at the same time, they can be employed as potential tools for subverting those same disciplinary forces.

Hayles's conclusions could be amplified, however, by also examining Burroughs's use of writing machines, which play a larger role in his work and in his working method. Hayles notes, for example, that Burroughs performed some of the tape recorder experiments he describes in *The Ticket that Exploded*, such as his attempts to externalize his sub-vocal speech or his experiments with 'inching tape', which are collected in the album *Nothing Here Now but the Recordings*, but even she admits that 'paradoxically, I found the recording less forceful as a demonstration of Burroughs's theories than his writing' because 'the aurality of his prose elicits a greater response than the machine productions it describes and instantiates' (1999:216). This paradox is resolved, however, if one considers the typewriter as Burroughs's primary tool for manipulating and subverting the parasitical 'word', and thus as the essential prototype for many of his theoretical media interventions. Throughout his life, Burroughs repeatedly emphasized that he was dependent on the typewriter and was incapable of writing without one: 'I can hardly [write] with the old hand' (Bockris 1981:1). Burroughs once attempted to use a tape recorder for composition, but this experiment proved to be a failure: 'In the first place, talking and writing are quite different. So far as writing goes I do need a typewriter. I have to write it down and see it rather than talk it' (Bockris 1981:6). When giving advice to young writers, Burroughs was also fond of quoting Sinclair Lewis: 'If you want to be a writer, learn to type' (*AM* 36). James Grauerholz notes that in 1950, Burroughs himself wrote his first book, *Junky*, 'longhand, on lined paper tablets', which were then typed up by Alice Jeffreys, the wife of a friend; however, Burroughs was soon 'disappointed with Jeffreys' work on the manuscripts [...] which he felt she had overcorrected, so he bought a typewriter and learned to type, with four fingers: the index and middle finger of each hand' (Grauerholz 1998:40). From the very beginning of his career, therefore, Burroughs was aware of the influence of writing technologies on the act of writing itself, and all of his subsequent works were mediated by the typewriter. This machine thus became a privileged site where the effects of media technologies were both demonstrated and manipulated.

The notion that the typewriter is inherently linked to the electric media environment—and, by extension, the digital media environment—has also become a popular theme in contemporary media studies. Friedrich Kittler, for example, argues that there was a rupture at the end of the nineteenth century when writing was suddenly seen as deficient and was stripped of its ability to store acoustic and optical information, resulting in their separation into three different media technologies: gramophone, film and typewriter (1999:14). Kittler also claims that the typewriter 'unlinks hand, eye, and letter', thus replicating the disembodying effects of electric media technologies (1990:195), and that the ultimate impact of this separation is that 'the act of writing stops being an act [...] produced by the grace of a human subject' (1999:203–4). Scott Bukatman similarly points out that '[w]hat first characterizes typing as an act of writing is an effect of *disembodiment*' (1993:634), and he extends this argument to the digital realm by suggesting that the typewriter 'produces an information space divorced from the body: a proto-cyberspace' (1993:635).

Burroughs's work repeatedly illustrates the notion that writing machines have an effect on subjectivity by mediating the act of writing, and writers are repeatedly described as disembodied agents, 'recording instruments', or even 'soft typewriters', who simply transcribe and store written information. While writing *Naked Lunch*, for example, Burroughs claimed that he was an agent from another planet attempting to decode messages from outer space, and within the novel itself he describes the act of writing as a form of spiritual 'possession' (*NL* 200). This notion is not simply a metaphor for creativity, but rather it reappears in descriptions of his own writing process: 'While writing *The Place of Dead Roads*, I felt in spiritual contact with the late English writer Denton Welch [...] Whole sections came to me as if dictated, like table-tapping' (Q xviii). The writer is thus removed from the actual composition of the text, and the act of writing becomes the practice of taking dictation on a typewriter. In the essay 'The Name Is Burroughs', Burroughs also reports a recurring 'writer's dream' in which he reads a book and attempts to remember it: 'I can never bring back more than a few sentences; still, I know that one day the book itself will hover over the typewriter as I copy the words already written there' (*AM* 9). In 'The Retreat Diaries', he claims that '[w]riters don't write, they read and transcribe' (*BF* 189), and he also describes dreams in which he finds his books already written: 'In dreams I sometimes find the books where it is written and I may bring back a few phrases that unwind like a scroll. Then I write as fast as I can type, because I am reading, not writing' (190). Burroughs even incorporates these dreams into the narrative of *The Western Lands*, where a writer lies in bed each morning watching 'grids of typewritten words in front of his eyes that moved and shifted as he tried to read the words, but he never could. He thought if he could just copy these words down, which were not his own words, he might be able to put together another book' (*WL* 1–2). The act of typing thus replaces the act of writing, because the words themselves have already been written and the writer's job is simply to type them out.

By disembodying the user and creating a virtual information space, Burroughs's writing machines also prefigure the globalizing impact of electric media technologies. John Tomlinson, for example, argues that contemporary information technologies have a 'deterritorializing' effect because 'they lift us out of our cultural and indeed existential connection with our discrete localities and, in various senses, open up our lifeworlds to a larger world' (1999:180). McLuhan also points out that the electric media environment not only fragments narrative and information, but also reconfigures geopolitical power. According to McLuhan, for example, the visual emphasis of typography led to both individualism and nationalism, because the printed book introduced the notion of point of view at the same time that it standardized languages: 'Closely interrelated, then, by the operation and effects of typography are the outering or uttering of private inner experience and the massing of collective national awareness, as the vernacular is rendered visible, central, and unified by the new technology' (1962:199). Electric media, on the other hand, represent a vast extension of the human nervous system, which emphasize the auditory over the visual and global awareness over individual experience: '[W]ith electricity and automation, the technology of fragmented processes suddenly fused with the human dialogue and the need for over-all consideration of human unity. Men are [...] involved in the total social process as never before; since with electricity we extend our central nervous system globally, instantly interrelating every human experience' (McLuhan 1964b:310–11). This leads to a greater degree of interdependence and a reduction in national divisions, because '[i]n an electrically configured society [...] all the critical information necessary to manufacture and distribution, from automobiles to computers, would be available to everyone at the same time', and thus culture 'becomes organized like an electric circuit: each point in the net is as central as the next' (McLuhan and Powers 1989:92). The absence of a 'ruling center', McLuhan continues, allows hierarchies to 'constantly dissolve and reform', and information technologies therefore carry the threat of 'politically destabilizing entire nations through the wholesale transfer of uncensored information across national borders' (McLuhan and Powers 1989:92). Rather than seeing this development as essentially negative, however, McLuhan adds that it will result in 'a dense electronic symphony where all nations—if they still exist as separate entities—may live in a clutch of spontaneous synesthesia, painfully aware of the triumphs and wounds of one other' (McLuhan and Powers 1989:95).

Burroughs also illustrates the deterritorializing effects of media technologies, and he frequently refers to the construction of national borders and identities as simply a function of global systems of control and manipulation. In his essay 'The Bay of Pigs', for example, Burroughs writes:

> There are several basic formulas that have held this planet in ignorance and slavery. The first is the concept of a nation or country. Draw a line around a piece of land and call it a country. That means police, customs, barriers, armies and trouble with other stone-age tribes on the other side of the line. The concept of a country must be eliminated. (*BF* 144)

The process of nation-building, in other words, is nothing more than the exercise of control. In 'The Limits of Control', Burroughs also points out that 'the mass media' has the power to spread 'cultural movements in all directions', allowing for the cultural revolution in America to become 'worldwide' (*AM* 120). The mass media therefore presents the possibility of an 'Electronic Revolution', which would not only cross national borders but also eliminate them (*Job* 174–203). By creating a sprawling, virtual information space, Burroughs's novels illustrate the ways in which media technologies could potentially fragment national identities and global borders; they also reveal the interconnections between information technologies and world markets, where cultural and economic exchanges gradually become inseparable.

THE ADDING MACHINE AND BUREAUCRATIC POWER

Bukatman's claim that the virtual information space of the type-writer is linked to the modern development of cyberspace can be most clearly seen by tracing the history of the Burroughs Adding Machine, which was patented by Burroughs's paternal grandfather in 1885. The Adding Machine was a device for both calculating and typing invoices, and thus it shared many common features with the typewriter, including a ribbon reverse that later became standard on all typewriters. Although the typewriter was often seen as a separate technology because it was designed for business correspondence rather than accounting, a brief look at the history of the Burroughs Adding Machine Company indicates that the divisions between calculating and typing machines were never that clearly defined. In the 1920s, for example, the company also marketed the Moon-Hopkins machine, which combined the functions of an electric typewriter and a calculating machine, and in 1931 it even began producing the Burroughs Standard Typewriter. This merging of calculating and typing machines reached its full realization with the development of business computers in the early 1950s, and the Burroughs Adding Machine Company was also involved in the earliest stages of this transition. In 1951, for example, it began work on the Burroughs Electronic Accounting Machine (BEAM), and in 1952 it built an electronic memory system for the ENIAC computer. In 1961 it also introduced the B5000 Series, the first dual-processor and virtual memory computer, and in 1986 it merged with Sperry to form the Unisys Corporation, which released the first desktop, single-chip mainframe computers in 1989. The Adding Machine and the typewriter thus both stand at the beginning of a historical trajectory, where the distinction between words and numbers became increasingly blurred and where typing gradually transformed into 'word processing'.

Burroughs clearly shares the legacy of this joint development of calculating and typing machines, as well as the development of a powerful corporate elite in America. The adding machine makes frequent appearances in his work, where it often represents the manipulative and controlling power of information. In *The Ticket that Exploded*, for example, Burroughs defines 'word' itself as 'an array of calculating machines' (*TE* 146). The novel also employs the linear, sequential and standardizing functions of calculating and typing machines as a metaphor to describe the mechanization of the body, or 'soft typewriter'. The narrator claims, for example, that the body 'is composed of thin transparent sheets on which is written the action from birth to death—Written on "the soft typewriter" *before* birth' (*TE* 159). Tony Tanner points out that the 'ticket' in the title of the novel also 'incorporates the idea that we are all programmed by a prerecorded tape which is fed into the self like a virus punchcard so that the self is never free. We are simply the message typed onto the jelly of flesh by some biological typewriter referred to as the Soft Machine' (1971:135). The 'soft typewriter' therefore represents the body as an information storage device, upon which the parasitical 'word' has been inscribed. The fact that the Burroughs Adding Machine Company also produced ticketeers and was an early innovator in computer punch card technology further emphasizes this notion of the parasitical 'word' as a machine or computer language—a merging of words and numbers into a system of pure coding designed to control the functions of the machine.

There are also moments in Burroughs's work when writing machines appear synonymous with the exercise of bureaucratic power, as can be seen in his description of the nameless 'Man at The Typewriter' in *Nova Express*, who remains '[c]alm and grey with inflexible authority' as he types out writs and boardroom reports (*NE* 130). This connection between machines and bureaucratic power is also illustrated in *The Soft Machine*, where Mayan priests establish an oppressive regime based on an information monopoly. They employ a regimented calendar in order to manipulate the bodies and minds of the population, and access to the sacred codices is strictly forbidden: '[T]he Mayan control system depends on the calendar and the codices which contain symbols representing all states of thought and feeling possible to human animals living under such limited circumstances—These are the instruments with which they rotate and control units of thought' (*SM* 91). The narrator repeatedly refers to this system as a 'control machine' for the processing of information, which is emphasized by the fact that the priests operate it by pushing 'buttons' (*SM* 91), like a typewriter or a computer. This connection between writing machines and bureaucratic authority is extended even further when the narrator goes to work at the Trak News Agency, whose computers actually invent news rather than record it. The narrator quickly draws a parallel between the Mayan codices and the mass media: 'I sus [sic] it is the Mayan Caper with an IBM machine' (*SM* 148). In other words, like the Mayan priests, who exercise a monopoly over written information in order to control and manipulate the masses, the Trak News Agency similarly controls people's perception of reality through the use of computers: 'IBM machine controls thought feeling and *apparent* sensory impressions' (*SM* 148–9).

The notion that the news industry manipulates and controls people's perceptions of reality is a recurring theme throughout Burroughs's work. In *The Third Mind*, for example, he writes:

> 'Reality' is apparent because you live and believe it. What you call 'reality' is a complex network of necessity formulae … association lines of word and image presenting a prerecorded word and image track. How do you know 'real' events are taking place right where you are sitting now? You will read it tomorrow in the windy morning 'NEWS' … (*3M* 27)

He also cites two historical examples where fabricated news became real: 'Remember the Russo-Finnish War covered from the Press Club in Helsinki? Remember Mr. Hearst's false armistice closing World War I a day early?' (*3M* 27). In the chapter 'Inside the Control Machine', Burroughs more explicitly argues that the world press, like the Mayan codices, functions as a 'control machine' through the same process of repetition and association:

> By this time you will have gained some insight into the Control Machine and how it operates. You will hear the disembodied voice which speaks through any newspaper on lines of association and juxtaposition. The mechanism has no voice of its own and can talk indirectly only through the words of others … speaking through comic strips … news items … advertisements … talking, above all, through names and numbers. Numbers *are* repetition and repetition is what produces events. (*3M* 178)

Like the Mayan codices, therefore, the modern media also illustrates the merging of words and numbers in a machinic language of pure control. Burroughs adds, however, that the essential difference between these two systems is that the 'Mayan control system required that ninety-nine percent of the population be illiterate' while 'the modern control machine of the world press can operate only on a literate population' (*3M* 179). In other words, the modern control machine is an extension of the printing press because it uses literacy in order to maintain social hierarchies and keep readers in a passive state of detachment. In order to overthrow these hierarchies, it is therefore necessary not simply to develop the literacy skills the Mayans lacked, but also to subvert the control machine itself and the standards of literacy it enforces.

THE 'FOLD-IN' METHOD AND AUDITORY SPACE

The narrator of *The Soft Machine* quickly discovers that understanding the nature of the Trak News Agency's control machine is the first step to defeating it: 'Whatever you feed into the machine on subliminal level the machine will process—So we feed in "dismantle thyself" [...] We fold writers of all time in together [...] all the words of the world stirring around in a cement mixer and pour in the resistance message' (*SM* 149). In other words, the narrator is able to dismantle the control system by manipulating the writing machine and disrupting its standard, linear sequence of information. This manipulation involves the use of a technique Burroughs referred to as the 'cut-up' or 'fold-in' method: 'A page of text—my own or someone else's—is folded down the middle and placed on another page—The composite text is then read across half one text and half the other' (*3M* 95–6). Burroughs frequently employed this method in his own work, and it is perhaps the clearest example of how the typewriter creates 'new kinds of subjectivity' by displacing the author as the controlling consciousness of the text. In a 1965 *Paris Review* interview, Burroughs explained the essential difference between this method and simply free associating at the typewriter: 'Your mind simply could not manage it. It's like trying to keep so many chess moves in mind, you just couldn't do it. The mental mechanisms of repression and selection are also operating against you' (Knickerbocker 1965:25). The ultimate goal of this technique, in other words, is to short-circuit the literate mind and use the typewriter to achieve a more primitive state of awareness, which McLuhan describes as precisely the effect of the electric media environment.

Burroughs's justification for the 'fold-in' method also emphasizes the basic inadequacy of print in comparison to developments in other media: '[I]f writing is to have a future it must at least catch up with the past and learn to use techniques that have been used for some time past in painting, music and film' (*3M* 95). Burroughs thus saw this method as enabling the typewriter to manifest the properties of other media, including sound recording. This connection between the typewriter and sound may appear confusing, as his novels remain essentially visual, but McLuhan points out that the distinction between visual and auditory space actually refers to the way in which media technologies structure information:

> Television, radio and the newspaper [...] deal in *auditory space*, by which I mean that sphere of simultaneous relations created by the act of hearing. We hear from all directions at once; this creates a unique, unvisualizable space. The all-at-once-ness of auditory space is the exact opposite of lineality, of taking one thing at a time. It is very confusing to learn that the mosaic of a newspaper page is 'auditory' in basic structure. This, however, is only to say that any pattern in which the components coexist without direct lineal hook-up or connection, creating a field of simultaneous relations, is auditory, even though some of its aspects can be seen. The items of news and advertising that exist under a newspaper dateline are interrelated only by that dateline. They have no interconnection of logic or statement. Yet they form a mosaic or corporate image whose parts are interpenetrating [...] It is a kind of orchestral, resonating unity, not the unity of logical discourse. (McLuhan 1963:43)

Burroughs's 'fold-in' method thus transforms standardized, linear texts into a 'mosaic' of information, which parallels the structure of television, radio, and newspapers. Even though Burroughs's 'cut-up' novels remain essentially visual, they create an auditory space because they provide connections between texts that are not based on 'logic or statement', and they behave more like the 'sphere of simultaneous relations created by the act of hearing'. Such an understanding of auditory space helps to explain Burroughs's notion of the 'fold-in' method as manifesting the properties of music, or McLuhan's paradoxical notion of the typewriter as both a tool that regulates spelling and grammar and 'an oral and mimetic instrument' that gives writers the 'freedom of the world of jazz' (1964b:230).

The function of this method can be most clearly seen in *The Ticket that Exploded*, where the narrator describes a 'writing machine' that

> shifts one half one text and half the other through a page frame on conveyor belts [...] Shakespeare, Rimbaud, etc. permutating through page frames in constantly changing juxtaposition the machine spits out books and plays and poems—The spectators are invited to feed into the machine any pages of their own text in fifty-fifty juxtaposition with any author of their choice any pages of their choice and provided with the result in a few minutes. (*TE* 65)

The machine thus performs the 'fold-in' method by fragmenting and rearranging texts, and it further disrupts the written word through the use of 'calligraphs': 'The magnetic pencil caught in calligraphs of Brion Gysin wrote back into the brain metal patterns of silence and space' (*TE* 63). The possibility of 'silence and space', therefore, is represented through a break with print technology. This is most clearly illustrated on the last page of the novel—an actual calligraph composed by Brion Gysin, in which English and Arabic words alternate in various permutations of the phrase 'Silence to say good bye' (*TE* 203). The function of the machine is thus mirrored in the construction of the book itself, which was also composed using the 'fold-in' method and contains passages spliced in from other authors, including lines from Shakespeare's *The Tempest*. Because the novel contains the formula for its own self-generating reproduction, Gérard-Georges Lemaire uses the term 'writing machine' interchangeably to refer to both the content and method of Burroughs's work, and he points out that Burroughs's machine not only 'escapes from the control of its manipulator', but 'it does so in that it makes it possible to lay down a foundation of an unlimited number of books that end by reproducing themselves' (*3M* 17). In other words, the parasitical 'word' is externalized from the writer's own consciousness and reproduces itself in a series of endless permutations.

TYPESETTING EXPERIMENTS, THREE-COLUMN CUT-UPS AND THE GRID

Another method Burroughs employs to transform the printed word into an auditory space can be seen in his typesetting experiments, which were clearly inspired by the structure of newspapers and magazines. By presenting a series of unrelated texts in parallel columns, the newspaper suggests interconnections which are not based on logic or reason, and many of Burroughs's stories from the 1960s and early 1970s reveal a growing interest in the effects of typesetting, one example being 'The Coldspring News'. When this piece was originally published in *White Subway*, it was divided into two columns, and the sections contained bold titles, thus imitating newspaper headlines (*WS* 39, see *BF* for a reprint without the three-column format). The title of the story was also designed to resemble a masthead, with Burroughs listed as 'Editor' rather than author (*WS* 39). Subsequent editions removed this formatting, but Robert

Sobieszek points out that Burroughs continued these experiments in his collages, many of which 'were formatted in newspaper columns and often consisted of phrases rearranged from front pages of the *New York Times* along with photos or other illustrations' (1996:55). Sobieszek also notes that in 1965 Burroughs created his own version of *Time* magazine, including

> a *Time* cover of November 30, 1962, collaged over by Burroughs with a reproduction of a drawing, four drawings by Gysin, and twenty-six pages of typescripts comprised of cut-up texts and various photographs serving as news items. One of the pages is from an article on Red China from *Time* of September 13, 1963, and is collaged with a columnal typescript and an irrelevant illustration from the 'Modern Living' section of the magazine. A full-page advertisement for Johns-Manville products is casually inserted amid all these texts; its title: 'Filtering'. (1996:37)

These experiments therefore offer another illustration of the ways in which the press mediates or 'filters' our experience of reality, and because the typewriter enables such interventions, allowing writers to compose texts in a standardized font that is easily reproducible, these collages offer a perfect illustration of McLuhan's claim that '[t]he typewriter fuses composition and publication' (1964b:228).

A similar kind of typesetting experiment can be seen in Burroughs's film scripts, such as *The Last Words of Dutch Schultz* (1975), where he uses multiple columns to describe the sound and image tracks of a non-existent film about the gangster Dutch Schultz. By using Hollywood terminology, as well as employing various gangster film clichés, Burroughs effectively imitates the language and style of Hollywood films. The script also includes photographs from Hollywood films and press clippings concerning the actual Schultz, thus blurring the boundaries between fictional and documentary sources and exposing the ways in which the mass media, including both the film industry and the world press, effectively determines and controls people's perceptions of reality. The script also performs a similar kind of intervention as his earlier typesetting experiments by employing separate columns for sounds and images. In other words, rather than following the strict format of traditional screenplays, Burroughs's script simultaneously represents both an imitation and a subversion of yet another institutional form of textual production. The sound and image columns are also reminiscent of the 'Exhibition' in *The Ticket that Exploded*, which isolates and manipulates sound and image tracks in order to create random and striking juxtapositions that draw the spectator's attention to the constructed nature of the media itself (*TE* 62–8).

The purpose of these interventions, therefore, is ultimately not to participate in the mass media but rather to subvert and dismantle its methods of presenting information. This is most apparent in Burroughs's three-column cut-ups, in which three separate columns of text are combined on the same page. Although these cut-ups resemble Burroughs's newspaper and magazine collages, the purpose of the juxtaposed columns is ultimately to subvert the newspaper format, not to replicate it. This method is clearly based on the theoretical tape recorder experiment Burroughs describes in *The Ticket that Exploded*, where he suggests recording various sides of an argument onto three tape recorders and allowing them to argue with each other (*TE* 163). The purpose of this experiment is to externalize language and remove it from the body, while at the same time deflating the power of words through their simultaneous and overlapping transmission in a nonsensical cacophony of sound. Like the three tape recorders, the three columns of text also produce multiple, competing voices simultaneously vying for the reader's attention, and the reader has to choose whether to read the columns in sequence from beginning to end, to read the individual pages in sequence, jumping between columns at the bottom of each page, or to read across the page from left to right, jumping between columns on every line. These compositions thus represent a radically new kind of information space—a proto-hypertext—in which the role of the author is displaced and linear structure is disrupted. In some of these compositions, such as 'Who Is the Third That Walks Beside You', Burroughs even decenters his own authority by combining found documents with excerpts from his novels (*BF* 50–2). He effectively makes these already cut-up passages even more disorienting by removing them from their original context, re-splicing them into new arrangements and setting them in juxtaposition to one another. As if to emphasize the purpose behind this procedure, he also includes a passage from *The Ticket that Exploded*, in which he encourages the reader to 'disinterest yourself in my words. Disinterest yourself in anybody's words, In the beginning was the word and the word was bullshit' [sic] (*BF* 51).

Burroughs's grids represent yet another method of manipulating written information. The grids follow the same logic as Burroughs's three-column cut-ups, although the vertical columns are also divided horizontally into a series of boxes, thus multiplying the number of potential links the reader is able to make between the blocks of text. Burroughs employs this method in many of his collages, such as *To Be Read Every Which Way*, in which he divides four vertical columns of text into nine rows, thus creating 36 boxes of text which can be read in any order (Sobieszek 1996:27). Much of this work was compiled for the original edition of *The Third Mind*, which was never published; however, in his essay 'Formats: The Grid', Burroughs describes this method as 'an experiment in machine writing that anyone can do on his own typewriter' (Burroughs 1964:27), and he illustrates the process using material taken from reviews of *Naked Lunch*:

> I selected mostly unfavorable criticism with a special attention to meaningless machine-turned phrases such as 'irrelevant honesty of hysteria,' 'the pocked dishonored flesh,' 'ironically the format is banal,' etc. Then ruled off a grid (Grid I) and wove the prose into it like start a sentence from J. Wain in square 1, continue in squares 3, 5 and 7. Now a sentence from Toynbee started in squares 2, 4 and 6. The reading of the grid back to straight prose can be done say one across and one down. Of course there are many numbers of ways in which the grid can be read off. (Burroughs 1964:27)

Like the 'fold-in' method, therefore, the grid illustrates the displacement of the author as the controlling consciousness of the text; other than choosing which texts to use, the author has little to no control over the ultimate arrangement. Burroughs adds, for example, that 'I found the material fell into dialogue form and seemed to contain some quite remarkable prose which I can enthuse over without immodesty since it contains no words of my own other than such quotations from my work as the critics themselves had selected' (1964:27). Burroughs also notes that these textual 'units are square for convenience on the typewriter', but that this grid represents 'only one of many possible grids [...] No doubt the mathematically inclined could progress from plane to solid geometry and put prose through spheres and cubes and hexagons' (1964:27). Like his three-column cut-ups, therefore, the grids also represent a kind of proto-hypertext, where the number of possible pathways and links between blocks of text are multiplied even further and the potential number of mathematical permutations seems virtually limitless. The grids are thus a logical extension of the auditory space created by the 'fold-in' method, and they seem to resemble Oulipian writing experiments, such as Raymond Queneau's *Cent Mille Millard de Poemes*, a sonnet containing 10 possible choices for each of the 14 lines, thus comprising 10^{14} potential poems.

WRITING MACHINES AND THE GLOBAL VILLAGE

Burroughs's writing machines not only illustrate the manipulation and subversion of information as a way of dismantling hierarchies of control, but they also illustrate the impact of media technologies on national identities and global borders by revealing the ways in which the electric media environment also reconfigures space and time. The revolutionary potential of the 'fold-in' method is even more pronounced in *The Soft Machine*, for example, because the act of shifting between source texts is played out within the narrative as shifts across space and time. 'The Mayan Caper' chapter opens with an astounding claim: 'I have just returned from a thousand-year time trip and I am here to tell you [...] how such time trips are made' (*SM* 81). The narrator then offers a description of the procedure, which begins 'in the morgue with old newspapers, folding in today with yesterday and typing out composites' (*SM* 81). In other words, the 'fold-in' method is itself a means of time travel, because 'when I fold today's paper in with yesterday's paper and arrange the pictures to form a time section montage, I am literally moving back to yesterday' (*SM* 82). The narrator is then able to overthrow the Mayan control machine by employing the 'fold-in' method on the sacred codices and calendars. By once again altering the time sequence, the priests' 'order to burn [the fields] came late, and a year's crop was lost' (*SM* 92). Soon after, the narrator leads the people in a rebellion against the priests: 'Cut word lines [...] Smash the control machine—Burn the books—Kill the priests—Kill! Kill! Kill!' (*SM* 92–3). This scene is perhaps the clearest illustration of Burroughs's notion that the electric media environment allows for the spread of cultural revolution worldwide, as media technologies like the newspaper enable information to be conveyed rapidly across space and time, regardless of national borders, thus emphasizing group awareness over individual experience and global interdependence over national divisions.

Because the borders between the blocks of text in Burroughs's grids are so fluid, they also seem to function as a corollary to the spatial architecture of the transnational 'Interzone' in *Naked Lunch*. This 'Composite City' is described as a vast 'hive' of rooms populated by people of every conceivable nation and race (*NL* 96). Because these inhabitants have clearly been uprooted from their 'discrete localities' and placed in a labyrinthine space, which appears completely removed from space and time, Interzone would appear to be the most perfect illustration of Tomlinson's notion of the deterritorializing effect of media technologies. Burroughs also describes Interzone as 'a single, vast building', whose 'rooms are made of a plastic cement that bulges to accommodate people, but when too many crowd into one room there is a soft plop and someone squeezes through the wall right into the next house' (*NL* 162). Interzone therefore represents a kind of virtual grid, in which people are converted into units of information that pass freely across barriers without resistance. The transfer of bodies through walls thus serves as a metaphor for the structure of the text itself, which contains rapid shifts and jumps that allow characters to travel inexplicably across space and time. These shifts are largely due to the method with which the book was originally written. Burroughs wrote the sections in no particular order, and the final version of the novel was ultimately determined by the order in which the pages were sent to the compositor. This process once again reflects the structure of hypertexts in that linearity is absent and the reader is free to choose multiple pathways: 'You can cut into *Naked Lunch* at any intersection point' (*NL* 203). Burroughs also emphasizes that the beginning and the ending of the novel are artificial constructs and that the novel includes 'many prefaces' (*NL* 203). The fact that the virtual information space of the text is essentially a product of writing machines is made even more explicit when Burroughs describes these shifts as the effect of 'a broken typewriter' (*NL* 86).

This rapidly shifting and disorienting atmosphere also reflects the drug-induced state in which Burroughs began writing the novel. His description of the city, for example, quickly merges with his description of the effects of *yagé*, which is further reflected in his apparently random and disconnected prose style: 'Images fall slow and silent like snow [...] everything is free to enter or to go out [...] Everything stirs with a writhing furtive life. ... The room is Near East, Negro, South Pacific, in some familiar place I cannot locate. ... Yage is space-time travel' (*NL* 99). This passage would seem to support McLuhan's claim that Burroughs's drug use represents a 'strategy of by-passing the new electric environment by becoming an environment oneself' (1964a:517), an interpretation which Burroughs rejects in his 1965 *Paris Review* interview: 'No, junk narrows consciousness. The only benefit to me as a writer [...] came to me after I went off it' (Knickerbocker 1965:23). Subsequent critics, such as Eric Mottram, have attempted to reconcile this disagreement by turning the discussion away from the effects of media on mental states and arguing instead that the essential similarity between Burroughs and McLuhan is their mutual interest in the globalizing power of electric media: 'Burroughs corrects McLuhan's opinion that he meant that heroin was needed to turn the body into an environment [...] But his books are global in the sense that they envisage a mobile environmental sense of the network of interconnecting power, with the purpose of understanding and then attacking it' (Mottram 1971:100). This disagreement can be resolved, however, by considering the difference between heroin, which 'narrows consciousness', and *yagé*, which eliminates individualism and effects a return to tribal ways of thinking. At the same time that Burroughs rejects McLuhan's claim, for example, he also adds that he wants 'to see more of what's out there, to look outside, to achieve as far as possible a complete awareness of surroundings' (Knickerbocker 1965:23). These are precisely the reasons why Burroughs sought *yagé*, and it is only under the influence of this drug that he effectively reproduces the conditions of the electric media environment within his own body.

The auditory space of the text therefore parallels the physical geography of Interzone, and any sense of the individual—including any sense of the author as the controlling consciousness of the text—dissolves in a larger awareness of human unity. Such a reading might imply that Interzone illustrates McLuhan's notion of a 'global village', which enables a greater degree of equality between nations. The narrator adds, however, that Interzone is also 'a vast silent market', whose primary purpose is to conduct business transactions (*NL* 96). Interzone therefore not only represents a deterritorialized space marked by fluid borders and rapid transfers, but it also illustrates the essential link between cultural and economic exchange because it is impossible to separate the sharing of cultural ideas and differences from the exchange of goods and services. According to Fredric Jameson, for example, the term 'globalization' itself refers to the combined effect of both new information technologies and world markets, and it 'affirms a gradual de-differentiation of these levels, the economic itself gradually becoming cultural, all the while the cultural gradually becomes economic' (1998:70). McLuhan was also aware that the effects of electric media technologies would be far more devastating on the Third World than on Western culture: 'In the case of the First World [...] electronic information dims down nationalism and private identities, whereas in its encounter with the Third World of India, China, and Africa, the new electric information environment has the effect of depriving these people of their group identities' (McLuhan and Powers 1989:165). Because Interzone illustrates both the economic and cultural effects of globalization, it is perhaps easy to understand why Interzone does not represent a more harmonious and egalitarian 'global village'. The loss of group identities and economic stability, and the constant presence of European colonials, only seem to heighten the level of corruption and inefficiency already present in the city, such as the 'drunken cop' who registers new arrivals 'in a vast public lavatory', where the 'data taken down is put on pegs to be used as toilet paper' (NL 98). Business itself is also represented as an essentially hopeless process, in which useless products are endlessly waiting to be passed through customs, and embassies direct all inquiries to the 'We Don't Want To Hear About It Department' (NL 163).

Like the 'global village', therefore, Interzone represents a virtual or deterritorialized space in which people of every imaginable nationality and race are able to meet and exchange information. But unlike the 'global village', Interzone is a labyrinth of both communication and economic exchange, which ultimately subdues and disempowers its inhabitants. The key to liberating the global space of the electric media environment, according to Burroughs, is to subvert and manipulate the media technologies themselves, thus drawing the hypnotized masses out of their waking dream and making them more aware of the degree to which media technologies condition their perceptions of reality. In Naked Lunch, for example, Burroughs states that the ultimate purpose of conventional narrative transitions is 'to spare The Reader stress of sudden space shifts and keep him Gentle' (NL 197). By manipulating the linear function of his own writing machines, Burroughs attempts to reject these conventions and transform the gentle reader into a potential revolutionary, who would no longer be passive and detached but rather aware and involved.

CONCLUSION

Burroughs most clearly represents the manipulation and subversion of electric media technologies through his own experimental methods of constructing texts. Burroughs also repeatedly represents writing machines within his work to illustrate the effects of information technologies on subjectivity, as well as their potential use for either positive or negative ends—as control machines or weapons of resistance. Burroughs similarly depicts the global impact of the electric media environment by illustrating the ways in which writing machines are capable of spreading either cultural revolution or cultural imperialism, depending on whether or not people are capable of appropriating and manipulating them. The texts which I have focused on in this chapter, which include examples of Burroughs's work from the 1950s to the early 1970s, can therefore be seen as exposing and subverting the influence of writing machines on the material conditions of their own production in order to provide a model of technological reappropriation that could potentially be extended on a global scale. Burroughs's work thus retains an empowering notion of human agency while also complicating the divisions between self and other.

REFERENCES

Bockris, V. (1981) *With William Burroughs: A Report from the Bunker*, rev. edition (New York: St. Martin's Griffin, 1996).
Bukatman, S. (1993) 'Gibson's Typewriter', *South Atlantic Quarterly* 92(4), pp. 627–45.
Burroughs, William S. (1964) 'Formats: The Grid', *Insect Trust Gazette*, 1, p. 27.
—— (1975) *The Last Words of Dutch Schultz: A Fiction in the Form of a Film Script* (New York: Viking), pp. 37–46.
Grauerholz, J. (1998) 'A Hard-Boiled Reporter', IN *WV* pp. 37–46.
Hayles, N. K. (1999) *How We Became Posthuman: Virtual Bodies in Cybernetics, Literature, and Informatics* (Chicago: University of Chicago Press).
Jameson, F. (1998) 'Notes on Globalization as a Philosophical Issue', IN Jameson, F., and Miyoshi, M. eds, *The Cultures of Globalization* (Durham, NC: Duke University Press), pp. 54–77.
Kittler, F. (1990) *Discourse Networks 1800/1900*, Cullens, C., and Metteer, M. trans. (Stanford: Stanford University Press).
—— (1999) *Gramophone, Film, Typewriter*, Winthrop-Young, G., and Wutz, M. trans. (Stanford: Stanford University Press).
Knickerbocker, C. (1965) 'William Burroughs: An Interview', *Paris Review* 35, pp. 13–49.
McLuhan, M. (1962) *The Gutenberg Galaxy: The Making of Typographic Man* (Toronto: University of Toronto Press).
—— (1963) 'The Agenbite of Outwit', *Location* 1(1), 41–4.
—— (1964a) 'Notes on Burroughs', *The Nation* 28 December 1964, pp. 517–19.
—— (1964b) *Understanding Media: The Extensions of Man* (New York: McGraw-Hill).

McLuhan, M., and Powers, B. R. (1989) *The Global Village: Transformations in World Life and Media in the 21st Century* (New York: Oxford University Press).

Mottram, E. (1971) *William Burroughs: The Algebra of Need* (Buffalo, NY: Intrepid).

Sobieszek, R. (1996) *Ports of Entry: William S. Burroughs and the Arts* (Los Angeles: Los Angeles County Museum of Art/Thames & Hudson).

Tanner, T. (1971) *City of Words: American Fiction 1950–70* (London: Jonathan Cape).

Tomlinson, J. (1999) *Globalization and Culture* (Chicago: University of Chicago Press).

7
Totally Wired: Prepare Your Affidavits of Explanation

Edward Desautels

The study of thinking machines teaches us more about the brain than we can learn by introspective methods. Western man is externalizing himself in the form of gadgets [...]
—William S. Burroughs (*NL* 23)

Benway, that great 'manipulator and coordinator of symbol systems' and expert in the methods of control (*NL* 20), takes special satisfaction in the way contemporary society has opened its kimono. So reports agent Lee (also known as William S. Burroughs, Bull Lee, El Hombre Invisible, and so on) who remains forever in the field, though the signal by which he transmits his communiqués daily grows more faint. You could say Lee's signal seems to weaken in direct proportion to the growing power of Benway's—never mind that both represent equally competent spirits in this magical universe. Still, Lee's is the work of an agent and an agent must report—particularly when the stakes are so high. We got Eddie the Sponge tuning in to Lee's signal, headphones slung like manhole covers over his jug ears. Eddie's face assumes the aspect of a French Surrealist in the throes of an automatic composition as he transcribes the report.

... At the New Reconditioning Center (NRC), Benway enlightens an apprentice: Our subjects are unaware of their status as subjects, being as they are unaware of many things. Unwittingly, they have bought our propositions wholesale. They have developed a reliance on their thinking prostheses and through these prostheses *we break them down*. It's a most agreeable situation. Tasty. Our efficiency is improving exponentially with every new device unleashed on the market ... laptop computers, mobile phones, personal digital assistants, automated bank teller systems, credit cards encoded with information at the point of sale, all capable of communicating over a network of networks, the so-called Internet, not only with each other, but with the data systems of commerce, education, and government. They got the special need, my dears. Even when confronted with facts of their exposure—facts that we ourselves feed them to effect, shall we say, a more benign posture—they only use *more* of this technology and more haphazardly than ever ... Snowy image of hapless citizen swiping cards at Circuit City in purchase of personal computer ... Secretary at local cable company dispatches a 'truck roll' for broadband Internet connection ...

It's worth noting our agent exhibited no inclination to explore the technology (Silberman 1997a). It is not difficult to understand why. His reports have always sought to 'wise up the marks', clue them in to the concept of word as virus, to the use of image and word as instruments of control, to the role played by technology and the mass media in this use of these instruments, to the command of mass media by the vested interests comprising the Control Machine (Skerl 1985:48–57). Certainly, he must have surmised a basic rottenness in a technology born out of the Department of Defense. It seems these reports fell on deaf ears ...

On the occasion of Burroughs's exit, *Wired Magazine's* web edition published an article attempting to position his legacy with regard to the Internet. In it, author Steve Silberman cites an 'uncanny correspondence between Burroughs's 1950s version of the "Interzone" ... and the Internet' (Silberman 1997b). In the same article, Levi Asher, architect of the website 'Literary Kicks', added, '[t]he Internet *is* an Interzone—a zone where no one's in control'. Agent Burroughs might find such notions naive. Rather than a control-free zone, the Internet and its supporting technology comprise an organ of control more closely resembling Benway's 'Reconditioning Center' and the locked-down society of 'Annexia'. The Internet makes possible *even more* lines of control, built on new languages/codes, through which the machinery of control may impose its will through manipulation of word and image. As Burroughs observes in *The Adding Machine*: 'No control machine so far devised can operate without words, and any control machine which attempts to do so relying entirely on external force or entirely on physical control of the mind will soon encounter the limits of control' (*AM* 117). The Internet is nothing if not an endless exchange of image and word, and sets up the perfect environment of mediation through which the Control Machine can indulge its addiction in a way that prevents the subject from contacting his enemy direct (*NL* 21).

Reports coming in from our agents in the field, pieced together here by Eddie the Sponge, suggest that the ubiquitous computerization of society—and more specifically the advent of the Internet—can be manipulated in ways that realize Agent Burroughs's darkest vision of the technological 'Control Machine' decried in his communiqués. Links between control and technology's ability to externalize its users manifest themselves both in subtle paradigm shifts regarding the nature of knowledge and productivity in our computerized world, and in less subtle, overt actions such as the emergence of comprehensive government surveillance systems.

TRANSMISSION CONTROL PROTOCOL/INTERNET
PROTOCOL

'Hey, we got an empty column to fill on page 3.'
'Don't sweat it, just run another Internet pump piece.'

Millions Flock to 'Net' Worldwide

San Francisco, March 2003—Global Reach, a leading market research firm providing demographic analysis of world Internet usage, estimates the number of Internet users world wide at 634.1 million. Global Research puts the number of European users at 224.1 million, those in Asia/Pacific at 179.4 million and the total in English-speaking countries at 230.6 million. English speakers comprise 36.5 percent of the so-called online population, while the greater majority of Internet users, 63.5 percent, are non-English speakers.[1]

Benway addresses an audience assembled in the NRC lecture hall: As you can see, these numbers confirm our success at infecting world populations with Internet technology. It is a beautiful thing to behold. They gots the bug and they don't care: a year 2000 study conducted by UCLA noted that as recently as 1997 the estimated number of American Internet users stood at a mere 19 million. This number exploded like a metastasizing neuroblastoma to 100 million in just two years. Penetration of Internet technology to American households reached the 30 percent mark within seven years of its general availability. Compare this with electrical wiring—the seminal technology without which we could not have dreamed of our present endeavor. It took us 46 years to achieve such penetration. Or, for that matter, television—our early, crude, but nonetheless effective attempt at a mind grab—which took 17 (Cole 2000:4–7). We are obtaining the desired effect. (Wild applause from the members, distinguished guests, and the nameless assholes in the visitors' gallery.)

Fortuitous sociopolitical trends have helped streamline our efforts. Like I always say, 'if you can't be beautiful, be lucky' (laughter from the assembly). The rapid technological development I've just described paralleled an era of significant cultural change. Just as our Internet initiative began to gain traction, the Soviet Union and Eastern Bloc began to dissolve. New markets there, as well as in China, opened up to the West. And, where there are markets there are avenues of control. Naturally, through no small effort on our part, these Eastern European and Asian nations were 'wired'. Welcome to the honey pot: new audiences discovered easy access to news and information they had previously been denied. English became the lingua franca of the Internet. Translation tools emerged enabling users to translate websites among the world's most widely spoken languages.[2] Let me tell you it gives me a special warm feeling every time I think about it.

F(a/e)ces in the Pentagon

Educate your minds, my dears, with the grand actuality of fact. The story of the Internet's conception and development begins in the Pentagon. It fell under the auspices of the Advanced Research Projects Agency (ARPA), a Department of Defense organ set up during the Eisenhower administration. ARPA's objective: end infighting and duplication of effort among the various branches of the United States Armed Forces by assuming overall control of most military research and development projects. When its initial mission to conduct missile research was co-opted by NASA, ARPA reorganized and set its sights on, interestingly, behavioral science research and research related to time-share computing systems for military command and control.

Under the direction of J. C. R. 'Lick' Licklider, the agency focused itself on research concerning Lick's ideas about 'man–computer symbiosis' (interactive computing). Flush with cash, ARPA is said to have funded 70 percent of computer science research in the US from the period of Lick's administration onward (Naughton 1999:81). The fruits of this research include the 'mouse' and the graphical user interface, enhancements that helped spread the contagion of computer use among the general public, who were justifiably wary of anything called 'command line interface'.

As ARPA's research agenda narrowed, the agency became a kind of 'skunkworks' in the Pentagon devoted to solving the problem of a workable packet-switched data network.[3] In 1969, ARPA awarded a contract to the Boston firm Bolt, Beranek, and Newman (BBN, for whom Licklider had worked in the 1950s) to design and build such a network. By 1973, the first e-mail message had been sent over the ARPANET and its reach had extended across the Atlantic to Britain and Norway. In 1986, the National Science Foundation implemented NSFNET, and in 1988 the dismantling of ARPANET began. In 1993, the National Science Foundation turned over (you might say 'unleashed') the Internet to commercial entities.

As society has become computerized, Lick's vision of man–computer symbiosis has become a reality. The batch-processing paradigm (in which a number of commands were prepared, then sent to the computer for processing) has been overthrown by the paradigm of truly interactive and instantaneous computing (in which, by the very nature of the process, the user makes of the computer a thinking prosthesis, often depositing information once held strictly between the ears on networked computer drives open to covert access). And so we thank Lick for instant, fingertip access to information which only decades ago would require hours of searching, sorting and sifting to discover. Thanks for the existential impulse of computerized home shopping. Thanks for the exchange of greetings, letters, documents, photographs, all without need of envelope, stamp, or a trip to the post office. How satisfying to instantly locate individuals who share our interests and assemble with them 'online' for discussion. Yes, thanks to Lick we can participate in societal and cultural exchanges online in ways never before possible.

... Signal detected: Pentagon has given us Internet. Pentagon has spawned man–computer symbiosis. Pentagon has turned over controls of Internet infrastructure to so-called private sector, to the boards and syndicates of the world. Think about all the websites you have visited. Think about all the e-mails you have sent. Think about the books you've purchased from online retailers. Think of the computers holding your credit history. Think of the computers holding your medical history. Think about the ability for advertisers—and others—to trace your movements on the web. You are not anonymous. Think of the information on your own Internet-connected computer, an open book to anyone possessing the right hack. Your hard drive is not only readable, but also 'writeable'. Who is writing to your hard drive?[4]

CERTAIN CONNECTIONS IN CERTAIN SOCKETS

Successful control means achieving a balance and avoiding a
showdown where all-out force would be necessary.
—William S. Burroughs (*AM* 119)

Benway: You've heard me say it time and again: 'I deplore brutality.'
So how do we proceed? We've done a good job manipulating the
drug issue: 'Anti-drug hysteria is now worldwide, and it poses a
deadly threat to personal freedoms and due-process protections of
the law everywhere' (*NL* xlvii). But there are other 'demographics'
to address. We can't, for one, depend on the middle classes like we
used to. Our operatives in the boards and syndicates are undertak-
ing subtle work, my dears. Our key requirement is for a bureaucracy
reinforcing the vested interest of power and/or money. This vested
interest is perhaps the most potent check we have on freedom of the
individual, which is both a threat to our position and a source of all
sorts of untidiness (*Job* 60). We need a bureaucracy so slick the rubes
will lay down their cold hard cash for it, a bureaucracy built on
something that blinds with the flash of the gewgaw but which also
stimulates a perception of functionality and purpose; something
consumable that forever keeps the subject one step behind by virtue
of its rapid cycles of obsolescence and renewal; something that facil-
itates indulgence in a variety of addictions and every sort of low
behavior; something operating with the efficiency of a machine, the
very use of which can lubricate the machinery of Control itself.

Computers! Data devices! Yes, we've run with Lick's man–computer
symbiosis paradigm and wired our subjects up but good. We are programming our subjects, as we do our machines, for optimal efficiency. Eavesdrop on their thoughts: I need a computer. I need a
better, more efficient computer. I need a bigger hard drive onto
which I can dump more and more of my *self*. I need to connect that
computer to other computers on the Internet, thereby expanding
my capacity for 'thought'. I need a broadband connection so I can
'think' faster. I need to acquire and learn new programs so I can do
more, do it faster, keep up.

The syrupy glide of this operation has been a thing of beauty.
Even when the cat got out of the bag, nobody truly believed it. Yes,
Jean-François (I like to call him 'Frankie the Frog') hit the nail on
the head in his '*rapport sur le savoir*' for the government of Quebec.
Twenty-five years down the road that little episode is but a hiccup,

despite the fact he laid it all out: the infusion of corporate dollars into scientific research, the consequent shift in the very way knowledge is created, the quiet evolution to a society operating on the input–output paradigm ever striving to minimize input and maximize output.[5] Walk into a neighborhood bar and witness capitulation: 'I don't see why our government *isn't* run like a business. Those business guys know how to get bang for their buck.' And Frankie? In some quarters discredited, in others thought passé: 'A metanarrative unto himself', I've heard him called.

So here (pointing to photograph of stooped middle-aged man bearing a slightly confused expression), we have a typical subject. Not only have we conditioned him to rely on his thinking prostheses, to think and operate along an input–output paradigm, so too have we subjected his body to control in the interest of productivity (Murphy 1997:84). I quote one of our analysts: 'The productive subject produces surplus value not only by laboring, but also by consuming, to appease the negative "desires" of which it is made' (1997:80). Consider the avenues to physical addiction the Internet opens up. My god, the porn glut alone has created an entire class of orgasm addicts ...

Eddie the Sponge recalls the remarks of the 'Death Dwarf' to inspector J. Lee and the district supervisor in *Nova Express*, a report plumbing the role of technology in the creation and maintenance of lines of control:

> Images—millions of images—That's what I eat—Cyclotron shit—Ever try kicking *that* habit with apomorphine?—Now I got all the images of sex acts and torture ever took place anywhere and I can just blast it out and control you gooks right down to the molecule [...] (*NE* 45)

A cyclotron is a particle accelerator. The cathode ray tube (CRT) on your television—and your computer monitor—is a particle accelerator. The CRT speeds electrons from the cathode, redirects them in a vacuum with electromagnets, and smashes them into phosphor molecules on the screen. Oh my god! The Death Dwarves are force feeding us cyclotron shit through our eyeballs! *Mmmmm. Must surf Net ...*

Nova NetMob

Look at America. Who actually controls this country? It is difficult to say. Certainly the very wealthy are [...] in a position to control and manipulate the entire economy.

—William S. Burroughs (*AM* 120)

Signal received: In 'The Limits of Control', Burroughs asserts that 'the technocratic control apparatus of the United States has at its fingertips new techniques which if fully exploited could make Orwell's *1984* seem like a benevolent utopia' (*AM* 117). One may ascribe such a comment to 'Burroughsian paranoia' (a notion most likely promulgated by the disinformation wing of the New Reconditioning Center), but all reports indicate the establishment of a worldwide technical control apparatus. Rotten with wormholes not apparent to the casual user, the Internet infrastructure slides into place. These wormholes are exploited daily by hackers, crackers, 'script kiddies' and others, even those with just a modicum of technical knowledge but possessed of an abundance of (some would say) ill intent. But the hackers aren't the only ones with the keys to the shithouse: the mechanisms to exploit the Internet's weaknesses with overarching surveillance systems are being set up in broad daylight by government bureaucracies.

Control's eye in the pyramid

The folks who brought you the Internet in the first place, DARPA (ARPA now overtly prefaced by 'Defense'), are pleased to introduce the 'Information Awareness Office' (IAO). Headed up by John Poindexter, former admiral and professional Iran-Contra liar, its 'Total Information Awareness' (TIA) program takes as its mission,

> to imagine, develop, apply, integrate, demonstrate and transition information technologies, components and prototype, closed-loop, information systems that will counter asymmetric threats by achieving total information awareness [...][6]

In other words, DARPA is implementing technology to suck as much data as it wants out of the systems it helped create and promulgate. Note the original emblem of the IAO: a modification of the Masonic 'All Seeing Eye' set in a pyramid (as you will also find on the US dollar bill). Wrapped in a circular band formed by the words 'Information Awareness Office', the eye casts a ray over the globe. Above pyramid and globe appears the acronym DARPA. Below lies the motto '*Scientia est Potentia*' ('knowledge is power'). A fitting complement, that, to the motto '*Novus Ordo Seclorum*' ('a new order of the ages'), which appears similarly positioned on the greenback. Cut to Benway at podium in NRC: Indiscretion, in this case, may have been the bitter part of candor: the logo was cause for some indigestion. DARPA, recognizing a public relations liability, removed the logo from its publications and replaced it with a new, corporation-style logo cleansed of hoary Masonic references. I like to think of it as a kinder, gentler logo; more in tune with the 'corporatization' of our government bureaucracies. The so-called news media commented on this change, as well as the general scaling back of information on the IAO and TIA sites. As has been our experience, the general populace did not care, did not notice, or was mollified by the usual stonewalling: 'A spokeswoman for the Information Awareness Office, which runs the TIA project at the Defense Advanced Research Projects Agency (DARPA), said she had no details on the deletions' (McCullagh 2003).[7]

Appetizing menu

Benway pointing to chart on screen: You see here just a sampling of programs being undertaken by the IAO. Allow me to elucidate.[8]

Program	Goal/Purpose
Genisys	*To produce technology enabling ultra-large, all-source information repositories.* In the beginning was the word. Information lies in the word. '[A]ll hate, all pain, all fear, all lust is contained in the word' (*Job* 15). Cut subjects' words with control words and play back to subject. 'With this simple formula any CIA son of a bitch can become God [...]' (15).
HumanID	*(Human Identification at a Distance) To develop auto-mated biometric identification technologies to detect, recognize and identify humans at great distances.* Currently, this constitutes a crude strategy at best. However, we are presently working through 'trusted' media to normalize the notion of bionics. Integration of networked technologies into the human subject will net exponential advances for our program (Greengard 1997).
EELD	*(Evidence Extraction and Link Discovery) EELD is devel-oping detection capabilities to extract relevant data and relationships about people, organizations and activities from message traffic and open source data.* So simple: hindsight being 20/20, and given such universal input, we can insinuate in the activities or our subjects, ex post facto, all manner of compromising connections.

IAO has armed itself with the following technologies to support its programs:

*   *Collaboration and sharing over TCP/IP networks across agency boundaries* (linking of government surveillance and security agencies by virtue of the Internet).
*   *Biometric signatures of humans* (retinal scans for every citizen, stored on file and required for access ...).
*   *Real-time learning, pattern matching and anomalous pattern detection* (once every subject's Internet and other activities are dumped into their vast central data repositories, these agencies use algorithms to establish 'normal' patterns of network data against which 'anomalous' activity will trigger alerts. Of course, we exert great influence over what is defined as 'anomalous').
*   *Story telling, change detection, and truth maintenance* (exactly whose 'truth' is to be maintained? Well, naturally, it's not the subjects' ...).
*   *Biologically inspired algorithms for agent control* (a work in progress, but sounds tasty, don't you think?).

In the interest of national security

Eddie the Sponge adjusts the squelch control to make out weakening signal, transcribes Lee transmission, fills in the gaps with BEGs (best educated guesses) ... Of course, DARPA positions these programs as necessary to 'classify and identify foreign terrorists'. It knows that in the post-September 11 environment, characterized by rampant anti-terrorism and amplified xenophobic hysteria, it could set up just about any odious surveillance system it wants 'in the interests of national security'. As Burroughs notes in *The Adding Machine*: ' "We acted in the interests of national security," they say smugly. It's the old war game, from here to eternity. Where would the military and the CIA be without it?' (156).

One needn't make a great intuitive leap to surmise that an agency such as the CIA is already taking advantage of any surveillance technology and systems growing out of DARPA. It will comb the information sucked up by the gigantic DARPA vacuum cleaner and sift through it using DARPA algorithms to detect 'anomalous' information. This technology will be used not only to detect the activities of 'foreign terrorists', but also to monitor the activities of *any* individual it deems a threat to the vested interests it serves. Think of the files compiled on US citizens by the FBI under J. Edgar Hoover using much less sophisticated technology. And the FBI is at it again. Its

'DragonWare Suite' (successor to earlier 'Carnivore' and 'Omnivore' programs) enables the FBI to access e-mail messages, downloaded files and web pages flowing over the networks of Internet service providers (Tyson 2002). US Attorney General John Ashcroft, lauding a court ruling supporting the sharing of surveillance information among government agencies, piously invokes the sacred words tailored to fit present circumstances: 'A coordinated, integrated and coherent response to terrorism was created [...] when the Patriot Act was passed' (Department of State 2002).

Both DARPA and the FBI make claims about protecting the privacy of American citizens in the exercise of these programs. A DARPA white paper opens: 'Privacy of personal data is an absolutely essential element of any information system that carries information about American citizens.' However, the concluding summation of this paper concedes that reconciling domestic espionage with privacy is a problem that's 'DARPA hard' (DARPA 2002). Must be wary when the government starts talking about privacy:

> In whose name is privacy being invoked? In the name of those who bugged Martin Luther King's bedroom and ransacked the office of Ellsberg's psychiatrist? And how many other bedrooms have they bugged? Does anyone believe these are isolated instances? That they were caught on the first job? (*Job* 11)

DARPA hard(er)

More disturbing intelligence: investigative reporter Nicky Hager has blown the whistle on ECHELON. Brainchild of the National Security Agency (NSA), ECHELON 'works by indiscriminately intercepting very large quantities of communications and using computers to identify and extract messages of interest from the mass of unwanted ones' (Jennings and Fena 2000:91). These communications include satellite phone calls, Internet communications (including e-mail), faxes and telexes. Communications are digitally sifted for keywords of interest. Nations involved in ECHELON include the United States, the United Kingdom, Australia, New Zealand and France. Hager's 1998 report on the matter, *Exposing the Global Surveillance System*, was received with predictable skepticism by the media and government officials on its publication. However, in September 2001, the European Parliament adopted a report it says confirms ECHELON's existence:[9]

> [T]he existence of a global system for intercepting communications, operating by means of cooperation proportionate to their capabilities

among the USA, the UK, Canada, Australia and New Zealand under the UKUSA Agreement, is no longer in doubt [...] [I]t seems likely, in view of the evidence and the consistent pattern of statements from a very wide range of individuals and organisations, including American sources, that its name is in fact ECHELON, although this is a relatively minor detail [...] [T]here can now be no doubt that the purpose of the system is to intercept, at the very least, private and commercial communications, and not military communications [...] [T]herefore, it is surprising, not to say worrying, that many senior Community figures [...] who gave evidence to the Temporary Committee claimed to be unaware of this phenomenon. (European Parliament 2001:11)

The toy company and the pickle factory

It has been demonstrated again and again that individuals can hack into your computer system (or a database system holding your credit, health or equally sensitive information), sniff your passwords, gain control of a system, monitor your online activity and write files to your computer. Automated hacking tools are widely available on the Internet, and, consequently, many hacks rely more on hacker persistence than they do on technical skill and knowledge. And, with a little sophistication, much is possible.

Consider the case of the 'DSSAgent' program shipped as part of Mattel software for children's computer activity products. (Get 'em when they're in short pants and lollipops.) The DSSAgent software was unwittingly installed by consumers with the legitimate software and silently ran in the background, communicating to Mattel whenever the computer went online (Garfinkle 2000). Though Mattel claimed 'the program does not send personal information to Mattel and does nothing to identify a particular user', one wonders about the covert manner in which Mattel operated. And even though the software was targeted to children, it took a highly computer-savvy adult to recognize the intrusion and go public with Mattel's duplicity. This technology can and has been easily adapted for more nefarious purposes. Any program loaded, any web page downloaded to your computer may contain this sort of 'Trojan horse'. The download contains an embedded program to be used for illicit purposes, or sends the illicit program as a masked e-mail attachment, or downloads it in a background operation when a web page is loaded by a 'victim' user. Unaware, the victim installs the program/opens the e-mail, or downloads the web page. At this point, all bets are off. The victim's hard drive is an open book. Imagine what the 'pickle factory' (CIA) could do/does with this accessible technology. There are even programs, available for purchase on the web, that will record the unwitting victim's every key stroke and forward this information to a designated networked system.

Consider this: if an individual claimed to have invented the gun, wouldn't the government have already developed the *machine* gun? As Burroughs observes, '[i]t is no exaggeration to say that all important research is now top secret, until someone lets a rat out of the bag' (*Job* 62). Given what organizations like the FBI and IAO have already let out of the bag, it staggers the imagination to consider what plans and systems they *haven't* made public.

CRAZIES FROM THE CRAZY PLACE, BREAK OUT!

Joe is a troublemaker. He has exposed secret government project 23 Skidoo in an online discussion board. One morning, there's a knock on the door. It's the Feds. Whaddaya want? We have a warrant for your arrest on grounds of child pornography. Uh oh. We also have a warrant to seize your hard drive, which we know to contain illegal pornographic images of children. There must be some mis—... Save it. One of the agents takes a seat at Joe's computer and begins searching his files. Yep, he thinks. Right where I put 'em.

Signal transcription: Potential virus from the technological organism has infected the biological organism. Has imprinted it with 'the mark inside', the one we can't beat, the one that delivers us into the hands of control. How else do we explain our refusal as a society, despite numerous warnings, to acknowledge the risk at which we place ourselves when externalized through our gadgets and engaged in the activities of a networked society?

The prognosis is not good. 'We have seen nothing reassuring in that direction [of a future made better by automation and technology], with the present people in power, the more efficient the technology the more of a menace they are' (*Job* 68). I'll encode my data with cryptography. Don't you think we got the algorithms to crack it? I'll set up a firewall in front of my computer. Swiss cheese, my dears. I'll tunnel my connections through a virtual private network. Now you're back to cryptography—child's play. I'll throw my computer away. Good luck getting along in the society *we're* building.

Here's what we're up against: a technological control bureaucracy determined to exploit the gadgetry through which society externalizes itself for purposes of surveillance and control; the dominance of multinational corporations whose funding of science research has effected a paradigm shift in the nature, production, and dissemination of knowledge to the extent that society begins to mirror the input–output efficiencies of its computers; a corporate culture producing and marketing cyber-surveillance systems to control its employees (a topic not addressed in this report); and an environment in which getting along without the technological gadgetry of the age is becoming an ever more difficult proposition. This set of conditions was not attained randomly. They are a construct.

How to break out? The implied threat of control through surveillance is hotwired to the subject's fear of having his private life made public and the resulting shame this would induce—'Adam experiences shame when his *disgraceful behavior* is played back to him' (*Job* 19). Perhaps one can jump the gun, overcome shame and open oneself completely *a priori*. Or, maybe, turn the playback mechanism around and create distracting noise in the machine; break ECHELON down like an overloaded thinking machine when every e-mail, every web page, contains the words:

Colonel, domestic disruption, smuggle, 15 kg, nitrate, Pretoria, M-14, enigma, Bletchley Park, Clandestine, nkvd, argus, afsatcom, CQB, NVD, Counter Terrorism Security, Rapld, 98G, 98F, Oklahoma City, fertilizer, Reaction, Corporate Security, Police, sniper, PPS, ASIS, ASLET, TSCM, Security Consulting, High Security, Security Evaluation, Electronic Surveillance, Counterterrorism, spies, Mafiya, Aum Shinrikyo, Tesla, eavesdropping, debugging, interception, COCOT, rhost, rhosts, SETA, Amherst, Broadside, Capricorn, Gamma, Gorizont, Guppy Ionosphere, Mole, Keyhole, Kilderkin, Artichoke, Black Panther, MLK, Branch Davidian, Badger, Cornflower, Daisy, Egret, Iris, Hollyhock, Jasmine, Juile, Sphinx ...

Meantime, lay low and make sure your affidavit of explanation is in good order.

NOTES (FROM THE TECHNICAL DEPARTMENT)

1. The figures for Internet usage are available from the Global Reach website at <http://global-reach.biz/globstats/index.php3>.
2. Note from the Technical Department: Demystify yourself! For details regarding the underlying technology of the Internet, consult Cisco Systems' *Internetworking Technology Handbook*. See <http://www.cisco.com/univercd/cc/td/doc/cisintwk/ito_doc/index.htm>.

130   Writing, Sign, Instrument

3. A packet-switched network divides messages into small units (packets, sometimes referred to as 'datagrams') and sends each packet to its destination by the most efficient route, for later reassembly.
4. For a technical analysis of the many ways the ill-intentioned compromise network data security through misuse of the Internet, see McClure, Scambray and Kurtz's book *Hacking Exposed* (2003). Also, see the Computer Emergency Response Team (CERT) website at <http://cert.org>.
5. Frankie the Frog composed *The Postmodern Condition: A Report on Knowledge*, by Jean-François Lyotard (see References).
6. Use a third-party computer for the Information Awareness Office site: <http://www.darpa.mil/iao/index.htm>.
7. Catch them if you can: at the time this report was being revised, the entire DARPA site seemed to be 'off the air'.
8. Refer to the IAO's website for 'complete' details on these programs.
9. The complete report is available on the European Parliament's website, at <http://www.europarl.eu.int/tempcom/echelon/rrechelon_en.htm>.

REFERENCES

Cole, J. I. et al. (2000) 'The UCLA Internet Report: Surveying the Digital Future' (Los Angeles: UCLA Center for Communication Policy, <http://ccp.ucla.edu>).
DARPA (2002) 'Security with Privacy', <http://www.darpa.mil/iao/secpriv.pdf>.
Department of State (2002) 'Ashcroft Hails Special Surveillance Review Court Ruling', 18 November 2002, <http://usinfo.state.gov/topical/pol/terror/02111902.htm>.
European Parliament Temporary Committee on the ECHELON Interception System (2001) 'REPORT on the Existence of a Global System for the Interception of Private and Commercial Communications (ECHELON Interception System) (2001/2098[INI])', <http://www2.europarl.eu.int/omk/sipade2?PUBREF=-//EP//NONSGML+REPORT+A5-2001-0264+0+DOC+PDF+V0//EN&L=EN&LEVEL=2&NAV=S&LSTDOC=Y>.
Garfinkle, S. (2000) 'Software that can Spy on You', 15 July 2000, <http://dir.salon.com/tech/col/garf/2000/06/15/brodcast/index.html>.
Greengard, S. (1997) 'Head Start', online edition, *Wired Magazine* 5, 2 February 1997, <http://www.wired.com/wired/5.02/esberger.html>.
Jennings, C., and Fena, L. (2000) *The Hundredth Window: Protecting Your Privacy and Security in the Age of the Internet* (New York: The Free Press).
Lyotard, J. F. (1979) *The Postmodern Condition: A Report on Knowledge*, Bennington, G., and Massumi, B. trans. (Minneapolis: University of Minnesota Press, 1999).
McClure, S., Scambray, J., and Kurtz, G. (2003) *Hacking Exposed*, 4th edition (New York: McGraw-Hill).
McCullagh, D. (2003) 'US Government Database Spy Site Fading Away', *CNET News*, 23 December 2002, <http://news.zdnet.co.uk/story/0,t269-s2127931,00.html?rtag=zdnetukhompage>.
Murphy, T. S. (1997) *Wising Up the Marks: The Amodern William Burroughs* (Berkeley: University of California Press).

Naughton, J. (1999) *A Brief History of the Future: Origins of the Internet* (London: Weidenfeld and Nicolson).

Silberman, S. (1997a) 'Burroughs Pops Online Cherry with Drag Queens', *Wired News*, 20 February 1997, <http://www.wired.com/news/culture/0,1284,2173,00.htm>.

—— (1997b) 'Burroughs Spun a Legacy of Naked Sense', *Wired News*, 5 August 1997, <http://www.wired.com/news/culture/0,1284,5771,00.html>.

Skerl, J. (1985) *William S. Burroughs* (Boston: Twayne).

Tyson, J. (2002) 'How Carnivore Works', *How Stuff Works*, <http://www.how stuffworks.com/carnivore>.

8

New World Ordure: Burroughs, Globalization and the Grotesque

Dennis McDaniel

The scion of a well-known banking family once told me a family secret. When a certain stage of responsibility and awareness has been reached by a young banker he is taken to a room lined with family portraits in the middle of which is an ornate gilded toilet. Here he comes every day to defecate surrounded by the family portraits until he realizes that *money is shit.* And what does the money machine eat to shit it out? It eats youth, spontaneity, life, beauty, and above all it eats creativity.

—William S. Burroughs (*Job* 73–4)

This anecdote from *The Job* reveals the important role of the grotesque in the work of William S. Burroughs. For Burroughs, the grotesque reveals the residue of the control system that too few recognize and from which too few profit. As Burroughs suggests, one of the most salient aspects of economic globalization is the sacrifice of the imaginative impulse to the profit motive. Burroughs's characterization of global control systems has proved to be prescient. Benjamin Barber, in his seminal analysis *Jihad vs. McWorld*, asserts that, as multinational conglomerates merge, cultural products are increasingly homogeneous and increasingly Americanized. 'Music, video, theater, books, and theme parks', Barber argues, 'are all constructed as image exports creating a common world taste around common logos, advertising slogans, stars, songs, brand names, jingles and trademarks' (2001:17). Reminiscent of Trak Services in *The Soft Machine*, the giants of the global economy preach free enterprise as they undermine variety and competition:

The very idea of a genuinely competitive market in ideas or images disappears and the singular virtue that markets indisputably have over democratic command structures—the virtue of that cohort of values

associated with pluralism and variety, contingency and accident, diversity
and spontaneity—is vitiated. (Barber 2001:89)

Burroughs attempts to fight these 'command structures' through
the concept of the grotesque, understood as a satirical imagery that
plays on the exaggeration of certain features of its object in order to
demonize or otherwise undermine it. The concept is double-edged,
and has been used against both minorities and majorities. Leonard
Cassuto traces its origins within European culture to the inability of
the majority to account for the differences that minorities embody:
'both off-color humor and anomalous human bodies somehow
threaten, in varying degrees and different ways, the shared beliefs
about what constitutes the "human"' (1997:7–8). By using the
grotesque, majority cultures can represent minorities as 'a constant
intrusion on order, an anomalous agent of chaos' (1997:9).
Contemporary readers are well aware of how xenophobic propaganda caricatures, often produced to prepare citizens for war or
racist legislation, depict the African-American as dark, big-lipped
and bulgy-eyed, the Jew as big-nosed, the Arab as demonically
bearded and swarthy, or the Asian as buck-toothed and grossly bespec-
tacled. Modern power structures rely on the defective, deformed
'Other' as a means of justifying and maintaining their power. As
Burroughs notes, '[t]he police have a vested interest in criminality.
The Narcotics Department has a vested interest in addiction.
Politicians have a vested interest in nations. Army officers have a
vested interest in war' (*Job* 61). The control addicts feed on the
unruly. But the grotesque has also been used as a means to destabi-
lize and subvert hegemonic powers, and it is in this sense that
Burroughs deploys it. Burroughs's work recognizes the power of the
grotesque to combine, as John Ruskin describes it in his chapter
'Grotesque Renaissance' in volume 3 of *The Stones of Venice* (1853),
the 'fearful' and the 'ludicrous' (1913:345). These elements, as
Philip Thomson has more recently pointed out, exist together as an
'unresolved clash of incompatibles in work and response' (1972:27).
Wolfgang Kayser's important study of the grotesque reveals its
power in the context of the postmodern world. He argues that, as
opposed to the glorification of the body in popular media, the
grotesque body alienates, disturbs and unsettles, revealing 'the
estranged world' in which items are loosened from their familiar
meanings. Kayser finds that, as readers encounter the grotesque,
they can no longer live in their customary world with the assurance

that their known categories still apply (1968:184–5). This use of the grotesque as a dramatization of the absurd and nihilistic is especially characteristic of the late twentieth century. The grotesque destroys the old world or renders it ugly and revolting, while alleviating the nausea through humor. This sense of the grotesque appropriately follows the dropping of the atom bomb and the holocaust, which brought about what Jeffrey Nuttall calls 'bomb culture'. Hiroshima, Belsen and Vietnam introduced us to horror, and their impact demanded that people grow callous (Nuttall 1968:118). To Nuttall, 'morality, pain, and compassion—the whole business of identifying with other people and thus sharing and helping their discomfiture—had to be dissolved in [in many cases sick] humor'. The bomb, thereby, aggravates 'sick' humor, which in turn makes the presence of the bomb livable (Nuttall 1968:119). Finally, Tim Libretti argues that American proletarian literature of the 1930s used the grotesque because, as a means of subversion, the grotesque 'challenges the fetishized consciousness of bourgeois life that comprehends the world as permanent, natural and unchanging by virtue of the operation of commodity relations' (1995:176).

Throughout his work, Burroughs challenges the cultural hegemony of the West by rendering its cultural products grotesque. The grotesque bodies and deformed and deconstructed sounds and images in Burroughs's work represent the West's failed experiments at colonizing and controlling the world through word and image. Like the escapees from Benway's Reconditioning Center, Burroughs's grotesque images and sounds run amok despite the efforts of censors and arbiters of taste. They mock those whose consciousness and identity are privileged due to money and power.

This chapter will explore Burroughs's use of the grotesque in his various artistic endeavors as part of his effort to resist the cultural homogenization imposed through the mechanisms of globalized capitalism. I situate Burroughs's use of the grotesque in the context of late twentieth-century oppositional art and culture that uses the grotesque to challenge the standardized consciousness imposed by multinational corporate enterprise, and I connect the uses of the grotesque in Burroughs's writings, shotgun art and tape experiments with grotesque contemporary art and British punk culture of the 1970s to reveal consistencies in their resistance to popular modes of thinking and feeling. Burroughs's taste for the grotesque has been his legacy to the oppositional art movements of the late twentieth and early twenty-first centuries.

These movements share Burroughs's understanding of the subversive power of the grotesque; how it blends disgust and humor and thereby awakens and stimulates awareness and moral reproach; how it undermines both the ideal and the real, distorting both. That the grotesque has become a hallmark of avant-garde art and radical popular culture owes much to Burroughs's writings and sensibility. Burroughs had often stated his admiration of the emancipating randomness of twentieth-century art, and, in collaboration with Brion Gysin and Ian Somerville, based his cut-up experiments on the montage style of modern art. In turn, contemporary artists, in their use of dissected, fractured and deformed bodies, reflect Burroughs's influence. Similar lines of influence and sympathy can be drawn between Burroughs and punk.

Burroughs's satirical 'Bugger the Queen' anticipated The Sex Pistols' 'God Save the Queen', a parodic commemoration of Elizabeth II's silver jubilee. When The Sex Pistols were verbally and physically attacked for this song as it hit number one on the British charts, Burroughs wrote them a letter in support. Burroughs came to be known as the Godfather of Punk: 'They were his children', remarks the Burroughs insider Victor Bockris (1981:xii). Burroughs himself characterized punk as an 'interesting and important phenomenon' (Bockris 1981:128). The punk phenomenon grew out of the economic recession of 1970s Britain, and the punks' characteristic deglamorization resisted the commodified images upon which the new economy drew. Reduced to irrelevancy through unemployment and despair, British punks of the 1970s played 'with the only power at their disposal: the power to discomfit' (Hebdige 1988:18). The impulses to deform, disconnect and destroy that characterize the grotesque in Burroughs, contemporary art and the punk scene bring about a new art and new forms of cognition, free from official control, radically unmarketable and hence fully liberated.

THE GROTESQUE BODY

Burroughs's principal means of producing the grotesque is through an emphasis on the body, especially on what Mikhail Bakhtin calls 'the material body lower stratum', with its most unsavory functions and in its most humiliating positions. Bakhtin argues that the grotesque body challenges the liberal humanist's concept of identity. The grotesque body is blubbery, hairy, odorous and obtrusive, exceeding healthy limits and expunging muscular definition. The

grotesque body's superfluousness mocks the gravity of classical stat-
uary's heroic poses. Bakhtin states that the grotesque stresses 'those
parts of the body that are open to the outside world, that is, the
parts through which the world enters the body or emerges from it,
or through which the body itself goes out to meet the world'
(1965:26). The nose, lips, tongue, fingers, breasts and nipples, penis,
feet and toes, and the body's solid, liquid and gaseous issues are the
raw materials of the artist of the grotesque (26). As Bakhtin's
account suggests, the grotesque body is imperfect and out of control. Nauseating to behold, it defies attempts to transform it into a
commodity. Likewise, the grotesque body challenges the capitalist
vision of the free individual; Georges Bataille states: 'Man willingly
imagines himself to be like the god Neptune, stilling his own waves,
with majesty; nevertheless, the bellowing waves of the viscera, in
more or less incessant inflation and upheaval, brusquely put an end
to his dignity' (1929:22).

Burroughs's images of pained and distorted bodies are the source
of much of the offense that his work has produced, and certainly
much of its power. In the excerpts of the obscenity trial transcript,
Norman Mailer finds that the humor in *Naked Lunch* has close
affinities with the grotesque: '[I]t is the sort of humor which flour-
ishes in prisons, in the Army, among junkies, race tracks and pool
halls, a graffiti of cool, even livid wit, based on bodily functions and
the frailties of the body, the slights, humiliations and tortures a
body can undergo' (*NL* xviii).

Burroughs's use of the body to effect horror and humor has its
most direct precedent in the satirical style of Jonathan Swift. In
A Modest Proposal (1729), Swift uses the grotesque to protest the mis-
treatment of the Irish poor. The implied author straightforwardly
and benevolently argues the ease, inexpensiveness and effectiveness
of ending poverty by having tenants breed infants to be sold as food
to their landlords. In *A Modest Proposal*, the humor arises from the
dissonance between the ghastly images of slaughtered children and
the professed and felt kindness of the voice describing them. The
ironic glee with which Swift's voice describes a young child as 'a
most delicious, nourishing, and wholesome Food; whether Stewed,
Roasted, Baked, or Boiled' or in a 'Fricasie, or Ragoust' (Swift
1729:504) still reads today as profoundly unsettling. In the
'Deposition: Testimony Concerning a Sickness', Burroughs claims
that he adopts Swift's technique in *Naked Lunch* to 'reveal capital
punishment as the obscene, barbaric and disgusting anachronism

that it is' (*NL* xli). Like Swift, Burroughs most offends the reader who refuses to accept the body stripped of its pretensions and contrivances. Only a Naked Lunch will wise up the marks: '[L]et them see what they actually eat and drink. Let them see what is on the end of that long newspaper spoon' (*NL* xlii). For both writers, savagely satirizing their readers' sense of their moral selves by depicting bodies in the grotesque manner most effectively counteracts the forces of unjust social control.

Naked Lunch portrays a number of grotesque characters, including Placenta Juan the Afterbirth Tycoon and the infamous 'talking asshole'. However, the characterization of Pantopon Rose supplies, perhaps, the sharpest image of Burroughs's depiction of the grotesque body. In the throes of her addiction, and without a vein to strike, Rose takes desperate measures:

> [Rose] seized a safety pin caked with blood and rust, gouged a great hole in her leg which seemed to hang open like an obscene, festering mouth waiting for unspeakable congress with the dropper which she now plunged out of sight into the gaping wound. But her hideous galvanized need (hunger of insects in dry places) has broken the dropper off deep in the flesh of her ravaged thigh (looking rather like a poster on soil erosion). But what does she care? She does not even bother to remove the splintered glass, looking down at her bloody haunch with the cold blank eyes of a meat trader. (*NL* 10)

Burroughs's description of Rose's body and her disregard of the harm she does to it evoke our horror and laughter. The description produces horror by depicting unsanitary instruments prodding diseased wounds, junk-sick flesh begging for satisfaction, self-mutilation, streaming gore and ghastly excrescence. Rose's body, horrifying in its abused, scarred condition, is simultaneously human, insect and mere meat. However, the pitiless distance of the narrator simultaneously undercuts and accentuates the horror. This disinterest is shared by Rose, who ignores her ravaged body to feed her 'insect' hunger, losing the dropper into the recesses of her flesh and looking like a 'poster on soil erosion'. Robin Lydenberg has noted that such bodily corruptions ultimately disgust the reader in order to provoke 'an emetic purging of his cultural inheritance' (1987:143).

Contemporary British art shares with Burroughs's work that irresolvable tension between the humorous and the horrible. The 2000

Sensations exhibition of the work of younger British artists shocked spectators through its frank, parodic renditions of dead, soiled and mutilated bodies in odd juxtapositions with bizarre combinations of media (perhaps most noticeably in Chris Ofili's elephant-dung spattered Madonna, *The Holy Virgin Mary*, which incited then-mayor Rudy Giuliani to propose an end to all public funding to the Brooklyn Museum of Art). Like Burroughs's images of the grotesque body, these works, especially those of Damien Hirst and Jake and Dinos Chapman, foreground wounding, disease and waste. Hirst's most viscerally disturbing works are his bisections of livestock. In *This Little Piggy Went to the Market, This Little Piggy Stayed Home*, the nursery rhyme title mocks the condition of the piglet that has been split lengthwise with each half enclosed in its own formaldehyde-filled encasement. The two encasements are placed side by side, with one side placed slightly ahead of the other to enable easy viewing of internal organs. As in Hirst's other livestock works, this is no dummy, but a real pig with viscera revealed for public inspection. Similarly, Hirst's *Mother and Child Divided* parodies the title of the Paul Simon song, 'Mother and Child Reunion', in that the art object so entitled includes a mother cow and her calf, both bisected with entrails exposed. On the one hand, by using (or abusing) farm animals as (damaged) spectacle, Hirst challenges the notion of farm animals as lovable creatures that have rights and deserve to be treated with dignity. On the other hand, by depriving these livestock of use value, Hirst's artwork undermines the mission of the agricultural industry because this livestock, having been slaughtered by a sculptor, cannot be sold or consumed as food or clothing, but only as art. Conversely, Hirst's presentation of packaged waste as art complicates modern art's 'ready-mades'. As in the livestock bisections, the titles of his 'waste' artworks balance the nauseating sight with snide humor. In *I'll Love You Forever*, stacks of fluorescent yellow and orange infectious waste containers, labeled with appropriate warnings, are locked inside a bright blue cage, permitting viewing but not handling. The sight of biohazards disturbs the viewer, but the colorful display enchants and entertains. The title reflects the presence of the containers marked 'Placenta' and the sentimentality of preserving afterbirth as a parent would preserve an infant's lock of hair. Hirst's 'waste' artworks refuse commodification even after they have been made into art; if purchased, they must be kept out of the reach of children.

Unlike Hirst's use of actual carcasses and waste, Jake and Dinos Chapman use lifelike mannequins in their work, though the effect of their postures of torture is no less startling. In *Great Deeds Against the Dead*, arguably a parody of Goya's work of the same name, two hyper-realistic, naked male mannequins are harshly tethered to a bomb-scorched tree, one male hanging from a branch by his arms, which are pulled impossibly behind his back. The other mannequin has been terribly dismembered, his headless, armless torso hanging upside down by his legs, his severed arms hanging next to the torso, and his head stuck onto another upright branch. Both mannequins have had their genitalia excised. The seemingly intentional artificiality of the mannequins complicates the horror that the image of tortured figures conveys. For example, the artists made no effort to use human-like hair; instead, hair, eyebrows and mustache have a doll-like quality, giving the figure the appearance of a mangled GI Joe. The viewer's realization that these are toys, not people, and that those who simulate war rather than those who actually plan or fight are the satire's targets, mocks the apparent intentions of Goya's original—to evoke the horror and degradation of war or to elicit compassion for war's victims. Jake and Dinos Chapman's works that use mannequins and toy soldiers strongly connect with the dirtied and disfigured children's toys of recently deceased American artist Mike Kelley, whose work spoils the homogenized prettiness of dolls with human excrement. Scarred, impaled and diseased bodies also mark the resistance of British punk rock of the 1970s to the global commerce that, to the punks, tamed rock 'n' roll and put British youth on the dole. Punk uses the body to elicit horror and humor.

As with Burroughs, the grotesque gave British punks a material and mood by which they could dramatize the contempt with which the selfish, smug and corrupt Tory government of mid-1970s Britain had treated them. Cultural critic Greil Marcus describes this contrived ugliness of British punks of the 1970s: 'they were fat, anorexic, pockmarked, acned, stuttering, crippled, scarred and damaged, and what their new decorations underlined was the failure already engraved in their faces' (1989:74). Dick Hebdige suggests that through self-mutilation and body art, punks could embody a kiosk of revolutionary signs (1988:18). Degrading the body by cutting it, piercing it and making it bleed, as Sid Vicious often did on stage, celebrates the punk's power over his or her body, a power that defies easy conversion into a commodity. As a declaration of independence, punks smeared shit upon themselves before others could.

British punks also displayed the grotesque body in fashion and in their interaction with performers. In England especially, clothing style indicates social class and, in Hebdige's term, one's 'spectacular subculture'. Punk clothing and jewelry, especially as Vivienne Westwood and Malcolm McLaren designed such accoutrement, determined the course of British punk rock style. Indeed, McLaren established The Sex Pistols to boost sales of bondage wear in his King's Road boutique, SEX. Rival designers were no less daring. As Jon Savage has documented, BOY (another Chelsea clothier) sold T-shirts stained with dried animal blood, images of the death's head of recently executed murderer Gary Gilmore, and jewelry made of contraceptive packets and hypodermic syringes, while also displaying forensic cultures that contained simulated severed body parts in its shop windows (1992:324). As the ultimate expression of worthlessness, some punks wore trash bags. In their interaction with performers, punk audiences developed the practice of 'gobbing', or spitting on the musicians. Johnny Rotten, the lead singer of The Sex Pistols, inadvertently began this practice when, having a terrible cold, he discharged upon the audience, who returned the gesture. At once expressing disgust and fellowship, gobbing showed appreciation through disdain—indeed, through expectoration and contamination. A direct challenge to propriety, health codes and personal privacy, gobbing transformed the expression of appreciation into the transmission of disease.

Punk lyrics draw on the grotesque body as well. The lyrics of the song 'Bodies' by The Sex Pistols form a demonic dramatic monologue in which the singer confirms his bestiality in the very act of denying it, though the lyrics defy any definitive interpretation. Perhaps because 'Pauline' has had an abortion, the singer accuses her of being an 'animal' and a 'bloody disgrace'. The chorus, however, suggests that the singer cannot distinguish his own identity. With the word 'Body' echoing in the background, the singer desperately asserts that he is 'not an animal', but the desperation of the statement and the continual repetition of the word 'animal' suggest otherwise. Perhaps because Pauline's aborted fetus doesn't appear to be human, or perhaps because it does, the singer describes it as a 'screaming, fucking bloody mess', a 'throbbing squirm', and most dismissively, a 'discharge/Another loss of protein'. The baby is so deformed that the singer—could it be his child? Could it be the singer himself?—denies paternity. In his refusal of responsibility, he himself effectively becomes a 'bloody disgrace' like the mother. But his denial recognizes his own 'bloody mess'. 'I don't want a baby who looks like that', he claims, yet in the last words of the song, he becomes the baby, calling for his 'Mummy'. By recognizing the grotesqueness of his own body, he substitutes for the aborted fetus, betrayed and lost.

British punk musicians and their counterparts in painting and sculpture, recognizing that the image of the perfect body sells food, pornography, cars, exercise equipment and even bodies themselves, follow Burroughs by distorting, defacing and distending the body. Like Burroughs, by ruining the body's mainstream commercial potential, these artists resist global capital's effort to profit from the body.

DISTORTING THE FAMILIAR

Burroughs's grotesque bodies challenge commodification with their unresolved tensions and paradoxes. Similarly, Burroughs distorts familiar sounds and images to evoke horror and humor. The audiotape experiments that Burroughs conducted with Ian Somerville in the early 1960s exemplify how Burroughs distorts by deforming and recontextualizing. Burroughs and Somerville's experiments with splicing, inching and cutting in tapes grew out of Burroughs and Gysin's use of textual cut-ups and fold-ins. The cutting and splicing of texts and audiotapes echo the method of cutting textual and audiotape records to break control mechanisms (see *The Soft Machine* and *The Ticket that Exploded*). The raw material for many of the audiotape experiments consists of radio broadcasts, mostly news and commercials. By distorting these found, manufactured sounds, Burroughs and Somerville release them from any claim to rational meaning or to any historical verification, yet create awesome, even frightening melodies and rhythms. In 'The Silver Smoke of Dreams' (early 1960s), for example, two vocal tracks are blended and 'inched' back and forth across the tape head, distorting what may be recognized as a human voice reading English sentences (*BTGR*). What emerges is a new, uncanny voice—a third voice synthesized from two—that resembles an actual voice, having its timbre and tone, but speaking in a new rhythm and with new sounds. It becomes a convergence of voices that has no single identity; rather, the effect is fluid and indefinable, alien and nonlexical. The terrible distortion strikes listeners, but its odd misshapenness amuses them, like seeing their images in a funhouse mirror. 'Inching' distorts the voice by suddenly speeding it up and then slowing it down, contorting its pitch and timbre. Similarly, in recordings like 'The Total Taste is Here, News Cut-Ups' (early 1965), various unrelated radio reports and jingles are spliced together, and the effect is at first discomfiting. After continual repetition, however, the voices merge and the stories begin to gel, not into a logical whole, but into a range of voices (*Best*). The clashing news reports suggest alternate meanings or, at least, the problem of stabilizing meaning in the electronic age.

Punk rock also drew from this legacy of auditory and visual distortions of the familiar. In his book, *England's Dreaming*, Jon Savage suggests that Burroughs's audiotape experiments inspired punk's effort to 'play the media's accelerated jumble of signals back at them' (1992:231). The razor-sharp voice of Johnny Rotten, the poses that parodied the classic rock star look, the unexpected accessorizing of ties, jackets, torn shirts, vestigial safety pins and short hair, all combined to jam media signals. Jamie Reid's Situationist International-inspired posters and record sleeves are emblematic of the confusion of signs that characterizes punk style. Reid's design for a flyer promoting The Sex Pistols' 'God Save the Queen' defaces the smiling Silver Jubilee portrait of Elizabeth II by piercing her lips with a safety pin. The safety pin dishonors the Queen's majesty by placing her in league with England's 'shame', and simultaneously validates punk culture; it is an image both appalling and comical. Similarly, the graphic design of punk fanzines placed incompatible elements in conflict. The cover of the December 1976 issue of *Sniffin' Glue* features a penciled caricature of sneering cover-boy Johnny Rotten, his jaw extended and broadened to grotesque size, glaring at the reader amid a background of drawings of conventional holly and tree ornaments (Perry 2000).

DESTRUCTION AS CREATION

Burroughs also effects the grotesque by destroying already manufactured items and celebrating the debris as art. His description of this process testifies to its unlikely randomness: 'I picked up a piece of wood and blasted it. Then I looked at the broken piece of plywood where the shots came out and in these striations I saw all sorts of things [...] I said, "My God, this is a work of art"' (*PG* 13). This method, like portraying the grotesque body and distorting the familiar, counters mainstream market forces that prize wholeness, physical integrity and traditional bourgeois notions of the creative process. Burroughs's shotgun art best exemplifies his method of destroying to create. In these works, the shotgun blast literally deconstructs an intact, artificial object, in many cases plywood, stripping away the layers that compose it and bringing about several paradoxes. The 'made' shotgun 'unmakes' another 'made' item, putting everything out of context and rendering all indeterminate. A building material that has apparently lost its value has actually increased in value due to its destruction. Similarly, a shotgun, a ballistic instrument, now renders whole, though the wholeness is as an art object defined by its lack of wholeness (or by the fact that it is full of holes). A killing machine now gives life, albeit through an explosion. Though Burroughs claimed that he never would have pursued painting without shotguns, an essay that Burroughs published before the shotgun incident entitled 'The Fall of Art' suggests some foreshadowing of the idea. In this essay Burroughs foresees 'exploding art ... A self-destroying TV set, refrigerator, washing-machine and electric stove going off, leaving a shambles of a gleaming modern apartment; the housewife's dream goes up behind a barrier of shatterproof glass to shield the spectators' (*AM* 61). In the future, Burroughs suggests, art will destroy the consumer's paradise that post-World War II American industry promised to the suburban family and later to the world; 'exploding art' releases the creativity that the global consumer economy stifles.

Individual works testify to the power to create by destroying and the horror and humor that arise from the effort (see Sobieszek 1996). *Sore Shoulder*, the first work of shotgun art created by accident, reveals that the networks of fiber that compose plywood can be beautiful in their decomposition. In subsequent pieces like *Screaming Ghost* and *The Curse of Bast*, paint cans were placed as targets before the plywood, rendering absurd, even malevolent, the process of painting—painting becomes target practice. In these works, the grotesque aspect of the shotgun art consists in the tension between the destruction of new plywood and its simultaneous rebirth as art. The effects of shotgun blasts can evoke terror, and the residue of the impact suggests the awesomeness and power that can render human flesh as vulnerable as the plywood here. The rent portrait of Nancy Reagan in Burroughs's *The Curse of Bast* and the exploded image of the fashion model on the recto of *Mink Mutiny* emphasize the menacing element of shotgun art. In other cases, the word is rubbed out, so to speak, by affixing newspaper texts and images on the plywood, which the shotgun then explodes. However, the fanciful existence of the artwork itself and the shattered images of celebrities both balance and offset the terrifying power of the shotgun blast. A shotgun blast producing art that could be exhibited in a gallery or a museum seems odd, if not ludicrous to bourgeois culture. Yet Burroughs claims, 'I want my painting to literally walk off the goddamned canvas, to become a creature and a very dangerous creature' (*PG* 34–5). In Burroughs's shotgun art as well as his other work, the grotesque resists being incorporated into market forces, as destruction by its nature removes that fetishized quality of commodities, revealing the guts of the completed products and thereby the process by which they have been created.

Punk rock had been predicated on the impulse to destroy. Destruction and negation are hallmarks of the British punk ethos. 'I wanna destroy passerby', cries Johnny Rotten, taking the persona of the antichrist/anarchist. Marcus has interpreted the destructive impulse in punk as a reaction to global forces that left British youth with no future: '[T]he whole of received hegemonic propositions about the way the world was supposed to work comprised a fraud so complete and venal that it demanded to be destroyed beyond the powers of memory to recall its existence' (1989:18). Punk negated all the lies that it could target: corporate rock, the celebrity system, hippies and the 'love generation', and Tory politics. Most importantly, the utter ugliness of punk negated its commercial potential, thereby freeing it to break images at will. From the debris of this destruction, anything was possible and everything was permitted. Though the British punk fanzine *Sniffin' Glue* was simple and intentionally sloppy anyway, publisher Mark Perry regularly defaced the magazine's cover art with magic marker, defying consumers to purchase it. Working against the typewritten columns as well as the pictures, the magic marker traces blotted out words and made messages unintelligible. However, despite Perry's efforts to destroy his own creation, sales increased rapidly after the first three issues. Chagrined at the prospect of popularity, Perry stopped publishing *Sniffin' Glue* after the twelfth edition and in that issue's editorial urged his readers to 'STOP READING [*Sniffin' Glue*] NOW AND BURN YOUR COPY' (Perry 2000). *Sniffin' Glue*, like British punk in general, in Marcus's words, 'was a moment in time that took shape as a language anticipating its own destruction' (1989:82).

To its many critics, economic and cultural globalization, and the standardized, homogenized commodities with which it gluts the marketplace and the mind, has wrought sufficient destruction through the inequality it creates, the international terrorism it breeds and the creativity it kills. Burroughs, as well as other artists of the grotesque, challenge globalization by reducing or eliminating the exchange value of its commodities. The ultimate effect is not the annihilation of the market, but its liberation from those hegemonic powers that seek not choice but compliance. Through his use of the grotesque in the form of disgusting bodies, distorted images and creative destruction, Burroughs smirks at efforts to make him cooperate. Shotgun cocked, Burroughs crouches in the golden toilet bowl on which the scion squats, ready to make art where the sun doesn't shine.

REFERENCES

Bakhtin, M. (1965) *Rabelais and His World*, Iswolsky, H. trans. (Cambridge: Harvard University Press, 1968).
Barber, B. (2001) *Jihad vs. McWorld* (New York: Ballantine).
Bataille, G. (1929) 'The Big Toe', IN *Visions of Excess: Selected Writings, 1927–1939*, Stoekl, A. ed. and trans. (Minneapolis: University of Minnesota Press, 1985).
Bockris, V. (1981) *With William Burroughs: A Report from the Bunker*, rev. edition (New York: St. Martin's Griffin, 1996).
Cassuto, L. (1997) *The Inhuman Race: The Racial Grotesque in American Literature and Culture* (New York: Columbia University Press).
Hebdige, D. (1988) *Hiding in the Light: On Images and Things* (London: Routledge).
Kayser, W. (1968) *The Grotesque in Art and Literature*, Weisstein, U. trans. (Gloucester, MA: Peter Smith).
Libretti, T. (1995) ' "What a Dirty Way of Getting Clean": The Grotesque in Proletarian Literature', IN *Literature and the Grotesque*, Meyer, M. ed. (Amsterdam: Rodopi), pp. 171–93.
Lydenberg, R. (1987) *Word Cultures: Radical Theory and Practice in William Burroughs' Fiction* (Urbana: University of Illinois Press).
Marcus, G. (1989) *Lipstick Traces: A Secret History of the Twentieth Century* (Cambridge, MA: Harvard University Press).
Nuttall, J. (1968) *Bomb Culture* (London: MacGibbon & Kee).
Perry, M. (2000) *Sniffin' Glue: The Essential Punk Accessory* (London: Sanctuary).
Ruskin, J. (1853) *The Stones of Venice*, vol. 3 (Boston: D. Estes, 1913).
Savage, Jon (1992) *England's Dreaming: Anarchy, Sex Pistols, Punk Rock, and Beyond* (New York: St. Martin's).
Sobieszek, R. A. (1996) *Ports of Entry: William S. Burroughs and the Arts* (Los Angeles: Los Angeles County Museum of Art/Thames and Hudson).
Swift, J. (1729) 'A Modest Proposal', IN *The Writings of Jonathan Swift*, Greenberg, R. A. and Piper, W. B., eds (New York: Norton, 1973).
Thomson, P. (1972) *The Grotesque* (London: Methuen).

9

Nothing *Hear* Now but the Recordings: Burroughs's 'Double Resonance'

Davis Schneiderman

In the second decade of the nineteenth century, a now famous progenitor of American letters wrote (in mockery of the naturalist Buffon) that 'all animals degenerated in America, and man among the number' (Irving 1819:809). While readers of the time might have been surprised to learn that the author of this statement, one Geoffrey Crayon, was also that famous New York historian Diedrich Knickerbocker, those who know the 'real' identity of both writers as Washington Irving recognize Irving's position in the American canon as that of a literary imitator. Irving's pseudonymous Crayon completely transformed the original German locations of 'The Legend of Sleepy Hollow' and 'Rip Van Winkle' into terrain seemingly indigenous to the new world.

I deliberately use the term 'real' to describe this author's identity— not to question the existence of the man known as Washington Irving, but to dramatize (in conjunction with American 'degeneration') that the position of the author is bound inextricably with the transformation of his subject matter, so that the resulting amalgamation might respond to the question: 'Wouldn't it be booful if we should juth run together into one gweat big blob' (*Q* 100). Such is also the case with the American transient William S. Burroughs, who jigged about the map in his effort to produce a corpus that exists *never* in only one place and time, but rather, finds itself moving toward what he calls a 'final ecological jump' (Zivancevic 1981:525) into *space*.

'Space' has at least two meanings when applied to Burroughs's work; first, he encourages the evolution of humans into a form best suited for cosmic nether-realms via a spirit body (see Russell 2001:155–87); second, 'space' can also signify a postmodern dissolution of Enlightenment-imposed limits in a world no longer bound by the flat logic of hegemonic 'reason'. This latter value acts as a continual hedge against the more fantastic elements of the Burroughsian cosmology, but also finds connection with the political struggles characterizing the emerging global economic order, where 'all of nature has become capital, or at least has become subject to capital' (Hardt and Negri 2000:272).

Accordingly, Burroughs's entreaties for humans to evolve from 'time' into 'space' can be productively analyzed in terms of the material vagaries of global politics that are contemporaneous with his movement, not away from writing, but into a creative *space* (in the second sense of the term) populated with a variety of multimedia projects. As noted by a number of critics (Miles 1992; Sobieszek 1996; Murphy 1997), Burroughs has a long engagement with aesthetics *beyond* the written form, and this engagement can be traced back to at least the late 1950s in his work with Brion Gysin and Ian Sommerville.

Significantly, such supplementary activity quickly assumed a prominent theoretical position in Burroughs's work, which became increasingly fixated on conceits of media as both resistance *and* control. This ambivalence is crucial, both deployed and circumscribed by the language of its articulation, so that Burroughs's work—offering a symbolic language of media production—always searches for opportunities to exploit formal processes as a means of scuttling the forces of commodification: Burroughs not only argued for the efficacy of cut-ups, but also used them as a production tool; he not only wrote *about* films and recordings, but also made them throughout his career. His reflexive empiricism thus carries the significance of his work beyond that of a simply innovative writer, providing it with a 'double resonance'—an awareness of its structural limits in terms of both content and production.

Robert A. Sobieszek notes that Burroughs's film and recorder projects 'startlingly anticipate MTV rock videos of the 1980s and 1990s as well as the devices of "scratching" and "sampling" in punk, industrial, and rap music of the same decades' (1996:20–1). Still, it is important not simply to perceive the sound manipulation techniques that we consider contemporary, including 'inching'— represented on *Break Through in Grey Room* (a 1986 collection of early Burroughs sound experiments)—as the progenitors of today's ubiquitous rap and DJ culture; worse yet, to consider this culture from the banal academic perspective that would label those techniques as still *effectively* 'resistant' ignores the mass culture's ability to absorb innovation. In both cases, such plaudits run the risk of paradoxically diluting the work into the neutralized extensions of Madison Avenue. Rather, we must examine subversive possibilities that remain *ever* wary of the media, while simultaneously exploiting the field's incessant desire to *cover*. Accordingly, media literacy campaigns dedicated to reversing a default one-way information flow (as per the 'Senders' of *Naked Lunch* and their 'biocontrol apparatus' [*NL* 148]) have found some success in recent years. Image-savvy groups such as the indigenous rights-oriented Zapatistas in Mexico, as well as the coalition of activists involved in the 'Battle of Seattle' protest at the 1999 meeting of the World Trade Organization and the similarly motivated 2000 protests against the World Economic Forum's Asia Pacific meeting in Melbourne, Australia, demonstrate that the anti-globalization movement not only 'manifests viscerally in local spaces but it also depends upon broad non-geographical media spaces' (Luckman and Redden 2001:32).

Significantly, the clutch of struggles affiliated with the anti-globalization movement is always locked into a split-level effort: on the one hand, such movements must attempt to prevent the pandemic erosion of public space and public resources (air, water, wilderness, and so on); at the same time they must battle against the co-optation and dissolution of their public voices into the droning mass of the culture industry—any middle-American mall-rat with a pocket full of allowance can purchase a Che Guevara T-shirt. Burroughs's sound collaborations, while always in danger of becoming just this sort of empty prattle, are nonetheless ideally positioned: not to overthrow the control machine by 'storming the reality studio'—a goal *too* idealistic to combat a control machine that routinely deploys the techniques of media-savvy dissent—but to map, onto the material effects of its own delivery systems, strategies of guerilla resistance imbued with enough reflexive potential to hold the grey room *after* the oft-envisaged 'break through'.

As Tom Hayden comments (on a poster at the 1968 Democratic Convention in Chicago): '[T]hose administering the regressive apparatus [...] cannot distinguish "straight" radicals from newspapermen or observers from delegates to the convention. They cannot distinguish rumors about demonstrations from the real thing' (cited by Walker 1968:36–7). Hayden's statement seems to imply the opportunity for guerilla intervention, but for Burroughs, there is no such 'resistance' that can avoid the possibility of being spun from a reverse angle. Thus, the 'double resonance' of his sound production has as much to do with the undesirability of supposedly 'transformative' technological identity cast in the *illusion* of hybridity, as it does with the possibility of producing aesthetic artifacts capable of exploding the limits of conventional discourse.

THE HIPSTER BE-BOP JUNKIE?

Regarding Burroughs's first official sound release, *Call Me Burroughs* (1965), Barry Alfonso remarks (on the reissue liner notes) on the 'antique metallic resonance' of Burroughs's voice—linked to the resounding 'echoes of older America'—which, with its metanarrative pronouncements from texts such as *Nova Express*, assumes meanings not possible on the page. On the same track, 'Where You Belong', the straight-ahead voice tells us: 'We pull writers of all time in together and record radio programs, movie soundtrack, TV and jukebox songs [...] all the words of the world stirring around in a cement mixer, and pour in the resistance message' (*CMB*). Still, the English-language portion of the original 1965 liner notes, written by Emmett Williams, oversimplifies the connection between Burroughs's voice and the cut-up 'message', misattributing interpretative clairvoyance to Burroughs's already prophetic reputation. For Williams, Burroughs reading Burroughs *might* be taken as 'an indispensable key to the arcana of *The Naked Lunch* and *Nova Express*' (*CMB* liner notes).

Is this the 'real' Burroughs then—the producer *and* interpreter of text through its own articulation? According to Williams's playful and perhaps hasty summation, we can envision Burroughs feeding himself media on the subliminal level, processing himself through performance, and thus producing a hyperbolic carnival version of his own narrative fête. Such *jouissance* might point to the 'real' Burroughs in the same way that Crayon or Knickerbocker were at various times associated with the early American 'degenerate' called Washington Irving. Any correlation beyond simple identification or attribution remains only *local*, no more emblematic of the essential Burroughs than the $25 T-shirt is representative of the South American revolutionary.

Despite Williams's desire to 'discover' in Burroughs's voice some vital essence, what may be most significant about Burroughs's early forays into visual and sound culture is that the work itself never surrendered to the 'countercultural myth' that characterized much avant-garde output of the time—as Thomas Frank calls the myth that resistance operated in binary opposition to the 'muted, uniform gray' of the business world (1997:6). Frank, for instance, notes Pepsi-Cola's early 1960s invention of a completely commodified populace who could be set against the apparently rigid mores of old America (in this case represented by Coca-Cola) for mercantile purposes: '[I]n 1961 [Pepsi] invented a fictional youth movement, a more wholesome version of Mailer's hipsters but still in rebellion against the oppressive demands of mass society' (1997:170). Such easy binaries are not to be found in Burroughs's arsenal; marked by the 'double resonance' of his content and production, the ambivalence of addiction along with its complete hold on the subject assures Burroughs's readers that they would be wise to remain continually suspicious of the standard counterculture line: 'The prolonged use of LSD may give rise in some cases to a crazed unwholesome benevolence—the old tripster smiling into your face sees all your thoughts loving and accepting you inside out' (*Job* 137).

Accordingly, we might investigate Burroughs's *later* sound production as a project evolving from his early tape recorder and film pieces, because once the mass media entered its current period of rampant self-reflective narcissism, Burroughs's rise as a pop-culture figure was on one level assured by the fact that he was still alive *and* producing. Popular constructions of Burroughs as junkie-murderer-Scientologist-Nike shill-painter-homosexual-et al. might be read as reminders of the control machine's adaptability; no doubt, these 'ports of entry' will each remain enticing gateways for the Burroughs mythology, but Burroughs's continued suspicion of language's 'ability' to offer a clear message can also countermand the accreted meaning and interpretation of his popular persona: 'If they write an article attacking the Olympia Press as sexualizing congruent accessibility to its heart of pulp fecundate with orifices perspectives in the name of human privacy they have placed their thesis beyond the realm of fact [...] The words used refer to nothing' (*Job* 107). Language betrays any attempt to hang Burroughs onto a particular commercial hook, but also compromises—'informs'—on his retorts.

Even so, Burroughs's multimedia collaborations might *still* be interpreted as 'lines of flight' from the structures of advanced capital. The 'double resonance' of Burroughs's work and cultural appropriation attempts to perform key reversals, what Saul Alinsky calls 'mass political jujitsu' (cited by Klein 2002:281), so that while the forces of commodification try to assimilate the viral seed of Burroughs's language, they remain unable to force the words into their desired meaning.

INVERSION I: WORKING WITH THE POPULAR FORCES

In his classic treatise *Noise: The Political Economy of Music*, Jacques Attali articulates our first inversion—that recorded music and sound have become representative of a fundamental shift in the relationship between performance and recording. Whereas the original purpose of recording was to preserve the live concert experience, Attali argues that the evolution of mass reproducibility and the concomitant rise of the 'recording star' changed the live performance into a *repetition of the recorded situation*. The authority of original production and that of the recording industry are both called into question (1985:85–6), guaranteeing that even in its popular manifestation of apparent countercultural forms (for example, the Beatles), the recording industry 'assured that young people were very effectively socialized, in a world of pettiness constructed by adults' (110).

Burroughs and Gysin, aware of the deep structural ambivalence of the linguistic medium, argued that '[t]he word was and is flesh [...] The word was and is sound and image' (*3M* 159), and thus focused their recording energies on pieces that would somehow cultivate a reproduction of 'aura' that could grow *through* replication, while at the same time questioning the efficacy of their own involvement in the control mechanisms of the pre-recordings. In the liner notes for *Apocalypse Across the Sky* by the Master Musicians of Jajouka featuring Bachir Attar (produced by Bill Laswell), Burroughs and Gysin position the special caste of musicians ('the 4000-year-old rock 'n' roll band') in an era pre-dating the traps of language and technological recording: 'Musicians are magicians in Morocco [...] They are evokers of djenoun forces, spirits of the hills and the flocks and above all the spirits of music' (*Apocalypse* liner notes). Yet, Burroughs and Gysin also admonish the consumers of the music to 'let the music penetrate you and move you, and you will connect with the oldest music on earth' (*Apocalypse* liner notes). In order to account not only for the apparent contradiction of discovering such 'auratic' magic in the technological medium, but also for Attali's sense that *recording* sound and music becomes subordinate to the replicated long-player of capital, we must determine how Burroughs uses such an inversion to his advantage.

'Burroughs Break', the first track from the Burroughs and Gus Van Sant collaboration *The Elvis of Letters* (1985), offers the line, 'Whatever you feed into the machine on a subliminal level, the machine will process', and this sample is seemingly copied straight from the *Call Me Burroughs* record (as are other portions of *Elvis*). Van Sant's twangy guitar backs up the majority of *Elvis*, most effectively perhaps on the second track, 'Word is Virus', which repeats the ideological mantra of *Nova Express*: 'Word begets image and image *is* virus' (48). While such exercises, which mix Burroughs's spoken word recording with musical accompaniment, are notable advances from the deadpan delivery on *Call Me Burroughs*, the potential of Van Sant's project to overcome the limiting interplay of sound and text, while always relying more heavily on spoken word material, remains in question.

The privileging of the Burroughs text on this record is evident in the resonance of such sound recordings to the events of global theater. Stash Luczkiw, writing in *Italy Weekly* of the beleaguered Prime Minister Silvio Berlusconi, attributes a connection between Burroughs's line, 'Word begets image, and image is virus' (Luczkiw 2003), and the co-opting power of image politics to the Italian media elite. Luczkiw cites a rumor concerning the outlawed Masonic Lodge, Propaganda 2 (P2), and a supposed 1976 document, the 'Plan for Democratic Renewal', detailing an objective 'to gain influence and, ultimately, control over the mass media by infiltrating various newspapers, publishing houses and TV stations'. Significantly, Luczkiw names Berlusconi as a 'former member of P2' (2003), but his essay represents *more* than the political application of Burroughs's paranoiac cosmic-opera ideas.

Applying Burroughs's work to theoretical materials that attempt to explain the metaphorical implications of his prose is certainly a viable critical tactic, yet even casually drawing such conclusions (as Luczkiw does) from a text used in *The Elvis of Letters* does not specifically address the *recorded* nature of the disk. For it is the *material* of the recording, to return to Attali, that puts a unique spin on the replicating inversion of the original/recording relationship within the space of global capital. In order to circumnavigate the trap of 'double resonant' production applied *only* along its single written dimension, we must more precisely trace the relationship between recording and original.

INVERSION II: BURROUGHS CALLED THE LAW CALLED
BURROUGHS

Expanding on Roland Barthes's 'death of the author' in the late-Structuralist moment, Michel Foucault offers a salient conception of the 'author function' that characterizes our second inversion. Foucault traces the history of the 'author function' as born from an alteration of the common cultural notion of the 'author' *preceding* the text that she constructs from the genius of her creative faculty. After demonstrating how the author has indeed become subject to the legal vagaries of advanced capital, including 'ownership' necessitated by the rise of copyright law, Foucault shows how this 'author function' does not precede the text in the same way as the humanist notion of 'Author', but how it assumes a limiting function for the text(s) that it accompanies. The 'author function' becomes a *projection* of the 'operations that we force texts to undergo' (1969:551)—a chimera made real by its own culturally sanctioned image and its ability to reinforce epistemological discursive limits.

As one embodiment of this 'author function' that is complicit with control, Burroughs, the author-cum-counterculture-icon, must somehow intervene *directly* into the milieu of control in order to alter the discursive practices that are 'natural' to the capitalist environment of his production as an 'Author'. This task is not unlike his oft-used comparison for the limits of the space program ('Yes sir, the fish said, I'm just going to shove a little aquarium up onto land there, got everything I need in it' [*PDR* 41]); language, understood as a virus, precipitates its own dissemination in a way that forces a certain limited *meaning* at every juncture. If the solution to this poststructural quandary, as offered in such texts as the 'Academy 23' section of *The Job*, is recourse to *pictorial* associative systems, how can we reconcile Burroughs's work with image/sound as being any more successful than his already circumscribed-by-capital *textual* production?

The key to this 'solution' lies in the second reversal mixed with the first: if recording has become a means to replicate the live act that is now constructed as a facsimile of the recording (Attali), and if the 'author function' is in part an illusory product of copyright-inspired capital transactions of ownership (Foucault), then any disruption must occur in a way that scuttles the efficacy of the signifying chain separating 'original' from 'copy' *while at the same time* destroying the relational mechanisms that authorize such compartmentalization through the function of the 'genius' author or intellect.

EL HOMBRE INVISIBLE

Jesse Bernstein: How do you see the relationship between your public image—there's a William S. Burroughs archetype—your body of work, and yourself, the actual man?
William Burroughs: There is no actual man.
—Jesse Bernstein, 'Criminal Mind'

One of the more interesting sound works of Burroughs's later period is the 1997 remix release version of the classic Material album *Seven Souls* (1989), a sort of unofficial soundtrack to Burroughs's last major novel, *The Western Lands* (1987). Significant to this discussion is the way that the music, along with Burroughs's readings, creates an interplay that moves *beyond* the reliance on written text; as Murphy notes about the track 'The Western Lands', excerpts from different sections of Burroughs's novel have come together in the song (1997:225), creating an orchestrated cut-up at the altar of the mixing table. The final track of both the original and the remix record, 'The End of Words', returns the listener to that assumed connection between the text and its performance, which features 'Middle Eastern scales and overdubbed chants' (Murphy 1997:225), before Burroughs drones through the final passages of *The Western Lands*, including, significantly: 'The old writer couldn't write anymore because he had reached the end of words, the end of what can be done with words. And then?' (*WL* 258)

Expressed as both text and sound versions, this passage is ostensibly the 'same' in each instance, yet the difference between the 'original' written iteration of this passage and its re-articulation on the remix record becomes more than just a refraction of the 'real' world of the text *into* a sound medium. Such movement between mediums is not simply, as the Critical Art Ensemble laments, 'trying to eat soup with soup' (1994:86). Rather, the context has been altered to locate this new articulation, as a *new* expression of the 'double resonance' that exploits Attali's retroversion.

In Attali's conception, the artist originally recorded her work as a way of preserving the live performance. In this case, at first analysis, the live performance of Burroughs's reading would comport, in the straight-ahead style of *Call Me Burroughs*, to the reverse structure that Attali attributes to the pattern of replication typified by advanced capital: Burroughs reads and records the text during a live performance, in order to *preserve* (as per the reversal), through voice, the 'original' written text and any 'original' live performances that presumably preceded its recorded articulation. Significantly, this live performance is recorded.

Yet, with Laswell's band not so much performing a cut-up on the text as radically recontextualizing it, the situation undergoes a subsequent and crucial *re-inversion*: the recording of the spoken word reading, which Laswell uses on his 1989 record, becomes *the original performance* of the aural material (or the articulation that serves as such within the new regime), and the Laswell-produced track 'The End of Words'—a new recording—works in Attali's formula as a way of not merely limiting the new original by reproducing it again, but changing the new original—which is not, of course, the 'real' original—through the *détournement* of its first and only temporary position in a tenuous chain of signification (as an aural copy of the written text, which has been elided from the sound process completely).

For Burroughs's work, the context has now shifted, and his 'end of words' proclamation becomes a prophecy that plays itself out in the inability of that language to fix the 'meaning' of its articulation. Just as Magritte's picture of a pipe is no longer a pipe itself, Burroughs's text about the 'end of words' is no longer a fixed written text that attempts to signify an insoluble concept through appreciable limits, because its recording and subsequent re-situation plays upon Burroughs's own narrative critiques of the insolubility of originality. The recording and mixing process redirects the specter of repetition, so that any relation to the 'original' is not one of only preservation and repetition (as per Attali's reversal), but, potentially, one of evolution.

Still, it may be clear from such an example that Laswell's work, while certainly innovative, is little more than a clever cross-application of the cut-up method to a sound medium, and thus, the new articulation quickly exhausts its apparent insight into the system of replicated reproduction. While manipulations of spoken word texts are by no means legion in the popular arena, enough of this type of activity has been performed that the reader might see the re-signification of Attali's reversal (complicated by Burroughs's own production techniques, discussed earlier) as subject to Frank's cogent analysis of the countercultural myth, or Foucault's notions of the complete penetration of the power apparatus in a society of control. Without discounting these critiques, let us lay down the 'second reversal', that of the 'author function', onto this track.

EL HOMBRE DI-VISIBLE

Recall that Foucault expresses that the 'author function' is born contemporaneously with the text, and is, in fact, the limiting agent to which the text is attributed, a sort of phenomenological enforcer of Burroughs's 'Board Books'. Burroughs's solution, offered throughout his career, might be cited as: 'Equipped now with sound and image track of the control machine [...] I had only to mix the order of recordings and the order of images' (*SM* 92). This possibility is developed in works such as the CD *Break Through in Grey Room* (due to the fact that a text that has as its subject 'recording' is then manipulated as a recording itself), but let us consider the remix of *Seven Souls* for a later iteration of this methodology as a *musical* concept once removed from the 'originating' consciousness of the idea as already developed by Burroughs.

The original 1989 'Soul Killer' track, also a collection of passages from *The Western Lands*, expands upon 'Total Death. Soul Death', the consolidation of energy that occurs in that mummy-controlled 'space' of the Western hegemonic afterlife. From the track: 'Governments fall from sheer indifference. Authority figures, deprived of the vampiric energy they suck off their constituents are seen for what they are: dead, empty masks manipulated by computers. And what is behind the computers? Remote control of course' (*WL* 116). On the most provocative remix from the 1997 record, DJ Terre Thaemlitz's 'Remote Control Mix' of 'Soul Killer', Burroughs's famous dictum that there is 'nothing here now but the recordings' (which also *ends* the 1989 Laswell version) closes with the same warning about the 'recordings': '[T]hey are as radioactive as an old joke' (*WL* 116). The familiar metallic timbre of Burroughs's voice gives way to the distorted soundscape that one reviewer notes 'evok[es] imagery of Morocco or somewhere equally as exotic' (Stoeve 2002). The sonic wasteland is ethereal enough to situate the few remaining and audible Burroughs sounds, no more than quick glitches in time, in a way that implies that the 'author'—the absent Burroughs—has been drowned by the same 'remote control technology' that he conducted an excursus upon in the 1989 recording. From the time of 6:30 to 7:00 on the remix, we hear almost inaudible and certainly defamiliarized fragments of what sounds like Burroughs's voice buried beneath the sands of the engineer's table: 'originally' words in the pages of *The Western Lands* (assuming erroneously but deliberately that typing/scripting is the origination point of language), these words are no longer 'words' at all.

Here we enter the realm that lies submersed beneath the ambient waves of the postmodern musical era, served under the imprimatur of direct noise that one might find on the records Greg Hainge cites in his essay, 'Come on Feel the Noise: Technology and its Dysfunctions in the Music of Sensation', including Reynol's *Blank Tapes* or Francis Lopez's *Paris Hiss* (2002:42–58). In the postindustrial wilderness that closes Thaemlitz's mix, the warning about the 'radioactivity' of the pre-recordings becomes the last completely audible (although manipulated) portion of the track, so that this final desert of the red night not only plays upon the radioactive nature of the 'old jokes'—the old America that contributes to the degeneration of its inhabitants—but also continues the 'double resonance' that infuses the best of Burroughs's spoken word material: remixed almost beyond aural recognition, the spoken word 'text', a mélange of the textual and sonic, a distorted re-recording of a previously manipulated recording of a live performance of a written 'original' (with multiple variations across a history of Burroughs's work) hopelessly spins the Attali equation on its head, but also pushes toward Foucault's vision of the text as no longer constrained by the author function (although Foucault always envisions some form of constraint). We need no longer lament the replication of a recorded text or performance in its live iteration, because all of these categories are problematized by the conflation of the original and the recording. The identity of the 'real' originator Burroughs (while still 'present' on the remix) finds his flickering persona fed into the recording machine in so many iterations, both through his own instrumentation and that of other like-minded collaborators, that it is cut backward and chopped apart until the computer sample of 'his' voice, the recording of a recording, implodes.

Burroughs's 'double resonance' provides a limit, a glass ceiling for him to vibrate toward in an attempt to 'rub out the word', so that it is only with a *soul death, a total death* effectuated—through the use of the recording process that seeks to eliminate his voice from his own descriptive passages—that we can see our way forward to Foucault's vision of a future without the 'author function'. Foucault's future is founded *not* upon a reversal that allows the 'author' to *again* precede the 'text', but with an acknowledgement of the signifying limits of the author that accelerate the evolutionary changes, suggesting, like Burroughs's buried and distorted clicks at the end of the 'Soul Killer' remix, that: 'All discourses, whatever their status, form, value, and whatever the treatment to which they will be subjected, would then develop in the anonymity of a murmur' (Foucault 1969:558). Listen as closely as you like to the Thaemlitz track's final minutes, between 6:30 and 6:50; rewind and replay as often as you can; wear noise-canceling headphones to better preserve the snippets of deconstructed Burroughs that pass through your ears—and you will still hear only the murmur of standard narrative intelligibility.

(IN)FLEXIBLE AUTHORITY

This murmur is an apt metaphor in its ethereality—in its ambivalence between presence and absence—to bring us toward closure. N. Katherine Hayles, upon listening to *Nothing Here Now But the Recordings*, expresses the disjunction between the 'explanatory' prose segments on sound manipulation and the practical application of the method: 'I found the recording less forceful as a demonstration of Burroughs's theories than his writing. For me, the aurality of his prose elicits a greater response than the machine productions it describes and instantiates' (Hayles 1999:216). Significantly, Hayles's analysis also identifies the danger of Burroughs's sound experiments to 'constitute a parasitic monologue' if not 'self-disrupted' (215) by manipulations that might counteract the trap of language—so that sound can be expanded to not only echo the sounds of the body (an internal engine), but in its self-deconstruction, become an external mechanism that produces 'a new kind of subjectivity that strikes at the deepest levels of awareness' (220). Elsewhere is this collection, Anthony Enns attends to Hayles's critique through the primacy of Burroughs's use of the typewriter, yet we must also consider her hesitancy to embrace Burroughs's sound recordings as a reminder of the difficulty in escaping the parasitism of the control machine that feeds on the iconic image.

This brief reading of Burroughs's sound-related projects cannot possibly approach an exhaustive study, nor can it imply that such current sound production will actually *produce* Hayles's new subjectivity, because in many ways the works of contemporary musicians/ sound performers, no matter how seemingly 'revolutionary', exist in a different cultural location than once-'obscene' texts such as *Naked Lunch*. Great gains have been made for provocative aesthetics; while I never read Burroughs as a student, his work routinely finds a place on my syllabus as a professor, representing a local manifestation of Kathy Acker's statement that 'we are living in the world of Burroughs's novels' (1997:3). Even though we might now simply view a picture of Burroughs holding court with Kim Gordon and Michael Stipe, or hear socially conscious rock band Radiohead sample lead singer Thom Yorke's live voice for immediate playback during performances of 'Everything in the Right Place' (an application of 'Burroughsian' principles), we must still force ourselves to reconcile the overwhelming persona of the speaker against the cult of the image that dilutes its message, while simultaneously applying the same concerns to the medium. Perhaps, as both Attali and Hainge suggest, the solution can be found in the productive power of noise, because 'in its limited appeal [...] the Noise genre subverts the relationship between product and demand in the age or repetition and mass consumerism' (Hainge 2002:56).

The inherent problem of such pronouncements is that the control machine also listens to its own noises—and it never hesitates to engage in playback. During the 'psyops' (psychological operations) phase of the 2003 Iraq war, the US military followed Burroughs's admonition in 'Electronic Revolution' to use sound as *'a front line weapon to produce and escalate riots'* (now in *Job* 175): 'The military also uses the recordings during tank assaults as "force multipliers", sound effects to make the enemy think the forces are larger than they actually are' (Leinwand 2003).

Burroughs would advocate fighting fire with a *recording* of fire, and while even the recent rise of file sharing protocols might create conditions (in the separation of recording from corporate ownership) to cut the association lines of the mass media, the fact that we cannot eat soup with soup also argues for constant vigilance against the corporate and commercial forces. If the cop not only needs the criminal, but also *is* the criminal, we must also see the dominant culture's ability to absorb the ideologically 'resistant' as the key to the 'double resonance' of Burroughs's sound projects. Senator Orrin Hatch, himself a musician of the patriotic/religious variety, recently advocated integrating viruses into Internet downloads to damage file sharing culprits, which, in Hatch's words, 'may be the only way you can teach somebody about copyrights' (Bridis 2003:2B).

If the corporate body can literally consume everything it tastes, there is no sense in hiding the food. Instead, Burroughs's position must be fed into the machine in so many ways, from so many coordinate points, that not only will that position overwhelm the machine on the subliminal level, but the machine will be fundamentally changed so that it no longer recognizes a *source* for the recordings at all. The best way to put Burroughs's concepts to use may be to get rid of 'Burroughs' altogether.

And at the same time, we must make of ourselves a meal.

REFERENCES

Acker, K. (1990) 'William Burroughs's Realism', IN *Bodies of Work: Essays* (London: Serpent's Tail, 1997), pp. 1–5.

Attali, J. (1977) *Noise: The Political Economy of Music*. Theory and History of Literature, vol. 16, Massumi, B. trans. (Minneapolis, University of Minnesota Press, 1985).

Bernstein, J. (1988) 'Criminal Mind,' IN Lotringer, S. 2001, pp. 707–10.

Bridis, T. (2003) 'Senator favors really punishing music thieves', *Chicago Tribune*, 18 June 2B.

Critical Art Ensemble (1994) *The Electronic Disturbance* (Brooklyn: Autonomedia).

Foucault, M. (1969) 'What is an Author?', IN Kaplan, C., and Anderson, W. D. eds, *Criticism: Major Statements* (Boston: Bedford/St Martins, 2000), pp. 544–58.

Frank, T. (1997) *The Conquest of Cool: Business Culture, Counterculture, and the Rise of Hip Consumerism* (Chicago: University of Chicago Press).

Hainge, G. (2002) 'Come on Feel the Noise: Technology and its Dysfunctions in the Music of Sensation', *to the QUICK* 5, pp. 42–58.

Hardt, M., and Negri, A. (2000) *Empire* (Cambridge, MA: Harvard University Press).

Hayles, N. K. (1999) *How We Became Posthuman: Virtual Bodies in Cybernetics, Literature, and Informatics* (Chicago: University of Chicago Press).

Irving, W. (1819) 'The Author's Account of Himself', IN Baym, N. et al. eds, *The Norton Anthology of American Literature*, 3rd edition, vol. 1 (New York: Norton, 1989), pp. 808–10.

Klein, N. (2000) *No Logo*, first rev. edition (New York: Picador, 2002).

Leinwand, D. (12 February 2003) 'U.S. Forces drop propaganda bombs on Iraq', *USA TODAY*, <http://www.usatoday.com/news/world/iraq/2003-02-12-psyops_usat_x.htm> (16 June 2003).

Lotringer, S. ed. (2001) *Burroughs Live: The Collected Interviews of William S. Burroughs 1960–1997* (USA: Semiotext[e]).

Luckman, S., and Redden, G. (2001) 'The Sense of Translocal Community: Mediating S11', *to the QUICK* 4, pp. 21–34.

Luczkiw, S. (6 June 2003) 'The "forza" in Forza Italia', *Italy Weekly*, <http://www.italydaily.it/Comment/2003/Giungo/6_6.shtml> (13 June 2003).

Master Musicians of Jajouka Featuring Bachir Attar (1992) *Apocalypse Across the Sky* [Axiom Records, 314-410 857-2].

Material (1989) *Seven Souls* [USA: Triloka Records, remix/reissue 1997].

Miles, B. (1992) *William Burroughs: El Hombre Invisible*, rev. and updated edition (UK: Virgin, 2002).

Murphy, T. S. (1997) *Wising Up the Marks: The Amodern William Burroughs* (Berkeley: University of California Press).

Russell, J. (2001) *Queer Burroughs* (New York: Palgrave).

Sobieszek, R. A. (1996) *Ports of Entry: William S. Burroughs and the Arts* (Los Angeles County Museum of Art/Thames and Hudson).

Stoeve, H. (2002) Review of *Seven Souls* (Remix), <http://www.silent-watcher.net/billlaswell/discography/material/sevensouls.html> (7 June 2003).

Walker, D. ed. (1968) *Rights in Conflict: The Violent Confrontation of Demonstrators and Police in the Parks and Streets of Chicago During the Week of the Democratic National Convention* (USA: Bantam Books).

Zivancevic, N. (1981) 'Life in Space,' IN Lotringer, S. 2001, pp. 522–5.

10
Guerilla Conditions:
Burroughs, Gysin and Balch
Go to the Movies

Jamie Russell

'Remember i was the movies'

—Mr Bradly Mr Martin (*TE* 201)

In the week of 10 September 2001, a rare screening of one of William S. Burroughs's experimental short films from the 1960s was planned in the arts cinema of the World Trade Center in downtown New York. The subject of the film was a fantastic guerilla assault—led by William S. Burroughs wearing a gas mask and combat fatigues—on the forces of twentieth-century capitalism. Somewhat presciently, the title of this eleven-minute slice of avant-garde cinema was *Towers Open Fire*. After two hijacked airplanes flown by Muslim fundamentalist terrorists hit the World Trade Center's Twin Towers on the morning of 11 September, the screening was cancelled indefinitely (Dannatt 2002).

A firm believer in the precognitive potential of art—especially his own cut-up texts—in predicting future events and catastrophes, Burroughs would doubtlessly have raised a brief, wry smile at the coincidence that led his 28-year-old film to be showing in New York during that tragic week in the city's history.

He might also, it seems fair to speculate, have been concerned by the new global order that has since risen out of the ashes of the World Trade Center. A staunch critic of America's fluctuating social and political landscape, Burroughs regularly complained that his native land was transforming itself into an authoritarian regime. In the light of the present global order, it's difficult not to believe that many of Burroughs's worst fears have been realized.

Surveying the reality of the New American Century—from the 'illegal combatants' held in Guantanamo Bay to the military attacks on Afghanistan and Iraq, mainstream discussions of torture as a

161

viable means of preventing future terrorist strikes, police brutality against anti-war demonstrators during the Iraq conflict, and the continuing demonization of drug users (propped up by the suggestion that recreational drug use funds terrorism)—it seems that the totalitarian police state Burroughs so often warned us about is becoming an ever more likely (global) reality. As the paranoiac has become a prophet, any who deviate from the anti-terrorist line are wont to come under suspicion of being terrorists themselves.

Burroughs perhaps more than most. Given his antagonistic stance toward authority, Burroughs's brand of subversion would undoubtedly receive short shrift in today's world. After all, from his fantastic visions of armed, gay insurrection against the heterosexual dominant to his sympathetic discussion of Timothy McVeigh, the Oklahoma Bomber (*LW* 241), Burroughs's attitude toward terrorism has always been a bloody-minded affront to politically correct liberalism.

Of course, none of this is likely to be surprising to anyone familiar with Burroughs's post-*Naked Lunch* work. Throughout the 1960s and 1970s, during the time of the Nova trilogy and Wild Boy novels, Burroughs was obsessed with fantasies of guerilla resistance and armed insurrection against the white, heterosexual, capitalist dominant. Indeed, by advocating at various times the use of the cut-up method, Scientology, recreational drugs, the dream machine, tape recorder experiments and gay sex as interlinked tools for challenging the dominant, Burroughs's work of this period could be read as a call to arms, a revolutionary how-to manual that veers between the fantastic (sex magic) and the outlandishly practical (using tape recorders and sound systems to disorientate riot police).

Such fantasies were not simply restricted to the literary sphere, however. Toying with the gadgets of hi-tech revolutionary practice, Burroughs's experiments with tape recorders, sound systems and film became important additions to his novels' vision of guerilla revolt. Of all these extra-literary activities, though, it was the cinematic shorts he made during the 1960s with the help of British commercials director Antony Balch as well as long-time friend and collaborator Brion Gysin that would form an integral part of Burroughs's guerilla project. In these films—*Towers Open Fire* (1963), *The Cut Ups* (aka *Cut-ups and Cut-Ups* 1967), *William Buys a Parrot* (1963), *Ghosts at Number 9* (1963/1967–82), and *Bill and Tony* (circa 1972)—Burroughs not only challenged conventional modes of cinematic representation, but launched a 'terror' attack on his audience, offering a cinematic shock therapy that would 'Wise up all the marks everywhere Show them the rigged wheel—Storm the Reality Studio and retake the universe' (*SM* 151).

In this chapter, I want to highlight the extent of this terror attack, its motivation, execution and aims. What seems particularly interesting about this project is the way in which it dovetails not only with the revolutionary ideas of some of Burroughs's contemporaries, but also with some current critical theorists' understanding of the symbolic importance of the attack on the World Trade Center on 9/11.

As philosophers such as Slavoj Žižek and Jean Baudrillard attest, the post-9/11 world is one in which the spectacular effects of Hollywood and the American mass media have become increasingly obvious facets of globalized control. In an age in which the US entertainment industry has become a global phenomenon and where, as Nathan Gardells claims, 'MTV has gone where the CIA could never penetrate' (2002:2–3), the guerilla conditions that Burroughs, Gysin and Balch's experimental cinema outlined in the 1960s might well be more important than ever before in alerting us to the realities of the new global order and teaching us how to resist it.

WILL HOLLYWOOD NEVER LEARN?

In *Empire*, their wide-ranging discussion of the new political order of globalization, Michael Hardt and Antonio Negri claim that the imperialist global hierarchy of the twenty-first century is one in which

> the liberatory potential of the postmodernist and postcolonial discourses that we have described only resonates with the situation of an elite population that enjoys certain rights, a certain level of wealth, and a certain position in the global hierarchy [...] The real revolutionary practice refers to the level of *production*. Truth will not make us free, but taking control of the production of truth will. (2000:156)

Burroughs, a writer whose inherent essentialism has always made him a poor postmodernist at the best of times, would certainly agree. After all, the guerilla action that his novels and non-fiction writing advocate is one that always attacks the dominant's production of truth. Whether styling the source of our enslavement as the word, the image, compulsory heterosexuality, the media, or the battle between the sexes, Burroughs's sci-fi fantasies consistently allow for the possibility of grappling with the centralized forces of power head-on so as to subvert their aims and methods for the partisan cause.

In this respect, cinema has always had an important position in Burroughs's work as a symbol of word/image control. In *The Ticket that Exploded*, Burroughs makes this quite explicit:

> You are to infiltrate, sabotage and cut communications—Once machine lines are cut the enemy is helpless—They depend on elaborate installations difficult to move or conceal—encephalographic and calculating machines film and TV studios, batteries of tape recorders—Remember you do not have to organize similar installations but merely to put enemy installations out of action or take them over—A camera and two tape recorders can cut the lines laid down by a fully equipped film studio [...] And always remember that you are operating under conditions of guerrilla war—Never attempt to hold a position under massive counterattack. (*TE* 111)

In a novel dominated by Hollywood metaphors—the opening passage 'see the action, B.J.?' is styled as a film pitch (*TE* 1–6) and the prose is frequently interrupted by *'Bulletin[s] from the Rewrite Department'* (*TE* 84)—Burroughs argues that the American movie industry is duping the world's population, stiffing us all with a 'Reality Con' concocted by a 'Grade B Hollywood who couldn't get their dead nitrous film foot in the door' (*TE* 137). This is the 'ticket' referred to in the novel's title, a movie theater ticket offering admission to a bankrupt reality that has become so untenable in its blatant deceptions that it is about to explode:

> The film stock issued now isn't worth the celluloid it's printed on. There is nothing to back it up. The film bank is empty. To conceal the bankruptcy of the reality studio it is essential that no one should be in a position to set up another reality set. The reality film has now become an instrument and weapon of monopoly. The full weight of the film is directed against anyone who calls the film in question [...] Work for the reality studio or else. Or else you will find out how it feels to be *outside the film*. (*TE* 151)

Presenting Hollywood as part of a global conspiracy that seeks to pacify the citizens of the world in order to control them, Burroughs is quite explicit about the ways in which this illusionary spectacle is a product of corporate capitalism: 'In three-dimensional terms the board is a group representing international big money who intend to take over and monopolize space [...] The board books are written in symbols referring to association blocks—Like this: $ ... %' (*TE* 139). The only possible response to such a situation, Burroughs argues, is to launch a strike against the film itself, storm the reality studio and reclaim the production of truth for ourselves.

In many respects, Burroughs's cinematic experiments with Balch and Gysin can be read as a literal enactment of this strategy. Grasping the nettle of film production, Burroughs sought to challenge the monopoly of the image, wrestling the production of truth from the dominant in order to reveal the spectacular nature of the reality film. No wonder, then, that the working title for this revolutionary cinematic project was 'Guerilla Conditions'; Burroughs, Balch and Gysin clearly envisaged themselves as a group of partisans—even terrorists—intent on upsetting the status quo, using film itself as their principal weapon in a radical act of Situationist-style *détournement*.

In *Towers Open Fire* (1963), this attack on the reality studio becomes an integral part of the narrative as an unnamed guerilla commander (played by Burroughs) leads an assault on the Board and its manipulative chairman (also played by Burroughs, suggesting the inescapable duality of power/resistance). The aim of the guerillas is to loosen the Board's all-controlling grip on the world economy and—perhaps more importantly—to disrupt their broadcasting system long enough to expose the spectacle for exactly what it is: a spectacle.

Marrying form to content, the non-linear structure of the film is a reflection of the guerilla war that is being waged against the reality studio. As the guerillas disrupt the Board's control, the film's world and the film itself are thrown into chaos, with flickering bursts of static and disjointed editing suggesting the impending collapse of the spectacle, as if, at any moment, the reality film's movie ticket might literally explode. Making the spectacle untenable through their aggressive actions, the guerillas storm the reality studio and force the broadcasting towers to open fire, turning them back on the Board themselves. The film stutters and flickers as the guerilla attack reaches its zenith, and the Board members disappear in a haze of static as if they were nothing more than insubstantial ghosts made real through some kind of sinister projection technology. The reality studio has been overrun; a jubilant young man (played by Michael

Portman) celebrates by dancing an impromptu jig outside of a symbol of the Board's power (a Rex cinema). But as the sky fills with a mass of blue dots (hand painted onto each frame of each print of the film by Balch), such celebration proves premature; the Board have returned with a new weapon ... color film.

With its denigration of what Burroughs's voiceover calls the 'two-bit narrative line from Walgreens', the cut-up structure of *Towers Open Fire* is an affront to the conventions of linear (Hollywood) narrative. As such, it has often been read in relation to the avant-garde cinema of the 1960s that was growing on both sides of the Atlantic. However, to read *Towers Open Fire* simply as a counterpart to the work of American avant-garde filmmakers such as Stan Brakhage or Jonas Mekas, or to Beat-influenced cinema such as Robert Frank and Alfred Leslie's *Pull My Daisy* (1959), would be a mistake, for although there are clear points of historical and aesthetic convergence (Burroughs's use of flicker effects bears comparison with the stroboscopic, headache-inducing visuals of Tony Conrad's legendary *The Flicker* [1966]), *Towers Open Fire*'s aims go far beyond those of the New York underground or London Filmmakers Co-op. Foregrounding many of the ideas expounded in *The Ticket that Exploded* about the spectacular nature of capitalist society and the ways in which the reality film is manipulated by (and for the benefit of) the dominant, *Towers Open Fire* actually owes more to the Situationists than the avant-garde filmmakers of the 1960s, in particular the Debordian vision of 'The Society of the Spectacle'.

As Timothy S. Murphy insightfully argues elsewhere in this volume in his chapter 'Exposing the Reality Film: William S. Burroughs Among the Situationists', Burroughs was certainly aware of the work of the Situationist International and was doubtlessly influenced by the theories of Debord while planning his resistance to the reality film. Given that the author was an intermittent resident in Paris during the 1950s and 1960s and had several meetings with Letterist provocateur Isidore Isou (Hussey 2002:36–7), it seems plausible that he may also have been familiar with Isou's obsession with a cinema that would, as Debord's biographer Andrew Hussey puts it, 'wreck reality and unleash pure subjective vision on the world' (2002:37). Whether Burroughs was familiar with Debord's foray into cinema, *Hurlements en faveur de Sade* (*Howling in Favour of Sade* [1952])—a flickering alternation of empty white and black screens—is a moot point, but it is interesting to note that it pre-empted Burroughs's own appreciation of flicker effects by several years.

The Situationist comparison that Murphy explicates seems additionally apparent if we consider what makes *Towers Open Fire* so distinctive from its American and British avant-garde counterparts: the way in which it marries its science fiction trappings to a critique of capital. One of the film's key sequences involves recycled Pathé newsreel footage of the 1929 Wall Street Crash, used to suggest that the Board hold a power over the economics of capitalism. In forcing the collapse of the stock exchange for their own ends, the real conspiracy of the Board is far removed from the magical, science fiction back-story Burroughs gives it; it's actually as banal as currency, exchange and capital. The guerilla attack enacted within the film is one that seeks to smash not only the Board, but also the whole capitalist spectacle that it supports.

In *The Cut-Ups* (1967), this idea is taken much further. Eschewing the science fiction elements of *Towers Open Fire*, the film doesn't so much present the guerilla attack as part of its action, as it *becomes* such an attack in and of itself. The aim is less to fantasize the revolution than to actually, on the level of cinematic representation and audience reception, induce revolution (much as one might induce an epileptic fit) through the use of the cut-up method.

Unlike *Towers Open Fire*, *The Cut-Ups* (as its title implies) faithfully adheres to the principles of the cut-up technique. Dividing the original negative into four sections and then cutting each section into foot-long strips of celluloid, Balch 'hired an editor to perform the mechanical task of taking one foot of film from each roll (1-2-3-4). The one-foot sections were joined in consecutive and repeated 1-2-3-4 fashion' (Friedberg 1979:173). Meanwhile, the soundtrack was comprised of four sentences from a Scientology processing routine— 'Yes. Hello'; 'Look at this picture'; 'Does it seem to be persisting?'; 'Good. Thank you'—read by Burroughs, Gysin and Ian Sommerville at different speeds. The result was a disjointed film that went far beyond even the confusing non-linear efforts of *Towers Open Fire*.

Despite the complexities of this structural experimentation, *The Cut-Ups* still pursues much the same aim as *Towers Open Fire*, but is far more explicit in identifying the links between the reality film and global, corporate capital. A significant portion of the film follows Burroughs in Times Square, thus setting the action against a background of American consumerism. Advertising hoardings (from Coca-Cola to Camel cigarettes) are shown in a series of close-ups, while other sections of the film foreground Hollywood cinema (there are several shots of movie theaters showing films like Russ

Meyer's *Lorna*, the James Bond movie *Goldfinger* and the Jack Lemmon vehicle *Good Neighbor Sam*).

Highlighting the socioeconomic forces that maintain the reality film, in particular the links between Hollywood cinema and advertising (a facet of consumer capitalism already hinted at in Burroughs's distrust of the 'two-bit narrative line from Walgreens'), *The Cut-Ups* asks us to acknowledge the way in which cinema is an integral part of the spectacle (there was of course a certain irony in having Balch, a former commercials director turned film distributor and exhibitor, lead such an attack).

The intent of *The Cut-Ups* is demystification through deconditioning. As the soundtrack's repetitive voiceover suggests, the aim of *The Cut-Ups* is to make us 'Look at this picture' afresh. It's a multifaceted request, since we end up looking not only at the pictures within the film (advertising hoardings, billboards, Gysin's paintings), but also the picture the film offers us of the subliminal impact of mass capitalism's marketing strategies. Only through demystifying the process that maintains the spectacle will it be possible for us to storm the reality studio and free ourselves from its influence for good. That, at least, was the theory. For the majority of the original audiences who encountered *Towers Open Fire* and *The Cut-Ups* in the 1960s (often with little or no knowledge of Burroughs's work), these films were not far short of cinematic terrorism. On the films' initial release in London, Balch took great delight in watching whole auditoriums full of middle-class cinemagoers flee toward the exit while he gleefully proclaimed: 'It shows we're really getting to them!' (*Sight & Sound* 1980:143).

Getting to them was definitely one of the primary aims of these cinematic events, which is why the filmmakers exploited Balch's position within London's film community—in particular his contacts among distributors and exhibitors—to ensure that both films had a more mainstream release than they would have normally received. As a result, *Towers Open Fire* and *The Cut-Ups* were screened not to the niche audiences of the underground film circuit or the London Filmmakers Co-Op but to white, bourgeois cinema patrons who had little idea what they were about to be confronted with.

When *Towers Open Fire* and *The Cut-Ups* were shown at The Academy cinema on Oxford Street in London, Gysin claims that the

> moviehouse finally asked if we could please take them off the screen
> because they had such a high incidence of people forgetting really

strange things in the theater. There were more ladies who had left their handbags or their pants or their umbrellas or their shoes—an extraordinary number of unbelievable objects that they had never seen left behind before. (Cantrill 1984:41)

According to Balch, the films' ability to cause psychological distress was near-impossible to define. 'People would come rushing out of the audience saying "It's disgusting", to which the staff would reply, "It's got a U certificate, nothing the censor objected to, what are you objecting to?" Half the audience would love it and half would hate it, women would be sitting there with their heads in their hands having headaches' (1972:14).

No wonder, then, that such terrorist cinema received short shrift from the critics, the censors and even the avant-garde practitioners themselves. In England, respected cinema journal *The Monthly Film Bulletin* dismissed *The Cut-Ups* out of hand, claiming that '[t]he point of the film is not immediately apparent [...] But the effect is to induce a progressive boredom', concluding, 'we are left with a cinematic *reductio ad absurdum*, a mechanical and quite pointless exercise' (*Monthly Film Bulletin* 1968:62). The journal's critics were less scathing about *Towers Open Fire*, claiming: 'Technically the film is highly confident, and it does have pace, a quality on the whole lacking from the products of the current American avant-garde' (*Monthly Film Bulletin* 1963:123).

Although initially caught unawares by the films' power, the censors eventually rectified their mistake as *Towers Open Fire* became unique in the history of British film censorship as the only film ever to have been passed for a general release and then reclassified with an 'X' certificate (synonymous with pornography) in 1975 (Rayns 1975:13). For Gysin, though, the surest sign of the project's disastrous success was when the New York art scene decided that each of these filmmakers was to be treated as *persona non grata*:

The whole New York art *establishment*, including Jonas Mekas, didn't want us, right from the start [...] We arrived with a heavy aura of reputation which nobody wanted to have anything to do with [...] They thought that both William and I were very dangerous. William particularly dangerous. (Cantrill 1984:42)

Being 'dangerous' was, of course, an integral part of Burroughs's self-mythology. Yet, it was also integral to the cinematic project that he,

Balch and Gysin undertook throughout the 1960s. More self-consciously obsessed with upsetting and confronting their audiences on a psychological level than other avant-garde filmmakers of the period, Burroughs and his collaborators would be happy only with a radical rupture of both cinematic representation and the audience's bourgeois faith in the same. More radical and energetic than Warhol's languorous single shots and less romanticized than Brakhage's films, these shorts were part of a carefully planned assault on 1960s cinema and its audience, an attempt to alert them to the pernicious influence of the capitalist spectacle through violent, cinematic rupture.

THE DESERT OF THE REAL

Four decades after they were first conceived, scripted and shot, Burroughs's cinematic collaborations still occupy a marginal position, both in the artist's own catalogue of work and in the history of avant-garde cinema. Neither appropriated into the mainstream under the 'Beat' banner that saw *Pull My Daisy* canonized alongside *On the Road* and *Howl*, nor critically regarded enough to be placed alongside the work of Warhol, Brakhage, Smith and Mekas as key texts of the 1960s avant-garde, the films have remained poised on the brink of obscurity. Indeed, after Balch's death in 1980, the original negatives of many of the Burroughs–Balch–Gysin collaborations were so disregarded that they were very nearly thrown onto the scrapheap—quite literally—and were only saved by the timely archival intervention of Genesis P-Orridge (Sargeant 1997: 187–8).

Yet in many respects, the films' attempt to expose the spectacular nature of capitalist reality through violent intervention now seems eerily prescient, as Burroughs's vision of the omnipresent reality studio has found an unexpected currency in post-9/11 discussions of the contemporary world order.

In his book *Welcome to the Desert of the Real!*, philosopher Slavoj Žižek meditates on the importance of the World Trade Center attacks. Writing to mark the first anniversary of 9/11, Žižek suggests that the goal of fundamentalist terror is 'to awaken us, western citizens, from our numbness, from immersion in our everyday ideological universe' (2002:9). As an expression of what Žižek calls 'the passion for the Real' (2002:9), such acts of terror are designed to shatter the 'insulated artificial universe' (33) of the First World through an act of violent, murderous rupture:

> It was before the WTC collapse that we lived in our reality, perceiving Third World horrors as something which was not actually part of our social reality, as something which existed (for us) as a spectral apparition on the (TV) screen—and what happened on September 11 was that this fantasmatic screen apparition entered our reality. (Žižek 2002:16)

The 'spectacular effect' of the attacks was—in Žižek's reading of the events of 9/11—more important to the terrorists than the actual 'material damage' (2002:11). The aim was to induce 'shock and awe' on an unprecedented scale in American history and thus drag the First World out of its insulated reality where Third World discontent and suffering are strictly virtual occurrences. Only through shattering the dominant's system of symbolic exchange, its spectacular hold over its citizenry, could the spectacle and the reality film be overturned. It is an argument that has found increasing currency among critical theorists. Jean Baudrillard, for instance, has suggested that, for the terrorists of 9/11, 'the tactic is to bring about an excess of reality, and have the system collapse beneath that excess of reality' (Baudrillard 2002:18). As he goes on to argue, such terrorism has subverted the spectacle for its own ends:

> We have to face facts, and accept that a new terrorism has come into being, a new form of action which plays the game [...] solely with the aim of disrupting it [...] [The terrorists] have taken over all the weapons of the dominant power. Money and stock-market speculation, computer technology and aeronautics, spectacle and the media networks—they have assimilated everything of modernity and globalism, without changing their goal, which is to destroy that power. (Baudrillard 2002:19)

So, in comparison with the Gulf War, a spectacular non-event (a war which, as Baudrillard famously remarked, never happened), the terrorist seeks to make the unreal real, bringing Žižek's 'fantasmatic screen apparition' into our reality by making it shockingly concrete.

As a result of this disruption of the symbolic sphere, these critical theorists have turned their attention on the unreality of the spectacle and, in particular, on the way in which it is mediated through Hollywood. Žižek is perhaps the chief proponent of this, and what is so fascinating about his discussion with regard to Burroughs's resistance to the reality film in the 1960s is his obsession with the role of cinema in creating this 'insulated' world. Taking the title of his book from a line spoken in *The Matrix* (1999)—a science fiction blockbuster in which a small band of partisan fighters wage a guerilla war against a computer-generated virtual reality which has enslaved the human race in a spectacle of epic proportions—Žižek goes on to trace the intersection of contemporary Hollywood, terrorism and the spectacle:

> So it is not only that Hollywood stages a semblance of real life deprived of the weight and inertia of materiality—in late-capitalist consumerist society, 'real social life' itself somehow acquires the features of a staged fake, with our neighbours behaving in 'real' life like stage actors and extras [...] Again, the ultimate truth of the capitalist utilitarian despiritualized universe is the dematerialization of 'real life' itself, its reversal into a spectral show. (2002:13–14)

Faced with such a spectral show, the terrorist seeks to break the insulation of the fake through an excess of the real, using the systems of the dominant against the spectacle itself. The similarities between this and Burroughs's own understanding of the reality film seem patently clear.

Given the intersection of film, politics and terror, it's perhaps fitting that the last word should belong to American film critic John Patterson. Writing in *The Guardian* newspaper at the height of the war in Iraq, Patterson invoked Burroughs and *The Ticket that Exploded* to comment on the spectacular, 'Hollywoodized' nature of the war:

> The entire war is starting to resemble some huge, unwieldy international co-production that is spinning financially out of control at its distant location shoot, where hostile conditions hold sway, the cameras keep jamming and the catering table offers only dried-out olives and braised goat hooves, all washed down with a mug of hot sand [...] Think of George Bush as the lean young studio head back at Pentagon Pictures, urging Rummy, his embattled but allegedly visionary chief of production, to bring back a money-spinning hit if he wants to hold on to that posh corner office suite. Imagine Franks as James Cameron making *Titanic* or Michael Cimino making *Heaven's Gate* (with less

success—remember bankrupt United Artists, then imagine a bankrupt United States), sending the studio's investors and shareholders into conniptions with his spiraling budgets and wanton disregard for his screenwriters. (Patterson 2003:1)

This vision of embattled producers struggling to keep the reality film together is overtly Burroughsian, something Patterson explicitly acknowledges in his concluding paragraphs, where he quotes a section from Burroughs's novel *The Ticket that Exploded*, adding his own gloss:

The film bank is empty. To conceal the bankruptcy of the reality studio it is essential that no one should be in a position to set up another reality set [Boom! There goes Al-Jazeera, decoupled from the New York Stock Exchange, then bombed for good measure.] The reality film has now become a weapon and instrument of monopoly. The full weight of the film is directed against anyone who calls the film itself into question [...] Work for the reality studio or else. (Patterson 2003:1)

As he concludes, 'Talk about the movie-ticket that exploded in our faces. Burroughs wrote that in 1964. Whoever said the old reprobate was paranoid? It sounds like tomorrow's news. Or maybe the day after' (Patterson 2003:1).

With each passing day, though, the spectacle grows and the opposition against it becomes more desperate. Trapped between spectacular deception and murderous violence, the libertarian aims of Burroughs's fantastic cinematic vision of resistance seem both quaintly utopian and frighteningly accurate:

'You see the action, B.J.? All these patrols cut off light-years behind enemy lines trying to get through to some fat-assed gum-chewing, comic-reading Technical Sergeant to Base Headquarters and there is no Base Headquarters everything is coming apart like a rotten undervest . . but the show goes on . . love . . romance . . stories that rip your heart out and eat it . . Now how's this for an angle? Are you listening B.J.?' (*TE* 6)

If, as Burroughs claims, this 'reality film is the dreariest entertainment ever presented to a captive audience' (*TE* 150), perhaps the world needs a new film pitch: see the action Dubya?

REFERENCES

Balch, A. (1972) 'Antony Balch Interview: Break Through in the Grey Room Towers Open Fire', *Cinema Rising* (1)1, pp. 10–14.
Baudrillard, J. (2002) *The Spirit of Terrorism and Requiem for the Twin Towers* (London: Verso).
Burroughs, W. S., and Balch, A. (1990) *Towers Open Fire and Other Short Films*, Mystic Fire Video [video: VHS].
Cantrill, A. (1984) 'An Interview with Brion Gysin on the Films *Towers Open Fire* and *Cut Ups*', *Cantrills Filmnotes* (43)44, pp. 38–42.
Dannatt, A. (2002) 'Art is Not the Only Thing', *The Art Newspaper*, <www.theartnewspaper.com>.
Friedberg, A. (1979) ' "Cut-Ups": A *Syn*ema of the Text', IN Skerl, J., and Lydenberg, R. eds, *William S. Burroughs At the Front: Critical Reception, 1959–1989* (Carbondale: Southern Illinois University Press, 1991), pp. 169–73.
Gardells, N. (2002) 'From Containment to Entertainment: The Rise of the Media-Industrial Complex', *New Perspectives Quarterly* (15)5, pp. 2–3.
Hardt, M., and Negri, A. (2000) *Empire* (London: Harvard University Press).
Hussey, A. (2002) *The Game of War: The Life and Death of Guy Debord* (London: Pimlico).
Monthly Film Bulletin (1963) 'Review of *Towers Open Fire*', *Monthly Film Bulletin* (30)355, p. 123.
Monthly Film Bulletin (1968) 'Review of *The Cut Ups*', *Monthly Film Bulletin* (35)411, p. 62.
Patterson, J. (2003) 'Pentagon Pictures Present', *The Guardian*, 11 April 2003, p. 1.
Rayns, T. (1975) 'Fear and Loathing in the Cinema', *Time Out* 278, pp. 10–13.
Sargeant, J. (1997) *Naked Lens: Beat Cinema* (London: Creation).
Sight & Sound (1980) 'Antony Balch Obituary', *Sight & Sound* (49)3, p. 143.
Žižek, S. (2002) *Welcome to the Desert of the Real!: Five Essays on September 11 and Related Dates* (London: Verso).

11
Cutting up Politics

Oliver Harris

Certain things you must take literally if you want to understand.
—William S. Burroughs (*3M* 133)

IT IS IMPOSSIBLE TO ESTIMATE THE DAMAGE

The first line of the 'First Cut-Ups' published in *Minutes to Go* (1960) was, according to Brion Gysin, 'a readymade phrase that simply dropped onto the table; several layers of printed material were laid one on top of the other and cut through with the Stanley blade', and when he put these pieces together, Gysin laughed out loud 'because the answers were so apt and so extraordinary' (Gysin and Wilson 1982:56). Answers presume *questions*; but in this material practice the order of causality and chronology has to be reversed. Magically, the cut-up text answered Gysin precisely by revealing to him his own question—that is to say: *What will be the effect of the cut-up project?* Four decades later, the reply he received at the supposed moment of the project's inception,[1] courtesy of his Stanley blade, may still stand: 'It is impossible to estimate the damage' (*MTG* 6).

Although the temptation to generalize is a basic error—to speak of 'the cut-up' is to falsify the great range of cut-up procedures, the enormous variety of texts they produced, and the multiplicity of purposes they served, all of which varied over time—this original cut-up is, in its equivocal potency, exemplary. On the one hand, it prophesizes the very powers of prophecy that Burroughs would almost immediately claim for the method;[2] on the other, it predicts the very impossibility of predicting the exact outcome of individual cut-up operations or of definitively measuring the efficacy of the project as a whole. Simultaneously, it promises that the method works—in unspecified destructive ways—and yet creates that meaning only in hindsight and only as an open question. When Burroughs looked back on that 'hectic, portentous time in Paris, in

175

1959' toward the end of his last major novel, *The Western Lands*, he would ponder both the 'prophetic' significance of *Minutes to Go*'s cryptic phrases and the 'damage' he thought he was doing, concluding skeptically that it 'reads like sci-fi': 'We all thought we were interplanetary agents involved in a deadly struggle... battles... codes... ambushes. It seemed real at the time. From here, who knows?' (*WL* 252).[3] From first to last, there is a standoff between claims for the methods' prophetic and performative power, an equivocation about the productivity of cut-ups as tools of war in 'a deadly struggle' that may or may not have existed.

This paradox has posed an intractable problem for critics. With very few exceptions,[4] they have recycled Burroughs's claims at face value and sidestepped evaluating not only their internal coherence and consistency but also their validity. Did cut-up methods reveal the future, because events are 'pre-recorded', or did they produce events, because the function of writing is to 'make it happen'? Were they revolutionary weapons or a private delusional fantasy, a kind of therapy or a form of pathology? Did they *work*? From here, who knows?

Inevitably, the one claim that critics have never taken literally is Burroughs's original and overriding insistence: that cut-up methods were 'for everyone' and 'experimental in the sense of being *something to do*. Right here write now. Not something to talk and argue about' (*3M* 31). For critics to take Burroughs's advice—put most bluntly to Allen Ginsberg: 'Don't theorize. Try it' (*YL* 59)—would this not mean abandoning criticism altogether in favor of practice? Perhaps so. But, short of this, what it must mean is putting the cut-up project back onto its *material* base, and this in turn demands an accurate chronology of its development and promotion. For this reason, the first task is to revise the standard critical verdict on *Minutes to Go*, the launching manual and manifesto of the method.[5]

At first sight—and criticism has never given it a second look—*Minutes to Go* seems largely irrelevant to what would follow; an exceptional, minor text of crude experimentalism that Burroughs put behind him as he worked on his trilogy of novels, *The Soft Machine, The Ticket that Exploded* and *Nova Express*.[6] The fundamental problem with this account is that it effectively reverses the historical priorities by abstracting form and content from *method*. As a result, even the very best critical analyses have been based on a false understanding of how Burroughs's methods developed over time. Robin Lydenberg, for example, begins by claiming that '*The Soft*

Machine provides a relatively accessible introduction to Burroughs's writing experiments during the 1960s' on the basis of its 'tentative and restrained use of the cut-up' (1987:56); but her claim precisely inverts the true situation, because the edition she analyses is the second, which shows the massive revisions Burroughs was forced to make in order to undo the originally *un*restrained use of cut-up methods that made the first edition of his first cut-up novel so *in*accessible.

Equally, it is no coincidence that these novels are generally identified as 'the *Nova* trilogy'—which emphasizes the apocalyptic urgency of their allegorical political scenario—rather than 'the cut-up trilogy'—which would recognize the primacy of the material methods by which, so visibly and uniquely, they were created.[7] But this primacy is more than formal, since *the methods determined the political scenario, too.* The essential historical question, 'To what political analysis were cut-up methods an answer?', has therefore to be turned around and rephrased: 'What political analysis did the methods themselves *produce*?' Most obviously, we can see this in the way the Nova conspiracy appropriates the method to 'set cut-up terrorists against a totalizing discursive apparatus' (Latham 1993:48), even as these narrative agents of interplanetary resistance generalize the fantasy scenario of the cut-up writer engaged in his 'deadly struggle'. But Burroughs's politics of method was not simply subsumed by form and content, since its point of departure was not only the material acts that resulted in his texts, but also the material acts that they in turn were intended to produce. This *prospective* function, which has multiple and disparate dimensions, requires that a historical approach to cut-up methods means situating Burroughs's texts not just in relation to a past or present reality, but also with reference to the *future*. Burroughs's cut-up politics came from his scissors in a number of different ways, but in each we see the determining significance of method motivated materially as well as historically by the predictive urgency announced at the outset in the very title of *Minutes to Go*.

THE OLD PAMPHLET DAYS

Although Burroughs's trilogy presents extraordinary problems, criticism has found ways to read it: by isolating themes, reconstructing scenarios, analyzing formal structures, and so on. But none of these interpretive strategies work for his short texts in *Minutes to Go*, and this is because their frame of reference is essentially quite different. To begin with, rather than understanding these texts as failures— one-off exercises which Burroughs quickly abandoned—it is more accurate to say that they demonstrated the *provisional* and *productive* character of results proper to an experimental method. This is the key point about *Minutes to Go*: that the very first examples of the practice were used to publicize it; Burroughs did not try to perfect the method first. Of course, the process itself was future-oriented, in the sense that cutting up pre-existent texts reverses the sequence that is axiomatic to mimesis, so that the sign *creates* its referent; production replaces reproduction, and meaning becomes contingent, a coded message awaiting the 'intersection point' that will decipher it. This is one reason why Burroughs constantly went back to *Minutes to Go*, recycling its most enigmatic phrases—such as 'Will Hollywood Never Learn?'—in new contexts to discover new significances.

Constant revision in the light of experience was inherent in the method, and this process explains the fate of Burroughs's trilogy. The fact that it was realized in six editions over a seven-year period has always been read as a calculated refusal of linear structure and textual closure. But, rather than embodying any *theoretical* position, Burroughs updated his trilogy into present time—'That was in 1962', he comments in one place (*TE2* 9)—because he was led by his own methods of textual production to apply to novel-length works an experimental logic initially devised for, and in certain respects better suited to, the publication of short pieces in pamphlet or magazine form.

Indeed, a narrow focus on the trilogy has made it easy to overlook the fact that parts of all these novels first appeared in a range of alternative or underground journals, and that this process continued as Burroughs revised his texts. By the time the first edition of *The Ticket that Exploded* was published in December 1962, Burroughs had already published some 50 magazine contributions, a figure rising to 100 by the time *Nova Express* appeared in November 1964 and to 200 by the time the final edition of *The Soft Machine* was published in July 1968. In this light, the three novels may even be seen as *aberrations*, extraordinary exceptions to the cut-up project rather than its necessary fulfillment.

What I'm suggesting is our need to rewrite the literary history of the cut-up project to counterbalance the effects of that most pragmatic of constraints; namely, the commercial availability of textual materials. Critical attention to the cut-up trilogy inevitably reflects that availability, while doubly reinforcing Burroughs's reception as a *novelist* (even though the term 'cut-up novel' is virtually an oxymoron). For to approach Burroughs as the author of *The Soft Machine, The Ticket that Exploded* and *Nova Express* relegates to the margins his enormous investment of energy not only in multimedia applications, but also the far broader field of textual experiment. The true scale of that field can only be gauged by referring to the 60 pages of periodical contributions listed in Maynard and Miles's bibliography *and* the several hundred more unpublished short cut-up texts listed in the *Descriptive Catalogue of the William S. Burroughs Archive*. Only a tiny fraction of the published texts have been made generally accessible—in *The Third Mind* and *The Burroughs File*—but, even then, their true significance is inevitably obscured: to read Burroughs's experimental layout texts collected and reprinted in book form is an entirely different experience to reading them in the context of their original magazine publications.

There is, I would argue, a complex *politics* to this mode of production and publication that derives directly from Burroughs's material practice. Since Burroughs's priority did not lie in the finished text or in texts with traditional 'finish', he was able to exploit the particular advantages structured into magazine dissemination. As Barry Miles observed: 'Burroughs could present to the reading public his cut/up experiences immediately. Naturally, this provoked a highly intimate encounter with his colleagues' (1976:10; my translation). Miles was thinking specifically of Burroughs's regular newspaper layout columns in the small-circulation, mimeographed pamphlet, *My Own Mag*, and in August 1964 Burroughs wrote to its editor, the poet Jeff Nuttall, clarifying the precise political ambition of his contributions; he had, he noted, 'always yearned nostalgically for the old pamphlet days when writers fought in the street'.[8] In fact, Burroughs's *nostalgia* could be seen as unrecognized prescience, since the proliferating mass of little magazines was, by the mid-1960s, already forming an expanding underground network of alternative communication. Burroughs would develop the radical political potentials of this network explicitly in *Electronic Revolution* (1971), where he identified the underground press as 'the only effective counter to a growing power and more sophisticated techniques used by establishment mass media', concluding that 'the underground press could perform this function much more effectively by the use of cut/up techniques' (*ER* 24).[9] Burroughs's hopes for the underground press were to generalize the incendiary intentions he had had for his first cut-up pamphlets, as indicated in a summer 1960 letter to Dave Hazelwood concerning *The Exterminator*, the sequel to *Minutes to Go*: 'I think you realize how explosive the material is [...] Are you willing and able to publish—To put it in the street? Please answer at once. Minutes to go believe me.'[10]

Burroughs's remarkable commitment to small press publications throughout the cut-up decade meant trading against his work's commercial value; as he told Ginsberg in 1960, his best bets were 'no-paying far-out magazines like *Yugen* and *Kulchur*'.[11] In terms of the experimental opportunities it afforded Burroughs, this commitment constitutes a 'textual politics' as defined by Michael Davidson—the 'seizing of one's means of literary production' (1997:179)—and locates Burroughs's practice in a broader contemporary cultural context. For example, Charles Olson grasped the importance of such magazines as Diane DiPrima and Leroi Jones's *Floating Bear* (which published six cut-up texts by Burroughs in 1961–62): the immediacy of communication relative to book publication narrowed significantly the gap between producer and consumer. This narrowing enabled avant-garde and underground small press magazines to operate through localized, specific networks of dissemination, and over time Burroughs learned to exploit the narrowed distances between both the time of composition and reception and between the writer and a specialized audience.

The nearly two-dozen contributions Burroughs made to *My Own Mag* between 1964 and 1966 are especially important in this context, because it was here that he introduced his own newspaper, *The Moving Times*. Specifically focused on temporal experiments using text arranged in columns, *The Moving Times* was a precursor to his pamphlets, *Time* and *Apo-33* (1965), and a logical conclusion to *Minutes to Go*, where eleven of Burroughs's 16 texts had cut up newspaper articles. Editing his own experimental magazine enabled Burroughs not only to address his readers directly, but also to invite their involvement in such experimental projects as writing in 'present time' through collecting 'intersection points': 'Try writing tomorrow's news today. Fill three columns with your future time guesses. Read cross column [...] Notice that there are many hints of the so-called future' (*BF* 150).

Burroughs solicited both correspondence and creative collaborations from his readership and it was, as Maynard and Miles noted, through *The Moving Times* that he began his substantial cut-up collaborations with Claude Pélieu and Carl Weissner (1978:128). The new channels offered by the alternative press therefore confirmed the importance of the mode of publication to Burroughs's development and promotion of cut-up methods—and, hence, their instrumental value for the political goal of recruiting other practitioners. One three-column text, 'Who Is the Walks Beside You Written 3rd?', ends with a general call to take back ownership of the production of reality from those who publish the official text: 'It is time to do our own publishing' (*BF* 76). In this respect, we might revise Timothy S. Murphy's formulation for the general 'context of political engagement' into which Burroughs sent his 'literary interventions': 'Such a context could be called an *audience*, a community of addressees' (1997:145). Burroughs's mass of small press cut-up contributions, specifically those using newspaper formats, materially constituted precisely such a context; the resulting community was not projected on the basis of reception alone, however, but on recruitment to future acts of production—acts that in turn promised to produce the future.

ALLIES WAIT ON KNIVES

Burroughs's nostalgia for 'the old pamphlet days' of street-fighting writers may also be seen as a reference back to the historical avant-garde, specifically the era of Dada. Burroughs's early identification of cut-up techniques with the prior example set by Tristan Tzara's performance of '*Pour faire un poème dadaiste*'—the recipe for making a poem by drawing out of a hat words cut from a newspaper—is of course well known, but to this we must add recognition of the importance of the specific context in which Tzara published; that is to say, the *manifesto*. In 1918, Richard Huelsenbeck attributed the principle of active, provocative campaigning to Tzara, proclaiming: 'The manifesto as a literary medium answered our need for directness. We had no time to lose; we wanted to incite our opponents to resistance, and, if necessary, to create new opponents for ourselves' (cited by Richter 1964:103). Primed by knowledge of such historical precedents, in June 1960, as he worked on a pamphlet to follow *Minutes to Go*, Burroughs was therefore confident he could predict its reception: 'Expect a spot of bother. Well there has been plenty of that already. You can not win allies without making enemies.'[12] The manifesto as a medium encouraged Burroughs to take the military metaphor of the avant-garde quite literally, and *Minutes to Go* represents a political mobilization of friends—'FUNCTION WITH

BURROUGHS EVERY MAN/ AN AGENT' (59)—and an identification
of enemies—'CANCER MEN … THESE INDIVIDUALS/ARE MARKED
FOE' (12)—while *The Exterminator* goes one better: ' "Let petty kings
the name of party know/ Where *I* come I kill both friend and foe" '
(Burroughs and Gysin 1960:v).[13]

Burroughs's call to arms is contextualized by the urgency of Tzara's
manifesto form ('We had no time to lose'), but the distinctive feature
of *Minutes to Go*—and one of the reasons for its neglect—is the
absence in Burroughs's texts of anything remotely resembling a direct
aesthetic or political statement. This is because, while his texts were
heterogeneous in form and content—several reworked newspaper
articles into prose or stanzas, some fragmented the words of a
Rimbaud poem, and so on—all of them gave priority to the material
process of cutting up over its products. In doing so, they identified the value of the method for the *practitioner*, rather than the
reader. The inference is that cut-up methods should be understood as
artistic only in the specific sense of a liberating life praxis. Certainly,
Gysin's injunction, 'Make your whole life a poem' (*MTG* 43), directly
resurrects the Surrealist maxims of Breton and Lautréamont (which
Burroughs would repeat, typically attributing them to Tzara): that
poetry should be *practiced* and that it should be made by *all*. Leaving
the polemical task entirely to Gysin, Burroughs allowed the method
to become his message. As one cryptic phrase has it: 'Allies wait on
knives' (*MTG* 21).

In this respect, another of his letters to Hazelwood in the summer
of 1960 is especially revealing:

> I find that people read MINUTES TO GO without ever using the cut up
> method themselves. But when they once do it themselves they see.
> Any missionary work you do among your acquaintance in showing
> people how the cut up system works will pay off in sales. People must
> be led to take a pair of scissors and cut a page of type.[14]

Although he uses economic terms for his publisher's benefit ('pay
off in sales'), this cannot conceal the true nature of Burroughs's self-
interest here, which is defined by his recognition that, for his texts
to work, people 'must be led' to practice the methods by which he
himself had made them. In fact, there are two sides to this motive.
On the one hand, Burroughs knew he needed to promote the
method in order to ensure an *understanding* of his work, which
could be guaranteed most effectively by creating an audience of

producers—an audience, in effect, made in his own image. On the other hand, his early experience of cut-up methods turned emphatically on the seductive pleasure and private insights they yield so enigmatically to the practitioner. A strictly *physical* dimension was integral to the act—across the entire range of aesthetic, magical, and therapeutic functions Burroughs claimed for it. The key word in his claim for the uncanny, prophetic potency of the method—'Cut-ups often come through as code messages with special meaning for the cutter' (*3M* 32)—is emphatically the last.

VIRUSES WERE BY ACCIDENT?

From the very outset, Burroughs fully understood the affective value of cutting up for the *cutter*; but it took him some time to understand the value of the resulting texts for *someone else*. This delay had far-reaching consequences for his novel-length texts, and from the wholesale revisions he made to *The Soft Machine* it is evident that Burroughs had only then learned what Kurt Schwitters, referring to his comparable collage methods, had discovered four decades earlier: 'I cannot write 500 pages of *Merz*' (Schwitters and Hausmann 1962:5). Or to be more exact, Burroughs learned the equal truth of the corollary; that it was barely possible for anyone to *read* such a text. While developing entirely new functions in his trilogy, he therefore also sought to approximate key features of the physical experience of cutting up—such as the uncanny sensation of recognition—in the temporal experience of reading: 'When the reader reads page ten he is flashing forward in time to page one hundred and back in time to page one—the *déjà vu* phenomenon can so be produced to order' (*3M* 96). But the very length and complexity of his cut-up novels that enabled them to achieve astonishing affects also meant that they could not model the material process of their making for their readers to apply—and this failure had consequences for the politics of method at work in those texts.[15]

Significantly, the first edition of *The Soft Machine* lacked any polemical or methodological instructions. The injunction to *cut* is a refrain that runs much more explicitly throughout the other texts in the trilogy, but it is displaced in two significant ways. On the one hand, it is tied to the representational science fiction narrative of the Nova conspiracy, and on the other, it is shifted polemically away from textual applications to media higher up the technological scale—particularly tape recorders in *The Ticket that Exploded*.

While the second move accurately reflects Burroughs's own multi-media development of cut-up methods, in a sense it also compensates for the effects of the first, which risked turning the technique from a *practical* method into an essentially *rhetorical* element located within a purely fictional narrative.[16]

In *Minutes to Go*, where there is no narrative scenario, the *exemplary* function of Burroughs's texts is the key to determining their politics. While the input is clearly calculated rather than arbitrary—Rimbaud had specific aesthetic and visionary associations; the newspaper articles focused on cancer, genetic research and viruses—the content is secondary, in the sense that its choice is already determined by the method. Burroughs chose strategically the material for his chance procedures, so that they might mechanically generate results that were indeterminate and yet desired. Thus his focus on recent DNA research, which now appears uncannily prescient: 'As to the distant future say 100 years Dr Stanley sees the entire code being cracked "We will be able to write out the message that is you"' (*MTG* 61). This prophecy, in which the determinism of the genetic code coincides with the determinism of language, confirms the political value of the random factor introduced by cut-up methods. Since these methods materially short-circuited any pre-codified expression, this thesis must itself appear in cryptic form, as a code message arrived at by chance; hence the open question posed in the title of one of Burroughs's texts: 'VIRUSES WERE BY ACCIDENT?' (*MTG* 15).

In *Minutes to Go* Burroughs minimized direct political reference, and in his correspondence he expressed an anxiety that anyone should mistake the politics of his texts. In another letter to Hazelwood concerning publication of *The Exterminator* as a sequel to *Minutes to Go*, Burroughs was emphatic:

> Important to indicate that these pamphlets are to be considered abstract literature observation and mapping of psychic areas. Not political propaganda or if so entirely by accident. I do not subscribe to any of the sentiments expressed necessarily [...] Do these plots really exist? How in the fuck should I know? Just a writer is all. Just an artisan. Not running for office.[17]

The question, 'Do these plots really exist?', anticipates by a quarter of a century the skepticism expressed in *The Western Lands* ('It seemed real at the time'); in other words, even *at the time* Burroughs felt the need for a certain equivocation. Given the urgency of these plots and the urgency with which Burroughs promoted cut-up methods, this might seem paradoxical. But the final phrasing ('Not running for office') indicates Burroughs's immediate recognition of the inappropriateness and danger of his own temptation to adopt a didactic and polemical mode of address. This recognition is emphasized in Burroughs's call to arms in *Minutes to Go*—'ANYONE CAN RECORD WORDS—CUT UP/ your own hustling myself' (*MTG* 60)— where the last phrase, taken from the ending of *Naked Lunch*, insists on the association between practicing the method and resisting authority—*especially* the authority of the master presumed to know and offer the truth. This recognition would also be structured into the stunning overture to *Nova Express*, where Burroughs's didacticism—'I order total resistance'—has to cancel itself out—'I offer you nothing. I am not a politician'—and has to be framed rhetorically as a letter delivered by his fictional persona, Inspector Lee (*NE* 6). The secret meaning of the couplet cited in *The Exterminator* now becomes clear: the emphasis in 'Where *I* come I kill both friend and foe' declares the dogmatic ego, no matter what its intentions, always fatal.

Burroughs's position was not produced by the cut-up project out of nowhere, of course. In the early 1950s he had already precisely deconstructed the prophet and the agent—the two key personae he would conflate in the figure of Hassan i Sabbah, the presiding genius of the cut-up project: recall the 'Wisdom-of-the-East routine' in *Queer* (where the holy man's answer is also 'How in the fuck should I know?' [82]), or the entire 'Prophet's Hour' routine in *Naked Lunch* (102–6); and recall the conspiracy scenario of agents and counter-agents sketched in his letters to Ginsberg ('But it is difficult to know what side anyone is working on, especially yourself' [*LWB* 269]), which returns in *Naked Lunch* as 'all Agents defect and all Resistors sell out' (186). Such critiques of unilateral authority and undivided agency underwrote the case Burroughs made to Ginsberg in April 1958, more than a year before he took up cut-up methods, that 'the answer is not in Politics':

> The main thing, as Bill says, is that any government, or person, who tries to put down a story saying that they are Right (& the enemy wrong)—is already putting down a big Maya con. Any attempt to force people to agree with you, or propagandize an opinion, is already an invasion of ego. (Ginsberg and Orlovsky 1980:158)

However, Burroughs's new methods gave him something that he could never have conceptualized before. To grasp the fundamental and radical shift made possible by cut-up methods, it is sufficient to imagine Burroughs trying to proselytize on behalf of his trademark creative device of the 1950s, the routine form—'Don't theorize, Allen. Try it!'—or to imagine a reader taking literally the claim that '*Naked Lunch* is a blueprint, a How-To Book' (*NL* 203). Any such ambitions depended on an *available technique*—and until he saw what Gysin's Stanley blade had done, Burroughs did not have one.

MILLIONS OF PEOPLE CARRYING OUT
THIS BASIC OPERATION

The politics of *Minutes to Go* turn on the claim to be modeling and advocating precisely such an available technique, offering a liberating means for individual production rather than selling a product for mass consumption. Perhaps, then, we should take seriously Burroughs's invocations of the *Communist Manifesto* noted by Timothy S. Murphy—or to be precise, not the calls in *Naked Lunch* ('Paregoric Babies of the World Unite' [*NL* xlv]) or in *The Western Lands* ('You have nothing to lose but your dirty rotten vampires' [*WL* 7]), but, because of its alliance with an *available technology*, his call in the 1967 edition of *The Ticket that Exploded*: 'Carry Corders of the world unite. You have nothing to lose but your prerecordings' (*TE2* 167). Here, Burroughs seems to come surprisingly close to literalizing Hardt and Negri's position that the 'real revolutionary practice refers to the level of *production*. Truth will not make us free, but taking control of the production of truth will' (2000:156). Indeed, the cut-up method appears to fulfill their concomitant claim for the true nature of revolutionary political militancy, namely that it is 'not representational but constituent activity' linked 'to the formation of cooperative apparatuses of production and community' (2000:423).

This ambition to dissolve the gap between the writer as sole active producer of meaning/truth and the reader as passive consumer is based, therefore, on strictly material and pragmatic grounds. Rather than functioning *analogously*, as in the *Tel Quel* model whereby the *texte* reflexively offers 'the materialism of an open play of the signifier' as a critique of authorial expression (Hutcheon 1980:127), cut-up methods fulfilled absolutely literally the terms of Walter

Benjamin's critique of the productive relations of literature, made in 'The Author as Producer':

> The crucial point, therefore, is that a writer's production must have the character of a model: it must be able to instruct other writers in their production and, secondly, it must be able to place an improved apparatus at their disposal. This apparatus will be the better, the more consumers it brings in contact with the production process—in short, the more readers or spectators it turns into collaborators. (1934:98)

The promise of the cut-up method, promoted freely according to the 'Open Bank' policy announced in *Minutes to Go* (*MTG* 43), is therefore material and literal—as Gysin put it in the title text: 'the writing machine is for everybody/ do it yourself' (*MTG* 5).

But in what sense, if any, did it *work*?

Timothy S. Murphy is surely right to observe that 'the most compelling measure of success of the *Nova* trilogy' turns on effects that last 'only for a moment' and only for 'a small group of readers' (1997:139). However, this assumes that Burroughs's constant, urgent promotion of cut-up methods as a mass tool is of no relevance, that it belongs in a separate dimension outside the textual economy of the trilogy. On the other hand, when this dimension *is* taken into account for Burroughs's cut-up novels (as distinct from his mass of short, exemplary or polemical magazine texts), the result is a worrying literalism, whereby the trilogy's science fiction scenario models a revolutionary success that can be duplicated by readers recruited to cut-up methods by these novels: 'Burroughs's readers are clearly cast', as Robin Lydenberg puts it, 'as revolutionary cadets in training', so that *Nova Express* is 'an advanced seminar review of what the reader *should* have learned' from the two previous novels (1987:96). In which case, where are all the cut-up revolutionaries?

In the first full-length critical study of Burroughs, French critic Philippe Mikriammos commented on the success of cut-up methods by observing that the number who had experimented with them is 'beyond any doubt, far greater than those who applied the method of Tzara' (1975:63; my translation). True enough—but then Tzara's promotion was a one-off stunt, while Burroughs campaigned full-time with messianic zeal for an entire decade, and never entirely stopped for another quarter of a century. How many have experimented? It is, surely, impossible to estimate. What we do know is something much more limited; namely, the number and range of *published* works based on cut-up methods. Success has been judged most often, therefore, by citing the method's fertile creative influence on a roll call of artists experimenting in various media, from Kathy Acker to John Zorn. This is a genuine measure of achievement, surely unmatched by any other writer. On the other hand, none of these figures took up the practice for long enough or in such a way as to become identified with it. In this regard, consider the fate of the cut-up community that formed in the so-called Beat Hotel. In his introduction to Harold Norse's collection of cut-up texts, titled *Beat Hotel*, the German cut-up artist Carl Weissner stated: 'All the other practitioners quickly faded away. But Harold Norse [...] has remained one of the "Old Masters"' (1983:xii). With due respect to Norse and Weissner, *everyone* who took up the practice faded away—except Burroughs.

Challenging Burroughs about 'the advisability of using the cut-up method in fiction', Paul Bowles recalled that Burroughs had replied that '"in the hands of a master" it became a viable technique' (1972:349). Since there was only ever one master, since only Burroughs could make it work—consistently, productively—then we have to wonder not so much about the success of the method, but whether, as a creative practice available to others, it ever properly constituted one. Equally, the notion of an 'Old Cut-Up Master' is revealing, because it so flatly contradicts the politics of the 'Open Bank' policy. And where did Burroughs end up, a decade after *Minutes to Go*? With *Electronic Revolution*, another text that promoted a technology available to *all*.

In *Minutes to Go*, the cut-up method had been publicized in anticipation of further technological development: 'be your own agent until we deliver/the machine in commercially reasonable quantities' (*MTG* 5). After six years of intensive experiments, Burroughs in effect gave up on the cut-up writing machine and reinvested his key claims for the methods in a different technology: 'As usual', he noted in 'A Tape Recorder Experiment', 'the tip off came from those who wish to monopolize and control the techniques by which so called "reality" is formed and directed' (1966:20). In 'The Invisible Generation' (1966), this became another call to arms: 'any number can play anyone with a tape recorder controlling the sound track can influence and create events' (now in *TE2* 207). As before, the therapeutic claims for an individual practice—'such exercises bring you liberation from old association locks' (now in *TE2* 206)—coincided with the potential for producing a critical mass to achieve collective political action: 'put a thousand young recorders with riot recordings into the street' (now in *TE2* 210). In *Electronic Revolution*, the goal once again is to break the monopoly of the production of reality through the mass recruitment of cut-up guerillas, only now Burroughs concludes by envisaging a thousand-fold scaling-up of the scrambling exercises in 'The Invisible Generation': 'Any number can play. Millions of people carrying out this basic operation could nullify the control system' (*ER* 18).

Aside from the belated publication of *The Third Mind* in 1978, the cut-up project reached its terminal point with *Electronic Revolution*, and what that text ended up projecting was not a literary readership of millions, but millions in the streets wielding portable tape recorders, practicing non-literary cut-up methods for political ends. This was the Burroughs hailed by Timothy Leary as 'the Nostradamus/Prophet of the electronic future' (1987). In which case, it is tempting to conclude by invoking the 'Political Manifesto' of Hardt and Negri. Inspired by Spinoza's materialist teleology, according to which '*the prophet produces its own people*' (2000:65), they deduce that powerlessness can be turned into power by usurping the tools of the existing system: '*Don't the necessary weapons reside precisely within the creative and prophetic power of the multitude?* [...] The kind of arms in question may be contained in the potential of the multitude to sabotage and destroy with its own productive force the parasitical order of postmodern command*' (2000:65–6). Hardt and Negri's terminology and analysis is foreshadowed by Burroughs's Nova mythology, with its colonizing virus enemy that can be sabotaged precisely by taking literally the equation of power structures (the global order) with symbolic interpellation (the order of language), and reordering both at once: 'I had only to mix the order of recordings and the order of images and the changed order would be picked up and fed back into the machine' (*SM2* 92); 'The counter move is very simple—This is machine strategy and the machine can be redirected' (*NE* 74).

But for three pragmatic political reasons, we have to hesitate. Firstly, the mechanical simplicity of cut-up methods, which was so essential to their promotion, determines in the trilogy a political analysis and mode of action that is too simplistic: Burroughs's proleptic declaration of victory—the 'control machine has been disconnected by partisan activity' (*TE2* 59)—too optimistically conflates success *in* the novels with the success *of* them. Secondly, there is Burroughs's revealing parenthetical aside in *Electronic Revolution*, when he looks back at the experiments advocated five years earlier in 'The Invisible Generation': '(I wonder if anybody but CIA agents read this article or thought of putting these techniques into actual operation)' (*ER* 15). In other words, not millions, not thousands, maybe no partisans at all—only Burroughs. Thirdly, the cut-up project evolved a theory of power that fully embodied Burroughs's libertarian values—via Hassan i Sabbah's last words: 'Nothing is true. Everything is permitted'—but that can only gesture toward positive social justice. Thus, while 'partisans are everywhere, of all races and nations', as he put it in a 1964 interview, Burroughs undercut the potential formation of a collectivity through his definition of terms: 'A partisan may simply be defined as any *individual* who is aware of the enemy' (Mottram 1965:12; emphasis added). Even the strident 'pay it *all* back' demand of Hassan i Sabbah at the start of *Nova Express* has to be followed by a 'word of warning': 'To speak is to lie' (*NE* 7).

The upshot, to recall the terms of Burroughs's own retrospective assessment in *The Western Lands*, is that the question of the reality of his deadly struggle is still overwhelmingly phrased negatively in terms of doing damage: 'And now the question as to whether scrambling techniques could be used to spread helpful and pleasant messages. Perhaps. On the other hand, the scrambled words and tape act like a virus in that they force something on the subject against his will' (*ER* 35). In other words, using cut-up methods to fight the virus of power means fighting fire with fire. A hybrid of art and science, the technique that Gysin called 'Machine Age knife-magic' (*3M* 51) was meant to be strong black magic, a radical tool for occult assassins wanting to throw a deadly hex.[18]

This is an essentially terroristic logic, one amply developed in the cut-up trilogy and embodied from the outset in the figure of Hassan i Sabbah, who not only appeared in *Minutes to Go* but whose imprimatur Burroughs intended to put on the titles of its planned sequels ('Minutes to Go from Alamout' and 'Exterminator? Watch Hassan i Sabbah').[19] In 'Comments on the Night Before Thinking' (1961), Burroughs identified—and identified with—Hassan i Sabbah as 'strictly a counter puncher', an 'Assassin of Ugly Spirits' who made no attempt to 'extend political power': '[H]e reached out with his phantom knife and a general a prime minister a sultan died' (1961a:32). But in the 1967 edition of *The Ticket that Exploded*

Burroughs went *beyond* this apparently clear political identification, defining his ideal terrorist organization as

> an equivocal group of assassins called 'The White Hunters'. Were they white supremacists or an anti-white movement far ahead of the Black Muslims? The extreme right or far left of the Chinese? Representatives of Hassan i Sabbah or the White Goddess? No one knew and in this uncertainty lay the particular terror they inspired. (*TE2* 9)

This equivocation—is he siding with friends or foes, agents or counteragents?—is fundamental to Burroughs's political identity. If it makes sense to call upon the framework of political philosophy, and the particular terms of Hardt and Negri's manifesto—and that is a big *if*: 'Just a writer is all'—then what Malcolm Bull says of *Empire* would apply to Burroughs's project also: 'You may be able to threaten the world with a Stanley knife, but you cannot build a new society with one' (2001:6).

PRE-SENT TIME/WHAT WASHINGTON? WHAT ORDERS?

Inaugurating the cut-up project, *Minutes to Go* signaled a preoccupation with *time*—and not only in its title or in the recurrence of the word across numerous texts. This insistence on temporality begs the question of the urgency invoked by the text's title. Of course, we could take this as calling upon the conventional avant-garde association between formal rupture and historical crisis, but the obvious context—the international resurgence of collage-based practices in the 1950s and 1960s—relates cut-up methods to the *détournement* of materials taken from a rapidly expanding consumer culture and global media industry, and in no way does this account for *Minutes to Go*'s injunction to read the method as a practical response to conditions of emergency. Alternatively, we might take the title to imply a countdown to nuclear doomsday, in line with a Cold War reading of the Nova conspiracy. But this context is conjured only by Gregory Corso's poem, beginning 'Bomb decade' (*MTG* 32), and the effect is strikingly anomalous. No, the missing dimension is not historical but *biblical* time. Burroughs's invocation of the Gospel according to St John—'In THEE beginning was THE word' (*MTG* 59)—points toward a literal rendition of the *apocalypse* promised in the book's title: a revelation of the future, the end of this world.

This context enables us first of all to understand the *evangelical* character of Burroughs's promotion of cut-up practices; getting others to see what he had seen was indeed a kind of 'missionary work'. Secondly, it allows us to interpret one of the key claims for cutting up texts: 'this is the terminal method for/ finding the truth' (*MTG* 5). In other words, we might see the activity as performing a version of biblical exegesis in the tradition of Christian eschatology: as a pre-millennial faith determines that history is written before it happens and all signs point toward the end of the world, so too the true meaning of contemporary events can be read through a literal interpretation of the prophetic Word. Burroughs's observation that *Minutes to Go* 'has turned out to be a prophetic book' (*Job* 73) only confirms its original intention. Although the internal evidence is minimal—one of Gysin's phrases declares, 'We have seen the future' (*MTG* 7); another cites ' "AFTER THE GREAT AWAKENING" ' (*MTG* 9)—*Naked Lunch* had already established Burroughs's mock self-identification, both generally—'This is Revelation and Prophecy' (*NL* 208)—and specifically: ' "Yes sir, boys, the shit really hit the fan in '63," said the tiresome old prophet can bore the piss out of you in any space-time direction' (*NL* 204–5).

While the sources of Burroughs's apocalyptic cut-up vision were diverse—from Spengler's *Decline of the West* to Gysin's knowledge of occult traditions—the point remains that this vision was far from anomalous.[20] In fact, we can locate it within the cultural history studied by, among others, Paul Boyer in *Time Shall Be No More: Prophecy Belief in Modern American Culture*. Here we find both local resonances—prophecy believers are, Boyer notes, very careful readers of the newspapers—and large ones. His conjunction of ancient belief and modern technology reads, for example, like a synoptic account of the Nova conspiracy: 'In an age of computers, space travel, and genetic engineering, a genre of visionary writing [...] shaped countless believers' views of what lay ahead for humankind' (1992:21). Above all, there is Boyer's observation that a culture of biblical apocalypticism has informed American politics, especially from the Cold War onwards. In this light, the most striking resonance properly concerns the *future*—that is, the present post-Cold War world, in which George W. Bush's American foreign policy has been drafted in theological terms as a global struggle between the forces of good and an axis of evil. Since the world stands, as I write (Present Time: 15 March 2003), on the brink of a war that would be as religious as it was geopolitical—sustained by an eschatological vision almost as much as by the doctrine of 'full spectrum dominance'[21]—the prophetic force of Burroughs's fiction can only seem grimly accurate.

As he put it in *Naked Lunch* (referring to the ill-omened last days in the Mayan calendar): 'The Ouab Days are upon us' (*NL* 211).

From this point, and with uncanny precision, it would be possible to read the Nova conspiracy as a historical analysis disguised as prophetic fiction, to see in the Biologic Courts a version of the United Nations, in the Nova Mob an Imperial America, and in Hassan i Sabbah an avatar of Osama bin Laden, even down to conflating the assassin's 'phantom knife', the cut-up artist's 'Stanley blade', and the box cutters used by the 9/11 hijackers. Such a 'retroactively' prophetic reading would apply to Burroughs's 'Word' the hermeneutic principles of religious fundamentalists who, for example, read Saddam Hussein as the Antichrist and the harbinger of Armageddon in both Gulf War I and Gulf War II.[22] It would also take literally Burroughs's status as a prophet—a status that critics usually acknowledge, but as if it had no bearing on their criticism. But an absolute literalism is entirely appropriate, for what Burroughs meant by a 'precise intersection point' does indeed work on this basis. Partly inspired by his reading of J. W. Dunne's *An Experiment with Time* (1927), Burroughs's obsessive activity of collecting cut-up 'coincidences' always assumed an element of apparently reductive literalism, such as finding the precise repetition of a name or a number. To read Burroughs in what he called 'pre-sent' time requires taking literally both the 'intersection point', defined as 'a decoding operation, you might say, relating the text to external coordinates' (*3M* 136), and his suggestion that some of his texts 'have a long germination period seeds you might say' (*3M* 122). Inverting our expectations of chronology and causality, this notion of the text as a *seed* projects its historical referent into the future. When this projection is recognized, our reading is necessarily predetermined as prophetic.

The specific seed I have in mind is found, with variations, in a number of Burroughs's cut-up texts, but appeared for the first time in 'Operation Soft Machine/Cut', a two-page piece published in the fall of 1961. Needless to say, this 'seed' has been the *answer* from which I started, in expectation that it would reveal to me my own question.

The first text to use a three-column newspaper layout, 'Operation Soft Machine/Cut' presents in a condensed, often cryptic and elliptical form, material mostly made familiar in the trilogy of novels (the piece is billed as 'from a work in progress'), while it recycles key elements from *Minutes to Go*—including its title, repeated as a refrain throughout. Starting 'IN THE BEGINNING WAS THE WORD. And the word is the virus instrument', the text introduces the basic Nova conspiracy plot with an equivocation ('Suspending disbelief that such an invasion deal has taken place HOW CAN it be re-written' [Burroughs 1961b:76]) and identifies itself as a manual for resistance: 'THE FOLLOWING PAGES ARE BATTLE INSTRUCTIONS FOR ANTI*TRAK AGENTS: Exercise in phantom positions of GUERRILLA WAR' (76). This is followed by Mao's famous 'sixteen character' formulation of military principles ('Enemy advance we retreat. Enemy retreat WE ADVANCE. ENEMY ENCAMP we agitate. Enemy tire WE ATTACK' [1961b:76]) and an unusually politicized economic context in which 'THE OUAB DAYS' are associated with 'the dollar blight'. There are then sections on the dangers of the autonomous computing machine (citing Wiener's cybernetics theory), the manipulations of the society of the spectacle ('Word and image machine of world press and Follywood controlling and downgrading' [1961b:77]), and an account of liberation through *détournement* ('The dummy revolt flashed round the world when they took it to Cut City and talked out of turn and threw the word and image back' [1961b:77]). Finally, there is an early version of Hassan i Sabbah's opening speech in *Nova Express* and a closing, apocalyptic vision of '[a]gents who operate outside the lines saying most awful things totally un-top secret to top annihilating all' (1961b:77).

This, then, is the context for the text's point of intersection with present time:

> THESE ARE BATTLE
> INSTRUCTIONS:
> Shift linguals/vibrate
> tourists/free door ways/ cut
> word lines/shift tangle cut
> all words lines/ 'I said the
> Chief of Police skinned alive
> in Bagdad [sic] not Washington D.C.'
> // CUT CUT 'Cholera epidemic in
> Stockholm' // 'Scotland Yard
> assassinates the Prime Minister
> in a Rightist coup' // 'Switzer/
> land freezes all foreign assets'
> // 'Mindless idiot you have
>   liquidated the Commissar' // (1961b:77)

In a first approach to these lines, we can read them as terroristic applications of the cut-up principle of *détournement*: counter-subversive orders to assassinate and destabilize are turned back against those who issued the commands by a simple reordering of them. Phrased as reports of cut-up operations that *worked*, these bulletins do not sabotage the media's representation of past events, but scramble the control machine's orders for the future.

In a second approach, we should note how these lines return in other texts, because Burroughs updated them in a specific way. In the 'Gongs of Violence' chapter in the revised editions of *The Soft Machine*, they recur with minor changes followed by a significant additional line that identifies the focus of attention: 'machine guns in Bagdad [sic] rising from the typewriter' (*SM2* 161; *SM3* 153). Variants of this new line occur in several texts from 1964 and 1965 ('Who Is the Walks Beside You Written 3rd?' and 'Old Photographer' in *The Burroughs File*; 'Introductions', 'In Present Time', and 'Formats: The Grid' in *The Third Mind*). 'Old Photographer' is especially significant, not only because the line generates four new versions (including 'empty oil drums in Baghdad'), but also because it is here that Burroughs developed his notion of the text as a 'seed' (*BF* 125). And so, while it is very likely that newspaper reports were his source material, it is very *unlikely* that Burroughs intended such phrases to function as cryptic historical references to events that had already occurred in Baghdad, such as the downfall of the monarchy in 1958, Iraq's claim to sovereignty of Kuwait in 1961, or the Ba'th Party rebellion in 1963. They function instead as proleptic 'references' to the future, awaiting their point of intersection in the present. Primed by Burroughs's thesis, and writing at a time when Washington is claiming it must attack Baghdad to prevent Baghdad from attacking Washington, I find in the report of an assassination intended for 'Bagdad [sic] not Washington D.C.' an intersection point that has an extraordinarily seductive potency. But what seduces me is not the uncanny illusion of prophecy—as if Burroughs knew more than he possibly could. The coincidence is not literally prophetic, but rather prophetically literal, a profoundly affective experience of intersection through which (in both senses of the word) I 'realize' Burroughs's experiment with time.

In a third approach, we should note how Burroughs's original lines recur in *Nova Express*, where they open the section 'Will Hollywood Never Learn?'. Here, their immediate context plays on Burroughs's equation of *Time* magazine with a machine for controlling the future rather than reporting the present ('Insane orders and counter orders issue from berserk Time Machine' [*NE* 62]), but they are also set up much earlier in the text by the Intolerable Kid: 'I'll by God show them how ugly the Ugly American can be [...] They are skinning the chief of police alive in some jerkwater place. Want to sit in?' (*NE* 12). This allusion to the Ugly American—the imperial fantasy identity of Burroughs's persona in *Queer*, a novel set in 'jerkwater' colonial South American locales (*Q* 53, 105)[23]—crucially establishes a specific *national* frame of reference. Although the Nova conspiracy appears to subsume the Cold War conflict between America and Russia—and so to anticipate the kind of transnational global order of Empire mapped by Hardt and Negri—the specific context identifies the proper interpretation of the reordered war commands: the cut-up principle of cybernetic *feedback* coincides with what the CIA termed *blowback*—that is, the backfire of America's imperial overreach. Rather than viewing contemporary terrorist networks such as Al Qaeda as alien throwbacks to a barbarian age, we can see them dialectically as the inner 'truth' of modern American policies of control, returned to sender as part of a self-feeding correspondence. In this sense, Burroughs's power of prophecy, like his embrace of the Ugly American cold warrior identity, is better understood as an insight realized by the continuation of historical factors: 'World politics in the twenty-first century', wrote Chalmers Johnson, 'will in all likelihood be driven primarily by blowback from the second half of the twentieth century— that is, from the unintended consequences of the Cold War and the crucial American decision to maintain a Cold War posture in a post-Cold War world' (2000:238).

Finally, the original passage from 'Operation Soft Machine/Cut' encrypts a narrative into which we can insert Burroughs himself. In 'I said the Chief of Police skinned alive in Bagdad [sic] not Washington D.C.', we might identify the speaker as a senior CIA officer, the addressee as a covert operation assassin, and the scrambling of orders the work of Anti-Trak agents acting on Burroughs's guerilla battle instructions. As is well known, during World War II, Burroughs went to Washington to join the OSS, the forerunner to the CIA, but was turned down. 'God knows what would have happened', he later mused; 'I could have wound up head of the CIA and I probably wouldn't have written what I wrote' (Lotringer 1981:539). Since what Burroughs *did* go on to write formed a kind of fantasy version of the career he did *not* enter, we are left with a paradoxical reading in which he both gives the orders to assassinate and cuts them up. Which side was Burroughs on? The only unequivocal answer is his warning against authority and agency that goes beyond the dialectic of 'sides': 'Where *I* come I kill both friend and foe.' This was the anti-political maxim of the cut-up project, Burroughs's program for the cutting up *of* politics.

NOTES

1. I say 'supposed' advisedly: Burroughs and Gysin—above all Gysin—were well aware that a new movement required a foundation story, and their often-repeated anecdotes should be seen as a creation myth rather than as a necessarily factual account.
2. In *The Job*, Burroughs's 'most interesting experience with the earlier techniques was the realization that when you make cut-ups [...] they do mean something, and often that these meanings refer to some future event' (28).
3. ' "Professor killed, accident U.S." This is an old cut-up from *Minutes to Go* (1960), waiting all these years for the place in the Big Picture jigsaw puzzle where it would precisely fit' (*WL* 182).
4. For the most notable exception, see Murphy 1997:139–40, 144–5.
5. For a more detailed textual account, see my forthcoming article, ' "Burroughs is a poet too, really": the Poetics of *Minutes to Go*' in *The Edinburgh Review* (forthcoming, 2004).
6. This chapter references multiple versions of two volumes from Burroughs's Nova/cut-up trilogy—*The Soft Machine* and the *Ticket that Exploded*. For specifics on the different editions, please see the Abbreviations page of this collection.
7. The generally preferred term appears to have changed over time: whereas Lydenberg (1987) and Miles (1992) use 'cut-up trilogy', Murphy (1997) and Russell (2001) use 'Nova trilogy'.
8. Letter to Jeff Nuttall, 20 August 1964 (Fales Library, New York University).
9. Most of the material published in *Electronic Revolution* also appeared in *The Job*.
10. Letter to Dave Hazelwood, 27 May 1960 (Bancroft Library, UCLA at Berkeley). After the actual date, Burroughs added 'No Time'. This was one of several ways in which he marked the *temporality* of his correspondence throughout the 1960s, the most common form appearing in *The Yage Letters*, where his letter of 21 June 1960 is followed by 'Present Time' and 'Pre-Sent Time' (1963:59). Such epistolary dating practices formed an important parallel to the deconstruction of the time of writing and reading carried out by Burroughs's formal cut-up experiments.
11. Letter to Allen Ginsberg, 10 November 1960 (Rare Book and Manuscript Library, Columbia University, Ginsberg Collection).
12. Letter to Bill [Dobson?], 11 June 1960 (Department of Special Collections, Kenneth Spencer Research Library, University of Kansas; The Ginsberg Circle: Burroughs-Hardiment Collection [MS 63 C: c:1]).
13. For the origin of this line, see *LWB* 298.
14. Letter to Dave Hazelwood, 26 July 1960 (Bancroft Library, UCLA at Berkeley).

15. Although his interest is aesthetic rather than political, Géfin has also addressed the 'problematics of reading cutups without actual cutup experience': '[T]he reader cannot be expected to duplicate the original collage experience [...] by being exposed to the *results* of that primary experience' (1987:95).

16. The problem of maintaining a consistent hold on the relationships between theory and method and between the practical and the rhetorical is revealingly illustrated by the self-contradictions in Todd Tietchen's (otherwise very productive) article. For example, on the one hand, he relates cut-up methods to the *détournement* strategies of the Situationists and to the postmodern activism of 'Guerilla Semiotics' and 'Culture Jamming', and on the other he notes: 'Historically speaking, cut-ups belong to the movement towards self-reflexive fiction that dominated much of American writing during the 1960s' (2001:124). Equally revealing (see note 7) is the fact that Tietchen refers to the '*Nova* books'.

17. Letter to David Hazelwood, 24 June 1960 (Department of Special Collections, Kenneth Spencer Research Library, University of Kansas; The Ginsberg Circle: Burroughs-Hardiment Collection [MS 63 C: c:3]).

18. The legacy of this occult political dimension is clearest in the work of Hakim Bey, in such texts as *T.A.Z.: The Temporary Autonomous Zone, Ontological Anarchy, Poetic Terrorism* (New York: Autonomedia, 1991).

19. Letter to Bill [Dobson?], 11 June 1960, and Letter to Dave Hazelwood, 27 May 1960.

20. For other accounts of Burroughs's relation to apocalypticism, see Frank Kermode (1967), Richard Dellamora (1995), Edward J. Ahearn (1996), and Peter von Ziegesar (1997).

21. As former President Jimmy Carter noted in March 2003, the only religious leaders to support the attack on Iraq as a 'just war' were 'a few spokesmen of the Southern Baptist Convention who are greatly influenced by their commitment to Israel based on eschatological, or final days, theology' (9 March 2003, <www.bushwatch.com>).

22. 'The Persian Gulf War of 1991', notes Boyer, 'triggered a wave of prophecy interest focused on Iraq's Saddam Hussein and his plans for rebuilding ancient Babylon, whose end-time destruction is foretold in the Book of Revelation' (1992:280); in March 2003, the *Bush Watch* website featured numerous articles on the same theme, one quoting the head of the Jerusalem Prayer Team, who believed that 'a war with Iraq could be a "dress rehearsal for Armageddon"—the fulfillment of biblical prophecy' (16 March 2003, <www.bushwatch.com>).

23. On Burroughs, *Queer* and the Ugly American, see Harris (2003), chapter 3.

REFERENCES

Ahearn, E. J. (1996) *Visionary Fictions: Apocalyptic Writing from Blake to the Modern Age* (New Haven: Yale University Press).

Benjamin, W. (1934) *Understanding Brecht*, Bostock, A. trans. (London: Verso, 1977).

Bowles, P. (1972) *Without Stopping* (New York: Ecco, 1984).

Boyer, P. (1992) *Time Shall be No More: Prophecy Belief in Modern American Culture* (Cambridge, MA: Harvard University Press).

Bull, M. (2001) 'You can't build a new society with a Stanley knife', *London Review of Books*, 4 October, pp. 3–7.

Burroughs, W. S. (1961a) 'Comments on the Night Before Thinking', *Evergreen Review* (5)20, September, pp. 31–6.

—— (Fall 1961b) 'Operation Soft Machine/Cut', *Outsider* 1, pp. 74–7.

—— (1966) 'A Tape Recorder Experiment', *Klactoveedsedsteen* 3, May, pp. 20–1.

Burroughs, W. S., and Gysin, B. (1960) *The Exterminator* (San Francisco: The Auerhahn Press).

—— (1973) *A Descriptive Catalogue of the William S. Burroughs Archive* (London: Covent Garden). Compiled by Miles Associates.

Davidson, M. (1997) *Ghostlier Demarcations: Modern Poetry and the Material World* (Berkeley: University of California Press).

Dellamora, R. ed. (1995) *Postmodern Apocalypse: Theory and Cultural Practice at the End* (Philadelphia: University of Pennsylvania Press).

Dunne, J. W. (1927) *An Experiment with Time* (New York: Macmillan).

Géfin, L. (1987) 'Collage, Theory, Reception, and the Cutups of William Burroughs', *Literature and the Other Arts* 13, pp. 91–100.

Ginsberg, A., and Orlovsky, P. (1980) *Strait Hearts' Delight: Love Poems and Selected Letters 1947–1980*, Leyland, W. ed. (San Francisco: Gay Sunshine).

Gysin, B., and Wilson, T. (1982) *Here to Go: Planet R-101* (San Francisco: Re/Search).

Hardt, M., and Negri, A. (2000) *Empire* (Cambridge, MA: Harvard University Press).

Harris, O. (2003) *William Burroughs and the Secret of Fascination* (Carbondale: Southern Illinois University Press).

Hutcheon, L. (1980) *Narcissistic Narrative: The Metafictional Paradox* (New York: Methuen).

Johnson, C. (2000) *Blowback: The Costs and Consequences of American Empire* (London: Time Warner, 2002).

Kermode, F. (1967) *The Sense of an Ending* (New York: Oxford University Press).

Latham, R. (1993) 'Collage as Critique and Invention in the Fiction of William S. Burroughs and Kathy Acker', *Journal of the Fantastic in the Arts* (5)3, pp. 46–57.

Leary, T. (1987) 'Cyberpunks', <http://www.textfiles.com.drugs/leary002.txt>, 29 January 2003.

Lotringer, S. (1981) 'Exterminating', IN Lotringer, S. ed., *Burroughs Live: The Collected Interviews of William S. Burroughs 1960–1997* (USA: Semiotext[e], 2001), pp. 526–44.

Lydenberg, R. (1987) *Word Cultures: Radical Theory and Practice in William S. Burroughs' Fiction* (Urbana: University of Illinois Press).

Maynard, J., and Miles, B. (1978) *William S. Burroughs, A Bibliography 1953–73* (Charlottesville: University Press of Virginia).

Mikriammos, P. (1975) *William S. Burroughs: la vie et l'oeuvre* (Paris: Seghers).

Miles, Barry (1976) 'Introduction', IN Burroughs, W. S., *Le métro blanc*, Beach M., and Pélieu-Washburn, C. trans. (Paris: Bourgois/Seuil).

—— (1992) *William Burroughs: El Hombre Invisible*, rev. and updated edition (UK: Virgin, 2002).

Mottram, R. (1965) *Recontre avec William Burroughs*, IN Hibbard, A. ed., *Conversations with William S. Burroughs* (Jackson: University Press of Mississippi, 1999), pp. 11–15.

Murphy, T. S. (1997) *Wising Up the Marks: The Amodern William Burroughs* (Berkeley: University of California Press).

Richter, H. (1964) *Dada: Art and Anti-Art*, Britt, D. trans. (London: Thames and Hudson, 1965).

Russell, J. (2001) *Queer Burroughs* (New York: Palgrave).

Schwitters, K., and Hausmann, R. (1962) *PIN* (London: Gabberbocchus).

Tietchen, T. (2001) 'Language out of Language: Excavating the Roots of Culture Jamming and Postmodern Activism from William S. Burroughs's *Nova* Trilogy', *Discourse* 23.3, Fall 2001, pp. 107–29.

Weissner, C. (1983) 'Preface', IN Norse, H., *Beat Hotel* (San Diego: Atticus), pp. x–xii.

Ziegesar, P. Von (1997) 'After Armageddon: Apocalyptic Art since the Seventies', IN Strozier, C. B., and Flynn, M. eds, *The Year 2000: Essays on the End* (New York: New York University Press).

Part III

Alternatives: Realities and Resistances

12
The Map and the Machine
John Vernon

Editors' note: This essay appeared first in The Iowa Review *in 1972 and then as the chapter 'William S. Burroughs' in Vernon's book* The Garden and the Map *(University of Illinois Press, 1973). It is printed here as it originally appeared, without page numbers or specific book titles given after quotations, reflecting the position that, after* Junky, *Burroughs's early works* (Naked Lunch *and the Nova trilogy) formed a complete oeuvre without clear dividing lines.*

The romantic image of the artist as madman becomes with William S. Burroughs the reality of the madman as artist. What writers like John Barth, Thomas Pynchon, Alain Robbe-Grillet, and others attempt to show, that if the properties of the real world are taken seriously enough there is something essentially insane about that world, is taken for granted by Burroughs in his novels *Naked Lunch*, *The Soft Machine*, *Nova Express*, and *The Ticket that Exploded*. Burroughs's world is reality; there can be no doubt about that. It is Martin's reality film, Luce's *Time-Life-Fortune* monopoly, the machinery of visual and auditory control—'encephalographic and calculating machines film and TV studios, batteries of tape recorders'. But it is also an assault upon reality, an attempt to storm the reality studio and blow it up, to splice all the tape recorders into each other. ('Communication must be made total. Only way to stop it.') What is real about Burroughs is precisely the image of the world as machinery that Zola and the nineteenth century saw. But this reality is so total as to be fantastic, insane, grotesque; it is a reality in the process of exploding—'Only way to stop it'. Thus it is a reality whose machinery has come to life, like the kitchen gadgets that assault the housewife in *Naked Lunch*. It is a world whose objects (as in Sartre's *La Nausée*) 'stir with a writing furtive life', and whose living beings are either programmed machines or Vegetable People who 'tend gardens of pink flesh'.

Burroughs's vision, as at the end of *La Nausée*, is one in which the world has flown into two opposing principles, a labyrinthine, external, mechanical structure and a reified organic content. I use the word 'content' in the same sense as it is used by McLuhan, who rightly sees Burroughs's origins in the Industrial Age, when Nature became a vessel of aesthetic and spiritual values, that is, a content (1964:517). The underlying roots of this condition lie in the schizophrenic structures of thought in the West, which can comprehend Nature only by siphoning it off into a pure, separate space. The romantic movement, by emphasizing the inner, the creative, the vital, the natural, against the outer, the mechanical, the static, and so on (see Carlyle's *Characteristics*, for example), reinforced rather than challenged those structures of thought. Its result can be seen in Burroughs, for whom the natural and the organic are always shaped by the repressive nature of the mechanical, so that their manifestations are always stained by violence and evil.

The most common image of the mechanical and external in Burroughs is the City, 'a labyrinth of lockers, tier on tier of wire mesh and steel cubicles joined by catwalks and ladders and moving cable cars'. Maps, bureaucracies, IBM punch cards, and machines are also common images of this principle, as is the recurring notion of the real world as a movie film. The most common image of the other polarity, of organic content, is protoplasm, the blob, jelly: 'Some way he make himself all soft like a blob of jelly and surround me so nasty. Then he gets wet all over like with green slime. So I guess he come to some kinda awful climax.' At times this organic content is given the traditional name of 'garden', for example, the Garden of Delights (G.O.D.) or the Amusement Gardens, both pure areas into which Nature as a reified entity has been channeled by the structures of the real world:

The Amusement Gardens cover a continent—There are areas of canals and lagoons where giant gold fish and salamanders with purple fungoid gills stir in clear black water and gondolas piloted by translucent green fish boys—Under vast revolving flicker lamps along the canals spill The Biologic Merging Tanks sense withdrawal capsules light and soundproof water at blood temperature pulsing in and out where two life forms slip in and merge to a composite being often with deplorable results slated for Biologic Skid Row on the outskirts: (Sewage delta and rubbish heaps—terminal addicts of SOS muttering down to water worms and gloating vegetables—Paralyzed Orgasm Addicts eaten alive by crab men with white hot eyes or languidly tortured in charades by The Green Boys of young crystal cruelty).

Structurally, the mechanical and the organic in Burroughs are exact opposites. A machine is comprised of discrete movable parts, each confined to its location, in no other location, and each related along its border areas to other parts. All these parts are brought together one by one to perform an action, the coordination of which is not a synthesis but rather a reified object itself, with its own space: a circuit, a map, or in an extended sense, a program or punch card. The organic, on the other hand, reverses the tendency of the machine to unfold and separate into isolated, discrete spaces. As in the Amusement Gardens, objects structured as organic content merge with each other; they become a diabolical parody of the romantic 'All' and of the fluid life of the original garden. Mergence in this sense approaches the same condition as the mechanical, that of isolation and confinement. This is seen most clearly in the plan of the Liquefactionists in *Naked Lunch*. They propose that everyone merge by protoplasmic absorption into one person, who would then be totally alone, as confined in his space as any discrete mechanical part in its space. Thus although the mechanical and organic in Burroughs are exact opposites, there is an underlying sameness to them, a kind of inert, imprisoned objectivity; this is why the mechanical and organic are often merged, as in the recurring image of 'metal excrement'.

All of this is schizophrenia. It is a making explicit of the schizophrenic nature of reality in our culture by a man diagnosed as schizophrenic (Burroughs mentions this fact in the Prologue to *Junky*), in ways that are appropriately schizophrenic, that is, hallucinatory. Burroughs's world is structured upon either–or polarities—the organic and the mechanical, consciousness and the body, the self and the Other. This is most apparent in the image of the body in his novels. The body is variously seen as a machine (a tape recorder, a camera, a programmed computer, a robot), as a soft, amorphous mass, transparent, wet, penetrable, and finally as a combination of the two, a 'soft machine'. As a 'soft machine', the body's shape, skin or surface is the external, mechanical principle that contains its soft, amorphous content (a view that derives ultimately from the reification of shape and form as properties of objects in Aristotelian thought). Thus bodies are 'boneless mummies', and people wear uniforms of human skin, their own skin, which they can discard for

206 Alternatives: Realities and Resistances

the purpose of merging their soft, skinless content with someone else's.

This combination of a kind of dismemberment and merging is seen most explicitly in an incident that occurs repeatedly in *Nova Express* and *The Ticket that Exploded*: the merging of two homosexuals by means of the dismemberment and flaying of their external bodies in a film.

> The screen shifted into a movie—Bradley was lying naked with the attendant on the cot—The divine line of his body burned with silver flash fire shifting in and out of the other body—rectal and pubic hairs slipping through composite flesh—penis and rectums merged on screen and bed as Bradley ejaculated—He woke up with other thoughts and memories in Cockney accent of that attendant standing there with a plate of food—saw himself eating on screen composite picture tasting food in the other mouth intestines moving and excrement squirming down to the divide line of another body [...]

Many significant features of the schizophrenic experience are expressed in this passage. There is a subject–object split, a polarization between one's self and one's image on a movie screen (the modern equivalent of objective mirror space); this split, coupled with the experience of being controlled or persecuted by an external power and with the experiences of dismemberment and merging, is a common element of schizophrenia.

Compare the passage by Burroughs with the following letter of a hospitalized schizophrenic patient to a television station, in which she accuses television personalities and fellow patients of stealing parts of her body:

> Dear Sir,
>   This not my shape or face Mary —— has given me her glass eye and she has my noise. Bob Hope. Crooked mouth Peter Lin Hayes, has given me his lop sided shoulder. & terrible mans figure. He sold his shape to Mr. Albright, I want my own things
>   Frances ——, Pinky tongue. She has my noise.
>   Cathy Crosby has most of my things I want them. I have little Reds Kork leg, from the —— Hotel he lives most of the time & a few other bad features I cant mention he gave me. I guess knowing him you must know what it is.
>   Dolores —— club finger & two other fingers she had smashed in a defense plant Ruth —— one finger she had off in a defense plant.

Peggy —— or Hildegard has my hands & has gave me her large
lump in the back of the neck & her large head:
Ida ——
Jeanette —— has my eyes & hair & other things so make her give
them back. I don't want these things any more the Contest is over.
I want my own things back & also my daughter.
Dr —— has patricia & I want her back immediately Im going to the
police. I know all her markings & I have all hers & my pictures with my
attorney. Patricia took 3 screen test I have proof for these I took one
also. (cited by Rosen and Gregory 1965:310)

The schizophrenic delusions expressed by both Burroughs's passage
and this letter are expressions of the schizophrenia that is the realistic and objective world. In both, the reality that consciousness
relates to exists as an image on a screen, either a movie screen or a
television set. Reality has taken on the condition of machinery; it is
a movable representation of what we are familiar with, only more
focused; it exists in a frame that delineates it from its surroundings
and gives it an authenticity and potency that the world it copies
lacks. This is the classical image of the real carried to its full technological embodiment; it is the structure of mirror objectivity and
map space in the realistic novel become what it always implicitly
was, mechanical. The camera metaphor of human perception,
subscribed to by Kepler, Galileo, Newton, Leibniz, and others
(Turbayne 1962:205), becomes literal in Burroughs, and the object-
world exists as an image, as something we face, something we see or
have, not something we are. Thus the dismemberment that is virtual, as in Fielding's mechanical descriptions of the actions of the
body in objective space, becomes actual in Burroughs, in a space
that is itself an object, a movie screen.

This dismemberment in space in Burroughs is pushed to the
extreme condition of a total atomization of all things. Burroughs's
world is the Newtonian world of discrete objects and entities existing in objective space, confined to their own locations, and it is this
world carried to such an extreme that space explodes, and each
object wraps its own space around itself. Space is polarized into the
totally frozen map space of administration (maps, punch cards,
bureaucracies), and the atomistic space of objects overflowing their
administration ('This book spill off the page in all directions'). This
kind of polarization cuts across many of the features of Burroughs's
novels. On one hand there is immobility and catatonia, a condition
made possible (as in Beckett's *Unnamable*) by the diffusion of space

208 Alternatives: Realities and Resistances

into total objectivity, into a void, to the extent that one exists
anywhere and cannot move: 'I lived in one room in the Native
Quarter of Tangier. I had not taken a bath in a year nor changed my
clothes or removed them except to stick a needle every hour in the
fibrous grey flesh of terminal addiction.' On the other hand there is
frenzied activity, frantic action, a salad of actions that increase to
maximum intensity as their space shrinks: 'Diamonds and fur
pieces, evening dresses, orchids, suits and underwear litter the floor
covered by a writhing, frenzied, heaving mass of naked bodies.'

In any world, space always exists as the relationship between
objects; in Newton's universe, objects are impenetrable, discrete,
and this relationship of exclusive juxtaposition generates absolute,
objective space, space as a container (Čapek 1961:54ff). The space
of Burroughs's world encompasses at one polarity this Newtonian
space: objects clash and bounce off each other, and the world generally exists in a shattered, fragmented state. But the space of
Burroughs's world also shrinks to the skin of objects and bodies
themselves, and this is why things don't always stand outside each
other—they can merge. In objective space, the shape or skin of an
object represents its absolute boundary, since that shape is made
possible by space as an absolute ground. This is why, carried to its
logical conclusion, Newtonian science (and the structures of
Western thought in general) posits shape as a thing-in-itself. And
this is why the rigid split between the external shape or surface of
the human body and its internal content exists also for any object
in space.

Burroughs clearly sees that when shape is a thing-in-itself, it is of
a different order of being from what it contains. If shape is hard,
content is soft. If shape keeps things apart, content wants to run
together and merge. And if shape is removed, or simply dissolves as
each separate thing wraps its own space around itself, then things
(and people) do, in fact, merge: 'The Vigilante, The Rube, Lee the
Agent, A. J., Clem and Jody the Ergot Twins, Hassan O'Leary the
After Birth Tycoon, The Sailor, The Exterminator, Andrew Keif,
"Fats" Terminal, Doc Benway, "Fingers" Schafer are subject to say
the same thing in the same words, to occupy, at that intersection
point, the same position in space-time.'

Thus there are two spaces in Burroughs; as well as being contained
by external, objective space, objects and bodies are able to contain
each other, to merge, to be each other's space. The rhythm of isolation and merging seen in Conrad, which according to R. D. Laing is

the final stage of schizophrenia, is in Burroughs a rhythm of the expansion and contraction of space. As space expands into objectivity, objects and bodies exist in a state of fragmentation and isolation. Each thing is frozen, timeless, and immobile, since it exists in a void and hence is trapped in itself. But as space contracts, those things (and people) are brought together, first in frantic activity ('a writhing, frenzied, heaving mass of naked bodies') and finally in complete mergence, so that people step out of their shapes and merge, or people and things lose their shapes entirely in 'Biologic Merging Tanks'. The space of Burroughs's world is the space of objectivity and subjectivity at odds with each other, the juxtaposed experience of an external map space with its absolute boundaries and of a mythic space by which bodies are not subject to the limitations of a map and can merge; the mutually exclusive presence of both, of external and of mythic space, Merleau-Ponty calls the basis of schizophrenia (1945:287ff).

One of the underlying structural characteristics of this dual space is the concept of 'image', which Burroughs refers to repeatedly. The image refers primarily to the camera metaphor of perception and hence to the space of reality as a movie, but it also refers to the discrete, atomistic entities that wrap space around themselves. 'The human body is an image on screen talking.' 'Word begets image and image is virus.' 'Junk is concentrated image.' Image, as in the last statement, is always a concentration, a focus, a fixation. It is completely objectified reality, reality broken into bits and served up for consumption, or addiction. But it is also a datum of consciousness. Image is the discrete entity that spatializes consciousness itself, that gives consciousness the same structure as external space. 'Images' in Burroughs are like James's 'states of consciousness', which are things, or like Locke's 'ideas', which exist as atomistic objects in the mind. Burroughs frequently refers to conditioning processes that depend upon the theory of association of ideas, and he even asserts, not entirely ironically, that a movie and sound track of sexual activity are as good as the real thing. In this respect, Burroughs's world is firmly anchored in the structures of classical Western thought, in such figures as Locke and Pavlov, whom he refers to now and then.

His world is anchored in structures of control. 'The scanning pattern we accept as "reality" has been imposed by the controlling power on this planet, a power oriented toward total control.' Image is a discrete entity, and the only organization discrete entities can have, since internal synthesis is impossible, is one of external control—a map, a circuit, or a punch card. Because image is both a datum of consciousness and an object of the public world, all organization is by necessity control; the condition of the world is one of total map-like administration: 'The point at which the criminal controller intersects a three-dimensional human agent is known as "a coordinate point" [...] Now a single controller can operate through thousands of human agents, but he must have a line of coordinate points—Some move on junk lines through addicts of the earth, others move on lines of certain sexual practices and so forth.' The counterpart of the map, which administers control of the society, is the IBM punch card, a virus that administers control of the body:

> Transparent sheets with virus perforations like punch cards passed through the host on the soft machine feeling for a point of intersection—The virus attack is primarily directed against affective animal life—Virus of rage hate fear ugliness swirling round you waiting for a point of intersection and once in immediately perpetrates in your name some ugly noxious or disgusting act sharply photographed and recorded becomes now part of the virus sheets constantly presented and represented before your mind screen to produce more virus word and image around and around it's all around you the invisible hail of bring down word and image.

The obsessive reproduction of images that Burroughs refers to is his own literature: an orbit of snapshots of 'ugly noxious or disgusting' acts, a camera that can't be shut off.

Control imposes violence. In Burroughs the act of contact itself is violent, for it is always a seizing, a taking over, and the body, since it is a mere object, is easily seized. In *Naked Lunch* the Latah attaches himself to a person and 'imitates all his expressions and simply sucks all the persona right out of him like a sinister ventriloquist's dummy'. Burroughs's apprehension of the world is one of frightening relevance: a society organized and administered by the map structures of control is necessarily sadistic, since everything exists by virtue of the fact that it is organized, by virtue of being an object, something to be used. The use of human beings as objects accounts for the most obsessively recurring action in Burroughs's novels, what he calls the 'orgasm death': homosexual rape coupled with murder by hanging or strangling of the passive partner at the moment of climax. For Burroughs, violence is an absolute space into which one enters—it is like madness or sex; it is the 'Other Half' that our culture has repressed, has siphoned off into a pure, separate area.

The recurring association of sex and death is due to their mutual occupation of this separate area, and that area is specifically flesh, the body, 'the "Other Half," a separate organism attached to your nervous system'. In one respect, the concept of 'Other Half' is an expression of the internal–external split of the body; the 'Other Half' is the body as an outer mechanical structure attached to an organism. But the 'Other Half' is the bottom half of the body as well, the seat of sexual energies and anal violence, which has become anal and violent, regressive, because it has been made Other. On top, the body exists as a consciousness and a mental structure, but beneath it is a private space that the schizophrenic forms of realism and objectivity have repressed. 'Sex words evoke a dangerous that is to say *other* half of the body [...] You see the caustic layers of organic material? That is what they need from earth: Three other boys to make more marble flesh, ass and genitals vibrated by the iridescent attendant—Orgasm death is to other half of the body [...]' The phenomenon of violence in our culture is to a large degree due to this schizophrenia, to the repression of the 'Other Half' of the body, its objectification, and its consequent association with evil. Burroughs says, 'Sex and pain *form* flesh identity'; that is, the body is the siphoned-off object of sex, the object of pain. Or at least the form of the body, its surface, is the object of sex and pain, which implies that inside there is a content, an organism, which experiences sex and pain.

Both dual structures of the body, its external-internal and its top-bottom schizophrenia, are perfectly suited to the sadist. The pleasure of sadism lies in the simultaneous knowledge that one treats the body as an object (the 'Other Half' of the body, its bottom half and its external half), yet that object contains an organism and a consciousness that feel and experience pain. The knowledge that the body one gives pain to contains an organism is titillating to the highest degree, for it enables all organic aspects of experience to ally themselves with the obscene and ugly, with pain and evil. This is the world Burroughs writes about: one in which sex has achieved the space of evil, by virtue of the objectification of both sex and evil, their mutual predisposition as Other: 'Another instrument of these pain tourists is the *signal switch* sir … what they call the "yes no" sir … "I love you I hate you" at supersonic alternating speed. … Take orgasm noises and cut them in with torture and accident groans and screams sir and operating-room jokes sir and flicker sex and torture film right with it sir.' Sex and torture are allied because they are subject to the same manipulative control that objectifies the world as image and that creates a pure separate image of violence. This is why Burroughs's roots are in the underground literature of the eighteenth and nineteenth centuries, the literature of the Marquis de Sade and of all the anonymous nineteenth-century pornographers, the 'Other Half' of the civilized Victorian era.

If control is the result of map structures (patterns, coded punch cards) applied to the content of reality, then one important means of control in a civilized society is the circulation of goods, the map that guarantees the distribution of movable objects. In Burroughs, movable objects control the body literally because they are junk. 'Junk' means both waste objects and heroin, and the two are collapsed into one symbol in Burroughs's world. Civilized society is the consumer culture; it produces objects for instant consumption, objects with their waste function built in, objects to be emptied of their use and thrown away. The object most repeatedly emptied of its use in Burroughs is the needle, and it is emptied into the body. The complements of sadism and its fantasy of control are masochism and passive homosexuality and their fantasies of being controlled. The drug experience is the perfect image of these, for its act is totally receptive, an act that is not an act but the object of one. Thus the junkie is the perfect consumer; his body awaits the distribution of goods and is totally controlled by the map of that distribution. 'The world network of junkies, tuned on a cord of rancid jissom ... tying up in furnished rooms ... shivering in the sick morning.' And junk, Burroughs is careful to point out, is 'the ideal product ... the ultimate merchandise. No sales talk necessary. The client will crawl through a sewer and beg to buy ... The junk merchant does not sell his product to the consumer, he sells the consumer to his product. He does not improve and simplify his merchandise. His degrades and simplifies the client.'

Junk seals the objectification of the body, for the junkie's life consists of a series of actions performed on himself for the purpose of fulfilling a need; the body becomes the medium of that need, the passive vessel of junk. 'Passive' is the important word. The heroin experience is an offering of oneself up to be penetrated, either by another or by one's own self as other. Junk satisfies the need to be passive, to be controlled, to be relieved of the burden of initiating any actions, to be fed, to incorporate, to consume. As Burroughs said in an interview, 'if drugs weren't forbidden in America, they would be the perfect middle-class vice. Addicts would do their work and come home to consume the huge dose of images awaiting them in the mass media' (Knickerbocker 1965:149). The extent to which drugs, especially pills, have in fact become a middle-class institution testifies to the truth of Burroughs's words.

To be controlled by a world of movable objects, of consumer goods, is a schizophrenic experience of the world—and again a kind of schizophrenia that reflects upon the nature of reality itself. Addiction in Burroughs is the natural outgrowth of the addiction to material goods found in, for example, *Moll Flanders*. The difference is that in Burroughs, material goods threaten the addict at the same time they fulfill his need. 'Every object raw and hideous sharp edges that tear the uncovered flesh.' The significance Burroughs invests in the material world is paranoid; objects spring to life and penetrate the body, and the world exists as a threat. 'In the beginning his flesh was simply soft, so soft that he was cut to the bone by dust particles, air currents and brushing overcoats.'

This is the same apprehension of the world by Sartre or Beckett carried one step further. Roquentin and Malone are fascinated by a world of movable objects, objects to pick up and touch, to count, to handle. Burroughs's characters are persecuted by that same world. They are like a schizophrenic patient of Minkowski who feared imminent punishment by a system called the 'residue politics':

> Every leftover, all residue, would be put aside to be one day stuffed into his abdomen—and this, from all over the world. Everything would be included without exception. When one smoked, there would be the burnt match, the ashes, and the cigarette butt. At meals, he was preoccupied with the crumbs, the fruit pits, the chicken bones, the wine or water at the bottom of the glasses. (1923:128)

The subject–object split that produces the external-internal structure of the body also produces a split between the hard-edged objects of the world and the vulnerable, soft body, a split that gives the world the continual character of attack, of bombardment.

This bombardment of objects in Burroughs's novels is the visible manifestation of a world fragmenting itself, refining itself through the map of administration to the degree that it becomes total administration, hence total clutter. In Burroughs's world everything is on the verge of achieving complete separation and complete autonomy; it is a world in the state of explosion. 'Explosion' is finally (and paradoxically) the most uniform quality of Burroughs's novels, the polarity toward which his world most consistently gravitates. Even administrative control and map space cannot finally help objects to cohere, since administration and maps have their own separate space.

This is why context and landscape in Burroughs always exist in pure states; they are the ground out of which objects fly and explode, but they are motionless and ideal, sealed off from those objects. There is the landscape of the City, a mechanical labyrinth, and the landscape of Nature, the Garden of Delights, a swamp, or a mud flat; these are not so much environments in which actions occur as they are pure spaces for themselves. Actions and incidents that have any continuity usually occur in ill-defined rooms or on an ill-defined plain. Between these, which become less frequent with each novel, the wanderings of consciousness describe objects in a constant state of permutation and explosion, objects deprived of their context, each one in the context of itself, in its own exclusive space:

> Lord Jim has turned bright yellow in the woe withered moon of morn-
> ing like white smoke against the blue stuff, and shirts whip in a cold
> spring wind on limestone cliffs across the river, Mary, and the dawn is
> broken in two pieces like Dillinger on the lamster way to the Biograph.
> Smell of neon and atrophied gangsters, and the criminal manqué
> nerves himself to crack a pay toilet sniffing ammonia in a Bucket. ... 'A
> caper', he says. 'I'll pull this capon I mean caper.'

Burroughs's solution to the repressive control that the image of real-ity imposes is to fragment it and mix it together, to erase all lines between things. If reality is a film, one loosens its grip by submit-ting it to a state of explosion, by cutting it up and splicing all spaces and times randomly together:

> 'The Subliminal Kid' moved in seas of disembodied sound—He then
> spaced here and there and instaff [sic] opposite mirrors and took
> movies each bar so that the music and talk is at arbitrary intervals and
> shifted bars—And he also had recorder in tracks and moving film mix-
> ing arbitrary intervals and agents moving with the word and image of
> tape recorders—So he set up waves and his agents with movie swirled
> through all the streets of image and brought back street in music from
> the city and poured Aztec Empire and Ancient Rome—Commuter or
> Chariot Driver could not control their word dust drifted from outer
> space—Air hammers word and image explosive bio-advance—A million

drifting screens on the walls of his city projected mixing sound of any bar could be heard in all Westerns and film of all times played and recorded at the people back and forth with portable cameras and telescope lenses [...]

Burroughs's explosion of the reality image, as this passage illustrates, is an explosion of language too, the very language he uses to describe that explosion. The flat space of the objective world exists as a page as well as a film. To break its regimental control over consciousness, one must 'Shift linguals—Cut word lines', two phrases that occur over and over in *Nova Express* and *The Ticket that Exploded*.

This is the feature of Burroughs's novels that has won him a great deal of attention—the cut-up method of writing, by which a text is cut into short phrases of six or seven words, shuffled around and pasted together. Burroughs claims that he used this method unconsciously in *Naked Lunch*, and later had it brought to his attention by Brion Gysin. Together with Gregory Corso and Sinclair Beiles, Burroughs and Gysin published *Minutes to Go*, a collection of cut-up poems and articles, in 1960. Burroughs's novels subsequent to *Minutes to Go* have all displayed a rhythm of cohesion and fragmentation made possible by cutting up passages and printing the cut-up text after the original. With each novel the lines between cohesive writing and cut-ups have been increasingly blurred, and Burroughs has shuffled in cut-up newspaper articles and cut-up literature as well (*Lord Jim*, *The Waste Land*, passages from Shakespeare and Rimbaud).

As Burroughs himself has indicated, the cut-up method is not entirely new. 'When you think of it, "The Waste Land" was the first great cutup collage, and Tristan Tzara had done a bit along the same lines. Dos Passos used the same idea in "The Camera Eye" sequences in *U.S.A.*' Of these three figures, the mention of Tristan Tzara is perhaps most important. Tzara founded the Dada movement, out of which Surrealism grew, and Burroughs's literary roots are deeply imbedded in Dada and Surrealism. The rationale for Burroughs's cut-up method has been best expressed by Brion Gysin—'the poets are supposed to liberate the words [...] [W]ho told the poets they were supposed to think?' (1964:60)—and this rationale stems ultimately from that of Dada. As the catalog of a Dada retrospective put it, 'Man Ray untiringly transformed his surroundings from the useful to the useless [...] setting them free, and us at the same time' (cited by *San Francisco Chronicle* 1968:50). Thus the typical Dada work of art wrenches an object out of the context of its use and juxtaposes it with other such objects, a bicycle wheel upside down on top of a stool, for example, or a fur-lined teacup. Burroughs accomplishes with words what the Dadaists did with objects; he cuts them out of the context that defines their use and that consequently binds us to the real world.

At the bottom of Dada's use of objects and Burroughs's use of words is a sense of contradiction. In Dada, objects become at once static and dynamic—static, purely objective, by virtue of their lack of function, and dynamic by virtue of the contradiction that strangles their function (as in a fur-lined teacup). Dada objects impose their inertness (as objects do in *La Nausée*), and they do so by the energy released through contradiction. Dada and Surrealism also apply this sense of contradiction to language. In poems by Tristan Tzara or André Breton, not only is there a general atmosphere founded upon what in realistic terms is contradictory, that is, an atmosphere that merges fantasy and reality, dream life and waking life, but there is also a focused contradiction in every image. As one critic has put it, 'in order for the surrealistic image to provoke us out of our passivity, it must have a strength greater than the mere comparison of two similar things. It gathers its peculiar intensity from an inner contradiction powerful enough to free the imaginer from banal ways of judging a familiar phenomenon' (Caws 1966:56). Or as Reverdy has said, the profundity of an image is in an exact ratio to the distance between its elements (cited by Caws 1966:59). This is why, according to Kenneth Burke, Surrealist images are always violent; by bringing together objects of reality that don't belong together, Surrealism rapes the order of reality (1940:576).

More precisely, Surrealism rapes the order of language, which is analogous to the order of reality. This is what Burroughs does also. As Steven Koch puts it, 'in literature, meaning and structure are virtually coextensive'; hence Burroughs gives words 'their affect priority over their roles as signs quite simply: by de-structuring, by destruction' (1966:26). The extent to which this destruction is a natural extension of Surrealism can be seen in Reverdy's formula for re-energizing language, which is precisely one of destructuring. He proposes to eliminate conventional syntax and punctuation, to have no linking words, no adjectives, and no adverbs, so that only the force of nouns clashing together would be left (Caws 1966:59). The next step, as Swift showed in Book III of *Gulliver's Travels*, would be to eliminate nouns and communicate simply by holding up actual objects (or not so simply, as Swift saw, since one's vocabulary would have to be carried around on one's back). Swift's joke is the reality of an important aspect of twentieth-century consciousness. When the structure of language is invisible, when language itself is transparent, as it necessarily is for the realist, then it exists only as a glue to hold objects together. Surrealism carried over, perhaps as an unconscious expression of its parody of realism, this invisible function of language; as Aragon said, 'the content of a surrealist text is decisively important' (cited by Nadeau 1944:81).

The space of language is invisible in Surrealism, just as the space of Surrealistic paintings is the invisibly 'real' space of academic perspective, space as a container. This is why Surrealism, to reverse Frost's definition of poetry, is what is *not* lost in translation. The content of Surrealism consists of the objects it juxtaposes, and thus consists of words themselves as objects. When language is only a glue, its grip on objects can be loosened; as Roquentin in *La Nausée* says, 'things are divorced from their names'. Consequently names themselves are things, are objects to be cut up and shuffled around, 'all the words of the world stirring around in a cement mixer', Burroughs says. Surrealism makes the invisible structure of language visible; it carries the objectification of words in realism necessitated by that invisible structure to its inevitable conclusion. In this sense Burroughs is the supreme realist: in the cut-up passages of his novels, his world is there, consisting of the words on the page. For example, 'And love slop is a Bristol—Bring together state of news—Inquire on hospital—At the Ovens Great Gold Cup—Revived peat victory hopes of Fortia—Premature Golden sands in Sheila's cottage?—You want the name of Hassan i Sabbah so own the unborn?—Cool and casual through the hole in thin air closed at hotel room in London [...]' Burroughs's world is one in which objects have become so objective, so one-dimensional, so thin, that they have dropped out of the words they are dressed in, leaving only those words—as objects—behind.

This is why there is no silence in Burroughs's world (although he strongly desires it, as he states several times), and no shadows. Silence is built into the expressive nature of language, into what R. P. Blackmur calls 'language as gesture' (see Blackmur 1952), not into language as an invisible structure. Just as there is no expressive synthesis to the body in Burroughs, so there is no expressive synthesis to language, and words are consequently objectified and fragmented.

This is how and why they can be exploded, cut up. Words are an image of separate existence, existence in a body, in flesh, which is torment for Burroughs. One of the most striking passages in Burroughs's works occurs at the end of *The Soft Machine*, when tentative humans are born into separate existence excrementally, and take on the condition of words through their birth:

> We waded into the warm mud-water. hair and ape flesh off in screaming strips. stood naked human bodies covered with phosphorescent green jelly. soft tentative flesh cut with ape wounds. peeling other genitals. fingers and tongues rubbing off the jelly-cover. body melting pleasure-sounds in the warm mud. till the sun went and a blue wind of silence touched human faces and hair. When we came out of the mud we had names.

This is Burroughs's version of the Garden of Eden—it is one of the few actually serene passages in all his novels, even though that serenity is laced with matter-of-fact violence. Eden is the childhood mud of excrement and anal pleasure, and childhood is the only peace possible for bodily existence, since it is polymorphously perverse—'body melting pleasure-sounds in the warm mud'—and the body hasn't channeled into its separate existence yet. For this reason the body hasn't channeled into the separate existences of its individual senses either, and there is 'a blue wind of silence'. The fall consists of emerging from childhood and receiving a name. Anality then becomes simply repulsive and can be enjoyed only in regressive fantasy and violence, since a name indicates a bodily existence, a separate existence in flesh: 'What scared you all into time? Into body? Into shit? I will tell you: "*the word.*" Alien Word "*the.*" "*The*" *word* of Alien Enemy imprisons "*thee*" in Time. In Body. In Shit.'

The solution to separate existence is to atomize it, to make it totally separate, to cut it up, to explode it. In this sense Burroughs, for all the fantastic nature of his novels, participates in the structures of realism. Realism's function is a separating one, and the primary separations it makes are between the self and the body, and the self and the world. Language is always invisible in realism because the body has disappeared and is no longer the intersection of self and world. Burroughs fastens upon the necessary fragmentation entailed by draining the cohesive force of the self out of the world of things, out of the body, and out of language. He aggravates that fragmentation, cuts it up, and completes the transformation from the invisible structure of language to the objectification of words, to the making of all words into names, a transformation that enables words to become an image of totally separate existence.

The cut-up, or more exactly, being cut up, accounts in part for the experience of time in the world of Burroughs's novels. Time, like other aspects of that world, exists at two polar extremes, the first of which is explosion, being cut out of a context, the experience of total transportation out of oneself, out of a location, out of materiality. This is the temporality of flying and of release; it is ejaculation, the experience of being emptied, the experience of weightlessness. One is emptied of the body and its corporeality: '[T]he soft bones spurted out in orgasm leaving a deflated skin collected by the guards.' This is why ejaculation is so often associated with flying. Boys masturbate in roller coasters, on high wires, in planes, or simply while flying through the air—'boys swing from rings and bars jissom falling through dusty air of gymnasiums'. The drug experience also is a 'high', and being high is flying, exploding, often an actual experience of leaving the body: 'I project myself out through the glasses and across the street, a ghost in the morning sunlight, torn with disembodied lust.'

When this experience exists in the body, it is temporality as frenzied activity, the body flinging itself in all directions, each organ at the pitch of its activity and pushing at its walls, eyes popping, throat screaming, arms and legs thrashing. This is temporality as overflow and overreach, the temporality of fire or of water as a fountain: 'This book spill off the page in all directions, kaleidoscope of vistas, medley of tunes and street noises, farts and riot yipes and the slamming steel shutters of commerce, screams of pain and pathos and screams plain pathic, copulating cats and outraged squawk of the displaced bull head, prophetic mutterings of brujo in nutmeg trances, snapping necks and screaming mandrakes.' At one polarity, temporality is the experience of boundlessness, specifically a release from the boundaries, the gravity, of the past.

At the other polarity, time is a being completely bounded, a being trapped, specifically by the body and by the decay of the body. If at one extreme, temporality can be seen orally as screaming, at the other it is orally a being devoured: 'This Sex Skin is a critter found in the rivers here wraps all around you like a second skin eats you slow and good.' Decay consists of this devouring as an action the body performs on itself, as the growth of the body over itself. The most explicit instance of this occurs at the end of the story of the talking asshole in *Naked Lunch*, when the anal function seizes control over the body and literally devours it:

> After that he began waking up in the morning with a transparent jelly like a tadpole's tail all over his mouth. The jelly was what the scientists call un-D.T., Undifferentiated Tissue, which can grow into any kind of flesh on the human body. He would tear it off his mouth and the pieces would stick to his hands like burning gasoline jelly and grow there, grow anywhere on him a glob of it fell. So finally his mouth sealed over, and the whole head would have amputated spontaneous [...] except for the *eyes* you dig. That's one thing the asshole *couldn't* do was see. It needed the eyes. But nerve connections were blocked and infiltrated and atrophied so the brain couldn't give orders any more. It was trapped in the skull, sealed off.

The result is 'one all-purpose blob', the body sunk into its own weight.

If time at one polarity is a being emptied, at the other it is a being filled, a filling itself and spreading into itself of the body. Thus weightlessness at one polarity becomes a total surrender to weight at the other, flying becomes falling, and being high on drugs becomes coming down. Temporality as fire and a fountain becomes temporality as a stagnant pool and inorganic matter; the last is Burroughs's definition of a virus—'the renunciation of life itself, a *falling* towards inorganic, inflexible machine, towards dead matter'. Temporality as exploding becomes temporality as the settling of debris after explosion. This settling can be seen in one of the frequent devices Burroughs uses to modulate his prose. After describing a frenzied activity, he elongates the description, flattens it out and allows it to echo through the narrator's unconscious. The effect produced is rhythmically like the aftermath of an explosion:

> The scream shot out of his flesh through empty locker rooms and barracks, musty resort hotels, and spectral, coughing corridors of T.B. sanitariums, the muttering, hawking, grey dishwater smell of flophouses and Old Men's Homes, great, dusty custom sheds and warehouses, through broken porticoes and smeared arabesques, iron urinals worn paper thin by the urine of a million fairies, deserted weed-grown privies with a musty smell of shit turning back to the soil, erect wooden phallus on the grave of dying peoples plaintive as leaves in the wind, across the great brown river where whole trees float with green snakes

in the branches and sad-eyed lemurs watch the shore out over a vast plain (vulture wings husk in the dry air).

This kind of rhythmic settling represents the settling of Burroughs's world as a whole, as it descends into the flat, shadowless and time-less consciousness of cut-ups in the Nova trilogy. If the first polarity of time in Burroughs represents the release of time from the bound-aries of the past, that is, explosion, then settling as the second polar-ity represents a return to those boundaries and a total release from the possibilities of the future.

The moment in Burroughs at which these two polarities intersect is the moment of his most recurring image, the 'orgasm death'. The most common manifestation of this is hanging; the hanged man in Burroughs always ejaculates at the moment of death, an act that combines the weightlessness and transportation of the body at the pitch of its activity with the sudden grip of the body's own weight, and its falling into the death of that weight. When time has been separated into schizophrenic polarities, as it has in Burroughs's world, only a totally violent act can hold time together, and that act is the orgasm death, 'the whole birth death cycle of action'. Burroughs's obsession with this image is a desperate attempt to overcome the frightening schizophrenia of his world, an attempt that is self-defeating the more it is returned to, not only because its violence feeds that schizophrenia but also because it fragments time into islands of repetition, into purely exclusive moments, repeated orgasm deaths, which are exclusive in that they are related to nei-ther the continuity of the past nor the becoming of the future. This is the result of Burroughs's polarization of time; temporality now lacks a past and is total explosion, it now lacks a future and is set-tling, and it now lacks a past and a future and is orgasm death. Temporality thus falls apart into discrete components; it doesn't ripen or become.

Time in Burroughs takes one step beyond the spatialization of time in realism, but a step that realism makes inevitable. Time as a line, or a series of converging and diverging lines—time as the plot and reified continuity of realistic fiction—hardens and becomes brittle for Burroughs, so that it shatters and exists as a series of dis-crete, atomistic points or moments (as it exists for Descartes). If real-ity is addicting, as Burroughs claims, the proper time of realism is the time of the addict, which is atomistic, discontinuous. As one psychologist, Von Gebsttattel, puts it, 'the addict, having lost the contextual continuity of his inner life-history, exists therefore only in punctuate fragmentation, at the moment of illusionary fulfillment, that is, discontinuously' (cited by Binswanger 1944:347). Burroughs's warnings against junk (as well as his warnings against the orgasm death) are thus warnings against reality and the control over temporality that reality imposes by repetition. Junk is image, and 'the image past molds your future imposing repetition as the past accumulates and all actions are prerecorded and doped out and there is no life left in the present'.

But despite his own warnings, Burroughs's world is most completely his world when it exists as pure repetition, when it is cut up. The cut-up world is the final condition of time, as it is of space, in early Burroughs: it is atomistic time, time as a series of separate instantaneous flashes, time objectified and shattered into pieces, thus no time at all. This is why the completely bizarre often becomes the completely monotonous in early Burroughs. Realism that has been amputated into pure fantasy, and therefore into an ultimate realism, simply repeats itself if it exists only by virtue of being amputated. Time in the cut-up world of Burroughs is the same as what Von Gebstattel calls manic time: 'The manic always does the same, experiences the same, and in the medium of experientially immanent time moves nowhere' (cited by Binswanger 1944:387). Burroughs's world is precisely this: a movement toward immobility, toward frozen space. He arrives at this immobility from a different route than, say, Beckett's characters. He imposes explosion, and Beckett imposes catatonia. But the result is finally the same: a 'real' world that consists of words as physical entities on the immobile space of a book's pages.

In many ways, Burroughs's world represents a direct attack upon the world of realism. 'I have said the "basic pre-clear identities" are now ended', he asserts in *Nova Express*, and indeed the concept of the world as 'identity', and of characters as 'identities', is destroyed by Burroughs. But Burroughs's destruction of reality is accomplished with the very tools of reality, not only with junk but with scissors. The result is an object-world whose pre-confusion, whose nonidentity, *is* its identity, and whose schizophrenia is precisely the accelerated schizophrenia of the real world. There is no plot in Burroughs's world, but its frozen space is similar, for example, to the frozen space of Fielding's world, to the extent that the permission Fielding grants the reader in *Joseph Andrews* to skip chapters becomes in Burroughs the permission to 'cut into *Naked Lunch* at any intersection point'.

Burroughs's novels thus become diabolical maps, maps whose surfaces have been so intersected with conflicting directions, so cut up, that they are unreadable; they are maps of hell. Even the 'conflicting directions', the sense of surrealistic contradiction in Burroughs, are finally neutralized by a cut-up world, a world existing in pieces that can't relate to each other enough to contradict. This is more true of *Nova Express* and *The Ticket that Exploded*, than it is of *Naked Lunch* and *The Soft Machine*. In *The Soft Machine* Burroughs makes his best use of cut-ups by establishing with them a dynamic rhythm of cohesion and fragmentation that becomes the experience of the novel. In *Nova Express* and *The Ticket that Exploded*, however, cut-ups come to seize their own space, to have less to do with other sections of the novels, except as waste bins to catch those sections when they drop. They become stagnant pools of amputated language and space through which the reader has to wade.

The amputation of language and space becomes also, at its extreme, an amputation of the body. Although the body in Burroughs is reified into two principles, an organic and a mechanical one, the mechanical is the final condition of the body, since even purely organic life, the body as blob, eventually swallows itself and falls into mineral existence, into death. Thus the objectification of the body in realism becomes in Burroughs a total dismemberment of the body, an explosion of it into separate existence, into pieces whose parts are all equal to each other and equal to any other object in the vicinity. This is the final condition of realism: schizophrenic atomism, living in pieces, in a world of pieces. Burroughs's world is the 'real' world broken down into the components that Democritus began 'reality' with, into atoms. Cut-ups finally strip away all the illusions Democritus talked about; they tear objects out of any context they may have created in combination and give their pure context back to them, so that 'in *reality*', as Democritus said, 'there are only Atoms and the Void'.

REFERENCES

Binswanger, L. (1944) 'The Case of Ellen West', Lyons, J., and Mendel, W. M. trans., IN May, R., Angel, E., and Ellenberger, H. F. eds 1958, pp. 237–364.

Blackmur, R. P. (1952) *Language as Gesture: Essays in Poetry* (New York: Harcourt Brace).

Burke, K. (1940) 'Surrealism', IN *New Directions 1940* (Norfolk, CT).

Čapek, M. (1961) *The Philosophical Impact of Contemporary Physics* (Princeton, NJ: Van Nostrand).

Caws, M. (1966) *Surrealism and the Literary Imagination: A Study of Breton and Bachelard* (The Hague: Mouton).

Gysin, B. (1964) 'Cut-Ups', *Evergreen Review* (8)32, April/May 1964.

Knickerbocker, C. (1965) 'William Burroughs', IN *Writers at Work: The Paris Review Interviews*, third series (New York: Modern Library, 1967), pp. 141–74.

Koch, S. (1966) 'Images of Loathing', *Nation*, 4 July 1966, pp. 25–6.

McLuhan, M. (1964) 'Notes on Burroughs', *Nation*, 28 December 1964, pp. 517–19.

May, R., Angel, E., and Ellenberger, H. F. eds (1958) *Existence: A New Dimension in Psychiatry and Psychology* (New York: Basic Books).

Merleau-Ponty, M. (1945) *The Phenomenology of Perception*, Smith, C. trans. (London: Humanities Press, 1962).

Minkowski, E. (1923) 'Findings in a Case of Schizophrenic Depression', Bliss, B. trans., IN May, R., Angel, E., and Ellenberger, H. F. eds 1958, pp. 127–38.

Nadeau, M. (1944) *The History of Surrealism*, Howard, R. trans. (New York: MacMillan, 1965).

Rosen, E., and Gregory, I. (1965) *Abnormal Psychology* (Philadelphia: Saunders).

San Francisco Chronicle, 18 October 1968, p. 50.

Turbayne, C. (1962) *The Myth Of Metaphor* (New Haven: Yale University Press).

13
The High Priest and the Great Beast at *The Place of Dead Roads*

Ron Roberts

UNCLE AL AND UNCLE BILL IN THE TWENTY-FIRST CENTURY

This chapter will construct a relationship between the figures of William S. Burroughs, the 'High Priest' of beatnik and punk culture, and Aleister Crowley, the 'Great Beast' of black magic.[1] There is a sense in which the work of both authors connects into a larger, more occult network of thought than that which influences popular culture, resulting in a 'feedback loop', reprocessing certain aspects of their work and influencing everything from musical projects to contemporary retellings of major superhero stories. The start and end point of this loop is Burroughs's treatment of magic(k)al practice, particularly in *The Place of Dead Roads*, and its relationship to Crowley's esoteric writings.[2]

William S. Burroughs and Aleister Crowley can be seen as dual influences in a number of late twentieth-century movements, both artistic and political. Artistically, the most famous of these is probably Genesis P-Orridge's Temple ov Psychick Youth [sic] of the 1970s and 1980s, who were heavily influenced by, and worked with, Burroughs. They applied his processes to music, video and writing, while at the same time reading and absorbing the work of Crowley the magician. In a similar vein, Scottish comic-book writer Grant Morrison—called in to overhaul ailing marquee titles such as *The Justice League of America* (1997–2000), *The X-Men* (2001–2003) and *The Flash* (1997–98)—wrote a Burroughsian-influenced conspiracy theory title, *The Invisibles* (1994–2000). Morrison's websites are hotbeds of debate concerning magical technique, Burroughs, Crowley, drugs, the Beats and related topics. Toward the end of

The Invisibles's (flagging) run, Morrison provided his readers with a page that was itself a mystical focus (or sigil) asking them to perform Crowleyian VIIIth Degree magic over it (a concept that we shall investigate later in this chapter), so that the comic might continue to be published.

It is not just in the realm of art and comic books that the presence of Burroughs and Crowley can be felt. Musically, Burroughs collaborated with figures as diverse as Kurt Cobain and The Disposable Heroes of HipHoprisy, while Crowley's influence on bands such as Led Zeppelin is well known (see Davis 1985). Finally, while neither Burroughs nor Crowley developed a strongly self-conscious political stance, elements of their politics can be identified within the pop-political movement of the late twentieth and early twenty-first centuries, particularly in the anti-globalization movement associated with such figures as Noam Chomsky, Naomi Klein, Douglas Rushkoff and Howard Zinn. It can be observed that the majority of work produced by these artists and theorists responds, from the vantage point of various interrelated perspectives on the complexities of Western civilization, to what is rapidly coalescing into a 'Westernized' global order.

BURROUGHS AND THE GLOBAL ORDER

An entry point into a salient discussion of the 'global order' through the work of both Burroughs and Crowley must consider that their respective writings on the emergence of a consolidated global political and economic system seem to move in different directions: one emphasizing technocratic restrictions, the other delivering a crypto-fascist attack on permissiveness and purposelessness. In *Naked Lunch* (1959), Doctor Benway is one of the ciphers through which Burroughs foretells the development of post-World War II Western society:

> Benway is a manipulator and co-ordinator of symbol systems, an expert on all phases of interrogation, brainwashing and control [...]
> 'I deplore brutality', he said. 'It's not efficient. On the other hand, prolonged mistreatment, short of physical violence, gives rise, when skillfully applied, to anxiety and a feeling of special guilt. A few rules or rather guiding principles are to be borne in mind. The subject must not realize that the mistreatment is a deliberate attack of an anti-human enemy on his personal identity. He must be made to feel that he

deserves any treatment he receives because there is something (never specified) horribly wrong with him. The naked need of the control addicts must be decently covered by an arbitrary and intricate bureaucracy so that the subject cannot contact his enemy direct.' (NL 20–1)

It could be said that something akin to these 'control addicts'— variously identified in Burroughs's fictions as 'Nova criminals', alien beings from Minraud and 'vegetable people'—today administer and propagate a global sociopolitical hegemony. Like the 'technocracy' of Theodore Roszak and Herbert Marcuse, Burroughs sees a highly scientific and efficient anti-human impulse in twentieth-century society that stands as the crowning achievement of the Enlightenment process. 'Under the technocracy', writes Roszak, 'we become the most scientific of societies; yet, like Kafka's [protagonist in The Castle] K., men throughout the "developed world" become more and more the bewildered dependents of inaccessible castles wherein inscrutable technicians conjure with their fate' (1969:13).[3]

In The Place of Dead Roads, the order outlined in Naked Lunch has come to fruition; the later novel's primary concern is with the main character's struggle against the forces of a 'global order' that seeks to limit human potential and homogenize the human race. The novel chronicles the battle between the Johnson family (a term lifted from Jack Black's 1926 vagrancy classic You Can't Win describing those vagrants who abided by the rules of 'tramp chivalry'), and the 'shits'— the forces of 'truth', 'justice' and 'moral order'. The Johnsons are a gang in the sense of the Old West, although with a conspiracy-theory spin that transforms them from honorable tramps into a global network of anti-establishment operatives, struggling against the depredations of the 'powers that be' (led in the novel by the bounty hunter Mike Chase). The villains in Burroughs's novels often perform a double function, rapidly shifting from innocuous lowlifes to enemies of humanity, depending on the scene. In The Place of Dead Roads, this trope is noticeable in the shift from western to sci-fi story. It is telling that after a scene in which Kim and his friends invoke a major demon (PDR 92–4)—described with a careful eye to accuracy that draws from both the style of Crowley's rituals and the fiction of H. P. Lovecraft—the narrative focus becomes more surreally 'globalized'. Kim's enemies cease to be homophobic cowboys, upstart gunslingers and lawmen; instead, a stranger and more insidious enemy is theorized: the body-snatching alien invaders of Nova Express. Old Man Bickford and his cronies operate as typical western villains, but their conflict with the Utopian program of Kim Carsons and his Johnson family betrays their identity as the 'alien' influence Burroughs sees as responsible for the propagation of Western capitalism and the denial of human potential. It is these 'aliens'—alien in the sense that they seek to limit individual freedom through control mechanisms and an enforcement of ignorance—who constitute a new global order. For Burroughs, it is this anti-humanitarian impulse (typified by those who vehemently enforce laws surrounding 'victimless crime', and those whose nefarious schemes affect governments and nation states) that represents the greatest evil of the post-World War II order. Thus, the global order could constitute everything from a local group opposing a gay bar or hash café, through to the IMF or World Bank controlling the 'development' of a nation.

Writing in the first half of the last century, Crowley never formulated a picture of the modern industrial order in as much detail as Burroughs. However, in a preface to his cryptic *The Book of the Law*, he states:

> Observe for yourselves the decay of the sense of sin, the growth of innocence and irresponsibility, the strange modifications of the reproductive instinct with a tendency to become bi-sexual or epicene, the childlike confidence in progress combined with nightmare fear of catastrophe, against which we are yet half unwilling to take precautions.
>
> Consider the outcrop of dictatorships [...] and the prevalence of infantile cults like Communism, Fascism, Pacifism, Health Crazes, Occultism in nearly all its forms, religions sentimentalized to the point of practical extinction.
>
> Consider the popularity of the cinema, the wireless, the football pools and guessing competitions, all devices for soothing fractious children, no seed of purpose in them.
>
> Consider sport, the babyish enthusiasms and rages which it excites, whole nations disturbed by disputes between boys.
>
> Consider war, the atrocities which occur daily and leave us unmoved and hardly worried.
>
> We are children. (1938:13)

It is not too difficult to connect Burroughs's 'control addicts' with the various mechanisms of control (or placation) that Crowley lists above. While Burroughs posits a class of controllers, Crowley tends to see humanity's regression as a self-inflicted condition. Crowley posits a future Age of Aquarius, or 'Aeon of Horus',[4] in which humanity will reach a stage of adolescence. At that time (some point in the twentieth century), decisions would be made affecting the evolution of the species over the next 2,000 years (the standard length of an astrological age); Crowley argues that without the widespread adoption of his Law of Thelema, 'Do what thou wilt shall be the whole of the Law', a combination of infantilism and dictatorial control will result in the stultification of the human race.

This theme of progressive human evolution is also evident in Burroughs's fiction: his work prophesies a time when human culture will advance, becoming truly post-human, capable of transcending temporal restrictions and making the great leap into space. The first stage in such an evolution is the dissolution of boundaries: geographical, psychic and physical. This doctrine is at one with Crowley's generalized transgressive maxim: 'But exceed! Exceed!' (1938:37)

Significantly, these boundaries are located both within the self and imposed upon us by 'control addicts' like Doctor Benway. These boundaries, then, fulfill a role not unlike that of ideology, 'fixing' the identity of the individual through a combination of internal and external factors. And both Burroughs and Crowley suggest various strategies for the reshaping of the external world through the destruction of internal restriction; that is, the destruction of, or escape from, 'ideology' as a negative force. Common to both writers is a belief in the 'magical' power of language. Burroughs's most famous dictum, of language as a virus, echoes Crowley's maxim that the Will (or Word) of the magician can cause measurable changes in external reality, offering the possibility that the 'language virus', this 'muttering sickness', may be capable of transforming, rather than simply destroying, its host.

SEX MAGIC

Early in Burroughs's *The Place of Dead Roads* comes a sequence that distills a few centuries' worth of cryptic alchemical and magical texts into a page or so of wild west science fiction:

> Once he made sex magic against Judge Farris, who said Kim was rotten clear through and smelled like a polecat. He nailed a full-length picture of the Judge to the wall, taken from the society page, and masturbated

in front of it while he intoned a jingle he had learned from a Welsh nanny:

> *Slip and stumble* (lips peel back from his teeth)
> *Trip and fall* (his eyes light up inside)
> *Down the stairs*
> *And hit the wallllllllllllllll!*

His hair stands up on end. He whines and whimpers and howls the word out and shoots all over the Judge's leg. And Judge Farris actually did fall downstairs a few days later, and fractured his shoulder bone. (*PDR* 19–20)

Kim Carsons, the novel's time- and dimension-traveling assassin protagonist, 'knew that he had succeeded in projecting a thought form. But he was not overly impressed [...] Magic seemed to Kim a hit-and-miss operation, and to tell the truth, a bit silly. Guns and knives were more reliable' (*PDR* 20).

Silliness aside, the above extract reflects the VIIIth Degree teachings of the Ordo Templi Orientis (OTO), an order of Knights Templar that, allegedly, brought back the secrets of Tantric Yoga (sexual yoga, where the object of intercourse is not 'mere' orgasm, but the ritual unification of participants as the male/female—Shiva/Shakti—principles of the universe) from India.[5] At the invitation of the German leaders of the order (who due to the nature of the young Englishman's knowledge initially believed him to have stolen their secrets), Crowley took over and restructured the British OTO in 1912, incorporating his own magical symbolism and interest in homosexual sex magic. Initiates were taught to project their sexual energy in a ritual context employing trappings such as mantras, incenses and visualizations to focus the energy and use it as fuel for the Will.[6] Esoteric sex and masturbation becomes, then, 'the Science and Art of causing change to occur in conformity with the Will' (1929:xii). Sex as an instrument allowing 'action at a distance' is commonplace in Burroughs's fiction, while the human Will is conceived of not as individual agency, but as part of a larger network. As Burroughs explains: 'I think what we think of as ourselves is a very unimportant, a very small part of our actual potential [...] We should talk about the most mysterious subject of all—sex. Sex is an electromagnetic phenomenon' (Bockris 1981:60). (There are clear parallels between this conception of sexual energy and Wilhelm Reich's theories of Orgone power—a topic of great interest to Burroughs—and Michael Bertiaux's work with the sexual radioactivity he terms 'Ojas'.[7])

The 'electromagnetic'—or otherwise mysterious, occult—force generated during sex, and sexual magic in particular, is an important weapon in the fight against the 'shits' on the side of order and repression. While Kim rejects magic as a means of performing relatively prosaic acts such as revenge, *The Place of Dead Roads* later advocates magic as a means for large-scale transformation of the human Will; indeed, in this novel Burroughs considers it necessary for the transformation of the *human species*. Using the example of the medieval assassins, a quasi-mythical sect led by the fabled Old Man of the Mountain, Hassan i Sabbah, Burroughs outlines the ways in which magical knowledge—especially the nourishment and cultivation of this electromagnetic sexual power—can be used to transform the consciousness into a new order of being. It is this new being that is capable of resisting control, placation and suppression: the homogenizing tools of the 'control addicts'.

Hassan i Sabbah, a recurring figure in Burroughs's fiction, acts as a Guardian Angel to Kim, his dictum 'Nothing is true, Everything is permitted' an early version of Crowley's famous Law of Thelema: 'Do what thou wilt shall be the whole of the Law' (see Bockris 1981:116). In *The Place of Dead Roads*, the Assassins serve as an example of the next step in human evolution, while in earlier novels such as *Nova Express* (1964) it is the disembodied voice and shadowy presence of Sabbah that stands in opposition to the forces of the 'control addicts'. The 'Slave Gods' of Western civilization demand nothing but servitude; Burroughs makes this clear in an eight-point description of the 'objectives and characteristics' of the Slave Gods and their alien followers (*PDR* 97). Primarily they must ensure that the human race remains earthbound; at all costs, mankind must be prevented from reaching higher realms of existence:

> So the Old Man set up his own station, the Garden of Alamut. But the Garden is not at the end of the line. It might be seen as a rest camp and mutation center. Free from harassment, the human artifact [sic] can evolve into an organism suited for space conditions and space travel. (*PDR* 172)

There is a clear link between the figures of the assassins and comments made elsewhere by Burroughs concerning his beliefs for the future of mankind. When asked if he sees 'Outer Space as the solution to this cop-ridden planet', Burroughs replied, 'Yeah, it's the only place to go! If we ever get out alive ... *if* we're lucky' (Vale and Juno 1982:21). Later in the same interview, Burroughs cites Dion Fortune's *Psychic Self Defence* (1952) and David Conway's *Magic: An Occult Primer* (1973) as essential texts for those wishing to resist the technocracy's less obvious control mechanisms.[8]

According to Burroughs, the transformative powers of the assassins came from the homosexual act—an act that does not depend upon dualism and rejects the creative principles of copulation. As we have already seen, the VIIIth Degree of OTO sex magic, with its emphasis on the projection of an outward manifestation of the Will, was rejected by Burroughs as too 'hit-and-miss'. However, the homosexual act constitutes the XIth Degree of sex magic, almost universally acknowledged in occult circles as the most powerful form of Tantric energy manipulation. Modern magician and Voudon houngan Michael Bertiaux agrees: 'Those who possess the technical knowledge admit that psychic ability is increased so that all of the forms of low mediumship and crude psychic powers are made perfect, while the higher psychic powers are fully manifested' (Bertiaux 1988:44).

Crowley gives the theoretical formula of the XIth Degree in his *Magick in Theory and Practice*. He notes that

> [s]uch an operation makes creation impossible [...] Its effect is to consecrate the Magicians who perform it in a very special way [...] The great merits of this formula are that it avoids contact with the inferior planes, that it is self-sufficient, that it involves no responsibilities, and that it leaves its masters not only stronger in themselves, but wholly free to fulfill their essential Natures. Its abuse is an abomination. (1929:27)

The homophobic stance adopted in the last sentence is clearly a statement Burroughs would have disagreed with; it is an example of the bisexual Crowley making his writing more 'palatable' to a wide audience. However, it suggests the same special power Burroughs attributes to the non-dualistic or non-reproductive use of sex magic.

To return to the magical universe explicated in *The Place of Dead Roads*, it becomes obvious that magic—especially sex magic—is an important weapon in the arsenal of resistance. Burroughs returns to the VIIIth Degree episode quoted earlier in this chapter, commenting that linear narrative itself is a trope used by any global order as an instrument of control. The Slave Gods and their minions, the control addicts, administrate the reality 'film' much as a person with a remote control has power over the progression of a video-taped movie. It is the role of the enlightened resistor to 'cut up' this straightforward A-B-C conception of time:

> Take a segment of film:
> This is a time segment. You can run it backward and forward, you can speed it up, slow it down, you can randomize it do anything you want with your film. You are God for that film segment. So 'God', then, has precisely *that* power with the human film.
> The only thing not prerecorded in a prerecorded universe is the pre-recordings themselves: the master film. The unforgivable sin is to tamper with the prerecordings. Exactly what Kim is doing. (*PDR* 218)

Burroughs then explicitly links the transcendental powers of sex magic (specifically the episode discussed earlier) with this 'tamper-ing' process—a means to resisting and transcending the global order of the twentieth and twenty-first centuries.

Despite specific differences that these sex magics maintain in their philosophy, each system proffers sex as a transformative 'force' capable of producing a potentially 'resistant' state of subjectivity. The vehicle for such change is the development of a 'hidden' body that coexists with the physical shell, a 'ghost in the machine', or Body of Light.

BURROUGHS AND THE BODY OF LIGHT

In his book *Queer Burroughs* (2001), Jamie Russell draws attention to Burroughs's use of Crowley's term 'Body of Light'. Crowley's term (there are many others, such as the Voudon 'Gwos Bon Anj') describes the astral (or etheric) body that coexists alongside/in the normal, physical self. It is this astral form that possesses the capacity for mag-ical acts and makes contact with other astral entities. Therefore, cul-tivation of the astral self, this 'Body of Light', is essential for acts of magical resistance.

Burroughs had a great interest in 'other beings', specifically those termed succubae and incubi, or 'sexual vampires'. He theorized that these 'sexual vampires' are not necessarily negative in their relation-ships with human beings. In *The Place of Dead Roads*, Kim Carsons encounters such an entity, and finds the experience both pleasurable and rewarding. Toby, his incubus companion, is a ghostly figure that merges wholly with Kim as they make love: 'Afterward the boy would slowly separate and lie beside him in the bed, almost transparent but with enough substance to indent the bedding' (*PDR* 169). However, sexual contact with disembodied entities brings more than just physical pleasure—the relationship can lead to the accumulation of powerful allies in the fight against those forces seeking to replicate a restrictive form of global order—for example, those working to limit the potential of human evolution, keeping us ignorant and earthbound, or stuck in Crowley's state of infantilism. Kim Carson finds himself surrounded by a small team of astral sex partners, each of whom brings a special talent to the fight against the enemies of the Johnson family (electronics work, demolition, causing accidents). These sexual familiars can be cultivated using the VIIIth and XIth Degree OTO ritual work: 'He should make a point of organizing a staff of such spirits to suit various occasions. These should be "familiar" spirits, in the strict sense; members of his family' (Crowley 1929:169).

Burroughs posits a more extreme use for such beings: as helpers and catalysts in the transformation from earthbound human to space-traveling post-human. Or, perhaps more radically, as potential allies in the conflict on earth:

> BURROUGHS: We can only speculate as to what further relations with these beings might lead to, my dear. You see, the bodies of incubi and succubi are much less dense than the human body, and this is greatly to their advantage in space travel. Don't forget, it is our bodies which must be weightless to go into space. Now, we make the connections with incubi and succubi in some sort of dream state. So I postulate that dreams may be a form of preparation, and in fact training, for travel in space [...]
>
> BOCKRIS: Are you suggesting that we collaborate with them in some way which would in fact benefit the future of our travel in space?
>
> BURROUGHS: Well, I simply believe that we should pay a great deal of attention to, and develop a much better understanding of, our relations with incubi and succubi. We can hardly afford to ignore their possible danger or use. If we reject a relationship with them, we may be placing our chances of survival in jeopardy. If we don't dream, we may die. (Bockris 1981:189)

Burroughs's conception of using these astral forms as aids to enlightenment/evolution is paralleled in Crowley's work. The invocation of minor spirits from medieval grimoires aside, the central aim of Crowley's magical practice was the 'Knowledge and Conversation of the Holy Guardian Angel' (HGA).[9] This HGA is quite distinct from any notion of a Christian angel, representing instead that part of the Self that transcends the wheel of karma, or analogously, Burroughs's 'prerecorded film'. This perfected self exists beyond the physical boundaries of our shared reality, yet remains a part of the individual. To have the HGA 'on side', as it were, advances the Self toward what Crowley terms 'disincarnation'. This disincarnation is a process of 'removing [...] impurities, of finding in [the] true self an immortal intelligence to whom matter is no more than the means of manifestation' (1929:185). Thus, with the help of alien intelligences, or perhaps just a more rarefied form of our own mind made alien by its perfection, it may be possible to escape this 'cop-ridden' planet once and for all.

There is also a relationship between Burroughs's 'some sort of a dream state' and the astral traveling of Crowley's system of magic. Just as Kim Carsons seems to fold in and out of various dimensions cognizant with, yet not identical to, our own (from the haunted 'wild west' to a twentieth-century United Kingdom on the brink of revolution to futuristic bio-warfare tests in the Middle East), so Crowley tells us of various 'planes' of existence coterminous with our own. These planes can be accessed through dream, meditation and the techniques of sex magic discussed earlier. Once there, the magician can begin to master the various forces of the astral plane, meeting and recruiting the sorts of strange beings with which Burroughs populates his novels.

'GUNS AND KNIVES ARE MORE RELIABLE'

Crowley's system of magic was intended solely for self-improvement. He eschewed the use of magic for 'petty' or mundane affairs; when your child is drowning, he stated, one does not attempt to summon water elementals. You must instead dive in. Similarly, in *The Place of Dead Roads*, Kim Carsons expresses a preference for *direct* methods, such as guns and knives, over magical manipulations. A sequence in the novel finds Kim working as an agent of the English Republican Party, a fictitious organization intent on removing the monarchy. In *The Revised Boy Scout Manual* (1970), a novel in the form of three one-hour cassettes, Burroughs cheekily provides the blueprint for an armed insurrection and revolution, including random assassinations, biological warfare and the use of Reich's concept of 'Deadly Orgone

Radiation'. However, the key to any successful revolution, according to this text, is the use of a right wing, crypto-fascist regime to wrestle power from the 'democratic' governance of the hegemonic 'shits':[10]

> Riots and demonstrations by street gangs are stepped up. Start random assassination. Five citizens every day in London but never a police officer or serviceman. Patrols in the street shooting the wrong people. Curfews. England is rapidly drifting towards anarchy.
>
> [...] We send out our best agents to contact army officers and organize a rightist coup. We put rightist gangs into it like the Royal Crowns and the Royal Cavaliers in the street. 1. *Time for ERP* [English Republican Party]! 2. *Come out in The Open!* (1970:10)

Then the revolution changes tack, just as the reign of terror starts to turn into a Fourth Reich. Burroughs continues:

> Why make the usual stupid scene kicking in liquor stores grabbing anything in sight? You wake up with a hangover in an alley, your prick tore from fucking dry cunts and assholes, eye gouged out by a broken beer bottle when you and your buddy wanted the same one—no fun in that. Why not leave it like it is? [...]
>
> [...]
>
> So we lay it on the line. 'There's no cause for alarm, folks, proceed about your daily tasks. But one thing is clearly understood—your lives, your bodies, your properties belong to us whenever and wherever we choose to take them.' So, we weed out the undesirables and turn the place into a paradise ... gettin' it steady year after year ... (1970:11)

In his blackly humorous way, Burroughs turns the military-industrial complex on itself, appropriating the methods of chemical warfare, guerilla fighting and urban pacification from their creators. Magic, mind control and meditation might be all well and good, but there is a voice in Burroughs's fiction that calls out for physical, as well as psychic, resistance.

In a similar sense, *The Book of the Law* suggests the use of force as the only *real* means of removing the mechanisms of a technocratic global technocracy. While he did not share Burroughs's passion for all things militaristic, the third chapter of the 'Holy Book of Thelema' issues the decree of Ra-Hoor-Khuit, the Egyptian god of war and vengeance. In his commentary, from *The Law is For All*, Crowley states, somewhat provocatively:

> An end to the humanitarian mawkishness which is destroying the human race by the deliberate artificial protection of the unfit. What has been the net result of our fine 'Christian' phrases? [...] The unfit crowded and contaminated the fit, until Earth herself grew nauseated with the mess. We had not only a war which killed some eight million men, in the flower of their age, picked men at that, in four years, but a pestilence which killed six million in six months. Are we going to repeat the insanity? Should we not rather breed humanity for quality by killing off any tainted stock, as we do with other cattle, and exterminating the vermin which infect it? (1996:157)

The suspicious, crypto-fascist tenor of this passage undermines Crowley's call to brotherly arms, though its rhetoric may suit the style of an ancient war god. Crowley had a complicated relationship with Fascism, admiring both Hitler and Mussolini, though it was the Italian dictator's Fascist regime that was responsible for Crowley's ejection from Sicily in 1923. Crowley also considered his Thelemic teachings to be the missing religious component of National Socialism, and tried to persuade German friends to open a direct channel of communication between himself and the German Chancellor. This relationship was tempered by his round rejection of Nazism's racialist policies (fuel for a permanent Race War, Crowley surmised), although not, as is clear from the above quotation, their eugenics.

Both writers, then, play with rightist ideas—militarism, eugenics and genocide—as necessary steps in establishing an alternative future: that is, a society free of shits and control freaks and based on a respect for individual freedoms.

Of course, a tolerant society is required for what might be the greatest passion that the two figures had in common: the use of drugs. Burroughs's relationship with pharmacopoeia hardly needs emphasizing; *Naked Lunch* was famously written under the effects of majoun, a fudge made from powerful hashish. He continued the use of various narcotics throughout his life. Works such as *Junky*, *The Yage Letters* and the Appendix to *Naked Lunch* outline his encounters with, and attitudes toward, various drugs.[11]

Crowley was also well aware of the effects of illegal substances, going so far as to draw up a table of Kabbalistic correspondences detailing which drug to take to contact a particular god. His *Diary of a Drug Fiend* (1922a), made popular by a reprint in the 1990s, is a thinly disguised autobiographical account of his heroin and cocaine addiction. However, a text more analogous with Burroughs's body of work is *The Fountain of Hyacinth* (1922b), a rare diary that details with candor his attempts to wean himself off cocaine and heroin.

LAST WORDS

The lives of both men present parallel obsessions with drugs, weird sex, weird philosophy, the writing of fiction and a rage against the order established by 'the shits'. Both struggled with the various mechanisms of social control that were ranged against them, and provided 'blueprints' for those activists, adepts, agents and Johnsons seeking to continue the fight. Some points of convergence in these programs of resistance, such as developing the 'Astral Body' and the use of ritual magic, may seem outlandish, but they tap into that part of the human psyche that both wishes to believe in such things, and is capable of making such activities fruitful practice. Even so, from a twenty-first century viewpoint, this part of their blueprint may be dismissed as part of the New Age movement, laudable in intent, perhaps, but of no real practical consequence. However, their insistence on the same 'last resort'—actual armed insurrection and extermination of the agents of global ideology—raises disturbing questions from our post-9/11 perspective. Abstract psychic dabbling is juxtaposed alongside rhetoric that seems to encourage a terroristic approach to anti-global protest and demonstration. That the writing and philosophy of both men still hold a fascination for activists wary of the West's imperialist imperative—though no countercultural figure has yet to advocate armed resistance on anything like the same scale—stands as testament to the continuing importance of their outrageous lives and works.

NOTES

1. Aleister Edward Crowley was, like Burroughs, a complex and contradictory man. After reading philosophy at Oxford, he embarked on several grueling mountaineering trips that led to no small amount of fame before his erotic poetry and black magic made him infamous in the British press. Despite the fact that this article concentrates on Crowley the magician, it is his contribution to the Western tradition of yoga and Buddhism (he was a lifelong student of both) for which Crowley should possibly be remembered.
2. The spelling of magic with a 'k' originates from Crowley's 1929 text *Magick in Theory and Practice*. Seeking a term that was ideologically

'neutral', unlike theosophy, mysticism and so on, Crowley lit on 'magick' as a term that he could both appropriate and imbue with new meaning. Throughout this essay, the conventional spelling is used.

3. Roszak states that technicians such as Benway will be the engineers of a new global order, rather than the temporary (and replaceable) heads of nation states or large corporations. With Benway, Burroughs predicts the intellectual 'conjuring' of spin doctors and think tanks throughout the 'civilized'—that is, technocratic—world.

4. The identification and instigation of new 'aeons' is a preoccupation of magicians and magical orders. The Aeon of Osiris, itself following that of Isis, preceded the Aeon of Horus. In terms of the development of human society, this progression equates roughly to matriarchy, the patriarchy of Judeo-Christian society, and the period of the 'modern world' (post-1900). Some magicians have concluded that the late twentieth century constitutes a new aeon, that of Ma'at (a female Egyptian deity representing justice). This conclusion has been reached in the belief that widespread feminism, particularly in the previously male-dominated magical orders, has transformed society past the limits of the Aeon of Horus. All of this is at odds with orthodox Eastern Tantra, which states that the last 40,000 or so years have all been under the jurisdiction of the Goddess Kali (the *Kaliyuga*, or Age of Kali).

5. The Knights Templar are a Masonic organization allegedly descended from the mediaeval Knights of the Temple of Solomon the King, fearsome warriors who made their fortune during the Crusades. Accused of devil worship and idolatry, they were disbanded and their leaders burned as heretics (while their enormous gold reserves were plundered by the French and the Vatican). Some accounts have Knights Templar fleeing persecution to Scotland, where they were instrumental in establishing the 'Antient [sic] and Accepted Rite of Scottish Freemasonry'. Regardless, they still exist as a semi-secret order run along Masonic lines. Literature on the Templar ranges from the serious and historic (Nicholson 2001) through to the more fantastic (Baigent and Leigh 1991).

6. Theodor Ruess and Karl Kellner reinvigorated the OTO in nineteenth-century Germany. It exists today in two forms, one claiming direct lineage, the other content with the fact that its founder was Crowley's personal secretary. The 'degrees' of the OTO are of the Masonic kind; the first seven are prosaic rituals. From the VIIIth to XIth degrees, initiates are taught the various rituals of sexual magic. It is of course an ironic side-effect of globalization that one can learn the secrets of this magical order with nothing more than access to a decent bookshop, a bibliography and a willingness to sift through endless coy metaphors concerning cups and lances.

7. Bertiaux posits a similar theory to both Burroughs and Wilhelm Reich: that the human being generates a field of energy while sexually aroused. This energy can be guided and manipulated by the experienced user (shaman/Voudoniste/magician) and used toward various ends (see Bertiaux 1988).

8. These books are among the 'standard' texts one might find in any major bookstore's occult or mind, body and spirit section. However, these

relatively mainstream titles would lead the reader toward more 'interesting' texts that involve the practicalities of what Burroughs discusses.

9. This concept was not Crowley's own, but taken from a book of magic written by a mediaeval magician known as Abra-Melin. Crowley performed the long and arduous (six-month) Abra-Melin working at his infamous home at Boleskine, Loch Ness. It was supposedly successful, the results forming the core of much of the material for *Magick in Theory and Practice*.

10. Burroughs's attitude toward a global order is perhaps best summarized in this text: 'Actually the Queen is simply a holograph symbol of subservience operated by American know-how. Vulgar chaps, by and large, but they do have the technology' (Burroughs 1970:10).

11. *The Yage Letters* contains a passage Burroughs sent to Allen Ginsberg in 1960; it is an attempt, in the form of a long statement by Hassan i Sabbah, to answer the poet's mystic breakdown under the effects of the drug. This statement urges the young Ginsberg to 'not believe a word of it': 'NO ONE IN HIS SENSE WOULD TRUST "THE UNIVERSE" ' (61).

REFERENCES

Baigent, M., and Leigh, R. (1991) *The Temple and the Lodge* (London: Arcade Publishing).

Bertiaux, M. (1988) *The Voudon Gnostic Workbook* (New York: Magickal Childe, 1989).

Black, J. (1926) *You Can't Win* (San Francisco: Nabat Press, 2000).

Bockris, V. (1981) *With William Burroughs: A Report from the Bunker*, rev. edition (New York: St Martin's Griffin, 1996).

Burroughs, William S. (1970) *The Revised Boy Scout Manual*, IN Vale, V., and Juno, A. 1982, pp. 5–11.

Conway, D. (1973) *Magic: An Occult Primer* (New York: E. P.).

Crowley, A. E. (1922a) *Diary of a Drug Fiend* (Boston: Weiser, 1970, reprint 2001).

—— (1922b) *The Fountain of Hyacinth* (London: Iemanja, 1992).

—— (1929) *Magick in Theory and Practice* (New York: Castle Books, 1991).

—— (1938) *The Book of the Law* (York Beach, ME: Samuel Weiser, 1976).

—— (1996) *The Law is For All* (Tempe, AZ: New Falcon Publications). First printing in unedited form, following version from 1974 and 1975.

Davis, S. (1985) *Hammer of the Gods: Led Zeppelin Unauthorised* (London: Pan, 1995).

Fortune, D. (1952) *Psychic Self Defence* (New York: Aquarian Books).

Nicholson, H. (2001) *The Knights Templar: A New History* (New York: Sutton).

Roszak, T. (1969) *The Making of a Counter Culture* (London: University of California Press, 1995).

Russell, J. (2001) *Queer Burroughs* (London: Palgrave Macmillan).

Vale, V., and Juno, A. (1982) RE/Search #4/5: *William S. Burroughs/Brion Gysin/Throbbing Gristle* (San Francisco: RE/Search Publications).

14
A Camera on Violence: Reality and Fiction in *Blade Runner, a Movie*

Roberta Fornari

William S. Burroughs wrote *Blade Runner, a Movie* in 1979. Although this short novella does not represent a turning point in his career, it is exceptional for the sharpness of its apocalyptic vision and the novelty of its presentation technique. Critical works and essays on Burroughs's corpus, however, have not often mentioned *Blade Runner*, despite the fact that its futuristic vision provides an unusual showcasing of Burroughs's political engagements, which often remain buried in other texts. From this point of view, *Blade Runner* is a good example of how (science) fiction goes beyond the writer's simple presentation of facts and enters the realm of social commentary. The book/film projects the raw facts of the contemporary American political and health care systems into a *possible* future, in which uncontrolled diseases, overpopulation and the breakdown of law and order provide the context for a struggle for freedom. In this future, middle class, bourgeois lifestyles are attacked by anarchic values that often become individual or collective violent interventions against an established rule; violence appears as resistance to social control and as a means of liberation for both masses (self-organized groups or gangs) *and* individuals in order to give human beings a chance to achieve a radically new form of freedom.

In this essay I will present the background and history of *Blade Runner* as an example of an innovative fiction-movie form and discuss the political, social and ethical implications of Burroughs's presentation of violence, which will be shown to be highly ambivalent, both stylistically and in terms of actual political content. Stylistically, many of the descriptions of violence in *Blade Runner* make use of *divertissement*,[1] a technique of textual variation that tends towards playful purposes and mockery, aiming to subvert the reader's expectations of conventional and stylistic clichés. The informal collective violence presented in *Blade Runner* is often resolved through comedic slapstick interludes that invoke *divertissement*. These scenes, in which disorder prevails, rather than any logical, political and ideological opposition aimed at changing social values, also provide the clue to Burroughs's 'politics' in *Blade Runner*. I argue that Burroughs's purpose is to present a revolution that is not oriented toward the establishment of a new form of the State or society, but one that is against established social order per se, as a precondition for a radically new form of freedom and independence. The target of revolt is therefore not simply the prevailing social order, but also all forms of coercion and discipline, all forms of superimposition and moralistic values that undermine individual freedom. This critique of order and control, a key feature within all Burroughs's works, is complemented by a strong utopian element, signaling a sometimes-tense interplay between his radical individualism and his recognition of the urgent necessity for humanity to find new methods of emancipation. The tension between these elements is also present as a stylistic feature in his refusal to use linear order and traditional storyline, so that the prominent meta-textual theme, exemplified in the 'characters' quest for freedom, comes to reflect, in various ways, the author's own struggle against control.[2] In *Blade Runner*, much of the violence and the struggle for freedom involves social forces implicated in global change, including the attempted superimposition of oppressive laws and arbitrary order and the chaos engendered by such impositions; therefore the book also functions as a prophetic announcement of the emerging conflicts surrounding globalization and its critics.

BLADE RUNNER, A MOVIE: HISTORY
AND BACKGROUND

Written in 1979, in the form of a screenplay and definable as a 'fiction film', *Blade Runner* utilizes Burroughs's typical satirical style and addresses the problems of health care, medicine distribution and the transformation of the urban social environment into an anarchic zone, as a result of the government's inability to deal with social problems and needs. Following three defeated Health Care Acts in the early 1980s, social riots erupt as a consequence of the administration's mistakes in coping with the problems of an overpopulated New York. Violence and social conflicts give rise to the future scenario within which the story takes place: New York looks like the aftermath of a nuclear attack—'Whole areas in ruins, refugee camps, tent cities. Millions who have fled the city will not return. New York is a ghost city' (*BR* 6th section). Beginning with the first lines of the story, the extra-diegetic narrator tells the facts to a projected character, B.J. (a 'character' also featured prominently in *The Ticket that Exploded*), in the immediacy of the present tense. He explains that this film is about different aspects of human life and social systems, and in particular about 'overpopulation and the growth of vast service bureaucracies. The FDA and the AMA and the big drug companies are like an octopus on the citizen' (*BR* 1st section). The narrator then turns to his 'listener', B.J.:

> [Y]ou are asking me to tell you in one sentence what this film is about? I'm telling you it is too big for one sentence—even a life sentence. For starters it's about the National Health Insurance we don't got. (*BR* 1st section)

The distinctive performative voice in Burroughs's novels, together with the cinematic quality of the prose, transforms the text into a series of metamorphic images of an imminent reality not far from our own. The use of cinematic technique in one of the only Burroughs works presented directly as a film script has to be understood in the context of his other experiments with such imagery.

There are many features in Burroughs's texts that have a cinematic influence and create a cinematic impression: the use of the present tense (a rhythmic verbal device typical of script descriptions and off-screen voices); the particularized descriptions of movements and acts that are veritable close-ups and long-shots (the shooting scenes in *The Place of Dead Roads*, the riots in *Blade Runner* which remind us of the similarly depicted riots in *Naked Lunch*); and the continuous back and forth focus on different single parts of the body, as if a camera eye was the observer and the writer only the 'recording medium' in the process. Through fragmentation and montage-like associations, these cinematic devices translate into words and give movement to the stillness of written language.

Burroughs worked directly with film as well as with sound recording in various media projects during the 1960s. These experiments shed light on his work with verbal language as well as on his interest in the relationship between images and words. Burroughs's work with Brion Gysin, Ian Sommerville and Antony Balch in London and Paris led to the short features *Bill and Tony, Towers Open Fire,*

The Cut-Ups and *William Buys a Parrot*, based to some extent on his written works ('Towers Open Fire' from *Nova Express*). The written works created in those years are understandably the most difficult to read in terms of linear order, but they are also the most cinematic in terms of the immediacy of their imagery and the resulting dream-like effects. The Nova trilogy and *The Wild Boys*, written with the cut-up method, blend science fiction and utopian fantasy with repeated images of violence, challenging conventional moral codes and requiring the reader to 'take sides' in the wild boys' conflict. The use of cut-ups interrupts the process of easily connecting episodes and story lines, forcing the brain to create new connections and associative lines—as in a movie with a hectic montage.[3]

The coupling of cinematic style and technique with a satire of social conventions is well exemplified in *Blade Runner*, which is very loosely based on *The Bladerunner*, a mainstream science fiction novel published in 1974 by Alan Nourse.[4] In an interview, Burroughs declared: 'The idea of the underground medicine was in the book, and I got the idea from that. Then I got in touch with Nourse and he said he would be glad to have the name used because he considered it good publicity for his book' (Skerl 1980:116). Whether the operation is a postmodern recycling process of sci-fi material or 'solidarity between two writers' is not important here. It is relevant, though, that Burroughs used the idea developed by another writer, transforming the story into a form that is not a movie and not exactly a script; it works as fiction but, as is often the case in Burroughs's stories, the fiction's political elements and implications are dreadfully similar to reality.

Nourse's book, as well as many other science fiction works (*Johnny Mnemonic* by William Gibson, for example), deals with the future of medicine and health care as a dystopia. In the first decades of the twenty-first century, public authorities establish a system to limit population growth. National health care is free on the condition that people affected by illness agree to be sterilized. Many people reject these draconian measures and an illegal medical system is created; doctors and nurses perform underground operations. The central character of Nourse's story is Billy, the bladerunner, who smuggles medical tools and equipment and serves as a vital connection between doctors and the people who need operations because they have been disenfranchised from the officially sanctioned system.

In Burroughs's version, the idea of underground medicine is drawn and transformed into a piece of avant-garde art and pamphlet-style *divertissement*, which calls attention to the general condition of humanity. The setting is New York, transformed into a sort of Interzone after riots erupt in the early 1980s against the Medicine Acts; New York City is divided into areas either patrolled by police or left, in their absence, to gangs or less-organized groups of local citizens.

The first sections of the screenplay describe the background for the events of the text in 2014, the year in which the movie would supposedly take place. Events previous to 2014 generate the post-atomic setting and are described by a voice that seems to emerge, by its language and rhythm, from a media broadcast (a more literary than cinematic device of telling a story): 'This film is about America. What America was and what America could be, and how those who try to stifle the American dream are defeated.'; 'This film is about cancer and that's a powerful subject.'; and 'This film is about a second chance for Billy the blade runner, and for all humanity' (*BR* 1st section).

The use of the metropolis as the setting for the film narrative has interesting parallels. Since the beginning of the twentieth century, the metropolis has been the protagonist in many movies, a place of alienation and political control (*Metropolis*; Fritz Lang 1927), a post-modern locus of mysterious implication (*Blade Runner*, Ridley Scott 1982; *Brazil*, 1984 and *12 Monkeys*, 1996, both by Terry Gilliam) and a virtual creation for total control over human bodies and energy (*The Matrix*, Andy and Larry Wachowsky 1999). Although we cannot be certain if these directors read Burroughs's work, they were undoubtedly influenced by the pervasiveness of the *zeitgeist* that he tapped into. *Blade Runner*'s New York becomes the 'world center for underground medicine, the most glamorous, the most dangerous, the most exotic, vital, far-out city the world has ever seen' (*BR* 1st section). It is the 'real' city, after all, that is not very different from the idea and stereotype we receive from movies: New York is a place where 'everything is possible', a city that has always presented its events (fictional and real) as absolutely exceptional, and Burroughs is certainly aware of the overlapping strains of fiction and reality. The difference is that in *Blade Runner*, the disenfranchised population of New York City possesses a clear narrative rationale for the riots and revolts: these events are precipitated by the discontent that follows the legalization and government distribution of heroin. What Burroughs calls the 'United States Health Service' took over distribution through government clinics, and built up an intricate bureaucracy of corrupt police and investigators, so that ' "[m]any people who were not addicts got on the program and made a comfortable living selling off their allowance" ' (*BR* 4th section). In *Blade Runner*'s fictional world, any attempt to regulate or impose 'order' marginalizes a social group, making the National Health Act as dangerous in its social effects as any other Act:

> Ironically, the high death rate was largely due to the government's efforts to forestall the outbreak by strict weapon-control measures. The National Firearms Registration Act of 1982 debarred anyone with a criminal record or any record of drug addiction or mental illness, and all those on the welfare rolls, from buying or possessing any firearms of any description including air guns. This left the disaffected middle-class in possession of more firearms than any other group. (*BR* 4th section)

This situation pushes the Percival's Soldiers of Christ, a racist and fascist group, to attempt to take over New York and 'slaughter all ethnic minorities, beatniks, dope-fiends', etc. As is usual in Burroughs's texts, warfare and riots give way to a humorous images, in this case of 'doctors, nurses and orderlies' fighting against the rioters with 'scalpels saws and bedpans' and other ready-made weapons. The Soldiers of Christ are defeated, 'split into small groups and, abandoning their holy crusade, take to raping, looting, killing in the middle class neighborhoods of midtown Manhattan ....' (*BR* 5th section). The result of the battles is a city divided into an 'anarchic' lower side where it is possible to be operated on and to find any drug, and the rest of the city, almost empty and abandoned, with 'shabby open-air markets and vegetable gardens in vacant lots. Some are crowded, others virtually deserted' (*BR* 3rd section).

BLADE RUNNER, A MOVIE AS
POLITICAL COMMENTARY

Blade Runner was written while Burroughs was living in New York, and has to be understood within the political context of American society at this time. If we choose to separate these fictional scenarios from the relevant political issues, we would miss the underlying 'ideology' of the novel: *Blade Runner* warns against every attempt to disrupt the ethical value of freedom and individual choice through 'top-down' political intervention. The urgent need for liberation and freedom from any superimposition, and above all political control, shows an ambivalence that I will try to follow step by step in its implications.

Political control in advanced industrial societies is organized through institutional authority and political structure, which together come to form the State apparatus. In order to govern and administer the public sphere the State needs control and authority over the actions of individuals and groups. The State exerts power (more or less coercive) over individuals on whom rules are imposed, and makes use of bureaucratically organized police, armed forces, public administration, education, health care and environmental management systems. Political control in modern states therefore exhibits strong tendencies toward centralization and bureaucratization, tendencies that are accompanied by increasing diffuseness of authority and operational inefficiency, giving rise to contradictions. In *Blade Runner*, political control has become so diffuse that its limits and contradictions arouse a disruptive diverse response: 'grassroots' groups of people fighting against the Health Care Acts and producing 'outlaw' medicine instead of universal health care, a corrupt medical lobby defending its power, and scores of individuals who struggle to survive.

Helicopter view of Manhattan ...
Overpopulation has led to ever-increasing governmental control over the private citizen, not on the old-style police-state models of oppression and terror, but in terms of work, credit, housing, retirement benefits, and medical-care: services that can be withheld. These services are computerized. No number, no service. However, this has not produced the brainwashed standardized human units postulated by such linear prophets as George Orwell. Instead a large percentage of the population has been forced underground. How large, no one knows. These people are *numberless*. (*BR* 3rd section)

The implication of the term 'numberless' is double since it functions first, simply, as an indefinite term (we do not know how many people live underground) and, second, as a political referent: to be numberless implies the impossibility of being cured in a hospital or in any other health care structure. 'So America goes underground. They all make their own medicines in garages, basements, and lofts, and provide their own service [...] All you need is access to the medications' (*BR* 1st section). The science fiction setting of underground laboratories, flooded lower tunnels giving rise to an 'underground

Venice', and buildings 'joined by suspension bridges, a maze of plat-
forms, catwalks, slides, lifts' (*BR* 1st section) is common to many of
Burroughs's works (especially the 'Interzone' of *Naked Lunch*). Such
imagery is not so futuristic if we compare it to the appearance of
cities in developing countries, or indeed to the emergence of 'third
world' conditions in modern, capitalist societies. We should remember that the future imagined by Burroughs is the reality of the 1980s
Ronald Reagan reforms that dismantled the New Deal and Great
Society social welfare initiatives. Burroughs's fictitious premises fit
the reality of recent history:

> By 1980, pressure had been growing to put through a National Health
> Act. This was blocked by the medical lobby, doctors protesting that
> such an Act would mean the virtual end of private practice, and that
> the overall quality of medical service would decline. The strain on an
> already precarious economy was also cited. Drug companies, fearing
> that price regulation would slash profits, spent millions to lobby
> against the proposed bill and ran full-page ads in all the leading news-
> papers. And above all, the health insurance companies screamed that
> the Act was unnecessary and could only lead to increased taxes for
> inferior service. (*BR* 3rd section)

In his article 'William Burroughs and the Literature of Addiction',
Frank D. McConnell points out that science fiction is the least futuristic of popular genres, 'attempting as it does a constant purification
of the present through the neo-romance landscape of the future'
(1967:97). From this standpoint, *Blade Runner* represents an attempt
to anticipate humanity's future through the representation of
the most dreadful risks in order to provide a 'second chance' for
mankind to achieve a 'stateless society'; Burroughs's political utopia
is therefore anarchic and anti-collectivist. In the story, Billy the
bladerunner becomes the character who can travel back and forth
in time, granting him a chance to correct his mistakes.

Aside from any possible interpretation of the screenplay's literary
genre, Burroughs offers an acute and realistic vision. Solving the
problems of health care and medicine distribution (especially in
developing countries) has become not only a political necessity in
terms of the economic satisfaction of public needs, but also one of
the main points of contemporary political struggle in Western countries. The welfare state is the organ of a general redistribution of
wealth among the population and is, above all, the expression of 'big

government' that has mutated into 'a set of despotic instruments of domination for the totalitarian production of subjectivity' (Hardt and Negri 2001:324, my translation).

As explained by Michael Hardt and Antonio Negri, ' "big government" leads the great orchestra of subjectivities transformed into commodities and establishes borders of desire and lines along which the work is being divided in the globalized order' (324, my translation). The activities carried out by bureaucracies, private institutions with public functions and private health care firms, are all exemplars of control structures foisted upon individuals in terms of their obligation to choose only from what 'the market offers'. But this 'market' tends more and more toward monopoly practices supported by big government. In reaction, Burroughs's extra-diegetic narrator in *Blade Runner* asserts a supposedly anarchic, hyperbolic position that in fact expresses the values of the traditional small-scale capitalist: 'Is this freedom? Is this what America stands for? [...] We have been taught that if you put a better product on the free market, the superior product will sell' (*BR* 1st section).

This is not to imply, however, that Burroughs ever intended to offer a classical political position. His anarchic view has always tended to favor forms of rebellion that are far from any acceptable political solution in a sociopolitical context of organized collectivities. His micro-societies (as in *The Wild Boys*), his rebel groups and gangs, always border on acceptability (depending on the moral code of their opposition)—waiting to be recognized as 'legitimate' groups while they are opposed to mainstream society. One of the main problems in analyzing Burroughs's political concerns lies in the fact that he always denies any political involvement, while at the same time proposing intrinsically political solutions.

In his novels, Burroughs was lucidly aware of the sociopolitical landscape of the times. He saw his works not only as literary fictions seemingly detached from reality and intended as 'hallucinations', but also as works of futurology, dealing with the political, social and economic possibilities of a world in which individuals' lives are increasingly controlled through specialized systems. In this ever-growing control system, the imaginative tracks of a story or novel may disturb and subvert the existing order; therefore, for Burroughs, the act of writing is an anarcho-political act. This anarchic position is perhaps a constant point in Burroughs's views of life, and the quasi-libertarian position represented in the struggle against power and control is a typical American vision (Tanner 1971). It is, indeed, an example of a distinctively American method of disrupting order and continuity in the name of personal and individual freedom, and is reflected in both Burroughs's style and his theoretical principles:

> This film is about the future of medicine and the future of man. For man *has* no future unless he can throw off the dead past and absorb the underground of his own being. In the end, underground medicine merges with the medical establishment, to the great benefit of both. (*BR* 1st section)

When Jennie Skerl asked Burroughs to comment on the idea contained in these lines, he explained: 'A man has to get beyond his conditioning, or his future is going to be a repetition, word-for-word repetition. I would say that for a great percentage of people, all they do is repeat their past. They really don't have a future at all. And it's only by a sort of break with the past that anything new and different will emerge—which is very rare—a very rare occurrence' (Skerl 1980:117).

VIOLENCE AS FREEDOM—VIOLENCE AS *DIVERTISSEMENT*

Generally, the search for a new condition in Burroughs's diegesis passes through the experience of rebellion, and more often violence. The most exemplary works in this respect are *Naked Lunch*, *The Wild Boys* and his last trilogy, *Cities of the Red Night, The Place of Dead Roads* and *The Western Lands*. In *Blade Runner*, the 'spectacle of violence' is supported by less serious manifestations, privileging satire and slapstick comedy. Consequently, political concerns seem to be overridden by the intrinsic fictional purpose of the story. Riots and rebellions become necessities in the overthrow of authority; individuals such as the bladerunners and the illegal doctors prefer to live in a destabilized underworld where it is possible to find drugs and weapons, to be operated on and, above all, to be free even if this freedom entails considerable risks of its own:

> The transplant operation is performed in a subway operating room by a delco plant. The delco is heard throughout this scene, sometimes sputtering ominously as the lights dim. All the equipment is home-made, requiring continual readjustment and tinkering. Billy goes to fetch The Hand, best operating assistant in the industry [...] The Hand

is a Blues addict. The Blues is a metallic variation on heroin [...] Blue is twenty times stronger than heroin. (*BR* 13th section)

The basic political element of rebellion is problematized by Burroughs, as he uses a stylistic *divertissement* through which ideological subversion is often denied or set apart from the seriousness of the subject matter in favor of a slapstick scene that reasserts the anarchic element essential for any (self) liberation. This ambivalence is the result of a profound political *and* stylistic anarchy on Burroughs's part. All his works are rooted in this way of thinking, and denote the struggle against any superimposition of authority.

In an interview with Larry McCaffery and Jim McMenamin (1987:171–95), Burroughs answered the question of his ambiguous presentation of violence—'a combination of horror, black humor, grim fascination, maybe even sympathy'—which could be related to the literary experience of both the Marquis de Sade and Franz Kafka as analyzed in *The Algebra of Need* by Eric Mottram (1971). Burroughs's response to the problem of presenting violence as an exorcism or a celebration is pragmatic rather than ethical. Nonetheless his fictional world is dominated by a strong moral conception of good and evil:

> There's a lot of violence in my work because violence is obviously necessary in certain circumstances. I'm often talking in a revolutionary, guerrilla context where violence is the only recourse. I feel a degree of ambivalence with regard to any use of violence. There are certainly circumstances where it seems to be indicated. How can you protect people without weapons? (McCaffery and McMenamin 1987:176)

In *Naked Lunch*, that ambivalence is exemplified in the words and acts of Doctor Benway, perhaps Burroughs's best achievement in terms of satirical characterization and black humor. Benway's psychological violence presents interesting parallels with the reality and fictional representation of violence in advanced industrial societies. Violence exerted by the agencies of the State—the police, the armed forces and other empowered institutions—acquires a legal status, particularly in its ultimate iterations in the forms of capital punishment and the legitimization of war, which allows it to escape the sanctions accorded to acts of violence on the part of non-state agencies. According to Ann Norton, and following Max Weber, we may distinguish four types of violence, further differentiated by two criteria: the conformity of the violent act to extant legal or customary forms, and the individual or collective nature of the act. The first criterion distinguishes those acts that are evidently rule-bound, taking place within existing structures. The second criterion considers acts that manifest a conscious participation in collective identity. The types of violence, according to these distinctions, are formal collective, informal collective, formal individual and informal individual (Norton 1993:146). War is a form of formal collective violence, whereas riots and revolts may be defined as forms of informal collective violence with an awareness that 'all collective action is political for it reflects the participation of individuals in a common, incorporeal, entity' (Norton 1993:146). From this standpoint we can consider that violence may also be intended as reaction to authority, in the forms of riots or revolts, sometimes limited to groups in unique circumstances. This informal collective violence will be considered 'illegitimate' by public or established authorities since the concept and distinction between 'legitimate' and 'illegitimate' is founded by the same authority that makes the rules. From this point of view, and according to Weber, only the State can possess a monopoly on violence. Weber's analysis defines the State as follows: 'A compulsory political organization with continuous operations will be called a "state" insofar as its administrative staff successfully upholds the claim to the monopoly of the legitimate use of physical force in the enforcement of its order' (Mann 1986:55). Hannah Arendt, elaborating on this theme, notes that the type of violence exerted by the State or internal police actions, though labeled legitimate, should be subsumed under the euphemistic rubric 'the exercise of authority' (1969:4).

For fiction, the approach must be different, since language, style, visual appeal and ethical implications are involved. In this context it is important to point out that Burroughs's approach toward violence as fiction contains a deep imaginary level of fantasy that is opposed to real circumstances. It is as if Burroughs's texts, and *Blade Runner* in particular, signal: This is the world we live in, this is the total power that rules our lives—this story is the response, the ultimate attempt to free human individuals.

Fictional violence always expresses, in one way or another, the real violence of its social context, including the phenomenal violence reported by institutional media (television above all). The way in which accounts of violence are told and reported can be compared to the way in which violence is experienced and culturally approached. In *Screening Violence*, Stephen Prince explains how in some cases filmmakers cannot control the reactions of viewers to the graphic violence they put on screen (Prince 1999:1). In the case of textual violence, the impact is less 'immediate' and the response is more directly related to stylistic and literary devices. To read a violent scene is to pass through a process of making a mental image of that scene, a requirement that changes substantially in the sharp immediacy of cinema.

In addition, movie images may be violent not only in content but also in their graphic representation of the violent act or event, depending on the director's style and use of the camera eye. Writers often turn to satire and comedy in order to render violent representation more 'acceptable', as do movie directors,[5] whose work can be hampered by both censorship and market forces. Since violence is often intrinsic to satire, it is also easier for an author to use satire as a vehicle for violence against established order *without* the risk of being refused or censored. The main risk, on the contrary, is the danger of misinterpretation or relegation to a genre below that of 'serious art'. Satirical written works elicit greater acceptance and tolerance of violence because the satirical intent is tempered by a form of cultural mediation that reflects the rebellion against moral conventions. In satirical works violence often uncovers the writer's beliefs and convictions, especially when the text's subject matter deals with contemporary problems.

Accordingly, there are two aspects to Burroughs's use of satirical style: the first one aims at attacking arbitrary moral conventions that limit individual freedom in order to show the profound ambivalence of any form of violence, whether legitimate or illegitimate; the second one is that his satirical language can be defined, especially in some passages marked by a pamphlet style, as verbal or textual violence. As Mottram describes, Burroughs uses a language that fits with the world he experienced:

> [A] loveless world whose control is entirely in the hands of capitalists, doctors, psychiatrists, con men, judges, police and military, whose aim it is to perpetuate mass infantilism, apathy and dependence [...] [Nausea] tends to become horror of the obscenity towards which total power necessarily grows. (Mottram 1971:43)

In such a condition it is necessary to use violence to resist such totalizing iterations of power in order to recover individuality and independence.

254 Alternatives: Realities and Resistances

The position taken by Burroughs against capital punishment is a perfect synthesis of both a violent style of writing and the violence exerted by 'civilized' countries. Its satirical intent, however, is not at all symbolic, but quite literal:

> These sections [in *Naked Lunch*] are intended to reveal capital punishment as the obscene, barbaric and disgusting anachronism that it is. As always the lunch is naked. If civilized countries want to return to Druid Hanging Rites in the Sacred Grove or to drink blood with the Aztecs and feed their Gods with blood of human sacrifice, let them see what they actually eat and drink. Let them see what is on the end of that long newspaper spoon. (*NL* xli–xlii)

The experience of being tortured, convicted or punished is significantly absent from *Blade Runner*; the scenes of violence are represented as riots and revolts in opposition to the forces of law and order. We can therefore read *Blade Runner* as concerned with the phenomenon of informal collective violence; riots and rebellion that may arise when public authorities, government and institutions are not present as social and democratic markers capable of improving living conditions, but when they are, on the contrary, overly intrusive in public privacy and inimical to individual freedom of choice. *Blade Runner* therefore addresses an ethical problem: The riots in the novella occur when the citizenry rebel against not only the welfare state and public authority, but also against the sterilization initiatives imposed upon those people who accept medical treatment. The resulting society becomes a chaotic city where power is totally corrupt, and authority has reached the worst of all possible conditions—arbitrariness.

The consequence of this arbitrariness is that the average person cannot influence the actions of bureaucrats and doctors, who remain free (a *dreadful* freedom that Burroughs describes as equally ambivalent) to perform *any* kind of experiment; the environment is as chaotic as the effect it produces:

> Room changes and now contains a number of people, ticker tape machines, telephones, TV screens. These are highly-placed officials, bored and cynical. One is doing a crossword puzzle. Two are sniffing coke [...] The bureaucrat is leafing through papers. He points to a graph on the wall.
>   Now look at these cancer statistics. We are dealing here not just with an increase in cancer but with an increase in *susceptibility* to cancer ... a

breakdown in the immunity system. Why does a cancer or any virus take a certain length of time to develop? Immunity. Remove the immunity factor, and virus processes can be accelerated. (*BR* 14th section)

Burroughs is ambivalent on this point: is it even desirable to want a society where violence is the only way to obtain freedom and independence? What form will a society where everything is possible ultimately assume? Is there indeed as sharp a distinction between reality and fiction as Burroughs's cinematic writing style implies? Are we really free once we have disrupted the regime of authoritarian order?

Burroughs's ambivalence is perhaps the only viable position to assume in our civilization today, as marked by the postmodern loss of trust toward what Jean François Lyotard (1979) calls the 'metanarratives' and the inability to detect and understand the forms of power that regulate our lives. What Burroughs implies with his satirical style is that these forms of power are now decentralized; they have turned into an octopus-like structure disseminated across a globalized continuum. That is why he writes of 'guerrilla' action rather than conventional revolution or war, which often possesses a 'legitimate' consensus. Guerilla actions are generally illegal, and result from emergency conditions; they are self-organized, violent responses to the 'legitimate' violence of authority.

Authorized violence, as a 'non-emergency' condition, can more easily assume forms that comport to the commonplace scenarios of late capital: weapons, money, media broadcasting. In this scenario of global capital embedded in *Blade Runner* (as well as in all Burroughs's works), the underground forces that use informal collective violence—as opposed to formal collective violence represented by the State, the police, and so on—need to be recognized, at least on the page, as a 'legitimate' presence with a legitimate right to be free from the imposition of an overly intrusive power apparatus. The freedom of the bladerunner is manifest in his ability to manage and organize his own life, yet his intervention is limited to local situations. His work does not have 'revolutionary' connotations; it is, after all, individual intervention, or, in some cases, limited to small groups.

The bladerunner is a rebel who follows a personal ethical conviction and fights against imposed order—but he is also alone, waiting perhaps to be followed by a multitude of other individuals. His freedom is also cast by Burroughs as a form of salvation: freedom to associate in 'underground' groups, homosexual and/or anarchic communities, and other autonomous networks outside the conservative and established social conventions. At the end of the novel, Billy achieves a meta-consciousness of his existence in a zone between the past and future, where he runs his blade haphazardly in and out of time, representing the possibilities of an undetermined future.

In conclusion, Burroughs's representation of violence forms a multilayered tapestry of sociopolitical expression formulated through disruptive and often satirical linguistic techniques that reflect ambivalence toward the use of violence bound up with the necessity for people to fight against the machination of superimposed order. In Burroughs's text, the disruption of the standard narrative story line, verbal language and linear methods of event presentation assume a hectic visual power, and the reading process approaches a 'pure' cinematic experience conveyed through words: *Blade Runner* is a novella written in the form of a screenplay, and as such it has the features of a virtual movie. Its scenes should be imagined as movie images, running on a 'mind screen' imbued with a capability of creative visualization. Burroughs's aim, after all, is to free language, structure, and individual experience from any structural superimposition of the 'reality film'. This project is carried out through the appropriation of film devices, transposed into destructured and meta-fictional narrative, that emerge freely during the production of the reality film. The page becomes a virtual space where 'nothing is true, everything is permitted', because whatever rules limit conventional narrative are deliberately disregarded. There are no rules that limit fantasy and fictional possibilities.

Burroughs's graphic vision of a future that extends the logic of control to such disciplinary extremes suggests its own antidote in not only the inability of control to become total, but also in the articulation of its possible expansion into the future. Burroughs's fictional works are a form of resistance against a 'civilization' that harnesses human potential to the *telos* of the exploitation of labor, the alienation of consumption and the control of desire. It is to this concept of 'civilization' that Burroughs's works—and *Blade Runner* in particular—offer violence as resistance and as liberation. Burroughs's texts are the legacy of this vision, and in the age of globalization, both a warning and a blueprint.

NOTES

1. The term *divertissement* was first used by Blaise Pascal, French philosopher of the sixteenth century, and then by Voltaire to define his literary works

and parodies. It can be a slapstick scene or a pantomime. A postmodern text that uses parody and pastiche may have a high level of *divertissement*.
2. Examples of fictional characters who reflect this tension between author and creation include the semi-autobiographical William Lee in *Junkie*, who opens the gallery of Burroughs's alter egos that will later be staffed by William Seward Hall/Kim Carsons in *The Place of Dead Roads* and Kim/Neferti in *The Western Lands*.
3. Burroughs wrote another text in the form of a film; for *The Last Words of Dutch Schultz* (1970), he mixed the cut-up technique with the transcripts of gangster Dutch Schulz's delirious final days.
4. Burroughs's *Blade Runner* has nothing to do with the movie directed by Ridley Scott in 1982. Scott's *Blade Runner* is based on Philip K. Dick's novel *Do Androids Dream of Electric Sheep?* (1968).
5. The case of Stanley Kubrick's *A Clockwork Orange* (1971) is exemplary.

REFERENCES

Arendt, H. (1969) *On Violence* (New York: Harcourt Brace, 1970).
Hardt, M., and Negri, A. (2001) *Impero* (Milano: Rizzoli).
Hibbard, A. ed. (1999) *Conversations with William S. Burroughs* (Jackson: University Press of Mississippi).
Lyotard, J. F. (1979) *The Postmodern Condition: A Report on Knowledge*, Bennington, G., and Massumi, B. trans. (Minneapolis: University of Minnesota Press, 1999).
Mann, M. (1986) *The Sources of Social Power*, vol. 1, (Cambridge: Cambridge University Press).
McCaffery, L., and McMenamin, J. (1987) 'An Interview with William S. Burroughs', IN Hibbard, A. ed. 1999, pp. 171–95.
McConnell, F. D. (1967) 'William Burroughs and the Literature of Addiction', IN Skerl, J., and Lydenberg, R. eds, *William S. Burroughs at the Front: Critical Reception, 1959–1989* (Carbondale and Edwardsville: Southern Illinois University Press, 1991), pp. 91–101.
Mottram, E. (1971) *William Burroughs: The Algebra of Need*, rev. edition (London: Marion Boyars, 1977).
Norton, A. (1993) *Reflections on Political Identity* (Baltimore and London: The Johns Hopkins University Press).
Nourse, A. E. (1974) *The Bladerunner* (Milano: Mondadori, 1981).
Prince, S. (1999) *Screening Violence* (New Brunswick, NJ: Rutgers University Press).
Skerl, J. (1980) 'An Interview with William S. Burroughs', IN Hibbard, A. ed. 1999, pp. 113–31.
Tanner, T. (1971) *City of Words: American Fiction, 1950–1970* (New York: Harper and Row).

15

William S. Burroughs, Laughter and the Avant-Garde

Katharine Streip

METAPHORS AND COMIC PRACTICE

How are avant-gardes identified and what practices account for that identification? What are the criteria that enable us to identify contemporary avant-garde artists and what do those criteria say about both the cultural establishments that recognize movements or artists as avant-garde and avant-garde practitioners themselves?

William S. Burroughs offers an exemplary test case for these questions. In spite of its significance, his work still has not received academic canonization and continues to rest on the margins of American literary culture because of its fragmentary structure, the apparent contradictions of its cultural critiques and its outrageous humor. It is difficult to reconcile Burroughs's humor with the aesthetic goals of canonical postmodernism or with any straightforward political critique. A crucial impediment to Burroughs's reception is his humor. And as Burroughs remarks, 'Much of my work is intended to be *funny*' (1984:266).

How does humor function as an avant-garde strategy? Humor as a strategic avant-garde tactic that both transgresses and aims at eliminating the separation of art from life has been under-theorized. This is not surprising, as comedy (and theorizing about comedy) continues, for the most part, to occupy a position within critical discourse which ironically parallels the position of 'female' in gender constructs: it is a genre and a practice viewed as superficial, minor, lightweight, trivial and disreputable. As Susan Purdie observes in *Comedy: Mastery of Discourse*, 'the criticism of comedy is a site on which the assumptions a critic makes about what is valuable and possible in our general experience become especially apparent' (1993:120). Laughter has traditionally been viewed with suspicion in Western cultures; even a

258

subject such as sex, a great inspiration for joke work, can pose a challenge to laughter. For example, Burroughs writes in a letter to Allen Ginsberg '(Note that sex and laughter are considered incompatible. You are supposed to take sex seriously. Imagine a Reichian's reaction to my laughing sex kick! But it is the nature of laughter to recognize no bounds)' (*LTG* 80).

Humor within Burroughs's work can be read as a social practice and as a formal and a performative strategy, a way to probe and to explore boundaries. Here, current work on theories of globalization can be useful in expressing the relation between Burroughs's humor and the fictional landscape of his work. Just as modernization frameworks characterized social science programs in the period after World War II (Tsing 2000:454), today, globalization theories encourage us to imagine a new world in the making. I am particularly interested in the metaphors that inform the discourses of globalization, how they function to add to the charisma of the notion of an era of globalization, and how these metaphors in turn can illuminate Burroughs's comic practice. For example, the effect of Burroughs's humor within his work can be compared to the shifts in landscapes constituted by global cultural flows. These flows, identified by Arjun Appadurai as ethnoscapes (the moving landscape of people), mediascapes (the distribution of electronic capabilities to disseminate information), technoscapes (the global configuration of technology), financescapes (the movements of global capital) and ideoscapes (a chain of ideas composed of elements of the Enlightenment worldview) (1996:50–53), qualify the nature, depth and even the very existence of a global culture that is post-nationalist, postcolonial, postmodern and cosmopolitan. Burroughs's humor as well shapes and qualifies the landscapes that he imagines in his fictions. Just as Appadurai's global flows 'give rise to a profusion of fluid, irregularly shaped, variously textured and constantly changing landscapes' (Hay and Marsh 2000:2), Burroughs's humor unsettles any stable reading of his fictional landscapes. Global interconnectedness suggests a world full of movement and mixture, contact and linkages, and cultural interaction and exchange (Inda and Rosaldo 2002b:2). As Jonathan Inda and Renato Rosaldo argue, this interconnectedness 'implies a speeding up of the flows of capital, people, goods, images and ideas across the world [...] suggest[ing] an intensification of the links, modes of interaction, and flows that interconnect the world' and producing 'a stretching of social, cultural, political, and economic practices across frontiers' (9). In consequence, 'while everyone might continue to live local lives, their phenomenal worlds have to some extent become global as distant events come to have an impact on local spaces, and local developments come to have global repercussions' (9). A question that frames many discussions of globalization is that of whether globalization necessarily leads to a cultural homogenization of the world, 'the installation worldwide of western versions of basic social-cultural reality: the West's epistemological and ontological theories, its values, ethical systems, approaches to rationality, technical-scientific worldview, political culture, and so on' (Tomlinson 1997:144). Tomlinson points out that cultural materials do not transfer in a unilinear manner, with what is called a hypodermic model of media effects (Morley and Robins 1995:126), but require the recognition of a context of complex reception. An appreciation of Burroughs's exploration of boundaries through humor demands a similar recognition of the complexity of the context of reception. Although humor and globalization may seem metaphorically distant, as Appadurai insists, '[t]he imagination is now central to all forms of agency, is itself a social fact, and is the key component of the new global order' (1996:49).

Anna Tsing makes an important point:

> Globalization draws our enthusiasm because it helps us imagine interconnection, travel and sudden transformation. [F]low is valorized but not the carving of the channel; national and regional units are mapped as the baseline of change without attention to their shifting and contested ability to define the landscape [...] We describe the landscape imagined within these claims rather than the culture and politics of scale making. (2000:456)

Burroughs's work with humor insistently reminds us of the culture, politics and values that shape our responses. It represents both a seduction into laughter and a call for a critical stance toward the assumptions and fantasies represented by his comic practice.

VAMPIRIC EMOTIONAL POSSESSION

Burroughs's use of the imagination and the effects of humor can be seen in the presence of routines, or comic monologues, throughout his work. Many of Burroughs's routines originate in letters he wrote to Allen Ginsberg in the 1950s after the end of their love affair.

Ginsberg describes these routines as 'conscious projections of Burroughs' love fantasies—further explanations and parodies and models of our ideal love schlupp together. I was somewhat resistant, so much of his fantasy consists of a parody of his invasion of my body and brain' (*LTG* 6). Timothy S. Murphy also identifies these routines as a 'means of seduction [...] Through these routines, Burroughs hoped to win the errant Ginsberg back' (1997:144). However, as Ginsberg points out, to 'schlupp' means 'to devour a soul parasitically'. If the routines in Burroughs's fiction establish a relationship with his readers similar to the relationship with Ginsberg as a recipient of his letters, we must ask, is Burroughs's humor intended to seduce his readers? Is it aggressively meant to devour interlocutors, as his consciousness effectively takes over ours and sets off a laughter mechanism? Or does Burroughs mean to warn us of the potential for a kind of vampiric emotional possession through our reception of his entertaining and disturbing routines? Jamie Russell certainly views Burroughs's routines as threatening because of their tendency to collapse boundaries: 'Both fantastic and realistic, the routine is monstrous. Its schizophrenic oscillation between opposed registers (real/fictional, comic/terrifying, masculine/ feminine) threatens to overwhelm the teller, turning him into a mere ventriloquist's dummy [...] In this respect, the routine feminizes the receiver, throwing him into a camp hysteria that is likely to tear him apart, bringing about his psychic disintegration' (2001:22). In the relationship set up by Burroughs's routines, the comic, who should be the ventriloquist here, becomes transformed into a ventriloquist's dummy (evoking the disturbing transfer of subjectivity between Burroughs's Carny man and the talking asshole), while the receiver, possessed by laughter, also risks the loss of a stable self. Russell tentatively recuperates this potential psychic disintegration by ascribing the prestige of a survivor who has confronted the danger of self-loss and reveled in bawdiness to the appreciative audience of Burroughs's routines, but the undermining potential for psychic dissolution remains.

In recognition of this psychic threat, Burroughs clearly does not offer a utopian presentation of humor. A haunting passage from *Naked Lunch*—the Sailor 'laughed, black insect laughter that seemed to serve some obscure function of orientation like a bat's squeak' (*NL* 47)—suggests that for Burroughs, laughter is an involuntary, automatic reaction that we would not necessarily recognize as human in volition, but which can serve as a tool for orientation. As the passage continues, 'The Sailor laughed three times. He stopped laughing and hung there motionless listening down into himself. He had picked up the silent frequency of junk' (*NL* 47). Laughter is addictive and compulsive, and can be compared to involuntary physical responses such as sneezing, hiccupping and coughing, as we see in an incident in *The Wild Boys*: 'The boys pulled their eyes up at the corners yacking in false Chinese. The effect was irresistibly comic. Then the boys laughed. They laughed and laughed laughing *inside* us all the officers were laughing doubled over holding their guts in. The boys sneezed and coughed. They posted themselves in front of the CIA man and began to hiccup' (*WB* 132). The boys' laughter collapses the boundaries between officers and wild boys as their laughter erupts from within the officers. The boys' irresistible pranks prevent the officers from reasserting their autonomy, as they are literally possessed by seizures of laughter, hiccups, coughs and sneezes. The body takes over, the contagion spreads, the boys grab guns and in seconds hundreds of soldiers lie dead.

Laughter involves and expresses contradictory registers of emotion. D. H. Monro, Gregory Bateson and other reception-oriented humor theorists claim that a single, discrete emotion does not cause laughter, but rather an abrupt movement from one 'emotional sphere' to another (Monro 1951:249) or the interval of affective 'oscillation' created by this movement (Bateson 1953:6). This oscillation brings about the 'sharp cold bray of laughter' that an ass-like *Le Comte* repeatedly 'emits' in *The Wild Boys: A Book of the Dead* (128,137) and *Port of Saints* (38, 52, as well as the French Consul, 37). Because laughter is multi-referential, with shifting agendas, it can engage our awareness of the elements involved in its circulation through Burroughs's work in its exploration of boundaries and social limits.

This oscillation of emotions informs definitions of the term 'prank', a comic practice specifically associated with Burroughs (if you search *Google* with the words 'William Burroughs prank' four out of the first five responses will describe the death of his wife Joan Vollmer, 'killed in a drunken prank'. According to Burroughs, this 'prank' was both a case of possession [Morgan 1988:198] with tragic consequences, and the enabling source of his becoming a writer—'I am forced to the appalling conclusion that I would never have become a writer but for Joan's death, and to a realization of the extent to which this event has motivated and formulated my writing. I live with the constant threat of possession, and a constant need to escape from possession, from Control. So the death of Joan brought me in contact with the invader, the Ugly Spirit, and maneuvered me into a lifelong struggle, in which I have had no choice except to write my way out' [Q xxii]). Is a prank a malicious act, a trick, a practical joke? Are there criteria for good and for bad pranks? V. Vale and Andrea Juno argue that

> the *best* pranks invoke the imagination, poetic imagery, the unexpected and a deep level of irony or social criticism [...] Great pranks create synaesthetic experiences which are unmistakably exciting, original and reverberating, as well as *creative, metaphoric, poetic* and artistic. If these criteria be deemed sufficient, then pranks can be considered as constituting an art form and genre in themselves. (1987:4)

Bad pranks, on the other hand,

> are characterized not only by unoriginality but by *conventionalized* cruelty, these pointless humiliations do nothing to raise consciousness or alter existing power relationships. They are deeds which only further the *status-quo*; they only perpetuate the acceptance of and submission to *arbitrary authority*, or abet existing hierarchical inequities. Basically these include all pranks recognizable as 'clichés'—those which contribute no new poetic imagery. (1987:4–5)

According to Vale and Juno, good pranks are both creative and critical and play an important role in the history of art, in world myths and in written literature. Bad pranks, on the other hand, are conservative and conventional. A good prank crosses borders: '[G]enuinely poetic/imaginative pranks resist facile categorization, and transcend inflexible (and often questionable) demarcations between legality and illegality, good and bad taste, and right and wrong social conduct' (1987:5). Rabelais's Panurge, the master prankster, provides a model here, in his challenge to boundaries in the world of the Renaissance, a period where laughter also responded to a new awareness of the global. And as Tsing reminds us, '[t]he idea that global interconnections are *old* has only recently been revitalized, muffled as it was for much of the twentieth century by the draw of nationally contained legacies, in history, and functionally contained social worlds, in anthropology; it seems unfortunate to lose this insight so quickly' (2000:459). Comic practices can both articulate and respond to the shifting borders of globalization.

THE GLOBAL AND THE LOCAL

As an example of Burroughs's appreciation of the circulation between the global and the local, we might look at a famous routine which speculates on the consequences that arise when body parts assume their own lives: states of consciousness, individual agency and autonomy, stable philosophical and theological values are put up for grabs. In a discussion of the global traffic in human organs, Nancy Scheper-Hughes points out, for example, that '[t]ransplant surgery has reconceptualized social relations between self and other, between individual and society, and among the "three bodies"—the existential lived body-self, the social, representational body, and the body political' (2000:272). While these concerns may seem recent, the literature of talking body parts, expressing anxiety and humor over autonomous organs, can be traced back to the Old French fabliaux, anonymous narratives dating from the twelfth to the fourteenth century, short humorous tales written in octosyllabic couplets that present bawdy anecdotes, practical jokes and tricks of revenge, including such stories as 'Le Débat du con et du cul' ('The Dispute between the Cunt and the Anus') (Bloch 1986:105). Burroughs's 'talking asshole' routine continues this legacy by probing the demarcations of the legal, of taste and of social conduct through humor.

A first version of this sequence occurs in a letter to Ginsberg dated 7 February 1954. Burroughs prefaces the routine with a description of how he procrastinates before he settles down 'to write something saleable'—emphasizing how the routine itself is a commodity that explores commodification:

> So finally I say: 'Now you must work' and smoke some tea and sit down and out it comes all in one piece like a glob of spit: The incredibly obscene, thinly disguised references and situations that slip by in Grade B movies, the double entendres, perversion, sadism of popular songs, poltergeist knockings and mutterings of America's putrifying [sic] unconscious, boils that swell until they burst with a fart noise as if the body had put out an auxilary [sic] ass hole with a stupid, belligerent Bronx cheer. (*LTG* 17–18)

Burroughs clearly draws a connection between America's putrifying unconscious, as expressed in the popular culture of movies and songs, and the routine of the chattering asshole that culminates in a brain assumed to be dead because there is no more feeling in the eyes 'than a crab's eye on the end of a stalk'. After the routine, Burroughs continues with a discussion of border crossings:

So what I started to talk about was the sex that passes the censor, squeezes through *between* bureaus, because there's always a space *between*, in popular songs and Grade B movies, as giving away the basic American rottenness, spurting out like breaking boils, throwing out globs of that Un D. T. [undifferentiated tissue—a crucial part of the talking asshole routine] to fall anywhere and grow into some degenerate, cancerous life form, reproducing a hideous random image. (*LTG* 19)

Burroughs then significantly equates himself, or his humor, with the asshole who takes over:

This is my saleable product. Do you dig what happens? It's almost like automatic writing produced by a hostile, independent entity who is saying in effect 'I will write what I please.' At the same time when I try to pressure myself into organizing production, to impose some form on material, or even to follow a line (like continuation of novel) the effort catapults me into a sort of madness. (*LTG* 20–1)

When Burroughs writes humor for consumption, according to this description, it is the asshole who speaks.

Not surprisingly, critical analysis tends to eliminate the humor and respond to the horror of the 'hostile, independent entity' within the routine. However, both humor and horror are emphasized in the talking asshole routine as it appears in *Naked Lunch*. In the frame for the routine, Schafer, who is not listening to Doctor Benway talk, realizes the human body is 'scandalously inefficient' and wonders 'why not have one all-purpose hole to eat *and* eliminate' (*NL* 119). Benway responds 'Why not one all-purpose blob?' and starts the routine. In Benway's description of the Carny act, the talking asshole is synaesthetic, like a good prank—you can smell the sound. It also moves the audience physically—to hear the ass talk fills the audience with the urge to excrete. The Carny owner of the asshole initially speaks for the ass, as a ventriloquist. His act is 'Real funny, too, at first', and then the asshole gains verbal independence and turns out to be an innovative comic—'After a while the ass started talking on its own [...] his ass would ad-lib and toss the gags back at him every time' (*NL* 120). The asshole, or now commodified act, begins to consume as well; the subject or Carny man thinks this is cute at first and builds another act around the eating asshole, but the asshole is not willing to exist only as an objectified commodity, part of an act, and collapses the boundary between art and life (think of Peter Bürger, who defines the avant-garde as a series of tendencies aimed at overcoming the separation of art from everyday life, as attempts to dismantle the institution of art and the aesthetic as an acknowledged cultural sphere [Bürger 1984]; and recollect the commercial success of Joseph Pujol, 'Le Pétomane' [Lydenberg 1987:25–6 and Zeldin 1977:703–4]) by talking on the street, asking for equal rights, getting drunk, wanting love and kisses like any other mouth. Completely out of control, it talks day and night; the Carny man beats it and screams at it and sticks candles up it but the final words we hear from the asshole (and at this point, even before the eruption of the undifferentiated tissue, we must wonder who exactly is the real asshole here) are '[i]t's you who will shut up in the end. Not me. Because we don't need you around here any more. I can talk and eat *and* shit' (*NL* 120). The asshole has not only learned the lesson of economy and profit, but his understanding of efficiency is superior to that of his teacher. Soon the Carny man's mouth seals over with undifferentiated tissue, and only the eyes remain—the eyes no longer signify consciousness, and might even assume the function of an asshole for the asshole, mediating between within and without (the only change in the routine in *Naked Lunch* from the original letter to Ginsberg lies in the description of how the brain is trapped in the skull, rather than in a shell, when it can't give orders any more, emphasizing a mammal's prison).

Critics of Burroughs tend to read this routine as distinctly uncomic, presenting a destabilizing revolution of 'lower' over 'higher' terms. Tony Tanner, for example, sees the anecdote as a 'parable of matter in a state of hideous revolt', where lower forms of life devour higher forms (1971:117). For Tanner, the rebellion of body parts is hideous rather than funny. Alvin Seltzer, using terms offered by both the initial letter and *Naked Lunch* in both their subsequent discussions of bureaus as parasites, reads the routine as 'a political statement of the evils of a democratic system. The talking asshole becomes an allegorical equivalent of bureaucracies that feed off their host' (1974:346). Neil Oxenhandler interprets the tale psychoanalytically as 'the struggle between the oral impulse and the anal impulse', with a false victory for the anal impulse as the oral irrevocably returns (1975:144). Robin Lydenberg emphasizes language and the body and asserts: 'In this bizarre tale, Burroughs dramatizes the problematic relationship of body and mind, and the role of language in that relationship; the arbitrary violence of language as a system of naming and representation; and the possibility of an ontology and an aesthetics based on negativity and absence' (1987:19). At least Lydenberg does point out that the story is funny as well as frightening (23) and notes that 'critical references to the story do not appear in the context of discussions of Burroughs' humor' (26). Wayne Pounds identifies the routine as a parody of the discourse of scientistic, behaviorist human engineering, a dystopic parody of Benway's (actually Schafer's) engineering utopia (1987:219). Jamie Russell argues that the routine 'is a very obvious morality tale that warns against the mimicry of the feminine that is the basis of the effeminate paradigm and camp' and shows how 'the hideously comic image' (48) makes it easy to overlook the importance of what Lydenberg calls the 'novelty ventriloquist act' (cited by Russell 2001:48).

That this routine can inspire so many powerful readings is remarkable, but read with attention to its humor, it can also provide insights into the dynamics of Burroughs's comic practice. Although eyes often symbolize the intellect in the Western tradition, both eyes and asshole are also parts of the body. Cultural maps of the body assign very different values to assholes and eyes—collapse these differences and the resulting oscillation of emotions produces laughter. There are many links between the asshole and the eye in Burroughs's work as he plays with corporeal hierarchies. Starting with an indiscriminate appearance of organs in *Naked Lunch* ('In his place of total darkness mouth and eyes are one organ that leaps forward to snap with transparent teeth ... but no organ is constant as regards either function or position ... sex organs sprout anywhere ... rectums open, defecate and close ...' [*NL* 10]), the connection becomes more explicit in the recording *Spare Ass Annie and Other Tales* (1993), which describes its eponymous heroine thusly: 'She had an auxiliary asshole in the middle of her forehead, like a painful bronze eye' (*SAA*). The announcements '[a]nother installment in the adventures of Clem Snide the Private Ass Hole' (*NL* 108), 'I am a private asshole' (*CRN* 35) and 'I change my address, he gets a private ass hole to find me' (*WL* 123) also identify the asshole with the eye and with detection. In Burroughs's work, neither asshole nor eye is privileged—both represent the physical, both mediate between inner and outer. In *The*

Western Lands, when mummification is posed as a potential vehicle for immortality, we are reminded that any preservation of the body must include the asshole and all its functions:

> The young question the mummy concept:
> 'To keep the same asshole forever? Is this a clarion call to youth?'
> 'It stinks like petrified shit.'
> 'Have you something better to offer?' says a serious young Scribe [...]
> 'To reach the Western Lands is to achieve freedom from fear. Do you free yourself from fear by cowering in your physical body for eternity? Your body is a boat to lay aside when you reach the far shore, or sell it if you can find a fool ... it's full of holes ... it's full of holes.' (*WL* 161–2)

Both eyes and asshole represent holes, physical vulnerability, concavities that facilitate physical survival.

DIALECTIC BETWEEN THE SERIOUS AND THE FRIVOLOUS

Burroughs's ambivalence over the body's fragility can be found throughout his later work: 'I see myself streaking across the sky like a star to leave the earth forever. What holds me back? It is the bargain by which I am here at all. The bargain is this body that holds me here' (*WB* 102). In the past, immortality was achieved through preservation of the body (mummies)—now the body can be seen as part of a greater, more insidious bargain:

> Audrey felt the floor shift under his feet and he was standing at the epicenter of a vast web. In that moment, he knew its purpose, knew the reason for suffering, fear, sex, and death. It was all intended to keep human slaves imprisoned in physical bodies while a monstrous matador waved his cloth in the sky, sword ready for the kill. (*CRN* 309)

Escape from the body, a privileging of the mental or spiritual over the crude physical accidents and mortal contingencies of the flesh, should presumably bring liberation.

Here we return to the role of laughter in achieving, marking or qualifying this potential freedom, when Burroughs's narrator observes:

> The Duad is a river of excrement, one of the deadliest obstacles on the road to the Western Lands. To transcend life you must transcend

the conditions of life, the shit and farts and piss and sweat and snot of life. A frozen disgust is as fatal as prurient fixation, two sides of the same counterfeit coin. It is necessary to achieve a gentle and precise detachment, then the Duad opens like an intricate puzzle. (WL 155)

How to escape the false values of disgust and fixation, how to arrive at detachment? And what does it mean when the Duad opens, when a river of excrement reveals itself to be a complex puzzle? Laughter offers a way of exploring the boundaries that limit us to the emotional polarities of disgust or fixation. Our reception of the metaphors that circulate within Burroughs's humor—'Jody can do a fake Chinese spiel that'll just kill you—like a hysterical ventriloquist's dummy. In fact, he precipitated an anti-foreign riot in Shanghai that claimed 3,000 casualties' (NL 101)—determine whether we are in some way possessed by the joke, like a ventriloquist's dummy, like a comic or an asshole, or whether we can discover detachment through the humor.

One can see an evolution in Burroughs's relation to possession, frequently expressed through humor, from Naked Lunch (' "Possession" they call it. . . . Sometimes an entity jumps in the body [...] and hands move to disembowel the passing whore or strangle the neighbor child in hope of alleviating a chronic housing shortage. As if I was usually there but subject to goof now and again. ... Wrong! I am never here. ... Never that is fully in possession, but somehow in a position to forestall ill-advised moves. ... Patrolling is, in fact, my principle occupation' [NL 200]) to the questions that inform the late trilogy: 'It is essential for immortalists to remember, do not take anything too seriously. And remember also that frivolity is even more fatal ... so, what now?' (WL 163). This dialectic between the serious and the frivolous culminates in a final glimpse of an old man who realizes that what he struggles against necessarily constitutes what he must struggle for:

I want to reach the Western Lands —right in front of you, across the bubbling brook. It's a frozen sewer. It's known as the Duad, remember? All the filth and horror, fear, hate, disease and death of human history flows between you and the Western lands. Let it flow! My cat Fletch stretches behind me on the bed. A tree like black lace against a gray sky. A flash of joy.
How long does it take a man to learn that he does not, cannot want what he 'wants'?

You have to be in Hell to see Heaven. Glimpses from the Land of the Dead, flashes of serene timeless joy, a joy as old as suffering and despair. (*WL* 257–8)

In what seems like a joke, the longed-for Western Lands are squarely on the other side of a brook that bubbles like the asshole of human history. And instead of trying to frantically cross to that other side, or becoming paralyzed with disgust, here the narrator accepts that flow. I sometimes wonder if one of Burroughs's final pranks on his audience is this insistence that the barren trees of winter, the suffering and despair that lead people in and out of their addictions, the control mechanisms that provide an unearthly solace and a taste of immortality, are for better or for worse, a necessary part of the landscape. Like a good prank, Burroughs's humor reminds us not to dismiss the body. If we commodify the asshole, it will in turn commodify us.

Laughter for Burroughs is both an involuntary automatic reaction that we would not necessarily identify as human, and a potential tool for orientation. A good prank is creative, critical and raises consciousness. A good prank can inspire creativity, flexibility and resilience through laughter. A bad prank leads to frozen immobility where we are trapped, rather than liberated, by the oscillation of laughter. Although Burroughs frequently depicts laughter as hostile, even deadly ('His loud, metallic laugh rings out across the dump, and the crowd laughs with him under the searching guns' [*NL* 166]; 'The onlookers snort and bray with laughter sharp as flint knives in sunlight' [*WL* 71]), its absence in his work also signals mortal corruption. ('He organized a vast Thought Police. Anybody with an absent-minded expression was immediately arrested and executed. Anyone who expressed any ideas that deviated in any way from decent church-going morality suffered the same fate. The American Moral Disease passed into its terminal stage. Laughing was strictly forbidden. Everyone wore identical expressions of frustrated hate looking for a target' [*POS* 22–3].) Because 'it is the nature of laughter to recognize no bounds' (*LTG* 80), laughter marks a place where boundaries can be both acknowledged and crossed, where conventional feelings are questioned and challenged:

The door to another dimension may open when the gap between what one is expected to feel and what one actually does feel rips a hole in the fabric. Years ago I was driving along Price Road and I thought

how awful it would be to run over a dog or, my God, a child, and have to face the family and portray the correct emotions. When suddenly a figure wrapped in a cloak of darkness appeared with a dead child under one arm and slapped it down on a porch:
  'This yours, lady?'
  I began to laugh. The figure had emerged from a lightless region where everything we have been taught, all the conventional feelings, do not apply. There is no light to see them by. It is from this dark door that the antihero emerges.... (PDR 300)

The outlaw, the anti-hero, and the avant-garde can be said to share a sense of humor. Carl Hill, in his investigation of wit, observes how

Witz has come to be identified with the side of human reason. The split between accepted knowledge and the faculty that does the knowing, along with the increasing identification of Witz with the latter, marks Witz as the avant-garde of the intellect. It is in the paradoxical position of being both the builder and the destroyer of knowledge, tradition, and culture. (Hill 1993:4–5)

A study of humor as an avant-garde strategy of provocation and engagement can provide a 'stranger', more compelling framework for theorizing than such familiar categories as aesthetics versus politics or containment (the release and ultimate structural support of comic relief) versus transgression (or subversion). As John Limon points out, 'if comedy performs a useful task for theory it is all in the reduction to nonsense of the distinction between containment and subversion models of art' (Limon 2000:38). Burroughs's practice of humor points to a globalization model that endorses interconnection and valorizes both flows and the carving of their channels, that maps the relations between the local and the global and explores the scales of values used to construct those relations.

  Burroughs's joke work, exploring the relation between local organs and global constructs, illuminates how globalization must be seen not just as a new era facilitating commercialism and scholarship, but also as something that has always been with us. As Tsing argues, 'we can investigate globalist projects and dreams without assuming that they remake the world just as they want. The task of understanding planet-wide interconnections requires locating and specifying globalist projects and dreams, with their contradictory as well as charismatic logics and their messy as well as effective encounters and translations' (2000:456). Any articulation of flows must remain conscious of riverbanks—those structures that shape and are being shaped through globalization. Burroughs's humor urges us to recognize contradiction and mess, to appreciate the complexity of contexts of reception that lead, for example, to such profound (and profoundly different) responses to a 'talking asshole routine'. Humor in Burroughs's work offers a tool for orientation, to help us navigate even the flow made possible by the riverbank of the Duad.

REFERENCES

Appadurai, A. (1996) 'Disjuncture and Difference in the Global Cultural Economy', IN Inda, J. X., and Rosaldo, R. eds 2002a, pp. 46–64.

Bateson, G. (1953) 'The Position of Humor in Human Communication', IN *Cybernetics: Circular Causal and Feedback Mechanisms in Biological and Social Systems* (New York: Josiah Macy Jr. Foundation), pp.1–47.

Bloch, R. H. (1986) *The Scandal of the Fabliaux* (Chicago and London: University of Chicago Press).

Bürger, P. (1984) *Theory of the Avant-Garde* (Minneapolis: University of Minnesota Press).

Burroughs, W. S. (1984) 'My Purpose is to Write for the Space Age', IN Skerl, J., and Lydenberg, R. eds 1991, pp. 265–8.

—— (1993) *Spare Ass Annie and Other Tales* (Island Records 162–535 003–2).

Hay, C., and Marsh, D. (2000) 'Introduction: Demystifying Globalization', IN Hay, C., and Marsh, D. eds, *Demystifying Globalization* (Houndmills and London: Macmillan).

Hill, C. (1993) *The Soul of Wit: Joke Theory from Grimm to Freud* (Lincoln and London: University of Nebraska Press).

Inda, J. X., and Rosaldo, R. eds (2002a) *The Anthropology of Globalization: A Reader* (Massachusetts, Oxford, Melbourne and Berlin: Blackwell).

—— (2002b) 'Introduction: A World in Motion', IN Inda, J. X., and Rosaldo, R. eds 2002a, pp. 1–34.

Limon, J. (2000) *Stand-up Comedy in Theory, or Abjection in America* (Durham and London: Duke University Press).

Lydenberg, R. (1987) *Word Cultures: Radical Theory and Practice in William S. Burroughs' Fiction* (Urbana: University of Illinois Press).

Monro, D. H. (1951) *Argument of Laughter* (Melbourne: Melbourne University Press).

Morgan, T. (1988) *Literary Outlaw: The Life and Times of William S. Burroughs* (New York: Avon).

Morley, D., and Robins, K. (1995) *Spaces of Identity: Global Media, Electronic Landscapes, and Cultural Boundaries* (London: Routledge).

Murphy, T. S. (1997) *Wising Up the Marks: The Amodern William Burroughs* (Berkeley: University of Berkeley Press).

Oxenhandler, N. (1975) 'Listening to Burroughs' Voice', IN Skerl, J., and Lydenberg, R. eds 1991, pp. 133–47.

Pounds, W. (1987) 'The Postmodern Anus: Parody and Utopia in Two Recent Novels by William Burroughs', IN Skerl, J., and Lydenberg, R. eds 1991, pp. 217–32.

Purdie, S. (1993) *Comedy: The Mastery of Discourse* (Toronto and Buffalo: University of Toronto Press).

Rabelais, F. (1532–64) *The Histories of Gargantua and Pantagruel*, Cohen, J. M. trans. (London and New York: Penguin, 1955).

Russell, J. (2001) *Queer Burroughs* (New York and Hampshire: Palgrave).

Scheper-Hughes, N. (2000) 'The Global Traffic in Human Organs', IN Inda, J. X., and Rosaldo, R. eds 2002a, pp. 270–308.

Seltzer, A. J. (1974) *Chaos in the Novel, the Novel in Chaos* (New York: Schocken Books).

Skerl, J., and Lydenberg, R. eds (1991) *William S. Burroughs at the Front: Critical Reception, 1959–1989* (Carbondale: Southern Illinois University Press).

Tanner, T. (1971) *City of Words: American Fiction 1950–1970* (New York: Harper and Row).

Tomlinson, J. (1997) 'Internationalism, Globalization and Cultural Imperialism', IN Thompson, K. ed., *Media and Cultural Regulation* (London: Sage Publications), pp. 117–62.

Tsing, A. (2000) 'The Global Situation', IN Inda, J. X., and Rosaldo, R. eds 2002a, pp. 453–85.

Vale, V., and Juno, A. (1987) RE/Search #11: *Pranks!* (San Francisco, RE/Search Publications).

Zeldin, T. (1977) *France 1848–1945, vol. 2: Intellect, Taste and Anxiety* (Oxford: Oxford University Press).

16
Lemurian Time War
Cybernetic Culture Research Unit (Ccru)

The account that follows charts William S. Burroughs's involvement in an occult time war, and considerably exceeds most accepted conceptions of social and historical probability. It is based on 'sensitive information' passed to Ccru by an intelligence source whom we have called William Kaye.[1] The narrative has been partially fictionalized in order to protect this individual's identity.

Kaye himself admitted that his experiences had made him prone to 'paranoid-chronomaniac hallucination', and Ccru continues to find much of his tale extremely implausible.[2] Nevertheless, while suspecting that his message had been severely compromised by dubious inferences, noise, and disinformation, we have become increasingly convinced that he was indeed an 'insider' of some kind, even if the organization he had penetrated was itself an elaborate hoax, or collective delusion. Kaye referred to this organization as 'The Order', or—following Burroughs—'The Board'.

When reduced to its basic provocation, Kaye's claim was this: *The Ghost Lemurs of Madagascar*[3]—a text dating from 1987 which he also referred to as the Burroughs Necronomicon—had been an exact and decisive influence on the magical and military career of one Captain Mission, three centuries previously. Mission appears in historical record as a notorious pirate, active in the period around 1700 AD; he was to become renowned as the founder of the anarchistic colony of Libertatia, established on the island of Madagascar. Kaye asserted that he had personally encountered clear evidence of Burroughs's 'impact upon Mission' at the private library of Peter Vysparov, where Kaye worked most of his life. The Vysparov collection, he unswervingly maintained, held an ancient illustrated transcript of *The Ghost Lemurs of Madagascar*, inscribed meticulously in Mission's own hand.[4]

Kaye assured us that the Board considered the 'demonstrable time rift' he was describing to be a 'matter of the gravest concern'. He explained that the organization had been born in reaction to a

nightmare of time coming apart and—to use his exact words—
spiraling out of control. To the Board, spirals were particularly
repugnant symbols of imperfection and volatility. Unlike closed
loops, spirals always have loose ends. This allows them to spread,
making them contagious and unpredictable. The Board was count-
ing on Kaye to contain the situation. He was assigned the task of
terminating the spiral templex.[5]

HYPERSTITION

Vysparov had sought out Burroughs because of his evident interest
in the convergence of sorcery, dreams and fiction. In the immediate
postwar years, Vysparov had convened the so-called Cthulhu Club
to investigate connections between the fiction of H. P. Lovecraft,
mythology, science and magic, and was at this stage in the process
of formalizing the constitution of Miskatonic Virtual University
(MVU), a loose aggregation of non-standard theorists whose work
could broadly be said to have 'Lovecraftian' connotations. The interest in Lovecraft's fiction was motivated by its exemplification of the
practice of hyperstition, a concept that had been elaborated and
keenly debated since the inception of the Cthulhu Club. Loosely
defined, the coinage refers to 'fictions that make themselves real'.

Kaye drew Ccru's attention to Burroughs's description of viruses
in 'The Book of Breething' segment of *Ah Pook is Here and Other
Texts*: 'And what is a virus? Perhaps simply a pictorial series like
Egyptian glyphs that *makes itself real*' (APH 102). The papers Kaye
left for Ccru included a copy of this page of the *Ah Pook* text, with
these two sentences—italicized in the original text—heavily underlined. For Kaye, the echo of Vysparov's language was 'unequivocal
evidence' of the Russian's influence upon Burroughs's work after
1958. Whether or not this is the case, such passages indicate that
Burroughs, like Vysparov, was interested in the 'hyperstitional' relations between writing, signs and reality.

In the hyperstitional model Kaye outlined, fiction is not opposed
to the real. Rather, reality is understood to be composed of
fictions—consistent semiotic terrains that condition perceptual,
affective and behavioral responses. Kaye considered Burroughs's
work to be 'exemplary of hyperstitional practice'. Burroughs
construed writing—and art in general—not aesthetically, but functionally—that is to say, magically, with magic defined as the use of
signs to produce changes in reality.

Kaye maintained that it was 'far from accidental' that Burroughs's equation of reality and fiction had been most widely embraced only in its negative aspect—as a variety of 'postmodern' ontological skepticism—rather than in its positive sense, as an investigation into the magical powers of incantation and manifestation: the efficacy of the virtual. For Kaye, the assimilation of Burroughs into textualist postmodernism constituted a deliberate act of 'interpretivist sabotage', the aim of which was to de-functionalize Burroughs's writings by converting them into aesthetic exercises in style. Far from constituting a subversion of representative realism, the postmodern celebration of the text without a referent merely consummates a process that representative realism had initiated. Representative realism severs writing from any active function, surrendering it to the role of reflecting, not intervening in, the world. It is a short step to a dimension of pristine textuality, in which the existence of a world independent of discourse is denied altogether.

According to Kaye, the metaphysics of Burroughs's 'clearly hyperstitional' fictions can be starkly contrasted with those at work in postmodernism. For postmodernists, the distinction between real and unreal is not substantive or is held not to matter, whereas for practitioners of hyperstition, differentiating between 'degrees of realization' is crucial. The hyperstitional process of entities 'making themselves real' is precisely a passage, a transformation, in which potentials—already-active virtualities—realize themselves. Writing operates not as a passive representation but as an active agent of transformation and a gateway through which entities can emerge: 'by writing a universe, the writer makes such a universe possible' (*AM* 176).

But these operations do not occur in neutral territory, Kaye was quick to point out. Burroughs treats all conditions of existence as results of cosmic conflicts between competing intelligence agencies. In making themselves real, entities (must) also manufacture realities for themselves: realities whose potency often depends upon the stupefaction, subjugation and enslavement of populations, and whose existence is in conflict with other 'reality programs'. Burroughs's fiction deliberately renounces the status of plausible representation in order to operate directly upon this plane of magical war. Where realism merely reproduces the currently dominant reality program from inside, never identifying the existence of the program as such, Burroughs seeks to get outside the control codes in order to dismantle and rearrange them. Every act of writing is a sorcerous operation, a partisan action in a war where multitudes of factual events are guided by the powers of illusion. Even representative realism participates—albeit unknowingly—in magical war, collaborating with the dominant control system by implicitly endorsing its claim to be the only possible reality.

From the controllers' point of view, Kaye said, 'it is of course imperative that Burroughs is thought of as merely a writer of fiction. That's why they have gone to such lengths to sideline him into a ghetto of literary experimentation.'

THE ONE GOD UNIVERSE

Burroughs names the dominant control program One God Universe, or OGU. He wages war against the fiction of OGU, which builds its monopolistic dominion upon the magical power of the Word: upon programming and illusion. OGU establishes a fiction, which operates at the most fatal level of reality, where questions of biological destiny and immortality are decided. 'Religions are weapons' (*WL* 202).

In order to operate effectively, OGU must first of all deny the existence of magical war itself. There is only one reality: its own. In writing about magical war, Burroughs is thus already initiating an act of war against OGU. The throne is seen to be contested. OGU incorporates all competing fictions into its own story (the ultimate metanarrative), reducing alternative reality systems to negatively marked components of its own mythos: other reality programs become Evil, associated with the powers of deception and delusion. OGU's power works through fictions that repudiate their own fictional status: anti-fictions, or un-nonfictions. 'And that', Kaye said, 'is why fiction can be a weapon in the struggle against Control'.

In OGU, fiction is safely contained by a metaphysical 'frame', prophylactically delimiting all contact between the fiction and what is outside it. The magical function of words and signs is both condemned as evil and declared to be delusory, facilitating a monopoly upon the magical power of language for OGU (which of course denies that its own mythos exerts any magical influence, presenting it as a simple representation of Truth). But OGU's confidence that fiction has safely been contained means that anti-OGU agents can use fiction as a covert line of communication and a secret weapon: '[h]e concealed and revealed the knowledge in fictional form' (*PDR 115*).

This, for Kaye, was 'a formula for hyperstitional practice'. Diagrams, maps, sets of abstract relations, tactical gambits, are as real in a fiction about a fiction as they are when encountered raw, but subjecting such semiotic contraband to multiple embeddings allows a traffic in materials for decoding dominant reality that would otherwise be proscribed. Rather than acting as a transcendental screen, blocking out contact between itself and the world, the fiction acts as a Chinese box—a container for sorcerous interventions in the world. The frame is both used (for concealment) and broken (the fictions potentiate changes in reality).

Whereas hyperstitional agitation produces a 'positive unbelief'— a provisionalizing of any reality frame in the name of pragmatic engagement rather than epistemological hesitation—OGU feeds on belief. In order to work, the story that runs reality has to be believed, which is also to say that the existence of a control program determining reality must *not* be suspected or believed. Credulity in the face of the OGU metanarrative is inevitably coupled with a refusal to accept that entities like Control have any substantive existence. That's why, to get out of OGU, a systematic shedding of all beliefs is a prerequisite. 'Only those who can leave behind everything they have ever believed in can hope to escape' (*WL* 116). Techniques of escape depend on attaining the unbelief of assassin-magician Hassan i Sabbah: nothing is true, everything is permitted. Once again, Kaye cautioned that this must be carefully distinguished from 'postmodern relativism'. Burroughs-Sabbah's 'nothing is true' cannot be equated with postmodernism's 'nothing is real'. On the contrary: nothing is true because there is no single, authorized version of reality—instead, there is a superfluity, an excess, of realities. 'The Adversary's game plan is to persuade you that he does not exist' (*WL* 12).

KAYE AND BURROUGHS

Kaye's story began in the summer of 1958, when his employer Peter Vysparov met William S. Burroughs whilst conducting occult investigations in Paris.[6] As a result of this meeting Kaye was himself introduced to Burroughs on 23 December of the same year, at Vysparov's private library in New York.

It is clear from public documentary material that Burroughs was predominantly a resident in Paris and London at this time. Ccru found no evidence of any trip to the US, although his biography is not sufficiently comprehensive to rule out an excursion to NY with confidence. There is no doubt, however, that shortly after the winter of 1958 Burroughs starts writing cryptically of visions, 'paranormal phenomena', encountering his double, and working with cut-up techniques.[7]

As Burroughs hunted through the library's unparalleled collection of rare occult works, he made a discovery that involved him in a radical, apparently unintelligible disorder of time and identity. The trigger was his encounter with a text that he was yet to compose: '[A]n old picture book with gilt edged lithographs, onion paper over each picture, The Ghost Lemurs of Madagascar in gold script' (Burroughs 1987:30). He could not then have known that Captain Mission had taken the very same volume as his guide three centuries previously (already describing it as 'old').

Flipping through the pages, Burroughs entered a momentary catatonic trance state. He emerged disoriented, and scarcely able to stand. Despite his confusion, he was more than willing to describe, with a strange sardonic detachment, the anomalous episode.[8] Twenty-nine years would pass before Kaye understood what had occurred.

Burroughs told Kaye that, during the trance, it felt as though silent communication with a ghostly non-human companion had flashed him forward to his life as an old man, several decades in the future. Oppressed by 'a crushing sensation of implacable destiny, as if fragments of a frozen time dimension were cascading into awareness', he 'remembered' writing The Ghost Lemurs of Madagascar— 'although it wasn't writing exactly', and his writing implements were archaic, belonging to someone else entirely, in another place and time.

Even after his recovery the sense of oppression persisted, like a 'new dimension of gravity'. The vision had granted him 'horrific insight into the jail-house mind of the One God'. He was convinced the knowledge was 'dangerous' and that 'powerful forces were conspiring against him', that the 'invisible brothers are invading present time' (now in TE 209). The episode sharpened his already vivid impression that the human animal is cruelly caged in time by an alien power. Recalling it later, he would write: 'Time is a human affliction; not a human invention but a prison' (GC 16).

Although there is no direct historical evidence supporting Kaye's description of events, the immediate period after the 1958 'episode' provides compelling symptomatic evidence of a transformation in

Burroughs's strategies and preoccupations during this period. It was then that Burroughs's writing underwent a radical shift in direction, with the introduction of experimental techniques whose sole purpose was to escape the bonds of the already-written, charting a flight from destiny. Gysin's role in the discovery of these cut-ups and fold-ins is well known, but Kaye's story accounts for the special urgency with which Burroughs began deploying these new methods in late 1958. The cut-ups and fold-ins were 'innovative time-war tactics', the function of which was to subvert the foundations of the pre-recorded universe.[9] 'Cut the Word Lines with scissors or switchblades as preferred ... The Word Lines keep you in Time...' (*3M* 71).

Burroughs's adoption of these techniques was, Kaye told Ccru, 'one of the first effects (if one may be permitted to speak in so loose a way) of the time-trauma'. Naturally, Kaye attributes Burroughs's intense antipathy toward pre-recording—a persistent theme in his fiction after *Naked Lunch*—to his experiences in the Vysparov library. The 'cosmic revelation' in the library produced in Burroughs 'a horror so profound' that he would dedicate the rest of his life to plotting and propagating escape routes from 'the board rooms and torture banks of time' (*NE* 43). Much later, Burroughs would describe a crushing feeling of inevitability, of life being scripted in advance by malign entities: '[T]he custodians of the future convene. Keepers of the Board Books: Mektoub, it is written. And they don't want it changed' (*GC* 8).

It was in the immediate aftermath of the episode in the Vysparov library that Burroughs exhibited the first signs of an apparently random attachment to lemurs, the decisive implications of which took several decades to surface.

Burroughs was unsure who was running him, like 'a spy in somebody else's body where nobody knows who is spying on whom' (cited by Douglas 1998:xxviii). Until the end of his life he struggled against the 'Thing inside him. The Ugly Spirit' (*GC* 48), remarking that: 'I live with the constant threat of possession, and a constant need to escape from possession, from Control' (*Q* xxii).

THE ESCAPE FROM CONTROL

In Burroughs's mythology, OGU emerges once MU (the Magical Universe) is violently overthrown by the forces of monopoly (*WL* 113). The Magical Universe is populated by many gods, eternally in conflict: there is no possibility of unitary Truth, since the nature of reality is constantly contested by heterogeneous entities whose interests are radically incommensurable. Where monotheistic fiction tells of a rebellious secession from the primordial One, Burroughs describes the One initiating a war against the Many:

> These were troubled times. There was war in the heavens as the One God attempted to exterminate or neutralize the Many Gods and establish an absolute seat of power. The priests were aligning themselves on one side or the other. Revolution was spreading up from the South, moving from the East and from the Western deserts. (WL 101)

Also, the OGU is described as 'antimagical, authoritarian, dogmatic, the deadly enemy of those who are committed to the magical universe, spontaneous, unpredictable, alive. The universe they are imposing is controlled, predictable, dead' (WL 59).

Such a universe gives rise to the dreary paradoxes—so familiar to monotheistic theology—that necessarily attend omnipotence and omniscience:

> Consider the One God Universe: OGU. The spirit recolls in horror from such a deadly impasse. He is all-powerful and all-knowing. Because He can do everything, He can do nothing, since the act of doing demands opposition. He knows everything, so there is nothing for him to learn. He can't go anywhere, since He is already fucking everywhere, like cowshit in Calcutta.
>
> The OGU is a pre-recorded universe of which He is the recorder. (WL 113)

For Kaye, the superiority of Burroughs's analysis of power—over 'trivial' ideology critique—consists in its repeated emphasis on the relationship between control systems and temporality. Burroughs is emphatic, obsessive: '[I]n Time any being that is spontaneous and alive will wither and die like an old joke' (WL 111); he notes also that '[a] basic impasse of all control machines is this: Control needs time in which to exercise control' (AM 117). OGU control codings far exceed ideological manipulation, amounting to cosmic reality programming, because—at the limit—'the One God is Time' (WL 111). The presumption of chronological time is written into the organism at the most basic level, scripted into its unconsciously performed habituated behaviors:

> Time is that which ends. Time is limited time experienced by a sentient creature. Sentient of time, that is—making adjustments to time in

terms of what Korzybski calls neuro-muscular intention behaviour with respect to the environment as a whole...A plant turns towards the sun, nocturnal animal stirs at sun set...shit, piss, move, eat, fuck, die. Why does Control need humans?
  Control needs time. Control needs human time. Control needs your shit piss pain orgasm death. (*APH* 17)

Power operates most effectively not by persuading the conscious mind, but by delimiting in advance what it is possible to experience. By formatting the most basic biological processes of the organism in terms of temporality, Control ensures that all human experience is of—and in—time. That is why time is a 'prison' for humans. 'Man was born in time. He lives and dies in time. Wherever he goes he takes time with him and imposes time' (*GC* 17). Korzybski's definition of man as the 'time-binding animal' has a double sense for Burroughs. On the one hand, human beings are binding time for themselves: they 'can make information available through writing or oral tradition to other SAP humans outside [their] area of contact and to future generations' (*GC* 48). On the other hand, humans are binding themselves into time, building more of the prison, which constrains their affects and perceptions. 'Korzybski's words took on a horrible new meaning for Burroughs in the library,' Kaye said. 'He saw what time-binding really was, all the books, already written, time-bound forever.'

  Since writing customarily operates as the principal means of 'time-binding', Burroughs reasoned that innovating new writing techniques would unbind time, blowing a hole in the OGU 'present', and opening up Space. 'Cut the Word Lines with scissors or switchblades as preferred...The Word Lines keep you in Time...Cut the in lines...Make out lines to Space' (*3M* 71). Space has to be understood not as empirical extension, still less as a transcendental given, but in the most abstract sense, as the zone of unbound potentialities lying beyond the purview of the OGU's already-written.

  'You can see that Burroughs's writing involves the highest possible stakes,' Kaye wrote. 'It does not represent cosmic war: it is already a weapon in that war. It is not surprising that the forces ranged against him—the many forces ranged against him, you can't overestimate their influence on this planet—sought to neutralize that weapon. It was a matter of the gravest urgency that his works be classified as fantasies, experimental Dada, anything but that they should be recognized as what they are: technologies for altering reality.'

THE RIFT

For almost 30 years Burroughs had sought to evade what he had been shown to be inevitable. Yet numerous signs indicate that by the late 1980s the Control Complex was breaking down, redirecting Burroughs's flight from pre-recorded destiny into a gulf of unsettled fate that he came to call 'the Rift'.

Kaye consistently maintained that any attempt to date Burroughs's encounter with the Rift involved a fundamental misconception. Nevertheless, his own account of this 'episode' repeatedly stressed the importance of the year 1987, a date that marked a period of radical transition: the 'eye' of a 'spiral templex'. It was during this time that the obscure trauma at the Vysparov library flooded back with full force, saturating Burroughs's dreams and writings with visions of lemurs, ghosts from the Land of the Dead.

1987 was the year in which Burroughs visited the Duke University Lemur Conservation Center, consolidating an alliance with the non-anthropoid primates, or prosimians.[10] In *The Western Lands*—which Burroughs was writing during this year—he remarks that: 'At sight of the Black Lemur, with round red eyes and a little red tongue protruding, the writer experiences a delight that is almost painful' (*WL* 248). Most crucially, it was in 1987 that *Omni* magazine commissioned and published Burroughs's short story *The Ghost Lemurs of Madagascar*, a text that propelled his entire existence into the Rift of Lemurian Time Wars.

For some time previously Kaye's suspicions had been aroused by Burroughs's increasingly obsessional attitude to his cats. His devotion to Calico, Fletch, Ruski, and Spooner[11] exhibited a profound biological response that was the exact inversion of his instinctual revulsion for centipedes. His libidinal conversion to a 'cat man' (see *CI*) also tracked and influenced an ever-deepening disillusionment with the function of human sexuality, orgasm addiction, and Venusian conspiracy.

'Cats may be my last living link to a dying species' (*CI* 67), Burroughs wrote in his essay *The Cat Inside*. For Kaye it was evident that this intensifying attachment to domestic felines was part of a more basic drive, manifesting an intimate familiarization with the 'cat spirit' or 'creature' who partakes of many other species, including 'raccoons, ferrets and skunks' (*CRN* 244) and numerous varieties of lemurs, such as 'ring-tailed cat lemurs' (*GC* 3), the 'sifaka lemur', 'mouse lemur' (*GC* 4), and, ultimately, 'the gentle deer lemur' (*GC* 18). As initiatory beings, mediumistic familiars, or occult door-keepers, these animals returned Burroughs to lost Lemurian landscapes, and to his double, Captain Mission.

Kaye was highly dismissive of all critical accounts that treated Mission as a literary avatar, 'as if Burroughs was basically an experimental novelist'. He maintained that the relation between Burroughs and Mission was not that of author to character, but rather that of 'anachronistic contemporaries',[12] bound together in a knot of 'definite yet cognitively distressing facts'. Of these 'facts' none was more repugnant to common human rationality than their mutual involvement with *The Ghost Lemurs of Madagascar*.

'We offer refuge to all people everywhere who suffer under the tyranny of governments' (*CRN* 265), declared Mission.[13] This statement was sufficient to awaken the hostile interest of the Powers That Be, although, from the Board's perspective, even Mission's piratical career was a relatively trivial transgression. Their primary concern was 'a more significant danger [...] Captain Mission's unwholesome concern with lemurs' (Burroughs 1987:28).

'Mission was spending more and more time in the jungle with his lemurs' (*GC* 11)—the ghosts of a lost continent—slipping into time disturbances and spiral patterns. Lemurs became his sleeping and dream companions. He discovered through this dead and dying species that the key to escaping control is taking the initiative—or the pre-initiative—by interlinking with the Old Ones.

> The Lemur people are older than Homo Sap, much older. They date back one hundred sixty million years, to the time when Madagascar split off from the mainland of Africa. They might be called psychic amphibians—that is, visible only for short periods when they assume a solid form to breathe, but some of them can remain in the invisible state for years at a time. Their way of thinking and feeling is basically different from ours, not oriented toward time and sequence and causality. They find these concepts repugnant and difficult to understand. (Burroughs 1987:31)

The Board conceived Mission's traffic with lemurs, his experiments in time sorcery, and his anachronistic entanglement with Burroughs as a single intolerable threat. 'In a prerecorded and therefore totally predictable universe, the blackest sin is to tamper with the prerecording, which could result in altering the prerecorded future. Captain Mission was guilty of this sin' (Burroughs 1987:27).

'Now more lemurs appear, as in a puzzle' (*GC* 15). Lemurs are denizens of the Western Lands, the 'great red island' (*GC* 16) of Madagascar, which Mission knew as Western Lemuria,[14] 'The Land of The Lemur People' (*NE* 110), a Wild West. It was on the island of Madagascar that Captain Mission discovered that 'the word for "lemur" meant "ghost" in the native language' (*GC* 2)—just as the Romans spoke of lemures, wraiths, or shades of the dead.[15]

In their joint voyage across the ghost continent of Lemuria, inter-linked by lemurs, Mission and Burroughs find 'immortality' through involvement with the native populations of unlife. In describing this process, Kaye placed particular emphasis on Burroughs's 1987 visit to the Duke University Lemur Center. It was this colony of lemurs that introduced Burroughs to the West Lemurian 'time pocket' (*GC* 15), just as 'Captain Mission was drifting out faster and faster, caught in a vast undertow of time. "Out, and under, and out, and out," a voice repeated in his head' (*GC* 17). If time travel ever happens, it always does.

He finds himself at the gateway, inside the 'ancient stone structure' (Burroughs 1987:28) with the lemur who is 'his phantom, his Ghost' (29). He is seated at a writing table ('with inkpot, quill, pens, parchment' [29]). He uses a native drug to explore the gateway. Who built it? When? The tale comes to him in a time-faulted vision, transmitted in hieroglyphics. He 'chooses a quill pen' (29).

It is difficult to describe where the text comes from, but there it is: '[A]n old illustrated book with gilt edges. The Ghost Lemurs of Madagascar' (Burroughs 1987:29); '[A]n old picture book with gilt edged lithographs, onion paper over each picture, The Ghost Lemurs of Madagascar in gold script' (30). The vision echoes or overlaps, time-twinning waves where Mission and Burroughs co-incide. They copy an invocation or summoning, a joint templex innovation that predates the split between creation and recording, reaching back 'before the appearance of man on earth, before the beginning of time' (*GC* 15).

'When attached to Africa, Madagascar was the ultimate landmass, sticking out like a disorderly tumor cut by a rift of future contours, this long rift like a vast indentation, like the cleft that divides the human body' (*GC* 16).

They feel themselves thrown forward 160 million years as they access the Big Picture, a seismic slippage from geological time into transcendental time anomaly. The island of Madagascar shears away from the African mainland,[16] whilst—on the other side of time— Western Lemuria drifts back up into the present. The Lemurian continent sinks into the distant future, stranding the red island with its marooned lemur people. 'What is the meaning of 160 million years without time? And what does time mean to foraging lemurs?' (*GC* 16–17).

Time crystallizes, as concentric contractions seize the spiral mass. From deep in the ages of slow Panic[17] they see the 'People of the Cleft, formulated by chaos and accelerated time, flash through a hundred sixty million years to the Split. Which side are you on? Too late to change now. Separated by a curtain of fire' (Burroughs 1987:31).

The Ghost Lemurs of Madagascar opens out on to the Rift, 'the split between the wild, the timeless, the free, and the tame, the time-bound, the tethered' (*GC* 13), as one side 'of the rift drifted into enchanted timeless innocence' and the other 'moved inexorably toward language, time, tool use, weapon use, war, exploitation, and slavery' (*GC* 49).

Which side are you on?

As time rigidifies, the Board closes in on the lemur people, on a chance that has already passed, a ghost of chance, a chance that is already dead: '[T]he might-have-beens who had one chance in a billion and lost' (*GC* 18). Exterminate the brutes ... 'Mission knows that a chance that occurs only once in a hundred and sixty million years has been lost forever' (*GC* 21), and Burroughs awakens scream-ing from dreams of 'dead lemurs scattered through the settlement' (*GC* 7).[18]

According to Kaye, everyone 'on the inside' knew about the bad dreams, certain they were coming from a real place. In this, as so much else, Kaye's reconstruction of the 1987 event depended centrally upon *The Ghost Lemurs of Madagascar*, an account he cited as if it were a strictly factual record, even a sacred text. He explained that this was an interpretative stance that had been highly developed by the Board, and that to respect the reality even of non-actualities is essential when waging war in deeply virtualized environments: in spaces that teem with influential abstractions and other ghostly things. Kaye consid-ered Bradly Martin, for instance, to be entirely real. He described him as an identifiable contemporary individual—working as an agent of 'the Board'—whose task was to seal the 'ancient structure' that provides access to the Rift.

The Board had long known that the Vysparov library contained an old copy of *The Ghost Lemurs of Madagascar*, which dated itself with the words 'Now, in 1987' (Burroughs 1987:34). It had been catalogued there since 1789. The text was a self-confessed time-abomination, requiring radical correction. It disregarded fundamental principles of sequence and causality, openly aligning itself with the lemur people. What the Board needed was a dead end. Burroughs was an obvious choice, for a number of reasons. He was sensitive to transmissions, amenable to misogyny and mammal-chauvinism, socially marginalized, and controllable through junk. They were confident, Kaye recalled, that the forthcoming 1987 'story' would be 'lost amongst the self-marginalizing fictions of a crumbling junky fag'.

On the outside it worked as a cover-up, but the Insiders had a still more essential task. They had inherited the responsibility for enforcing the Law of Time, and of OGU: defend the integrity of the timeline. This Great Work involved horrifying compromises. Kaye cited the hermetic maxim: strict obedience to the Law excuses grave transgressions. 'They're speaking of White Chronomancy', he explained; 'the sealing of runaway time-disturbances within closed loops.'[19] What Mission had released, Burroughs had bound again. That is how it seemed to the Board in 1987, with the circle apparently complete.

Confident that the transcendental closure of time was being achieved, the Board appropriated the text as the record of a precognitive intuition, a prophecy that could be mined for information. It confirmed their primary imperative and basic doctrine, foretelling the ultimate triumph of OGU and the total eradication of Lemurian insurgency. Mission had understood this well: 'No quarter, no compromise is possible. This is war to extermination' (GC 9).

It seems never to have occurred to the Board that Burroughs would change the ending, that their 'dead end' would open a road to the Western Lands.[20] Things that should have been long finished continued to stir. It was as if a post-mortem coincidence or unlife influence had vortically reanimated itself. A strange doubling occurred. Burroughs entitled it The Ghost of Chance, masking the return of the Old Ones in the seemingly innocuous words: 'People of the world are at last returning to their source in spirit, back to the little lemur people' (GC 54). The Board had no doubt—this was a return to the true horror.

Yet, Kaye insisted, for those with eyes to see, The Ghost Lemurs of Madagascar announced its turbular Lemurian destination from the beginning, and its final words are 'lost beneath the waves' (Burroughs 1987:34).

Kaye's own final words to Ccru, written on a scrap of paper upon which he had scrawled hurriedly in a spiderish hand that already indicated the tide of encroaching insanity, remain consistent with this unsatisfactory conclusion: 'Across the time rift, termination confuses itself with eddies of a latent spiral current.'

NOTES

1. Ccru first met 'William Kaye' on 20 March 1999. He stated at this, our first and last face-to-face encounter, that his purpose in contacting Ccru was to ensure that his tale would be 'protected against the ravages of time'. The irony was not immediately apparent.
2. We have recorded our comments and doubts, along with details of his story, in the endnotes to this document.
3. This story was commissioned and published by *Omni* magazine in 1987. The only constraint imposed by the magazine was that there should not be too much sex.
4. Kaye was adamant that the existence of these two texts could not be attributed to either coincidence or plagiarism, although his reasoning was at times obscure and less than wholly persuasive to Ccru.
5. The concept of the 'spiral templex', according to which the rigorous analysis of all time anomalies excavates a spiral structure, is fully detailed in R. E. Templeton's Miskatonic lectures on transcendental time travel. A brief overview of this material has been published by Ccru as 'The Templeton Episode', in the Digital Hyperstition issue of *Abstract Culture* (volume 4).
6. Kaye insisted, on grounds that he refused to divulge, that this meeting was not a chance encounter but had in some way been orchestrated by the Order.
7. See Burroughs's letters from January 1959.
8. Kaye noted that both Vysparov and Burroughs had been mutually forthcoming about their respective experiences of a 'mystico-transcendental nature'. Although this openness would seem to run counter to the hermetic spirit of occult science, Kaye described it as 'surprisingly common amongst magicians'.
9. Burroughs described his production methods—cut-ups and fold-ins—as a time travel technology coded as a passage across decimal magnitudes: 'I take page one and fold it into page one hundred—I insert the resulting composite as page ten—When the reader reads page ten he is flashing forwards in time to page one hundred and back in time to page one' (*WV* 96).
10. There are two sub-orders of primates, the anthropoids (consisting of monkeys, apes, and humans) and the prosimians, which include Madagascan lemurs, Asian lorises, Australian galgoes (or bushbabies), and the tarsiers of the Philippines and Indonesia. The prosimians constitute a branch of evolution distinct from, and older than, the anthropoids. Outside Madagascar, competition from the anthropoids has driven all prosimians into a nocturnal mode of existence.
11. The extent of Burroughs's attachment to his feline companions is evidenced by his final words, as recorded in his diaries: 'Nothing is. There

is no final enough of wisdom, experience—any fucking thing. No Holy Grail. No Final Satori, no final solution. Just conflict. Only thing can resolve conflict is love, like I felt for Fletch and Ruski, Spooner and Calico. Pure love. What I feel for my cats present and past' (LW 253).

12. Ccru was never fully confident as to the exact meaning of this pronouncement. Kaye seemed to be suggesting that Mission and Burroughs were the same person, caught within the vortex of a mysterious 'personality interchange' that could not be resolved within time.

13. Burroughs writes of Madagascar providing 'a vast sanctuary for the lemurs and for the delicate spirits that breathe through them' (GC 16). This convergence of ecological and political refuge fascinated Kaye, who on several occasions noted that the number for Refuge in Roget's Thesaurus is 666. The relevance of this point still largely escapes Ccru.

14. Puzzling consistencies between rocks, fossils, and animal species found in South Asia and Eastern Africa led nineteenth-century paleontologists and geologists to postulate a lost landmass that once connected the two now separated regions. This theory was vigorously supported by E. H. Haeckel, who used it to explain the distribution of Lemur-related species throughout Southern Africa and South and South-East Asia. On this basis, the English Zoologist Phillip L. Sclater named the hypothetical continent 'Lemuria', or Land of the Lemurs. Lemurs are treated as relics, or biological remainders of a hypothetical continent. living ghosts of a lost world.

Haeckel's theoretical investment in Lemuria, however, went much further than this. He proposed that the invented continent was the probable cradle of the human race, speculating that it provided a solution to the Darwinian mystery of the 'missing link' (the absence of immediately pre-human species from the fossil record). For Haeckel, Lemuria was the original home of man, the 'true Eden', all traces of which had been submerged by its disappearance. He considered the biological unity of the human species to have since been lost (disintegrating into twelve distinct species).

As a scientific conjecture, Lemuria has been buried by scientific progress. Not only have palaeontologists largely dispelled the problem of the missing link through additional finds, but the science of plate tectonics has also replaced the notion of 'sunken continents' with that of continental drift.

Now bypassed by oecumenic rationality as a scientific fiction or an accidental myth, Lemuria sinks into obscure depths once again.

15. In the late nineteenth century, Lemuria was eagerly seized upon by occultists, who—like their scientific cousins—wove it into elaborate evolutionary and racial theories.

In the Secret Doctrine, a commentary on the Atlantean Book of Dzyan, H. P. Blavatsky describes Lemuria as the third in a succession of lost continents. It is preceded by Polarea and Hyperborea, and followed by Atlantis (which was built from a fragment of Western Lemuria). Atlantis immediately precedes the modern world, and two further continents are still to come. According to Theosophical orthodoxy, each such 'continent' is the geographical aspect of a spiritual epoch, providing a home for the series of seven 'Root Races'. The name of each lost continent is used ambiguously to designate the core territory of the dominant root race of that age, and also for the overall distribution of terrestrial land-mass during that period (in this latter respect it can even be seen as consistent with continental drift, and thus as more highly developed than the original scientific conception).

L. Sprague de Camp describes Blavatsky's third root race, the 'ape-like, hermaphroditic egg-laying Lemurians, some with four arms and some with an eye in the back of their heads, whose downfall was caused by their discovery of sex' (1978:58). There is broad consensus among occultists that the rear-eye of the Lemurians persists vestigially as the human pineal gland.

W. Scott Elliot adds that the Lemurians had 'huge feet, the heels of which stuck out so far they could as easily walk backwards as forwards'. According to his account the Lemurians discovered sex during the fourth sub-race, while interbreeding with beasts and producing the great apes. This behavior disgusted the spiritual Lhas who were supposed to incarnate into them, but now refused. The Venusians volunteered to take the place of the Lhas, and also taught the Lemurians various secrets (including those of metallurgy, weaving and agriculture).

Rudolf Steiner was also fascinated by the Lemurians, remarking that '[t]his Root-Race as a whole had not yet developed memory' (2002:68). The 'Lemurian was a born magician' (73), whose body was less solid, plastic, and 'unsettled'.

More recently, Lemuria has been increasingly merged into Churchward's lost pacific continent of Mu, drifting steadily eastwards until even parts of modern California have been assimilated to it.

Although Blavatsky credits Sclater as the source for the name Lemuria, it cannot have been lost upon her, or her fellow occultists, that Lemuria was a name for the land of the dead, or the Western Lands. The word 'lemur' is derived from the Latin lemure—literally, 'shade of the dead'. The Romans conceived the lemures as vampire-ghosts, propitiated by a festival in May. In this vein, Eliphas Levi writes of '[l]arvae and lemures, shadowy images of bodies which have lived and of those which have yet to come, issued from these vapours by myriads' (Levi 2001:126).

16. According to current scientific consensus, Burroughs's figure of 160 million years is exaggerated. Burroughs's geological tale is nevertheless a recognizably modern one, with no reference to continental subsidence. With the submergence of the Lemuria hypothesis, however, the presence of lemurs on Madagascar becomes puzzling. Lemurs are only 55 million years old, whilst Madagascar is now thought to have broken away from the African mainland 120 million years ago.

17. Burroughs remarks of Mission: 'He was himself an emissary of Panic, of the knowledge that man fears above all else: the truth of his origin' (GC 3).

18. Burroughs drifts out of the White Magical orbit as his lemur commitments strengthen—to the Board, his support for the cause of lemur conservation (the Lemur Conservation Fund) must have been the final and intolerable provocation.

19. The physical conception of 'closed time-like curves' invokes a causality from the future to make the past what it is. They work to make things

come out as they must. If this is the only type of time travel 'allowed' by nature, then it obviously shouldn't require a law to maintain it (such as the notorious 'don't kill granny'). The rigorous time-law policies of the Board, however, indicate that the problem of 'time-enforcement' is actually far more intricate.

20. 'The road to the Western Lands is by definition the most dangerous road in the world, for it is a journey beyond Death, beyond the basic God standard of Fear and Danger. It is the most heavily guarded road in the world, for it gives access to the gift that supersedes all other gifts: Immortality' (*WL* 124).

REFERENCES

Burroughs, W. S. (1987) 'The Ghost Lemurs of Madagascar', IN Datlow, E. ed., *Omni Visions One* (North Carolina, Omni Books, 1993).

Camp, L. S. de (1978) *Lost Continents: The Atlantis Theme in History, Science and Literature* (New York: Dover Press).

Douglas, A. (1998) ' "Punching a Hole in the Big Lie": The Achievement of William S. Burroughs', IN *WV* pp. xv–xxviii.

Levi, E. (2001) *The History of Magic*, Waite, A. E. trans. (New York: Weiser Books).

Steiner, R. (2002) *Atlantis and Lemuria* (NL: Freedonia Books).

Contributors' Notes

Ccru is a decentralized intelligence agency involved in the investigation, documentation and analysis of time disturbances and cultural anomalies. More on Ccru is available at <www.ccru.net>.

Ed Desautels lives in Pittsburgh, PA. He served for several years as a technical communications specialist with Internet pioneer BBN, as well as with the Internet security firm Arbor Networks. He is the author of the novel *Flicker in the Porthole Glass* (MAMMOTH, 2002). His short fiction and hypertexts have appeared in *Hayden's Ferry Review, Pennsylvania English, The Little Magazine* and the CD *Gravitational Intrigue: An Anthology of Emergent Hypermedia.* He is currently writing a novel based on the life of French Dadaist, gigolo, and suicide, Jacques Rigaut.

Anthony Enns is a Ph.D. candidate in the Department of English at the University of Iowa. His work on literature and media has appeared in such journals as *Postmodern Culture, Journal of Popular Film and Television, Popular Culture Review, Studies in Popular Culture, Quarterly Review of Film and Video, Currents in Electronic Literacy,* and *Science Fiction Studies,* and in the anthology *Sexual Rhetoric: Media Perspectives on Sexuality, Gender, and Identity* (Greenwood, 1999). He is also co-editor of the anthology *Screening Disability: Essays on Cinema and Disability* (University Press of America, 2001).

Roberta Fornari works as a translator in English and French and is a Ph.D. candidate in Literatures of English Language at La Sapienza University, Rome. She has written a thesis on William S. Burroughs's metafiction and is writing a Ph.D. dissertation on 'Violence in Postmodern American Fiction'. She has published on William S. Burroughs's *The Western Lands* and has presented the paper 'William Burroughs and Jonathan Swift's Satirical Worlds'. She also writes articles on cinematic techniques in movie magazines (*The Scenographer*) and is translating *The Great Unraveling* by Paul Krugman.

After completing a Ph.D. on Burroughs's collage aesthetic at Oxford in 1988, **Oliver Harris** has specialized in textual scholarship, editing *The Letters of William S. Burroughs, 1945–1959* (Penguin, 1993) and *Junky: The Definitive Text of 'Junk'* (Penguin, 2003). He has published numerous critical articles on Burroughs, the Beats, the epistolary, and film noir, and the book *William Burroughs and the Secret of Fascination* (Southern Illinois University Press, 2003). He is a professor of American Literature and Film at Keele University, England, where he lives with his wife Jenny and their three daughters, Ella, Mia, and Nina.

Allen Hibbard has edited *Conversations with William S. Burroughs* (University Press of Mississippi, 2000) and is the author of *Paul Bowles: The Short Fiction* (Macmillan, 1993). His reviews, articles, translations (from Arabic), stories and essays have appeared in numerous journals. He taught at the American

University in Cairo from 1985 to 1989 and at Damascus University, as a Fulbright lecturer, from 1992 to 1994. Currently he teaches at Middle Tennessee State University, where he serves as Director of Graduate Studies. He is now working on a biography of Alfred Chester. His most recent book, *Paul Bowles, Magic & Morocco*, is due out from Cadmus Editions in the spring of 2004.

Jon Longhi is the author of four books—*Bricks and Anchors, The Rise and Fall of Third Leg, Flashbacks and Premonitions*, and *Wake Up and Smell the Beer*—all published by Manic D Press. He regularly does public readings of his work and has toured nationally in the United States. He lives in San Francisco.

Dennis McDaniel is an Associate Professor of English at Saint Vincent College in Latrobe, Pennsylvania, where he also serves as Director of Freshman Writing. He received his Ph.D. in British Renaissance Literature at Duquesne University and has published and presented in areas ranging from Edmund Spenser to writing pedagogy to punk rock.

Jason Morelyle is a Ph.D. candidate in the Department of English at the University of Calgary and a sessional instructor at both the University of Calgary and Mount Royal College. He is also a policy analyst for a private, philanthropic foundation in Calgary.

Timothy S. Murphy is Associate Professor of English at the University of Oklahoma. He is the author of numerous studies of modern and contemporary literature, including *Wising Up the Marks: The Amodern William Burroughs* (University of California Press, 1997), editor of the scholarly journal *Genre: Forms of Discourse and Culture*, co-editor of the scholarly journal *Angelaki*, and translator of works by Gilles Deleuze and Antonio Negri.

Ron Roberts is a lecturer in English, Media and Composition at Reid Kerr College near Glasgow.

Jamie Russell finished his Ph.D. on William S. Burroughs and queer theory at London University's Royal Holloway College in 2000 (published as *Queer Burroughs*, Palgrave, 2001). Since then he has been working as a freelance film journalist in London, writing for a variety of publications including *Sight & Sound, Total Film, FHM, SFX*, and the BBC's film website, while also broadcasting on radio and television. He has written several books, including volumes on *The Beat Generation, Vietnam War Movies* and a guide to David Lynch's labyrinthine *Mulholland Drive*; he has recently completed *Dead Men Walking: The Complete History of Zombie Movies*. He is currently working on his first screenplay and can be contacted at <www.jamierussell.org>.

Davis Schneiderman is Chair of the American Studies Program and an assistant professor of English at Lake Forest College. His critical work on Burroughs has appeared in the journal *Revista Canaria de Estudios Ingleses* and the volume *Literary Modernism and Photography* (Greenwood Press, 2003), and he has written on subjects ranging from Kathy Acker to Jerry Springer to Radiohead. His creative work has been nominated for a Pushcart Prize and has appeared in numerous journals including *The Iowa Review Web*,

Clackamas Literary Review, Exquisite Corpse, Quarter After Eight, The Little Magazine, Gargoyle, and *Happy.*

Jennie Skerl is Associate Dean of the College of Arts and Sciences at West Chester University. She has published *William S. Burroughs* (Twayne, 1985), *William S. Burroughs at the Front: Critical Reception, 1959–1989,* co-edited with Robin Lydenberg (Southern Illinois University Press, 1991), and *A Tawdry Place of Salvation: The Art of Jane Bowles* (Southern Illinois University Press, 1997). She also edited the Winter 2000 special issue of *College Literature* on teaching Beat literature and was a major contributor to the *Dictionary of Literary Biography* volume on the Beats (edited by Ann Charters, 1983). A new collection, *Reconstructing the Beats,* is forthcoming from Palgrave in 2004. She has published essays on Burroughs, Jane Bowles, Paul Bowles, Beckett, Joyce, and narrative theory.

Katharine Streip is an assistant professor in the Liberal Arts College at Concordia University, Montreal, Quebec and received a Ph.D. in Comparative Literature from the University of California at Berkeley. She has published articles on Marcel Proust, Jean Rhys and Philip Roth, and is currently working on three projects: an analysis of humor in Marcel Proust's *Recherche* and French comic periodicals of the late nineteenth and early twentieth centuries; a discussion of parody in James Joyce and Raymond Queneau; and a study of the image of the child in Stevenson's *Dr. Jekyll and Mr. Hyde* and Nabokov's *Lolita.*

John Vernon is the author of ten books, including the book of poems *Ann,* the memoir *A Book of Reasons,* and the novels *La Salle, Lindbergh's Son, Peter Doyle, All for Love: Baby Doe and Silver Dollar,* and *The Last Canyon.* His work has appeared in *Harper's, Poetry, American Poetry Review, The Nation, The Los Angeles Times,* and *The New York Times Book Review,* and many other magazines, journals, and newspapers. Two of his books have been named New York Times Notable Books of the Year, and he has been awarded two National Endowment for the Arts grants. Professor Vernon is the 21st faculty member at Binghamton University to be named a Distinguished Professor; he teaches in the spring semester each year.

Philip Walsh is Assistant Professor in the Department of Sociology/ Anthropology at the State University of New York, College at Cortland, where he teaches sociological theory. He has published articles on Hegel and Nietzsche and is the author of a forthcoming book from Palgrave, provisionally entitled *Skepticism, Modernity and Critical Theory.*

Index

dualism – *continued*
  sexual, 22, 232, *see also*
    sex/sexuality
  of human nature, 66
Dunne, J.W., 193

Eberhardt, Isabel, 26
Edinburgh Festival, 31
Editions Champ Libre, 44
ego (Freud), 66, 67, *see also*
  psychoanalysis; dreams
  and superego, 66
Eisenstein, Sergei, 38
Electronic Revolution (Burroughs), 44,
  100, 160, 179, 188–90, 197n9,
  see The Job; Burroughs,
  cinema/film,
  production/experiments of;
  Burroughs, sound
  production/experiments of
Eliot, T.S., 38
Elizabeth II, Queen of England,
  135, 142
Ellison, Ralph, 18
Ellsberg, Daniel, 126
Elvins, Kells, 17
The Elvis of Letters (Burroughs and
  Van Sant, audio recording),
  151–2
  'Burroughs Break', 151
  'Word is Virus', 152
Empire (Hardt and Negri), 163, 191
empire, concept of (Hardt and
  Negri), 5, 54, 55, 163, 191,
  196
ENIAC, computer, 101
enlightenment, 16, 64, 67, 146,
  227, 234, 259
  dialectic of (Adorno and
    Horkheimer), 64
  see also reason
environmental disasters, 13, 63
Ernst, Max, 90
essentialism, 23, 163
Estrada, Joseph (former President of
  Philippines), 6
European Parliament, 126, 130n9
*Exposing the Global Surveillance
  System* (Hager), 126

The Exterminator (Burroughs and
  Gysin), 180, 182, 184–5, *see also*
  Burroughs, cut-up/fold-in
  method

fascism, 19, 36, 59, 226, 228, 236,
  237, 246
Federal Bureau of Investigations
  (FBI), 53, 125, 126, 128
Feminist Studies (journal), 27n3
Ferlinghetti, Lawrence, 32
fetishism, 70, 134, 144
Fiedler, Leslie, 21
Fielding, Henry, 207, 222
The Flash (Morrison, comic), 225
Flaubert, Gustave, 26
The Flicker (Conrad, film), 166
Floating Bear (DiPrima and Jones,
  journal), 180
'Formats: The Grid' (Burroughs),
  109, *see The Third Mind*
Fortune, Dion, 232
Foucault, Michel, 17, 74, 152–3, 157
  and power, 76–85, 155
  and freedom, 85
  and discourses, 77
  on discipline/disciplinary society,
    53, 78, 79
  History of Sexuality, 21
  see also subjectivity; author
    function
Fountain of Hyacinth (Crowley),
  238
Frank, Robert, 166
Frank, Thomas, 149–50, 155
Frankfurt School, *see* critical theory
'Frankie the Frog', 121, 130, *see also*
  Lyotard, Jean-Francois
Franks, Thomas (US general), 172
Freud, Sigmund, 65, 66, 68, 71n7,
  89, *see also* psychoanalysis
Friedman, Milton, 3
Fukuyama, Francis, 3

gadgets, 70, 116, 128, 129, 162, 203,
  see also Naked Lunch;
  Burroughs, science and
  technology
Gardells, Nathan, 163